Metamorphosis in Music

METAMORPHOSIS IN MUSIC

The Compositions of György Ligeti in the 1950s and 1960s

Benjamin R. Levy

OXFORD
UNIVERSITY PRESS

OXFORD
UNIVERSITY PRESS

Oxford University Press is a department of the University of Oxford. It furthers the University's objective of excellence in research, scholarship, and education by publishing worldwide. Oxford is a registered trade mark of Oxford University Press in the UK and certain other countries.

Published in the United States of America by Oxford University Press
198 Madison Avenue, New York, NY 10016, United States of America.

© Oxford University Press 2017

Library of Congress Cataloging-in-Publication Data
Name: Levy, Benjamin R.
Title: Metamorphosis in music: the compositions of György Ligeti in the
1950s and 1960s / Benjamin R. Levy.
Description: New York, NY: Oxford University Press, [2017] |
Includes bibliographical references and index.
Identifiers: LCCN 2016039508 | ISBN 9780199381999 (hardcover) |
ISBN 9780199382019 (oxford scholarly online) | ISBN 9780199382002 (updf) |
ISBN 9780190857394 (epub)
Subjects: LCSH: Ligeti, György, 1923–2006—Criticism and interpretation. |
Music—20th century—History and criticism.
Classification: LCC ML410.L645 L45 2017 | DDC 780.92—dc23
LC record available at https://lccn.loc.gov/2016039508

9 8 7 6 5 4 3 2 1

Printed by Sheridan Books, Inc., United States of America

For my father, mother, and sister, who have been constant sources of advice and inspiration

CONTENTS

ACKNOWLEDGMENTS

As one of the aims of the book that follows is an investigation of the complex network of influences that left traces on Ligeti's compositions, I am acutely aware that my own work, too, bears the marks of numerous interlocutors and owes a debt of gratitude to more people than I can succinctly name. Like any project that has spanned a number of years, it has intersected with various facets of my life, following me through different places, positions, and friendships. My thanks go to Thomas DeLio, who encouraged my early interest in Ligeti, channeled my scholarly instincts in productive directions, and advised my dissertation, which informs parts of chapters 2 and 3 of this book. Mike Boyd, Stephen Lilly, Stacey Mastrian, Jenny Snodgrass, Kristian Twombly, Steve Wanna, and many others from my graduate-school cohort remain close friends and collaborators who helped shape my views and opinions during this formative period and who continue to provide stimulating discussions and observations.

My research was also supported by the Paul Sacher Foundation in Basel, first in the form of a Research Stipend while I was working on my dissertation in 2004, but continuing in immeasurable ways ever since. The foundation has been most helpful and accommodating on several subsequent visits (in 2009, 2011, and 2014) and especially generous in granting permission to use and reproduce material for this publication. I thank the director, Felix Meyer, as well as the musicologists Hermann Danuser, Angela Ida De Benedictis, Matthias Kassel, Simon Obert, and Robert Piencikowski, all of whom took time out of their own work to talk to me about different projects. I am particularly grateful, however, to Heidy Zimmermann, who oversees the Ligeti Collection and has always offered her expertise and advice generously, and to Evelyne Diendorf, the librarian and archivist who graciously filled the numerous requests for materials from the archive that form the basis of this book.

Conversations with countless other scholars at archives, conferences, and lectures have allowed me to refine my ideas over the years. While a full list is too long to recount here, I have been particularly touched and heartened by the continued interest that Maureen Carr, Jennifer Iverson, Severine Neff, and Christoph Neidhöfer have taken in my work. The Ligeti scholars in North America and Europe—whose names you will see throughout the references—have not only provided a fertile intellectual environment for my work but have proven to be as congenial and encouraging a group as one could hope to find. The Hungarian translations in the book are my own, but I owe a great deal to both Peter Laki and Klára Móricz, who looked over many passages, offering suggestions and improvements.

I have been extremely fortunate to have held positions—first at Arizona State University and now at the University of California, Santa Barbara—where I could find supportive departments, sympathetic colleagues, and students who have kept me energized and motivated through their own intellectual curiosity. Both institutions helped fund research trips that were critical in fueling this project as it expanded from its earliest conception into its present form. Moreover, Glenn Hackbarth, Sabine Feisst, and Simone Mancuso were at the heart of a new music community that formed some of the most rewarding experiences of my time at Arizona State. In Santa Babara, I feel doubly lucky to have found, once again, a group of co-workers whom I can also call friends.

Suzanne Ryan and others at Oxford University Press have shown patience toward and confidence in this project for which I am most appreciative. They have been extraordinary in their efficiency and professionalism at every step of the process. My gratitude goes out to Wolfgang Marx, whose detailed review greatly improved the manuscript, as well as to Michael Searby and the still-anonymous reviewers who provided initial feedback and comments. Thanks are also due to Gene Caprioglio at C. F. Peters Corporation and to Caroline Kane at Schott Music Corporation for facilitating the rights to reproduce excerpts from Ligeti's scores. Similarly, I am grateful to the editors at PFAU Verlag, *Perspectives of New Music*, and *Twentieth-Century Music*, where I published articles that have been adapted into parts of the book.

Finally, but most deeply, I wish to thank my family. My parents, David and Lynne, and my sister, Beth—all more experienced scholars and writers than I am—read over drafts of every chapter, offering both practical suggestions on the manuscript and infinitely more valuable advice about weathering the ups and downs of life that went along with writing it. This book is lovingly dedicated to them.

Metamorphosis in Music

Introduction

Technique and imagination influence one another in a constant interchange. Every artistic innovation in the craft of composition ferments the whole spiritual edifice, and every change in this edifice demands constant revision of compositional procedure.

György Ligeti, "Metamorphoses of Musical Form"

György Ligeti wrote these words in the midst of one of the most remarkable transitional periods in contemporary music. Through the 1950s and 1960s he went from composing in the style of his countryman Béla Bartók to working at the cutting edge of the Western European avant-garde. His technique was constantly in fluctuation, and through this metamorphosis he created some of the most original works of art of the period, including *Artikulation, Atmosphères, Aventures*, the Requiem, *Continuum*, and the Chamber Concerto: compositions that attracted immediate attention at their premieres and continue to be performed and recorded today. As Ligeti has entered the canon of twentieth-century composers, his innovation and imagination have been widely recognized, but the techniques by which he arrived at these new developments have often been harder to discern. This is due, in part, to his secrecy about the specifics of his working methods, the often messy and incomplete nature of his sketches, and not least the relative obscurity of the Hungarian language.

Analyses of Ligeti's works have often eschewed the details of construction in favor of an abbreviated discussion using brief quotations from his interviews, simple descriptive references to prominent features at the surface of the music, or general observations about his aesthetic. In fact, many early discussions of his works were written by members of Ligeti's circle, and they take the form of a portrait of the composer, remaining uncritically close to

Ligeti's own descriptions.[1] Other analyses, such as Harald Kaufmann's reading of *Atmosphères* as a type of requiem or of the Second String Quartet in light of Samuel Beckett's *Endgame*, are highly interpretive and idiosyncratic.[2] Erkki Salmenhaara made major strides in the analysis of Ligeti's music, although it is often still presented as an introduction to the general features of the composer's style using a limited number of pieces.[3] Herman Sabbe makes a conscious effort to move past the composer's own descriptions and provides deeper and more purely analytical insights, although he addresses common features synchronically from across Ligeti's mature style, rather than arranging his study chronologically to show its development.[4] Much of the English-language scholarship focuses on the later years of Ligeti's career, although notable articles by Jonathan Bernard[5] and Jane Piper Clendinning's work concerning Ligeti's microcanonic and pattern-meccanico works[6] make valuable observations about pieces from the earlier period as well. The longer

1. Ove Nordwall, to whom Ligeti entrusted many of his manuscripts and sketches, is one clear example of this trend. Nordwall included interviews and personal correspondence with the composer as part of his book *György Ligeti: Eine Monographie* (Mainz: Schott, 1971). His other works about Ligeti, listed in the bibliography, follow much the same model. Monika Lichtenfeld, another close friend of the composer, and editor of *György Ligeti Gesammelte Schriften* (Mainz: Schott, 2006, as volume 10:1–2 of the Publications of the Paul Sacher Stiftung), henceforth abbreviated *GS*, also strongly reflects the composer's comments in her earlier essays "György Ligeti, oder das Ende der seriellen Musik," *Melos* 39, no. 2 (1972), 74–80, and "Zehn Stücke für Bläserquintett von György Ligeti," *Melos* 39, no. 6 (1972), 326–33. Works in English, including Paul Griffiths, *György Ligeti*, 2nd ed. (London: Robson, 1997) and Marina Lobanova, *György Ligeti: Style, Ideas, Poetics*, trans. Marc Shuttleworth (Berlin: Kuhn, 2002), also follow this pattern, often including interviews and the composer's program notes and never straying far from this line of interpretation.

2. Harald Kaufmann, "Ligetis Zweites Streichquartett," *Melos* 37, no. 5 (1970), 181–86, and "Strukturen im Strukturlosen: Über György Ligetis 'Atmosphères,'" in *Spurlinien: Analytische Aufsätze über Sprache und Musik*, 107–17 (Vienna: Verlag Elisabeth Lafite, 1969), a book in which Kaufmann also discusses *Aventures*: "Ein Fall absurder Musik: Ligetis 'Aventures & Nouvelles Aventures,'" 130–58.

3. Erkki Salmenhaara, *Das Musikalische Material und seine Behandlung in den Werken "Apparitions," "Atmosphères," "Aventures" und "Requiem" von György Ligeti* (Regensburg: Bosse, 1969).

4. Herman Sabbe, *György Ligeti: Studien zur kompositorischen Phänomenologie*, Musik-Konzepte 53 (Munich: edition text + kritik, 1987).

5. Jonathan Bernard, "Inaudible Structures, Audible Music: Ligeti's Problem, and His Solution," *Music Analysis* 6, no. 3 (October 1987), 207–36; "Voice Leading as a Spatial Function in the Music of Ligeti," *Music Analysis* 13, nos. 2–3 (July–October 1994), 227–53; and "Ligeti's Restoration of Interval and Its Significance for His Later Works," *Music Theory Spectrum* 21, no. 1 (Spring 1999), 1–31.

6. Jane Piper Clendinning, "Contrapuntal Techniques in the Music of György Ligeti," (PhD diss., Yale University, 1989); "The Pattern-Meccanico Compositions of György Ligeti," *Perspectives of New Music* 31, no. 1 (Winter 1993), 192–234; and "Structural Factors in the Microcanonic Compositions of György Ligeti," in *Concert Music, Rock and Jazz since 1945*, ed. Elizabeth West Marvin and Richard Hermann, 229–56 (Rochester: University of Rochester Press, 1995).

scholarly works in English include exemplary biographies by Richard Toop and Richard Steinitz that provide a good picture of the composer's life, if not as thorough an examination of his works.[7] Yet Ligeti insisted that technique and imagination are interdependent and inseparable, each responding to the other. This book helps complete the picture of Ligeti's musical metamorphosis by examining not only the aesthetic goals and features of the music but also the compositional techniques by which Ligeti was able to bring his imagination to fruition, as documented in the sketch materials held at the Paul Sacher Foundation in Basel, and by analyzing the resulting scores in detail.

The use of sketches in the analysis of twentieth-century music has a long and growing history, including landmark studies of Stravinsky's music,[8] as well as the work of scholars such as Friedemann Sallis and Patricia Hall.[9] Like Stravinsky in the first half of the twentieth century, Ligeti has come to be an emblematic figure whose career moved through numerous styles and touched on most of the different artistic trends of the second half of the century—a time when modernist ideals were splitting off in a myriad of postmodern directions. A close study of Ligeti's sketches can reveal much about the nature of these interchanges. In examining the move away from a common, tonal language, reference to the compositional sketches and drafts can be extremely useful in coming to an understanding of a contemporary composer's individual method. In her monograph *A View of Berg's* Lulu *through the Autograph Sources*, Hall has pointed out that "sketches are most helpful for highly defined theoretical systems, which, because of their complexity or unapparent relationships, we do not yet fully understand."[10] Ligeti's evolving compositional technique is a different matter than Berg's serialism, to be sure, yet the

7. Richard Toop, *György Ligeti* (London: Phaidon, 1999); Richard Steinitz, *György Ligeti: Music of the Imagination* (Boston: Northeastern University Press, 2003). In the introduction Steinitz mentions that his book was originally intended as "a stylistic and analytical study of a wonderful body of music" (xv) but that in the process it had become a biography. It is, indeed, one of the best biographical studies of Ligeti, but is more comprehensive as such than as an analytical study. It contains excellent analytical details about works from later in Ligeti's career including the *Three Pieces for Two Pianos* and the Études for Piano but considerably less detail about pieces from the late 1950s and the 1960s.

8. Notable among the theoretical books about Stravinsky that include detailed study of the composer's sketches are Pieter C. van den Toorn's *Stravinsky and the* Rite of Spring: *The Beginnings of a Musical Language* (Berkeley: University of California Press, 1987), and Maureen Carr's *Multiple Masks: Neoclassicism in Stravinsky's Works on Greek Subjects* (Lincoln: University of Nebraska Press, 2002) and *Stravinsky's* Pulcinella: *A Facsimile of the Sources and Sketches* (Middleton, WI: A-R Editions, 2010).

9. Patricia Hall and Friedemann Sallis, eds., *A Handbook to Twentieth-Century Musical Sketches* (New York: Cambridge University Press, 2004). Hall's work on Berg is exemplary, especially *A View of Berg's* Lulu *through the Autograph Sources* (Berkeley: University of California Press, 1996), and Sallis's *An Introduction to the Early Works of György Ligeti* (Cologne: Studio, 1996) is also highly relevant for the first chapter of this study.

10. Hall, *View of Berg's* Lulu, 11–12.

sketches are useful in similar ways. While Ligeti's compositional language is idiosyncratic and complex, he does compose using theoretical systems with well-defined procedures that come into clearer relief in the early stages of composition than they do in the final score.

Many of the problems and benefits that Hall identifies in her study of Berg's sketches apply to the work of Ligeti. First, sketches may aid in the identification of features that, although present in the finished score, can be more directly observed in the sketches and can lead to a more focused analysis. For example, they may help us recognize the harmonic scheme in such pieces as the Chamber Concerto, even in sections that seem polyphonic on the surface and whose individual lines might otherwise obscure the underlying harmonic structure. Second, sketches may allow for the recognition of an underlying model when the finished score presents only a substantially altered version of that model. Ligeti often establishes a system only to break it down during the course of a composition, and so sketches can be essential in determining what this system is and how the process of dissolution works against it. The repertoire of durations used in *Apparitions* is one of the earliest examples of the deterioration of a clear system; by the end of the work it is so extensively modified that it would be impossible to recognize it in the final score without information from the sketches.

Finally, sketches may work together with the composer's prose remarks to provide a more complete picture of the evolution of technique; here, however, also lies one of the pitfalls of this type of analysis. Ligeti spoke freely about his own works in interviews and essays, but his comments were often abbreviated, occasionally misremembered, and usually geared toward a particular audience; he positioned himself differently at different points in his career.[11] Likewise, Ligeti's sketches abound with written commentary, which must be read carefully and in context. In the heart of this period, there was a clear tendency for Ligeti to start with the verbal and work through the graphic or symbolic stages of sketching before arriving at the final score. Although this working method is not an absolute process, and at times Ligeti would go back and forth between these stages or mix them, his tendency was to move from the general verbal descriptions to the more specific graphs and score drafts.[12] Analyses of *Aventures* and *Lux aeterna* in chapters 4 and 5 show that

---

11. Insightful observations about Ligeti's rhetoric and the careful construction of his self-identity can be found in Charles Wilson, "György Ligeti and the Rhetoric of Autonomy," *Twentieth-Century Music* 1, no. 1 (2004), 5–28.

12. Jonathan Bernard makes similar observations in his essay "Rules and Regulations: Lessons from Ligeti's Compositional Sketches," in *György Ligeti: Of Foreign Lands and Strange Sounds*, ed. Louise Duchesneau and Wolfgang Marx, 149–67 (Woodbridge, UK: Boydell, 2011). Bernard categorizes Ligeti's sketches into five types, which he calls jottings, drawings, charts, tables, and musical notation. He arranges his discussion in "an order roughly general to specific" (151), but noting that Ligeti's sketches are almost never dated, he hesitates to attribute to them a chronological

numbering systems or abbreviations developed in the early stages of composition often appear in later stages as well, confirming the basic shape of his creative process. The verbal stages often read like brainstorming sessions, and though they contain ideas that elucidate features of the resulting work, many times they also contain ideas that do not materialize in the final version or do so only indirectly and can lead to an overly speculative interpretation of the completed work. Proceeding with caution, conservatively, along these lines, nevertheless can shed light on important issues in Ligeti's career—that he definitively knew of Giacinto Scelsi while writing the Cello Concerto, for example, even if the extent of this knowledge remains unclear.[13] The goal of this type of analysis, then, is not to work toward a "definitive" interpretation but, rather, to search for parallel discoveries in the composer's prose, sketches, and finished scores—discoveries that augment one another and lead to an enriched appreciation of these already multifaceted works.

Along these lines, one must be careful about offering unequivocal conclusions concerning the evolution of Ligeti's career and the sea of influences that he navigated; the narratives, both imposed and self-constructed, that circulate around this period of compositional development split off in numerous directions. At different points in his career Ligeti gave differing accounts of his involvement with contemporary schools of compositional thought. Shortly after his emigration to the West, for example, he tended to minimize the importance of his Hungarian background, which could be seen as provincial and unsophisticated, emphasizing instead the new opportunities and experiences he found in Cologne. In the late 1960s he began to talk about his Hungarian background again, though in a very stylized way, emphasizing the different mindset he brought with him to the West as a way of distinguishing himself from other figures in the avant-garde.[14] The importance of such figures as Bartók and Webern, the remnants or influences of tonal composers,

order. My conception of the sketches equates Bernard's prose "jottings" to the verbal stage and his drawings, charts, and tables to my graphic stage, before arriving at drafts.

13. Richard Steinitz also brings up this reference to Scelsi in the sketches for the Cello Concerto in his "À qui un hommage? Genesis of the Piano Concerto and the Horn Trio," in *György Ligeti: Of Foreign Lands and Strange Sounds*, ed. Louise Duchesneau and Wolfgang Marx, 169–214 (Woodbridge, UK: Boydell, 2011), esp. 174–75. It is a particularly fascinating case because elsewhere (particularly in "Fritz Cerha, herzlichst zum siebzigsten Geburtstag," in *GS* 1:473–78) Ligeti claims not to have known Scelsi until much later. The most intuitive connection between the Cello Concerto and Scelsi's work would be the use of unisons and even octaves that are then inflected with different timbres, attacks, or deviations; the sketch, however, refers specifically to double stops that ironically do not appear in the final piece, ultimately leaving more questions than answers.

14. In addition to Charles Wilson's "György Ligeti and the Rhetoric of Autonomy," see Rachel Beckles Willson, *Ligeti, Kurtág, and Hungarian Music during the Cold War* (New York: Cambridge University Press, 2007), for further observations on Ligeti's relationship to his native country and Hungarian identity.

and the degree of his involvement in various schools or movements, including Fluxus and Darmstadt, are all subject to reinterpretation throughout his career. Once again, the evidence this book presents is not aimed at validating some influences and discarding others but, rather, is intended to provide a fuller picture of the period, to examine another, often more private line of documentation that counterbalances the line of rhetoric Ligeti advanced both during and after this time.

This book begins by establishing the starting point of the composer's stylistic transformation, in which he used Bartók as his model, as shown in Ligeti's *Musica ricercata* (1951–53) and the String Quartet no. 1, *Métamorphoses nocturnes* (1953–54). Chapter 1 also examines the more experimental impulse found in these pieces, which continues through the choral works *Éjszaka* and *Reggel* (1955). While many of these early works have been thoroughly explored by Friedemann Sallis, the chapter also presents sketches for several incomplete and unpublished works dating from 1955–56: the prelude to a setting of Sandor Weöres's *Istar Pokoljárása* (1955), *Chromatische Phantasie* (1956) for piano, *Variations Concertantes* (1956) for small orchestra, and the first draft of a Requiem (1956), all of which show experimentation with Schoenberg's twelve-tone technique and may better reveal the extent of Ligeti's knowledge of dodecaphony than did his public statements at the time.

Chapter 2 deals with Ligeti's work in the electronic music studio of the Westdeutscher Rundfunk (WDR) in Cologne, just after his emigration in 1956. Drawing on sketches for these pieces, since no scores are available,[15] enables a detailed look at their construction and comparison with the techniques of the works that follow. *Apparitions* (1958–59) and *Atmosphères* (1961) are the focus of chapter 3; these landmark works were turning points in Ligeti's career and, along with the electronic works, lie at the heart of the debate over which of Ligeti's ideas originated before his arrival in the West and which were inspired by his first contact with Karlheinz Stockhausen, Mauricio Kagel, and other figures of the avant-garde. To that end, this chapter also contains a discussion of two orchestral works written before he left Hungary, *Víziók* and *Sötet és Világos* (both 1956), the composer's first attempts at creating a static musical surface before achieving his breakthrough with *Apparitions*.

Like many of his contemporaries in postwar Europe, Ligeti became preoccupied with absurdity in the early 1960s and was on the fringes of the Cage-influenced Fluxus movement. His involvement, though brief, had a lasting effect on his music, and subject matter tending toward the absurd and darkly comic lasted throughout his career, leading to the opera *Le Grand Macabre* (1974–77) and beyond. This period resulted in several conceptual, satirical,

---

15. The exception is Rainer Wehinger's retrospectively constructed "Listening Score," developed independently from the composer and published as *Ligeti—Artikulation: Electronische Musik, eine Hörpartitur* (Mainz: Schott, 1970).

and provocative pieces, *The Future of Music* (1961), *Trois Bagatelles* (1961), *Fragment* (1961), and *Poème Symphonique* (1962) but also had a clear influence on the more major works, *Volumina* (1961–62), *Aventures* (1962), and *Nouvelles Aventures* (1962–65). These three works, in particular, are the main focus of chapter 4, as they turned Ligeti's compositional skills—as shown by the more extensive sketch materials—toward an increasingly intricate and nuanced exploration of the absurd and theatrical.

With the Requiem (1963–65), Ligeti took yet another turn in his technique, a more conscious desire to codify and define his system of micropolyphony. His style is often divided into two distinct types, a "static" type drawing from *Apparitions* and *Atmosphères* and a "wild" or "gesticulating" type epitomized by the *De die judicii* sequence and drawing from *Aventures*.[16] Chapter 5 discusses the sketches where these procedures are developed in the Requiem and refined in *Lux aeterna* (1966), the related work *Lontano* (1967), and the Cello Concerto (1966).

This codification then enabled the fruitful period from 1967–70, discussed in chapter 6: Two Études for Organ (1967, 1969) and *Continuum* (1968) for harpsichord, the *Ten Pieces for Wind Quintet* (1968) and the String Quartet no. 2 (1968), and the ensemble works *Ramifications* (1968–69) and the Chamber Concerto (1969–70). Although several of these adopt techniques from earlier compositions, Ligeti's use of harmony and rhythm continued to evolve through these works. Starting with the organ étude *Harmonies* (1967), he began to branch out from the cluster-based harmonic ideas used extensively in his previous works to new, more widely spaced harmonic networks, which in turn supported new melodic ideas in works such as the Chamber Concerto. Along with these new harmonies, Ligeti began to use rhythmic structures built from fast repeated patterns often described as "pattern meccanico,"[17] from the mechanical presentation of the harpsichord work *Continuum*, in which these patterns develop independently in each hand, changing in length and giving the impression of a machine falling into disorder. Moreover, in the more substantial works from this period, Ligeti shifts between these different

---

16. This distinction and the lineage of these two styles were first noted in Salmenhaara, *Das musikalische Material*, and also mentioned in Ligeti's interview with Péter Várnai in *Ligeti in Conversation* (London: Eulenburg, 1983), henceforth abbreviated LiC.

17. The term "pattern meccanico" was coined by Clendinning, "Contrapuntal Techniques." It has been adopted by many others since, including Bernard, "Ligeti's Restoration of Interval," and Michael Hicks, "Interval and Form in Ligeti's *Continuum* and *Coulée*," *Perspectives of New Music* 31, no. 1 (Winter 1993), 172–90, but it is also the source of some disagreement between Clendinning and Miguel Roig-Francolí as to the composer's general or specific use of "meccanico" and "net-structure." This matter is discussed in more depth in chapter 6. See Roig-Francolí, "Harmonic and Formal Processes in Ligeti's Net-Structure Compositions," *Music Theory Spectrum* 17, no. 2 (Fall 1995), 242–67, and Clendinning's review of this article in *Music Theory Online* 2, no. 5 (July 1996), http://www.mtosmt.org/issues/mto.96.2.5/mto.96.2.5.clendinning.html.

textures and means of construction—sometimes abruptly but at other times through meticulous and gradual transitions.

With this outpouring of music between 1967 and 1970, we see a relatively stable period in Ligeti's style: a well-developed repertoire of techniques used across a body of works marking the completion of this stage of his musical metamorphosis. During the 1970s Ligeti's production began to trail off again as he devoted more time to the composition of his opera *Le Grand Macabre* and began to experience a stylistic crisis. Although the works from the early 1970s seem to move in the direction of more expressive titles—notably, *Melodien* (1971), *Clocks and Clouds* (1972–73), *San Francisco Polyphony* (1973–74), and *Monument-Selbstportrait-Bewegung: Three Pieces for Two Pianos* (1976)—these often merely intensify the ideas already present in such works as *Continuum* and the Chamber Concerto. Moreover, the expressive concerns explicit in the titles of these works are already implicitly present in the more abstractly titled works of the late 1960s. The conclusion of the book is devoted to ideas of form and expression in these later works. In a lecture given as part of the colloquium "Form in New Music" at Darmstadt in 1965, Ligeti insisted on the role of memory, and therefore history, in the perception of musical form, pointing out that "the historical aspect . . . relates not only to the form of the individual musical work but also to formal connections that develop between the individual works. The function of a work's segments can really not be explained from the inner musical connections of the work in question" but rather are meaningful only "in relation to the more general characteristics and schemes of connections that arise from the totality of works within a stylistic area or tradition." [18] These remarks complement his earlier "Metamorphoses of Musical Form" and are equally relevant to the pieces composed at the turn of the 1970s. While it is clear that they drew on ideas from throughout this transitional period, reexamining these late pieces, aided by the references to the works of other composers including Mahler, Bruckner, and Couperin found throughout the sketches from this period, we may also see how they touched on historical tradition. They were the culmination of Ligeti's metamorphosis, by which he arrived at an individual repertoire of techniques that he could use for a variety of expressive means; he established his own voice and could use it to comment on tradition. Ultimately, through this book and through the analysis of public statements, sketches, and scores that it presents, we may arrive at an intimate and detailed picture of Ligeti's mature style, his confident new voice, and its union of technique and imagination.

---

18. György Ligeti, "Form," in *Contemplating Music*, vol. 3, *Essence*, ed. Carl Dahlhaus and Ruth Katz, 781–96 (New York: Pendragon, 1987), 783. The lecture was originally issued in two parts in July 1965, was subsequently published in the *Österreichische Monatsblätter für kulturelle Freiheit* 13, nos. 148–49 (1966), 291–95, and is reprinted as "Form in der Neuen Musik," in *GS*, 1:185–99.

CHAPTER 1

Discontent and Early Experiments (1950–56)

At the outset of the 1950s György Ligeti was frustrated with the options available to him in his native Hungary, and the roots of his stylistic transformation lie in this precarious time and his resulting discontent. In August 1950 he returned to Budapest from Romania, where he had spent most of the previous year collecting and transcribing folk songs, and he found the situation in Budapest to be difficult at best in the face of censorship and governmental pressure. Any optimism left from the early postwar years had now dissolved as the government of Mátyás Rákosi extended its reach into the nation's cultural and educational institutions and into the everyday affairs of its citizens. Since 1948 the effort to bring Hungarian art and music into alignment with the Stalinist and Zhdanovist vision of socialist realism had grown steadily more intrusive, and in 1949 the Soviet-style Hungarian Musicians' Union (Magyar Zeneművészek Szövetsége) had taken control of musical life in the country. As Ligeti was starting his position as a lecturer in music theory at the Liszt Academy in September 1950, his compositions had to go before panel hearings run by the Union in order to be considered for broadcast on the radio or for public performance at events such as the Hungarian Music Weeks. Hungarian musical life was being transformed in radical ways, and musicians were responding in equally radical ways. Ligeti's teacher, Sándor Veress, had already left the country, having accepted a teaching position in Bern in 1949; these pressures were to compel Ligeti to embark on his own physical and artistic journey away from Hungary and toward new opportunities, experiences, and environments in the West.

The push toward a Soviet model led to the suppression of dissonant music by Bartók and by younger composers. Endre Szervánszky (1911–77) and Pál

Kadosa (1903–83), composers whom Ligeti admired and praised in print,[1] initially argued for the compatibility of even Bartók's modernist music of the 1920s with socialist ideals. Ligeti, too, was attached to the idea of "progressive" use of modern materials, and even at the end of 1948 he had hoped for an open and productive dialogue between those committed to a new understanding of tonality and those advancing twelve-tone composition—what he described as the two directions in new music.[2] Moreover, he expressed an idea similar to Szervánszky's: that Bartók's late works, including the *Concerto for Orchestra* and the *Third Piano Concerto*, represented a balance of abstraction and accessibility and a possible direction forward. This position, however, was not persuasive in the Union or in the government, and as Danielle Fosler-Lussier has shown, "between 1948 and 1950 those who cherished modernist styles would be compelled either to reevaluate and defend their opinions or to withdraw into silence."[3] Bartók's more dissonant works were effectively banned starting in 1949, while his work with folk music was emphasized as the true measure of his legacy. Ligeti found himself in a similar position; many (though by no means all) of his arrangements and folk-influenced works found an audience, but his ventures into a more modernist style were found unsuitable for performance and suppressed. Works including his *Régi Magyar társas táncok* (Old Hungarian Ballroom Dances, 1949), *Négy lakodalmi tánc* (Four Wedding Dances, 1950), and *Kállai kettős* (Double Dance from Kálló, 1950) became relatively popular, while *Concert Românesc* (1951), the choral work "Háj, ifúság!" (Oh, youth!, 1952), and the Cello Sonata (1953) were barred.[4]

After his return from Romania, Ligeti submitted for consideration his *Concert Românesc*, a mixture of folk melodies and newly composed material in the same spirit. The fate of this piece in the committee hearings exemplifies some of the problems that led to Ligeti's discontent. Rachel Beckles Willson has unearthed the minutes of these hearings and recounted the peculiar mixture of "serious engagement with the music"[5] with self-criticism and political

1. See György Ligeti, "Neue Musik in Ungarn," *Melos* 16, no. 1 (1949), 5–8 (written at the end of 1946), and "Neues aus Budapest: Zwölftonmusik oder 'Neue Tonalität'?," *Melos* 17, no. 2 (1950), 45–48 (written at the end of 1948). Both are reprinted in *GS*, 1:51–55 and 56–60, respectively. The praise of Kadosa is muted in the later article, Kadosa having regressed from the bolder harmonies of his earlier works.
2. Ligeti, "Neues aus Budapest," *GS*, 1:56–57.
3. Danielle Fosler-Lussier, *Music Divided: Bartók's Legacy in Cold War Culture* (Berkeley: University of California Press, 2007), 4.
4. This is not a complete list of Ligeti's banned works; accurately identifying them all is complicated by the vagaries of Ligeti's memory and official recordkeeping. Some sources also include *Pápainé* (1953) and *Öt Arany-dal* (1952). See Ove Nordwall, *György Ligeti: Eine Monographie* (Mainz: Schott's Söhne, 1971), 60; Richard Steinitz, *György Ligeti: Music of the Imagination* (Boston: Northeastern University Press, 2003), 50–52; and Paul Griffiths, *György Ligeti*, 2nd ed (London: Robson, 1997), 21.
5. Rachel Beckles Willson, *Ligeti, Kurtág, and Hungarian Music during the Cold War* (New York: Cambridge University Press, 2007), 41. See also Fosler-Lussier, *Music Divided*, for more on the cases of Andras Mihály and Endre Székely.

theater that made these hearings so tense and precarious, especially when striking the wrong tone in matters of party ideology could have severe consequences. After apparently being approved for inclusion in the first Hungarian Music Week, the work was rejected without a clear reason at another meeting two weeks later. Ligeti maintained that the reason for its rejection was its use of dissonance, particularly in the fourth movement, where an F♯ appears in the key of F major.[6] The unpredictable outcomes of these hearings, where even a strongly folk-influenced work could be found too dissonant and modern and the vote of one committee could be overturned without a clear rationale, pushed Ligeti and many of his contemporaries to work in secret, writing some works for public approval but keeping others private—an activity Ligeti described as "composing for the bottom drawer."[7]

Amid these political pressures and dangers Ligeti was able to find pockets of freedom and outlets for his creative impulses when they diverged from official guidelines—and it is in these more private activities, as recorded in sketches and commentary, that his musical metamorphosis began to take shape. Ligeti recalled that his position as an instructor of theory, rather than composition, often shielded him from direct scrutiny. He was able to direct some of his creative activity into traditional outlets—textbooks on classical harmony published in 1954 and 1956[8] as well as his folk-song arrangements—while reserving his more adventurous experiments for the bottom drawer. As an instructor at the Liszt Academy and a member of the Musician's Union, Ligeti had other opportunities, too, but he remembered clearly the paradoxical feeling of being both "elevated and privileged, and at the same time enslaved."[9] Through the Union he had access to materials including the German periodical *Melos*, for which he reported on musical developments in Hungary several times in 1949 and 1950. From this journal he could also learn some of the goings-on in Western Europe, including the schedules of radio programs that featured modern music, although these broadcasts were often jammed. Moreover, through contacts who lived or traveled abroad, he had acquired books including Thomas Mann's *Doktor Faustus*, René Leibowitz's *Introduction à la musique de douze sons*, and Theodor Adorno's

6. This is a much later recollection; see György Ligeti, "Über mein *Concert Românesc* und andere Frühwerke aus Ungarn," written in 2002 for liner notes to the Teldec CD on which this work was first released, reprinted in *GS*, 2:152. Beckles Willson, *Ligeti, Kurtág*, 40, suggests, on the basis of Ligeti's notes, that the piece was in fact performed, although likely at less prestigious events.

7. Ligeti uses this wording frequently; for example, in "Über mein *Concert Românesc*" he calls this "Musik für die Schublade," *GS*, 2:152. Steinitz, *Ligeti*, 62, also repeats this wording.

8. György Ligeti, *Klasszikus összhangzattan: Segédkönyv* (Budapest: Zeneműkiadó, 1954) and *A klasszikus harmóniarend* (Budapest: Zeneműkiadó, 1956).

9. György Ligeti, *"Träumen Sie in Farbe?" György Ligeti im Gespräch mit Eckhard Roelcke* (Vienna: Paul Zsolnay Verlag, 2003), 69 (Wir waren herausgehoben und privilegiert und gleichzeitig Sklaven).

Philosophy of New Music, in about 1952. Ligeti could apply to stay at the Rákoczi Castle in northeast Hungary, which had been converted into a house for artists; he recalled going there on several occasions and being able to work in peace—in fact, *Concert Românesc* was composed there. Once he had gained the trust of colleagues at the academy, Ligeti also found allies in the committee hearings and confidants with whom he could speak frankly, if only behind closed doors.

Perhaps because of the ongoing debates circulating around Bartók, and perhaps owing to his convictions about progressive ideas in music, Ligeti spoke of a desire that arose in the 1950s to escape this complicated legacy and move in his own direction. The start of his *Melos* article "Neue Musik in Ungarn" acknowledges a deep admiration for Bartók but also addresses the degree to which he overshadowed the next generation of Hungarian composers.[10] In a 1978 interview with his countryman Péter Várnai about his conflicted relationship with Bartók, Ligeti maintained,

all my compositions dating back to Hungary show Bartók's influence very strongly, and to a lesser extent that of Stravinsky and of Berg's *Lyric Suite*. In the post-war years in Hungary we did not know much about other modern composers. Then, in the early '50s, I began to feel that I had to go beyond Bartók. It did not mean repudiating him, of course; stylistically, I have always maintained very strong links with him. What I felt I had to abandon were traditional forms, a musical language of the traditional kind, the sonata form. That gave me the impulse to "break with Bartók."[11]

At other times, however, as when speaking with Josef Häusler in 1968, Ligeti made it appear that this break was more sudden and complete, downplaying the enduring stylistic links.[12] Throughout these comments one finds a strong sense of the necessity of musical progress (akin to what he could have read in Adorno) and an implicit fear that Hungary's isolation meant falling behind developments in the West. This anxiety, compounded by the political situation in Hungary, was another significant motivation for the dramatic changes in Ligeti's life and art that would follow.

MUSICA RICERCATA (1951–53)

In later years Ligeti would point to his piano work *Musica ricercata* as a critical point in finding his own voice as a composer, describing it as a moment of "Cartesian" doubt, when he questioned all his previous assumptions about

10. Ligeti, "Neue Musik in Ungarn," in *GS*, 1:51–52.
11. Interview with Péter Várnai in *Ligeti in Conversation (LiC)*, trans. Gabor J. Schabert et al. (London: Ernst Eulenburg, 1983), 13.
12. Interview with Josef Häusler, in *LiC*, trans. Sarah E. Soulsby, 88–90.

music, "as if to build up a new kind of music starting from nothing."[13] This goal, however, like Ligeti's break from Bartók, was stated well after the fact, and the details of the piece itself suggest that Ligeti remained quite attached to models he found in previous music and to traditional working methods. As we will find in this chapter, the process of creating a unique compositional voice was by no means simple or immediate; it incorporated and synthesized diverse influences, and *Musica ricercata* was merely the beginning of a more gradual metamorphosis with lines of continuity that reach back to his original influences and others that lead forward to the innovations that define his later work.

Part of the reputation of *Musica ricercata* as a work of sudden stylistic change has to do with its radical approach to pitch organization—a "formalist" scheme that surely had no chance of getting past the censors. The first movement uses only one pitch class (A) for the majority of its duration, adding a second pitch class (D) at the very end. Each successive movement increases this count by one, so that by the eleventh and final movement, Ligeti arrives at the complete chromatic collection. Although this piece has the air of a recreation from nothing and of a complete reconsideration of received presumptions about pitch, it is clear that Ligeti knew what the results of this experiment would sound like and that established models were never far from his mind. The pitch scheme is most conspicuous at the beginning of the work, but as more pitches are added in later movements Ligeti begins to rely, once again, on familiar structures, scales, and ideas—especially those from Bartók's musical idiom.

Movement I

The first movement of the work is in many ways the most striking and original of the set. If Ligeti was questioning the use of pitch material, the problem is most clearly presented in this movement: "What can I do with a single note?"[14] The severe restriction on pitch, however, opens up other musical elements as areas of real invention. The opening tremolos create a suspenseful, unmetered introduction, and the use of pedal and silently depressed keys at the end of the movement attunes one to the possibilities of timbre and resonance, features that become more important in his later output. Ligeti experiments with rhythm, density, and register in the body of the movement, developing recognizable rhythmic motives, shifting them on or off the beat, adding octave displacements, and bouncing figures off one another playfully in different registers, doublings, and syncopations. It is only the final passage, leading to the introduction of the D, that uses different divisions of the beat (triplets, quintuplets, sextuplets, and septuplets) hammering *tutta la forza*

13. Ligeti, "Anlässlich *Lontano*" (1967), quoted in Steinitz, *Ligeti*, 54, following an uncredited translation in the liner notes to Wergo LP 2549 011.
14. Ibid.

through a written-out acceleration using the outer extremes of the keyboard. In place of the development of pitch, then, these other parameters contribute most significantly to the growth of the movement.

Movements II and V

The pitch structure of the second movement is almost as radical as that of the first, but it begins to betray the work's debt to Bartók through other features. It develops from a simple chromatic figure moving back and forth between E♯ and F♯, adding a third note, G, in dramatic fashion in measure 18, approximately halfway through the movement. Despite the limitations on the pitch material, the movement does develop a theme. Through the first four measures the melody articulates three points of arrival, each ending on a longer held note, marked *tenuto, non-legato*, as shown in example 1.1. The first unit moves from E♯ to rest on F♯, then reverses this motion in the second, and Ligeti expands this idea with a continuation in the third unit; the division into 5+5+10 beats echoes the sentence structure common to Beethoven's themes. As in the first movement, the theme's development occurs not by motivic variation but by presentation with different voicing, pedaling, dynamics, and registers—doubled in octaves and pushed to the extreme ends of the keyboard. The dramatic arrival of G has the potential to create a wider network of semitone neighbors, but instead G remains separate, always appearing as a repeated note, first presented in acceleration and then as quickly as possible. This kind of percussive acceleration was found in the first movement as well, but here it moves from a radically austere setting to a more familiar one, echoing elements of Bartók's "night music" style. This same pattern can be found in the repeated xylophone figures in the third movement of *Music for Strings, Percussion, and Celesta*, the "Music of the Night" movement of *Out of Doors*, and in an even closer parallel in piano music, the Bagatelle no. 12 from op. 6.[15] The *quasi parlando* marking in the third statement of the theme (m. 10) is also found in many of Bartók's folksong transcriptions and is another indication of his continuing influence.

This synthesis of Bartók, folk music, and chromaticism also marks the fifth movement of the set. The performance indications (*rubato, lamentoso*) and the opening chromatic neighbor figures recall the *parlando* style of the second movement, as does the phrasing of the theme in two short statements followed by a longer continuation. With the expanded pitch resources of the fifth movement, however, Ligeti develops another Bartókian idea—an octatonic

15. David Schneider, *Bartók, Hungary, and the Renewal of Tradition* (Berkeley: University of California Press, 2006), makes a compelling case that the "Night Music" style as originated in Bartók became a musical topic closely connected to Hungarian identity

Example 1.1. *Musica ricercata*, II, mm. 1–4

subset made of two minor trichords, placed a tritone apart (B–C#–D and F–G–A♭); near the dramatic climax of the movement, in measure 21, this allows a variant of the theme to occur in dissonant, parallel tritones.

Movements III and VII

In addition to the attachments to Bartók and folk music, some movements remain similar to Ligeti's own previous compositions, despite his claim to be creating something entirely new. Movements III and VII of *Musica ricercata* are adaptations, respectively, of the first and second parts of Ligeti's Sonatina (1950).[16] In accordance with the pitch scheme of the new work, the third movement pares down the original Sonatina movement's chromatic pitch content to only four pitches: C, E♭, E, and G, which form a triad with both the major and the minor third, a common construction in both Stravinsky and Bartók. The conflict between E and E♭ at first plays out in different registers but becomes more fused as the work goes on, appearing in direct chromatic succession rather than in separate motivic statements. As with the other movements, the limitations in pitch bring out creative use of other parameters such as register, dynamics, articulation, and rhythm.

The seventh movement is based on a melody Ligeti first used in the Sonatina and to which he returned again and again, using it four decades later in the second movement of his Concerto for Violin and Orchestra (1990, revised 1992). Whereas the Sonatina presents this melody simply, *andante* and accompanied in parallel triads—a technique found in both Debussy and Bartók—the newer version develops in novel ways. The accompaniment, shown in example 1.2, features a pentatonic pattern in the left hand, repeated swiftly, continuously, and evenly but altogether independent from the melody in the right hand, marked *cantabile, molto legato*. Along with the pitch content of the first movement, the rhythmic character of the seventh stands

and to a poetic tradition of depictions of the night and the stars. Ligeti's place in this tradition is worth further exploration, given the works with titles evoking the night or darkness discussed below.

16. Friedemann Sallis, *An Introduction to the Early Works of György Ligeti* (Cologne: Studio, 1996), connects the Sonatina to a series of other works (100–121), and a more detailed comparison of the two works can be found in Márton Kerékfy, "'A "new music" from nothing': György Ligeti's *Musica ricercata*," *Studia Musicologica* 49, nos. 3-4 (2008), 203–30.

Example 1.2. *Musica ricercata*, VII, mm. 1–4

out as one of the most original features of the set, yet even here Friedemann Sallis has pointed to a precedent in Sándor Veress's *Billegetőmuzsika*, a set of progressive piano pieces that Ligeti had reviewed favorably in the periodical *Zene-pedagógia* (Music Pedagogy).[17] The melody also develops through several variations that increase in complexity, first adding harmonization in thirds and then the use of imitative, echoing figures in the right hand.

There are evocations of folk music in this melody as well, although they are abstracted from their original sources. Its structure and character seem to match Bartók's description of Romanian "long song" as having "no rigid structure at all; indeed, it is performed like an improvisation, using a few standard patterns rather freely."[18] Although the particular figures do not resemble most of Bartók's transcriptions of long song, many of the melodic ideas appear in the "Hora Lungă" movement of Ligeti's Sonata for Solo Viola (written in 1991–94, about the same time as the Violin Concerto), reinforcing this connection. One of these recurring figures—a cadential move to the second scale degree (G, over the repeated left-hand ostinato, which emphasizes F) is a feature that Bartók identified in Yugoslav folk music.[19] The melody, then, appears to be a synthetic blend of Romanian and Yugoslav features, while the accompaniment uses a pentatonic collection, the foundation of Hungarian folk song.

Movement IV

Movement IV, cast as a waltz—another traditional genre that appears repeatedly in Ligeti's works from this period—is tonally centered on G, but it balances this tonal focus with symmetrical pitch structures. The pitches used in

17. The review appeared in *Zene-pedagógia* 2, no. 3 (March 1948), 43; see Friedemann Sallis, "We Play the Music and the Music Plays with Us: Sándor Veress and His Student György Ligeti," in *György Ligeti: Of Foreign Lands and Strange Sounds*, ed. Louise Duchesneau and Wolfgang Marx, 1–16 (Woodbridge, UK: Boydell, 2011).

18. Béla Bartók, *Rumanian Folk Music* (The Hague: Nijhoff, 1967), 2:25.

19. See Benjamin Suchoff, "Bartók and Yugoslav Folk Music," in his *Béla Bartók: A Celebration* (Lanham, MD: Scarecrow, 2004), 213; also see Bartók's *Mikrokosmos* no. 40, "In Yugoslav Style."

Example 1.3. *Musica ricercata*, IV, mm. 55–60

the opening of this movement (F♯, G, A, and B♭) are a symmetrical arrangement found as a subset of the harmonic minor scale on G. As with other movements in the set, Ligeti reserves the introduction of the final pitch of the movement for a dramatic effect, only introducing the tone G♯ (completing the chromatic pitch-class content of the movement) at measure 54. The emphasis on symmetry interacting with diatonicism is evident from the chords, which follow the introduction of G♯ and expand out from G♯ directly to the dyads G–A and F♯–B♭, shown in example 1.3. This symmetrical section over a pedal G♯ bass (placed at the approximate golden section of the movement[20]) serves as a brief bridge before the return of the G minor subject.

Movements VI and VIII

Even when Ligeti is introducing more pronounced dissonances into the work, he follows models based on Bartók and on folk music; movements VI and VIII both have strongly folklike characters, but they employ more striking dissonances, accentuating features that Ligeti observed in ensembles while in Romania—and exactly the kind for which the *Concert Românesc* was purportedly banned. In his report on Romanian folk music Ligeti notes with particular interest the use of dissonance in an ensemble he studied in Covăsinț.[21] He observed dissonances arising from the use of ostinato and heterophony and as a side effect of a kind of improvised harmonic accompaniment in which chords supporting the tonic alternate with neighboring chords that usually are step related but sometimes are varied or interpreted differently by members of the ensemble, resulting in strident dissonances. These dissonances also arise in movements VI and VIII. The strongly pentatonic opening of the sixth movement, along with the syncopated rhythms, mark this piece as folk-influenced;

---

20. The golden section is a proportion derived from the ratio of successive numbers in the Fibonacci series and is commonly approximated at 0.618. This concept was very important to Ernő Lendvai, an acquaintance of Ligeti's discussed further below.

21. Ligeti, "Ein rumänisches Ensemble aus dem Komitat Arad," *GS,* 1:69–76.

heterophonic dissonance is particularly evident in measures 11–12, where two lines begin in octaves but diverge into ninths before coming back together.

The eighth movement also gives the aural impression of folk music, following precedents found in Bartók's treatment of similar material. The melody is situated in an inner or lower voice with an upper voice acting as a drone and sometimes creating harsh dissonances as the melody moves against it—something Ligeti had observed in Bartók's "Bear Dance," a work he analyzed while a student at the Liszt Academy.[22] Melodies in inner voices also occur in pieces from *Mikrokosmos*, including many passages from the "Six Dances in Bulgarian Rhythm" from Book 6, which are also similar to Movement VIII's fast tempo and uneven $\frac{7}{8}$ meter.[23] The melody and drone often strike perfect fourths or fifths on the downbeats of measures imitating the sound of open strings, another feature of folk music. Starting in measure 11, however, Ligeti begins to cycle these through the circle of fifths, extending the diatonic pitch content of the opening into more chromatic territory. While this move toward more chromatic writing is common in Ligeti's works from this period, some of the later movements of *Musica ricercata*, which date from 1953, have more specific connections to the String Quartet no. 1 (begun in the same year), even acting as study pieces for sections of the larger work. In this case the upper drone, resulting dissonances, and Bulgarian rhythm of movement VIII are incorporated into the passage starting at measure 600 of the quartet.

Movement IX

We have found consistent references back to Bartók throughout *Musica ricercata*, but movement IX bears an explicit dedication to the memory of the older composer. Márton Kerékfy has pointed out that the opening of the piece uses the 3:1 model scale—alternating minor thirds and half steps, which Ernő Lendvai[24] posited as one of the scalar models that Bartók derived from the

22. Ligeti's analysis was published in *Zenei Szemle* 2 (1948), reprinted in *GS*, 1:309–14; György Kurtág remembers the elegance of his analysis, and in particular the placement of the melody in an inner voice, in *György Kurtág: Three Interviews and Ligeti Homages*, ed. Bálint András Varga (Rochester, NY: University of Rochester Press, 2009), 99.

23. See, e.g., Bartók, *Mikrokosmos*, no. 150, mm. 5–22.

24. Ernő Lendvai was a classmate of Ligeti's who went on to lecture at the Liszt Academy (1954–56). His analyses of Bartók's works place much importance on the Fibonacci sequence and the "golden section" proportions derived from them. His main writings are available in English as *Béla Bartók: An Analysis of His Music* (London: Kahn & Averill, 1971) and *The Workshop of Bartók and Kodály* (Budapest: Editio Musica Budapest, 1983). Lendvai's work has been criticized for many reasons—including inconsistencies in his methodology and more philosophical objections—and it has provoked polarized responses geared toward improving his methods, on the one hand, and toward refuting his work, on the other. See Roy Howat, "Bartók, Lendvai and

Fibonacci sequence—before filling out the rest of the pitch-class content of the movement (the chromatic scale minus E and G).[25] In keeping with the movement's dedication, we can find several direct connections to the third movement of the *Concerto for Orchestra*, "Elegia," which itself has a memorial character. It also uses this 3:1 scale in the woodwind lines (starting m. 10) as well as the same short-long, double-dotted rhythms (starting m. 32) and extensive use of tremolos and trills, which Ligeti also features at the ending of his memorial.

Movement X

The Bartókian technique of interval expansion is clearly present in the tenth movement of *Musica ricercata*, although a curious page in the sketches points to other sources on Ligeti's mind at the time. The theme is presented chromatically at first, but in its second statement (starting in m. 18) the half-steps are expanded to thirds. These statements are shown in examples 1.4a and 1.4b. This kind of interval expansion is seen in Bartók's Fourth String Quartet, for instance, between the chromatic theme of the second movement and the diatonic variation of that theme in the fourth, uniting these parallel spots in the five-movement arch form.[26] Here, however, the particular change from half-steps to alternating major and minor thirds expands the chromatic opening into the diatonic set, establishing a meaningful contrast that persists throughout the movement. The chain of major and minor thirds appears in

the Principles of Proportional Analysis," *Music Analysis* 2, no. 1 (March 1983), 69–95. Jonathan Kramer provides more general information in his "The Fibonacci Series in Twentieth-Century Music," *Journal of Music Theory* 17, no. 1 (Spring 1973), 110–48. Critiques of Lendvai can be found in Malcolm Gillies, "Review Article: *Ernő Lendvai: The Workshop of Bartók and Kodály*," *Music Analysis* 5, nos. 2–3 (July–October 1986), 285–95; Gillies, "Bartók Analysis and Authenticity," *Studia Musicologica Academiae Scientarum Hungaricae* 36, nos. 3–4 (1995), 319–27; Paul Wilson, *The Music of Béla Bartók* (New Haven: Yale University Press, 1992), esp. 203–8; and János Kárpáti, "Axis Tonality and Golden Section Theory Reconsidered," *Studia Musicologica Academiae Scientarum Hungaricae* 47, nos. 3–4 (September 2006), 417–26.

25. Kerékfy, "'A 'new music' from nothing,'" 215–16, also mentions Lendvai's 2:1 (octatonic) and 1:1 (chromatic) models, which are likely derived from the interlocking minor thirds. The missing minor third—a particularly Bartókian interval—in the overall pitch content of the movement may also suggest the absence of Bartók. It is also tempting to find Lendvai's golden section in this movement; it would fall (depending on whether one counts according to measures or beats and with what consideration for changing tempo—all grounds on which Lendvai has been thoroughly critiqued) near the *fff* climax in m. 21.

26. Bartók's Fourth Quartet has been analyzed many times in many ways. A brief overview of these features can be found in Halsey Stevens's *Life and Music of Béla Bartók*, 3rd ed. (New York: Oxford University Press, 1993) or in Amanda Bayley, "The String Quartets and Works for Chamber Orchestra," in *The Cambridge Companion to Bartók* (New York: Cambridge University Press, 2001), esp. 161–62.

Example 1.4a. *Musica ricercata*, X, mm. 2–9

Example 1.4b. *Musica ricercata*, X, mm. 18–25

Moritz Hauptmann's writing about the tonal system, where it helps define tonal space through the fifth-related primary triads (IV–I–V in a major key), and Ligeti must have been aware of the tonal implications of this cycle: the two-sharp collection used by the right hand comes to rest first on D (m. 39) and then on B (m. 43), clearly suggesting the major and relative minor, even while the left hand sustains its own cycle of thirds, creating half-step dissonances with the right.

Many of these ideas return in the String Quartet. Interval expansion in general plays a significant role in motivic and thematic variation in that piece, but other ideas reappear as well. A tentative draft of the quartet uses a very similar theme as its opening, although it does not appear in the final version. The cycle of thirds, however, does reappear in the quartet at measure 243, again contrasting with the highly chromatic material of other sections. Edward Gollin has described Bartók's use of similar chains as "compound-interval cycles" extending beyond diatonic use and bridging into fully chromatic ideas.[27] Ligeti's use of the compound-interval cycles of major and minor thirds follows in the same vein.

One of the more peculiar moments in the sketches comes from this movement. Originally cast as a longer movement labeled "11-Note Variations" (11-Hg Variációk), the sketch contains a satirical quotation of the opening of the bridal chorus from Wagner's *Lohengrin* example 1.5, but it is not used in the final work. The phrase is written out twice in the last two lines (starting where the bass clef occurs in the right hand), each time introducing playful ⅜ measures in alternation with bars of ²⁄₄, undercutting the seriousness of the original. The quotation of one of the most banal and diatonic passages of Wagner—a composer celebrated for his chromaticism—takes a particularly ironic turn in a context where the chromatic and diatonic versions of the theme play out in earnest conflict. In the wider context of the piece as a whole,

27. Edward Gollin, "Multi-Aggregate Cycles and Multi-Aggregate Serial Techniques in the Music of Béla Bartók," *Music Theory Spectrum* 29, no. 2 (Fall 2007), 143–76.

Example 1.5. *Musica ricercata*, X, sketch with Wagner quotation. Reproduced with kind permission from the György Ligeti Collection of the Paul Sacher Foundation, Basel

which seems to reaffirm the chromatic, we might take this as a rejection of Wagnerian chromaticism as Ligeti upholds more systematic approaches to using all twelve tones. Despite Ligeti's later claims that this set represented a "new kind of music starting from nothing," he is betrayed by another point of reference in previous music, albeit more criticism than homage, that shows these sources of traditional influence to have been very much on his mind.

Movement XI

The final movement of *Musica ricercata* identifies another source of influence on the young Ligeti; the piece is subtitled *Omaggio a Girolamo Frescobaldi* and is based on the "Ricercar cromatico" from his *Missa degli Apostoli*. The idea of the ricercar, then, presumably also informs the title of the whole set. Ligeti's interest in Frescobaldi may have also come by way of Bartók. Benjamin Suchoff has pointed to Bartók's transcriptions, including those of works by Frescobaldi and other figures of the Italian Baroque, as important turning points in his compositional style.[28] Whereas Frescobaldi used three-note chromatic cells, always anchored to a functional scale degree, however, Ligeti's version (example 1.6) uses directed chromatic motion to complete the aggregate. At various times later in his career, Ligeti addressed his use of the full chromatic in different ways, in some cases acknowledging that his idea for this passage came from a time when he had a "vague notion of a sort of twelve-tone music" and at times downplaying the connection entirely.[29] As we shall see below, he was already interested in the idea of twelve-tone composition, and in the years immediately following, he became more actively engaged with it.

Although the extension of the theme to include all twelve pitches, each occurring only once, must have been a deliberate statement, the rest of the movement has little to do with twelve-tone technique. Like the fugue from Bartók's *Music for Strings, Percussion, and Celesta*, the theme is transposed through the circle of fifths. Ligeti takes the theme through the entire circle, at regular three-measure intervals, using pervasive descending chromatic scales as the countermelody. After twelve statements he begins another cycle, this time in stretto, with entrances every three beats. Augmentations and diminutions begin a few measures later, at which point the pattern of entrances becomes less regular, first reversing the circle of fifths and then repeating and skipping entrances to guide the theme back to a form of tonal closure. The last statement begins on

28. Benjamin Suchoff, "Impact of Italian Baroque Music on Bartók's Music," in his *Béla Bartók*, 71–80.

29. György Ligeti, notes to *György Ligeti, Edition 6: Keyboard Works*, Sony CD SK 62307 (1997), 11. Compare this statement to the passage of "Anlässlich *Lontano*" quoted in Steintiz, *Ligeti*, 54, cited above, where he claims to have been "totally oblivious of Schoenberg's method."

Example 1.6. *Musica ricercata*, XI, mm. 1–3

sempre p, sempre legato (sehr gleichmäßig / very evenly)

E, like the opening of the movement, and ultimately comes to a close on A, the note that received so much emphasis in the first movement.

Musica ricercata began to take shape when the rejection of the *Concert Românesc* was fresh, yet Ligeti had not yet given up on having his instrumental works passed through the committee of the Hungarian Musicians' Union. He arranged his *Six Bagatelles* from movements III, V, and VII–X, representing the least austere and dissonant, and therefore the most performable, of the set. These went before the committee in December 1953. They were approved for performance, but, owing to the vagaries of the Union's inner workings, they were not actually performed until 1956, and even then without the last movement. Ligeti's next composition, the String Quartet no. 1, *Métamorphoses nocturnes*, seems not to have been presented to the censors at all.[30] The quartet has been frequently compared to the music of Bartók. Rachel Beckles Willson, for example, calls it "transparently an extension of the elements of Bartók that were most at odds with Soviet demands."[31] Yet in this extension Ligeti also builds on *Musica ricercata*'s experiments in pitch, including its reaffirmation of chromaticism, at times approaching a primitive type of twelve-tone writing. In addition to Bartók's middle quartets, Ligeti cited Alban Berg's *Lyric Suite* as an influence on this work, although he had only examined the score and had no recording or opportunity to hear it. This fascination with Berg's work, however, indicates a growing hunger for knowledge about developments in the West that would only intensify as more materials, including scores and recordings sent from abroad, became available in the unstable time following the death of Stalin and the rise of Imre Nagy to replace Rákosi.

STRING QUARTET NO. 1, *MÉTAMORPHOSES NOCTURNES*

Ligeti described his String Quartet no. 1 as a variation form with no theme, but rather a "fundamental intervallic idea"[32] of two interlocking major seconds serving as the germinal motive. The sense of thoroughgoing metamorphosis conveyed by the subtitle is thus more apt than the idea of a true theme with variations. The complexity of the work has led to conflicting

30. Beckles Willson, *Ligeti, Kurtág*, 52–53.
31. Ibid., 52.
32. György Ligeti, "Streichquartett Nr. I *Métamorphoses nocturnes*," *GS*, 2:162 ("intervallische Grundgedanke").

Example 1.7. String Quartet no. 1, synopsis of the form

	Measures	Tempo and Character	Sonata Cycle	Arch Form
Part I	1–68	Main Subject and Development	Theme 1	A (seconds)
	69–103	Transition and Secondary Theme	Theme 2	
	104–209	Variations on the Secondary Theme		
Part II	210–38	Adagio	Slow Movement	B (thirds)
Part III	239–367	Presto	(Interlude)	C (fourths)
	368–538	Prestissimo		
Part IV	539–73	Andante Tranquillo	(Slow Movement)	B (thirds)
Part V	574–99	Tempo di Valse	Dance Movement	(thirds)
	600–54	Subito Prestissimo (Bulgarian Rhythm)		(seconds)
Part VI	655–59	Subito: molto sostenuto	"Rondo Finale"	A (seconds)
	660–97	Allegretto un poco giovale		
	698–745	Poco più mosso		
	746–80	Subito allegro con moto		
	781–1030	Prestissimo		
	1031–59	Allegro comodo giovale, Prestissimo		
Coda	1060–1215		Coda	Coda

interpretations of its form. Most of these try to reconcile the sense of a set of variations with other features that suggest an arch form, as in Bartók's Fourth and Fifth quartets, or that suggest a sonata cycle presented as one movement (perhaps owing something to Liszt or to the continuous, multi-part form of Bartók's Third Quartet).[33] example 1.7 provides a synopsis of the form with features that suggest both a sonata cycle, on the basis of tempos and character, and an arch form, on the basis of interval expansion of the main motive of the piece.

The fundamental idea of the work occurs with the first violin entrance in measure 7 (example 1.8a). Along with the form of the piece, this main building block shows a debt to Bartók, again suggesting that Ligeti's move away from this model was more gradual than he later implied. The quartet's motive imitates an idea common in Bartók's writing and perhaps most explicit in the Fifth String Quartet, a work Ligeti knew well enough to write an introductory analysis for inclusion in the score in spring of 1957. The ending motive of the first movement of the Bartók (example 1.9), itself derived from ideas embedded in the second and third themes of the exposition (see violin I, mm. 26–27,

33. See Pierre Michel, *György Ligeti: Compositeur d'aujourd'hui* (Paris: Minerve, 1985), 186–94; Sallis, *Early Works*, 122–67; Steinitz, *Ligeti*, 63–64; and Bianca Țiplea-Temeș, "Ligeti's String Quartet no. 1: Stylistic Incongruence?" *Studia Universitatis Babes-Bolyai—Musica* 2 (2008), 187–203.

Example 1.8a. String Quartet no. 1, main theme, mm. 7–19, violin I

Example 1.8b. String Quartet no. 1, second subject, mm. 83–89, violin II

Example 1.8c. String Quartet no. 1, capriccioso figures, mm. 93–94, violin I

Example 1.8d. String Quartet no. 1, adagio theme, mm. 211–16, violin II

and cello, m. 48, for example), presents a nearly identical idea in ascending and descending forms. In Ligeti's quartet this idea grows organically from the opening four-note motive to a six-note presentation of these interlocking seconds, setting the stage for developmental variation through the rest of the movement. The continuation of the theme contains several other motives that are developed more or less independently later in the string quartet, especially the descending chromatic motive (D–D♭–C) leading into measure 13 and the motive wedging outward from E♭, leading into measure 15. Large-scale features of the theme include the articulation of another particularly Bartókian feature—the "Z-cell" identified by Leo Treitler—through the opening G, the progressive motion toward C to end the first phrase, and

Example 1.8e. String Quartet no. 1, presto theme, mm. 242–54, viola and cello

Example 1.8f. String Quartet no. 1, prestissimo theme, mm. 369–76, violin I

Example 1.8g. String Quartet no. 1, andante theme, mm. 539–40

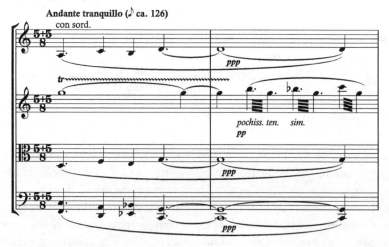

Example 1.8h. String Quartet no. 1, waltz theme, mm. 576–83, violin I

Example 1.8i. String Quartet no. 1, Bulgarian rhythm, mm. 600–3, violin I

Example 1.8j. String Quartet no. 1, rondo theme, mm. 661–64, viola

Example 1.9. Bartók, String Quartet no. 5, I, mm. 216–18

long-held notes of the cadential motive of the second phrase (D♭–C–F♯).[34] The interaction of whole tones, semitones, and Z-cells brings the motivic language of the quartet squarely in line with the chromatic idiom of Bartók as exemplified by his Fourth Quartet.

The subsequent passage, up to measure 69, helps set the tone of the rest of the work and shows its challenges to form and analysis. The theme is divided between the cello and the viola, at first alternating between statements of the primary motive in its original form and in inversion. This division leads to progressive fragmentation and dissolution; different motives identified in the theme receive more isolated attention, and the theme itself is broken down almost as soon as it is presented. This emphasis on developmental material and on individual motives, rather than on thematic identity, is at the heart of the formal interest of the work; in this passage there are no discrete lines between variations of the entire theme, but rather a gradual shift of emphasis from one motivic idea to another. Though clearer character variations occur later in the piece, this opening passage sets a more fluidly evolving precedent that is crucial to Ligeti's concept of metamorphosis.

A *vivace* transition (measures 69–79) leads to what Sallis calls the second subject (example 1.8b). The head motive of the first theme remains present in the music, but it is now placed in the accompanimental figures in the low strings. The second subject can also be seen as an outgrowth of the expanding motive of the first subject, but here the contours of the chromatic cell lead inward rather than outward. Although it is not related by a strict retrograde motion or inversion, this relationship is nevertheless audible.

The transitional passages on either end of the second subject introduce another important idea for the quartet: the *capriccioso* figures. Here the upper strings play passages based on perfect fourths and fifths, a minor second apart (from the down beat of m. 93, note the stack of descending fourths, D♭6–A♭5–E♭5–B♭4–F4–C4–G3, that underlies the passage shown in example 1.8c). Several movements of *Musica ricercata* began to use interval cycles in creative ways, but these passages in particular have a similarity to Berg's *Lyric Suite*, using cycles of fourths or fifths to complete the chromatic collection. Ligeti had studied the score of the *Lyric Suite*, and though it is doubtful that he could have discerned all the intricacies of Berg's twelve-tone technique, it seems quite likely that the systematic use of interval cycles, and in particular the use of embedded chains of perfect fourths or fifths within the basic row, made an impact on Ligeti's quartet.

---

34. Leo Treitler, "Harmonic Procedures in the 'Fourth Quartet' of Bela Bartók," *Journal of Music Theory* 3 (1959), 292–98. The Z-Cell has the intervallic set class (0167), and its structure can be thought of as two tritones a semitone apart, two semitones a tritone apart, or as two perfect fourths or perfect fifths a tritone apart.

The section marked Adagio, mesto (m. 210) brings a more dramatic change in character to the string quartet, with an abrupt arrival at a slow section accompanied by a striking transformation of the head motive through interval expansion. The interlocking major seconds of the opening now expand to interlocking minor thirds (example 1.8d), which are also reordered (ascending, then descending). Again, the development is rather free, but clearly audible, and the use of the same ending motive—a descending semitone plus tritone—reinforces the relationship with the main theme. This section also bears a resemblance to the ninth movement of Ligeti's *Musica ricercata*; as they do in the Bartók memorial (also marked Adagio, mesto), the minor thirds and minor seconds develop an octatonic sound before filling out the rest of the chromatic set. The use of dotted rhythms, especially when they gain violent force at measure 227, also recalls the earlier piano work.

Reminders of aspects of *Musica ricercata* are even more apparent in the passage that follows. The Presto section (m. 239, example 1.8e) alternates between modal scales and arpeggios created by alternating major and minor thirds, in a manner similar to that used in the tenth movement of *Musica ricercata*. Here, though, Ligeti is not bound by the earlier work's pitch scheme (which used only eleven notes) and is free to use all twelve pitch classes, extending this cycle of alternating major and minor thirds more strictly, while overlapping different statements with changes in direction and different starting points.

The central section (m. 368), marked Prestissimo, is a critical junction in the piece; this is the section that is hardest to reconcile with both a sonata-cycle interpretation and an arch form. In the former, the presto and prestissimo sections are ancillary interludes in the middle of two slow sections, but in the arch-form interpretation, the Prestissimo is the middle point of the entire structure. It is here that the head motive appears again, now expanded further to become interlocking fourths, a major second apart (example 1.8f). While the importance of fourths is, of course, set up by the early *capriccioso* figures, here they operate as a version of the theme, exhibiting the same motivic repetition and growth that previous thematic statements have all shared.

The second slow section, then, is either a continuation of the first slow movement after a two-part interlude or the return to B material as part of the arch form of the work. In either interpretation it connects back to the material at measure 210 in a number of ways. Most notable here is the return to interlocking minor thirds, now presented in a chorale texture, paired with an exact inversion in the bass, and with each part stacked in parallel fifths (example 1.8g). In addition to the motivic recollection, the muted instruments, with added trills, tremolos, and later, harmonics, connect this section to the world of Bartók's night music—the source of the previous slow section and the movement of *Musica ricercata* as well.

The ending of the quartet builds up speed through a pair of dance sections before reaching its frenetic conclusion. As with previous sections, these dances can be related to movements of *Musica ricercata*. The waltz theme (m. 574, example 1.8h) recalls, of course, the fourth movement, although here the melody also derives from the rhythm of the earlier *capriccioso* figures, replacing their fourths and fifths with the same kind of cycle of thirds (alternating major and minor, though often voicing them as sixths) found in the Presto passage at measure 239. This dissolves into descending three-note chromatic figures, which both recall the chromatic motive of the initial theme and help prepare the rising three-note motive of the finale.

The passage at measure 600 (example 1.8i) is a dance in Bulgarian rhythm (largely $\frac{7}{8}$) featuring the same rhythm and folk-influenced use of an upper drone that we observed in the eighth movement of *Musica ricercata*. More subtly, however, this section brings back the head motive below the drone, in its original form in seconds. This recall becomes stronger at measure 655—close to the golden section in terms of timing, if not by measure numbers—where the theme comes back in the high register of the first violin before the acceleration toward the end.

Richard Steinitz has described the passage from measure 660 to the end as a "rondo-style finale,"[35] and indeed, this passage has characteristics of a five-part rondo form (ABACA). Ligeti's use of chromaticism in this section is particularly varied, mixing more traditional approaches with more radical ones. The A theme of the rondo (example 1.8j) uses a three-note rising gesture, repeated, with its continuation rising higher, using the same kind of sentence structure that was seen in *Musica ricercata*. One passage, at measure 764, deserves mention for the type of development it exhibits and for the precedent it sets for later techniques. The instruments begin in a close canon (another device common to Bartók's quartets), and the three-note chromatic motive [1+1] (reading intervals in semitones from low to high) expands regularly and systematically, shifting patterns by semitone until it reaches the intervals of a perfect fourth and a tritone: [1+2], [2+2], [2+3], [3+3], [3+4], [4+4], [4+5], [5+5], [5+6].

From this basic chromatic beginning, the two contrasting themes develop in different ways. The first violin's B theme emerges "imperceptibly" from the ostinatos in the lower strings at measure 709. The theme itself is a rising chromatic line, voiced in wide intervals and marked *molto espressivo* as it crescendos and establishes itself as the primary melodic focus. The violin completes two exact iterations of the chromatic scale before it changes directions in measure 726. At this point the other instruments join in, each entering in canon a semitone from the previous entrance. Sallis has remarked on Ligeti's knowledge of Thomas Mann's *Doctor Faustus* and Adorno's *Philosophy of New Music* at this time, and he reads the self-conscious use of the chromatic scale in this section as an early experiment with twelve-tone technique—and the

35. Steinitz, *Ligeti*, 64. Sallis, *Early Works*, 133, labels this as his third subject.

similarity to the later *Chromatische Phantasie*, analyzed below, may support such a reading.[36] If so, however, then the contrast between the rondo's B and C themes is quite significant. The C theme, beginning at measure 781, is clearly Bartókian in its origins. It uses exactly the type of polymodal chromaticism that Benjamin Suchoff has identified in Bartók as a way of regulating the chromatic.[37] Together the Lydian scale in the viola and the Phrygian scale in the cello—both centered on F and building the same kind of repeated and rising motives of the A theme—use all the notes of the chromatic scale. This pattern is then taken through the entire circle of fifths. The coexistence of a polymodal approach to chromatic writing with transpositions by fifth, and an approach based purely on the chromatic scale, is noteworthy in light of Ligeti's position between Bartók and Schoenberg, articulated in his prose and compositional writing in the following years.

The body of the quartet uses a full range of coloristic effects—trills and tremolos, glissandi, double stops, accented pizzicatos, and muted echoes— the coda is remarkable for its use of harmonics and glissandi. The adventurous timbres of the rondo finale may owe something to Berg's Allegro misterioso, especially in the last section's quiet but frenetic interplay of sul ponticello and sul tasto. The coda, however, moves beyond this into a shadowy texture that captures the nocturnal mood of the work as a whole, referencing the delicate effects of Bartók's night music (and perhaps some of the supernatural moments in Stravinsky's ballets), but unlike these precedents, the finale transcends this environment of suspense and mystery and begins to create a nearly static background, anticipating moments in Ligeti's later works in particular, the ending of his *Atmosphères*.

TWELVE-TONE EXPERIMENTS OF 1955–56

Métamorphoses nocturnes is the culmination of Ligeti's Hungarian-period works, but it is also a significant point of departure for an interest in fully chromatic and even twelve-tone or serial music. The political situation in Hungary was quite turbulent after the death of Stalin in March 1953; Imre Nagy took over the premiership from Rákosi and looked to implement a "New Course" of reforms, softening some of the harshest restrictions of the Stalinist period. The power struggles between the two sides continued between 1953 and 1955,[38] but in this unstable time leading up to the tenth anniversary of Bartók's death,

36. Sallis, *Early Works*, 155–57.
37. See Suchoff, *Béla Bartók*, 147*ff*, which draws on Bartók's "Harvard Lectures," in *Béla Bartók, Essays*, ed. Benjamin Suchoff (Lincoln: University of Nebraska Press, 1976), esp. 367*ff*.
38. Fosler-Lussier, *Music Divided*, 150–53.

there were opportunities for musicians to speak up for reform. Bence Szabolcsi, whose Bartók seminars Ligeti praised in *Melos*, was one of the first to attempt to rehabilitate Bartók publicly.[39] András Mihály, who had been censured and stripped of power for his previous statements about Bartók,[40] followed soon thereafter, and Ligeti's own 1955 essay "Remarks on Several Conditions for the Development of Bartók's Chromaticism"[41] can be read as a contribution to this project. It can also be considered a defense of his classmate Ernő Lendvai's analyses of Bartók, which had been published earlier that year and ventured into areas of formal analysis that were extremely controversial.

The argument of Ligeti's essay—and of others articulating support for Bartók—rests on a contrast between the chromaticism of Bartók and that of Schoenberg's twelve-tone compositions. The former, it was claimed, rested on the established significance of certain intervals and relationships between notes and thus was seen as a "natural" evolutionary outgrowth of modal and tonal systems. The latter, however, in which only the row defined the significant intervals and relationships between notes, was cast as arbitrary or artificial. The Mephistophelian associations found in Mann's *Doctor Faustus* colored this line of argumentation and set Bartók as the protagonist against this nefarious "other."[42] In this public attempt at rehabilitating Bartók's more challenging works, however, Ligeti may have drawn on another line of reasoning. Adorno's advocacy of Schoenberg rather than Stravinsky in *The Philosophy of New Music* relies on the same kind of evolutionary argument about the historical progress of material. By Adorno's reckoning, however, modernist music was the more desirable side, against which the aesthetic of clear tonality and simple folksong settings seemed primitive, artificial, and even false.[43] This argument resonated with many Hungarians who, rather than valuing the folklorist idiom promoted by the state, "came to associate Bartók's most difficult music with the idea of political freedom" and, in Fosler-Lussier's formulation, began to consider Bartók himself as a "speaker of difficult truths."[44] As the allure of these ideas became stronger, and as more examples of and sources concerning the second Viennese school became available, Ligeti's works and writings from this period came

39. Ligeti, "Neues aus Budapest," *GS*, 1:60.
40. See Fosler-Lussier, *Music Divided*, 117*ff*.
41. György Ligeti, "Zur Chromatik Bartóks," *GS*, 1:295–301, translated into German by Éva Pintér (originally "Megjegyzések a bartóki kromatika kialakulásának egyes feltételeiről," *Új Zenei Szemle* 6, no. 9 [1955], 41–44. An English translation appears in Sallis, *Early Works*, 256–61.
42. Beckles Willson, *Ligeti, Kurtág*, 35–36, comments on the role of Mann's novel in public discourse concerning Bartók and Schoenberg.
43. See Theodor W. Adorno, *Philosophy of New Music*, trans. and ed. Robert Hullot-Kentor (Minneapolis: University of Minnesota Press, 2006), 32: "Not only are these sounds obsolete and unfashionable. They are false."
44. Fosler-Lussier, *Music Divided*, xv, 151.

to represent not only a definite move towards chromaticism after *Musica ricercata*. They also represented a kind of synthesis of Schoenbergian and Bartókian approaches very much along the lines of another idea of Adorno's, namely, that Bartók's "best works . . . in many respects sought to reconcile Schoenberg and Stravinsky."[45]

It is in this problematic context of misinformation, demonization, and rehabilitation that we must consider György Ligeti's relationship to serialism and twelve-tone technique, especially when examining his drafts, sketches, and compositions from 1955–56. This relationship has been the source of much debate, and yet the extent of his exposure to dodecaphony while still in Hungary remains particularly hazy. The composer himself downplayed his knowledge of serial techniques before his emigration, insisting at various points later in his career that he was "totally oblivious of Schoenberg's method"[46] and that he "knew nothing about serial practices."[47] The commonly accepted narrative has come to be something along the lines of Alex Ross's formulation that "in secret, Ligeti dabbled in twelve-tone writing, though his understanding of the method was gleaned haphazardly from the pages of Mann's *Doctor Faustus*, which he read in 1952."[48]

We can see how this narrative might be flattering to Ligeti, and perhaps why he would let this version of the story go unchallenged or even encourage it, since it makes his swift mastery of these concepts all the more remarkable. To all appearances, he went from knowing practically nothing when he left Hungary in December 1956 to producing the first major analysis of Pierre Boulez *Structures Ia* in February and March 1957.[49] Sallis, however, has pointed out the implausibility of this claim, drawing on personal conversations and other sources to show that in 1955 Ligeti not only had books by Leibowitz and Adorno but also had Hanns Jelinek's *Anleitung zur Zwölftonkomposition*.[50] This seems to have been a particularly valuable source of Ligeti's knowledge of the serial techniques with which he had become fascinated. Moreover, the unfinished works and unpublished sketches reveal wider knowledge and more extensive experiments than Ligeti commonly acknowledged. Nor are

---

45. Adorno, *Philosophy of New Music*, 8.
46. Ligeti, "Anlässlich *Lontano*," quoted in Steinitz, *Ligeti*, 54.
47. *LiC*, 127.
48. Alex Ross, *The Rest Is Noise* (New York: Farrar, Straus, and Giroux, 2007), 466.
49. György Ligeti, "Entscheidung und Automatik in der *Structure Ia* von Pierre Boulez," *GS*, 1:413–46, was written during this time in early 1957 but only published in *Die Reihe* in 1958. The English edition appears as György Ligeti, "Pierre Boulez: Decision and Automatism in Structure 1a," trans. Leo Black, in *Young Composers: Die Reihe* 4, English ed., 36–62 (Bryn Mawr, PA: T. Presser; London: Universal Edition, 1960).
50. Hanns Jelinek, *Anleitung zur Zwölftonkomposition*, first part (Vienna: Universal Edition, 1952). The second part appeared in 1958; citations of this later in the chapter refer to the second edition, 1967. See Sallis, *Early Works*, 204*ff*.

Example 1.10. Chronology of works and unfinished projects

Mátraszentimrei dalok (1955)	Published Folksong Settings
Éjszaka, Reggel (1955)	Published Choral Pieces
Istar pokoljárása (1955)	Sketches, dated Dec. 1955, include a relatively complete prelude to a much longer, ongoing work
Chromatische Phantasie (1956)	Complete but unpublished
Variations Concertantes (1956)	Incomplete
Requiem (1956)	Incomplete
Sötet és Világos (1956)	Incomplete, related to *Apparitions*
Víziók (1956)	Lost, related to *Apparitions*

these documents an isolated cul-de-sac of experimentation, but, rather, they occupy an important place in Ligeti's development and relate directly to many of his published works, forming a continuous record of his exploration of compositional ideas.

Only two of Ligeti's compositions from 1955 and 1956 have since been published and entered his official works list, but he appears to have had many simultaneous projects under way during this time, as shown in example 1.10. Because of the overlapping chronology of these pieces, the discussion that follows proceeds from the simpler to more involved projects.

Chromatische Phantasie

The *Chromatische Phantasie* is Ligeti's simplest twelve-tone experiment, although it is also the most complete and self-contained piece among these drafts and sketches. In it Ligeti uses the chromatic scale itself as a type of row in a work he described as "absolutely orthodox twelve-note music."[51] The notes of the scale appear in descending order but are presented in a variety of registers and durations, resulting in different note combinations. At several points the piece moves towards clusters, as seen in example 1.11, measures 10–11.[52] The use of silently depressed keys in measure 15 shows attention to timbre and resonance, as well as, perhaps, a debt to Bartók—especially when combined with the percussive acceleration, a characteristic found in Bartókian night music, which Ligeti had already explored in the second movement of *Musica ricercata*. The passages framing this cluster repeat gestures—and the order of positions in the row—successively collecting two-, three-, and then five-note

51. Griffiths, *Ligeti*, 14.
52. The transcription and those that follow preserve the notes, rhythms, and other markings of the sketch but not the exact layout on the page.

Example 1.11. *Chromatische Phantasie*, sketch transcription, mm. 1–19

ideas, first in ascending gestures emphasizing major sevenths in measures 13–14, then in descending gestures using minor ninths in measures 17–18, a type of quasi-inversion but without changing the form of the row. The use of Fibonacci numbers in these groupings is another indication that even in this serial experiment, Bartók was not far from Ligeti's mind.

This type of descending chromatic line occupies an interesting place in Ligeti's music, pointing backwards as well as forwards. It recalls the passage of the String Quartet no. 1 discussed above in relation to nascent twelve-tone ideas, but it also connects to the descending "Lamento" motive, as it is found throughout Ligeti's oeuvre.[53] There is a moment about halfway through the

53. The Lamento motive has been discussed by several authors including Richard Steinitz, "Weeping and Wailing," *Musical Times* 137, no. 1842 (August 1996), 17–22 and Stephen Taylor, "The Lamento Motif: Metamorphosis in Ligeti's Late Style" (DMA

Phantasie when the piece comes to a halt and the simple descending motive is heard alone in the uppermost register. It is a moment of dénouement, clearly revealing the chromatic row as the conceptual origin of the entire work, not merely as a trope, an isolated reference point, or a motive within a piece but as a full-fledged technique, the exploration of which could generate an entire composition, with diverse means of expression.

Variations Concertantes

The orchestral *Variations Concertantes* (example 1.12) has many similarities with the *Chromatische Phantasie* but proves to be a more expansive and ambitious project. It uses a chromatic wedge as the basic row, starting on D and expanding outward, adding E♭, then D♭, and so forth, in regular alternation. For the first hexachord, each note is presented in a distinct register and instrumentation, creating a suspenseful, atmospheric effect similar to the opening of the *Phantasie*. Ligeti presents simple differences in timbre and register in turn, and then overlapping in layers with semi-regular durations in each instrument: D occurs in the piano, tripled in octaves and initially spaced 7 beats apart; E♭ in the harp, every 6 beats, followed by D♭ in the celesta, E in the piano, C in the low instruments, and F in the high xylophone accelerate to complete the hexachord.

In contrast, the second hexachord, starting in the second half of measure 7, stays in the middle register, where instruments combine to blur the open fifth between B3 and F♯4, expanding each note outward into three-note chromatic clusters. The accelerating rhythms also recall features of the *Phantasie*, and its lineage back to Bartók, but this experiment has several characteristics that show a greater awareness of the possibilities of twelve-tone technique. First is the move away from the chromatic scale as a row. Hanns Jelinek, whose *Anleitung zur Zwölftonkomposition* Ligeti had acquired the previous year, explicitly forbade the use of the chromatic scale and the circle of fifths as possible rows because of their undifferentiated interval content.[54] Another notable feature is the demarcation of hexachords as structural units in the opening of this piece—something lacking in the *Phantasie*.

Other features in the passage that follows also seem to stem from exposure to the *Anleitung*. Jelinek stressed that the row is primarily a melodic

diss., Cornell University, 1994). Amy Bauer discusses the idea of lament more broadly, as a musical topic, genre, and as an underlying concern related to the composer's historical and cultural contexts, in *Ligeti's Laments: Nostalgia, Exoticism, and the Absolute* (Burlington, VT: Ashgate, 2011).

54. Jelinek, *Anleitung*, 11.

Example 1.12. *Variations Concertantes*, sketch transcription (reduced from full score), mm. 1–11

construction,[55] and he frequently demonstrated means of creating melodic variation and motivic coherence within the twelve-tone system. We can focus on three of his principles for accomplishing this: first, the development of different characters (demonstrated by Jelinek's model compositions, which are often character pieces); second, the gradual development of coherent gestures or motives; and third, using different partitions or groupings of the row, so that motives—often unified by contour and rhythm—vary in their starting notes and emphasize different aspects of a single underlying row.

These principles are reflected in the subsequent passage of the *Variations* (example 1.13). After the introduction of the two hexachords, Ligeti begins a twelve-tone waltz, using the transposition of the row to E♭. The use of a transposed row is in itself a move toward a (relatively) more refined technique, but the way it is used is also striking. The initial note, E♭, is heard in the bass, allowing the melody to start on D and thus maintaining an emphasis on this pitch class, even while changing the row. Perhaps this also creates a more diatonic feeling in the opening of the waltz melody, which then progresses through the extent of the row to A and back through most of the retrograde, while the

55. Ibid., 29 ("Eine Zwölftonreihe ist primär eine melische Anordnung"). See the discussion of principles of melodic variation more generally throughout 29–38.

Example 1.13. *Variations Concertantes*, sketch transcription (reduced from full score) mm. 12–15

bass repeats the opening trichord, marking the beats of the $\frac{3}{4}$ waltz. The point where the row reverses—the note A, at the end of measure 13—is related in a significant way to Jelinek's principles; Ligeti uses the last note of the row as an anacrusis to the next statement of the leaping motive, so that the retrograde seems to be a strong continuation of the development of the main waltz theme, preserving the contour and character of the motives, while varying the order positions used. The continuation, introducing a countermelody, furthers this type of melodic development, and in measure 19 statements of the original melody begin accumulating in canon through the few remaining measures of the draft.

Like the descending lament in the *Chromatische Phantasie*, the wedge in *Variations Concertantes* is an important link in a continuous chain of ideas found throughout Ligeti's works. In particular, the material present here harkens back to Bartók's second Bagatelle, op. 6, as well as to Ligeti's earlier *Invenció* (Invention, 1948) and his adaptation of Frescobaldi in the last movement of *Musica ricercata* (1951–53). The *Variations* also anticipate wedge-like formations used in compositions throughout the 1960s, for example, the Requiem (1963–65) and the ninth *Piece for Wind Quintet* (1968), discussed in chapters 5 and 6.[56] Throughout these pieces other serially derived ideas occur, and the chromatic wedge never fully loses its connection to these early dodecaphonic underpinnings.

The sketches for *Variations Concertantes* include an extensive verbal planning phase, the first extant example of a working method that becomes increasingly common in Ligeti's later works. And though many of the ideas never materialized in drafts of the *Variations*, the sketches are a fascinating repository of ideas that do resurface in later works, as well as a record of Ligeti's expanding knowledge of contemporary composers. In several pages of sketches. Ligeti brainstormed different types of variations using verbal descriptions. At one point, he listed fifty-five different variations

56. Jane Piper Clendinning discusses the wedge-like formations in Ligeti's micropolyphony in "Contrapuntal Techniques in the Music of György Ligeti" (PhD diss., Yale University, 1989), 66–67.

grouped by tempo (very fast, fast, medium-fast, moderato, slow, and very slow). He later revisited that list, bringing the total number of variations to more than sixty. The variation descriptions range from the conventional (march, waltz, chorale variations, chromatic fugue, and perpetuum mobile) to the exotic (including "fast jazz," "large gamelan," and "birds") and even to the fantastic, including wording that reappears in pieces including *Apparitions* and *Aventures*. Descriptions such as "large automata, demonic clocks," (nagy automata, gonosz órák) and "bug scherzo, (muted)" (bogár scherzo [sord]) figure in *Aventures* (see chapter 4), while "dark—light" (sötét—világos) and "web (snot)" (szövevény [takony]) figure in the drafts of *Apparitions* (see chapter 3).[57] On another page this reference is expanded and more explicitly connected to the childhood dream he often cites as an inspiration for *Apparitions*: "web (snotty dream) with imprisoned blocks" (szövevény [taknyos álom] fogvatartott blokkokkal).[58] One very slow variation marked "row presentation" (Reihe-bemutat) may have indicated a moment of dénouement like that in the *Chromatische Phantasie*. Finally, several of the variations reveal knowledge of and specific associations with contemporary composers. Besides a reference to a "totally primitive Bartók (xylophone)" (teljesen primativ Bartók [xyl]), there are references to "Henze trumpet fanfare" (Henze trombiták fanfár), to Webern as being "completely broken apart" (teljesen attört [Webern]), and to "Boulez," whose name is given in quotation marks every time it appears and unfortunately has no other associative descriptions, other than being listed as a slow variation. Other sketches name Karlheinz Stockhausen and Luigi Nono, who are associated with sudden dynamic changes and with use of the entire keyboard.[59] These references date the sketch to after Ligeti's correspondence with Stockhausen in the summer of 1956, and though none of these associations betray an especially deep understanding of the music of the Western European avant-garde, they do show at least a passing familiarity with some of its features.

57. The word "szövevény," which occurs frequently in Ligeti's sketches, means "a web, weave, tangle, or network" and is translated here as "web" but elsewhere as "network," especially when describing the more regular organization of harmonic networks in chapter 6. The term "gonosz órák," literally "evil clocks," also occurs in several places, and is translated here as "demonic clocks," following Ligeti's rendering as "Horloges Démoniaques" in *Nouvelles Aventures*.

58. This dream is recounted in multiple places including *LiC*, 24–25, and as "Zustände, Ereignisse, Wandlungen: Bemerkungen zu *Apparitions*" in *GS*, 2:170–73. It was originally written at about the time of the premiere of *Apparitions* and was published first in *Bilder und Blätter* 11 (1960), 50–57, was republished in *Melos* 34, no. 5 (1967), 165–69, and translated by Jonathan Bernard as "States, Events, Transformations," in *Perspectives of New Music* 31, no. 1 (Winter 1993), 164–71.

59. These notes are contained in sketches for *Sötét és Világos*, but they appear to be intended for a set of piano pieces that were never realized.

In the unfinished Requiem, as opposed to the previous two examples, the row does not play out in immediate tone successions but, rather, guides the completion of an aggregate over a larger section. The work is scored for two SATB choirs, with divisi in all parts, making in effect a sixteen-voice setting. The completed section builds from the bass parts up, using a dotted quarter–eighth–quarter rhythm (setting the text "Requiem") in different offset and overlapping rhythms to introduce the notes A and B in measures 4–9, adding D and E in measures 9–18, and bringing in the tenors with the same rhythm on G, and then more melodic gestures adding B♭, C, and E♭. The texture builds to a unison F in the male voices (dotted eighth–sixteenth–quarter) before the final notes of the aggregate are introduced in massive chords using all the voices, bringing the first section to a close.

This would not necessarily stand out as a twelve-tone piece, yet Ligeti identifies it as such in a later interview.

My first draft for a Requiem is in an archaic kind of Bartók style. In the early '50s I started work on another draft; it is twelve-note music although I did not know Schoenberg or Webern but had heard about their music and worked out a kind of pentatonic serialism. The series consisted of two pentatonic scales—with two pien notes they add up to twelve.[60]

The sketches support this reading of the piece (even if they also place the draft closer to the mid 1950s than the early 1950s). example 1.14a shows a transcription of the "series" made up of two pentatonic scales plus two "pien" notes (borrowing a Chinese term for a type of ancillary note). This transcription is a detail occurring underneath the first system of a sketch of the piano-vocal score, and it matches the order of the introduction of pitch classes in the opening, summarized in the analytical reduction of example 1.14b. Other sketch pages showed this same series in retrograde and inverted forms, but the completed draft, only forty-three measures, ends with the chords that complete this first aggregate. Unfortunately, there is no way to tell how (or if) Ligeti would have used the other versions of this series.

Éjszaka, Reggel

The choral pair *Éjszaka* and *Reggel* (Night and Morning) is one of the few published works from this period. Written in 1955, they suggest that Ligeti was already exploring stylistic elements seen in the 1956 Requiem. It is tempting

60. *LiC*, 47–48.

Example 1.14a. Requiem (1956), series, sketch transcription (detail)

Example 1.14b. Requiem (1956), analytical reduction of the opening section

Basses, mm. 4-18   Tenors, mm. 19-38   Tutti Chords, mm. 39-43

Example 1.15. *Éjszaka*, mm. 1–5, basses and tenors

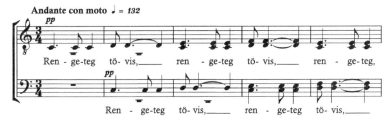

to say that these works may have served as study pieces for the abandoned Requiem. Their use of pentatonic and diatonic segments to complete the chromatic aggregate suggests a synthesis of Bartók and dodecaphony—or at least the infusion of a type of rigor from twelve-tone writing into the chromatic idiom of Bartók's works of the 1920s. In *Éjszaka*, the use of canonic entries to build clusters like those in the Requiem, and in fact using the same rhythmic idea, is quite apparent in the opening bars (example 1.15). This effect has precedent in Bartók's use of canon and perhaps a closer model in the *a cappella* choral writing of Zoltán Kodály's *Hegyi Éjszakák* (Mountain Nights, movement 1, 1923; movements 2–4, 1955–56), which is similar in its use of diatonic clusters, as well as in its nocturnal theme.

In this setting Ligeti has stripped away many of the more romantic sentiments present in Sándor Weöres's original poem, focusing only on the repetition of two lines: "rengeteg tövis" (countless thorns), set with canonic lines using the white-key diatonic collection, and "csönd" (silence), set to static chords on the black-key pentatonic collection. Another line, "én csöndem: szívem dobogása . . . éjszaka" (my silence, my beating heart . . . night), is stated once at the end.[61] The removal of the poem's more romantic middle

---

61. Sallis, *Early Works*, 171, and Beckles Willson, *Ligeti, Kurtág*, 71–72, discuss the changes to the text in greater detail. The translation used here follows Sallis.

lines parallels an emphasis on technical construction and on capturing the initial image of the poem rather than on emotional expression. The change from the first line to the second (and thus from diatonic to pentatonic, completing the aggregate) occurs precisely at the golden section of the piece, a formal device that Lendvai claimed was the basis for much of Bartók's music. The stark dualism—seen in the pairing of two movements, "Night" and "Morning," as well as in the two main ideas within the first movement—is another feature that may owe a debt to Lendvai's writings about Bartók. Whatever its ultimate source may be, this contrast becomes a fixture in Ligeti's music; it is seen in *Apparitions* and its drafts, in particular, where two-movement forms, often slow-fast and often emphasizing a move from a low register to a high one, also carry connotations of darkness and light.[62]

Reggel has a livelier, more folk-like character, but sketches for it show a now-familiar type of logic behind its large-scale pitch structure. One sketch includes the passage shown in example 1.16a, built from a compound-interval cycle, alternating minor thirds and major seconds—intervals that are common to the pentatonic scale and that help form the primary motive of the movement. The repetition of a minor third (C♯–E–G) allows for the completion of the aggregate by the sixteenth note of the cycle, something Ligeti tracks by marking the pitches in order of introduction (labeling repeated notes with the number of their first appearance).

The actual introduction of pitches in the work uses the same building blocks—minor thirds and major seconds—but assembles them in a slightly different way. The main motive of the piece is first transposed by fifths to create the pentatonic collection (C–E♭–F plus G–B♭–C in measures 1–4), achieved by transpositional combination of the (025) intervallic cell[63] in a way similar to that shown in the sketch, if one reads the chain of alternating major seconds and minor thirds in the opposite direction (that is, descending in register,

62. Ligeti discusses associations of color with music in his conversation with Péter Várnai, *LiC*, 58.

63. This book makes limited use of conventions of atonal set theory, especially for representing the prime form of interval-based structures. In set theory, intervals are represented by their distance in semitones. Prime form—shown in parentheses and read from left to right, as the pitch structure from low to high—represents the closest possible spacing of a pitch-class set and also treats sets and their inversions as reducible to a single representation, taking the intervallic structure most weighted toward the bass. Thus (025) can represent either a major second (two semitones) below a minor third (3), adding up to a perfect fourth (5), or it can represent a minor third below a major second. An overview of set theory and prime form can be found in Joseph Straus, "A Primer for Atonal Set Theory," *College Music Symposium* 31 (1991), 1–26. A more extensive treatment is in his *Introduction to Post-Tonal Theory*, 3rd ed. (Upper Saddle River, NJ: Pearson, 2005).

Example 1.16a. *Reggel*, stacked thirds, sketch transcription

Example 1.16b. *Reggel*, analytical reduction of mm. 1–6

F–E♭–C–B♭–G–F–D; see example 1.16b).[64] Further transpositions expand this to the two-flat diatonic collection (although E♮ also occurs in the tenor briefly in measures 11 and 17, it is not emphasized). The moment of contrast comes in measure 25 with a new tempo and a switch to repeated notes. Ligeti completes the large-scale aggregate by focusing on another diatonic collection in the second part of the piece, the four-sharp collection, which has the maximally distant relation of a tritone to the collection used in measures 1–24. The second collection, though built differently, is still made up of combinations of minor thirds and major seconds, as the initial melodic ideas can be parsed as E–F♯–A and G♯–B–C♯. Ligeti described these pieces as being "not twelve-tone, but also not any more Bartók."[65] Here, too, Ligeti is perhaps overstating his distance from Bartók's legacy at this stage of his career, while emphasizing the deliberate new approach in pieces like these and the Requiem, drawing these familiar pentatonic and diatonic ideas toward the rigor of a serial approach to fully chromatic writing.

Istar pokoljárása

Istar pokoljárása (Istar's journey to hell) was a much more expansive project, an oratorio based on Weöres's telling of the Babylonian legend. It is among the earlier of the pieces discussed above, but Ligeti's work on it extended through his last years in Hungary, and many of the more experimental ideas taken from his early dodecaphonic studies found their way into this composition. György Kurtág recalled, "In 1955–56, he worked on Weöres' *Istar pokoljárása* (Istar's Descent into Hell). True, all that remains of it are a few sheets of sketches, but

---

64. Richard Cohn has discussed Bartók's use of transpositional combination, an important precedent. See his "Inversional Symmetry and Transpositional Combination in Bartók," *Music Theory Spectrum* 10 (Spring 1988), 19–42.

65. Griffiths, *Ligeti*, 14.

we talked about it so much at the time that it has fixed itself in my memory as a special, major work."[66]

Istar truly shows the depth of Ligeti's study. In actuality the sketches come to seventeen pages, including abstract planning—row forms, derivations, and manipulations of the basic material—as well as two relatively continuous versions of the prologue of the work. The row manipulations begin with the familiar chromatic wedge of *Variations Concertantes* but take it through a complex series of transformations, generating new material that touches on the all-interval properties of the row (like the row in Berg's *Lyric Suite*, the chromatic wedge contains an instance of all of the possible intervals), as well as the interval cycles and other symmetries inherent in its construction.

Several of Ligeti's sketches follow the orthography for twelve-tone rows recommended in Jelinek's *Anleitung*. This included both the "quaternion" of basic forms and, below it, the master table of all forty-eight versions, written out in semitone transpositions. Jelinek gives explicit directions for the quaternion: it should include the row, followed by the retrograde (starting on the last note of the row) and, aligned underneath, the inversion and the retrograde inversion, making a symmetrical square.[67] He does allow for other row forms that might highlight invariance or other significant connections, but otherwise is exacting about how the quaternion and row table should appear, and in several of his sketches Ligeti follows these instructions precisely.

In another sketch, reproduced in example 1.17, Ligeti uses a novel method of deriving new orderings by skipping notes of the original row—something not found in the *Anleitung* but uncannily reminiscent of the work of Alban Berg. Although Ligeti knew and greatly admired the score for the *Lyric Suite*, it is unclear whether he could have modeled some of his row-derivation procedures on Berg directly or on the meager secondary literature available to him, or whether he discovered these independently by examining their own internal logic.[68]

Ligeti systematically derives material by skipping notes of the row (kimarad, "leave out or omit"). First he omits one note, then two, and so on. At each step of the process he recreates the quaternion, writing out the retrograde, and below it the inversion and the retrograde inversion, to make a symmetrical

66. Quoted in Varga, ed., *Kurtág*, 107.

67. Jelinek, *Anleitung*, 14–15.

68. It is possible that Ligeti had access to a copy of Willi Reich's *Alban Berg: Mit Bergs eigenen Schriften und Beiträgen von Theodor Wiesengrund-Adorno und Ernst Krenek* (Vienna: Herbert Reichner Verlag, 1937). The Paul Sacher Foundation's Sándor Veress Collection has a copy of this book inscribed and dated "Budapest, 1948." We know that Ligeti and Veress had a close relationship, and when Veress resettled in Switzerland in 1949, he trusted Ligeti with his piano (see Sallis, "Sándor Veress and His Student György Ligeti," 5), so it is within the realm of possibility that Ligeti had access to this book or an awareness of its content through his teacher.

Example 1.17. *Istar pokoljárása*, sketch of row derivations. Reproduced with kind permission from the György Ligeti Collection of the Paul Sacher Foundation, Basel

square. Yet he often constructs the quaternion not on the basis of the entire row but on certain significant segments of the row, each of which highlights consistent symmetrical interval patterns revealed through this process. Skipping over one note at a time yields the odd order positions (1, 3, 5, 7, 9, and 11, written above the first line of the sketch), followed by the even order positions, each making a linear chromatic hexachord, first ascending and then descending. In the next system Ligeti skips over two notes at a time, taking three passes through the row. This process yields symmetrical segments based on minor thirds and similar to traditional seventh chords. Skipping over three notes at a time, he finds a variety of whole-tone segments, both ascending and descending. Here, too, the hexachords would create the all-combinatorial diatonic (Guidonian) hexachord, precisely the one used by Berg in the *Lyric Suite* and in *Lulu*. Skipping four notes at a time, Ligeti derives another row with complementary hexachord types (012378) and (012567). After an aborted process of skipping five at a time (labeled "etc." [stb.])—deriving results similar to those in the second system—Ligeti moves to the process of skipping six at a time. He finds results similar to those he derived by skipping four. In fact, the entire row is a rotation of the retrograde of that line of the sketch. This rotation, however, yields another all-combinatorial hexachord, (012678). And it is this hexachord-type, consisting of two chromatic trichords, a tritone apart, that he uses exclusively in the work's prologue.

This hexachord is then reordered to become the "table of rows" (Istar jegyz. sorok) shown in example 1.18, arranging the content to focus on minor seconds and perfect fourths, with a major third at the end and a tritone from the end to the beginning. This chart shows Ligeti's selection of hexachords, arranged in tritone and minor-third transpositions that place invariant forms in the first two columns and the complementary forms in the third and fourth. This pattern extends through all four basic row forms, thus showing at least an implicit awareness of the all-combinatorial properties of this hexachord.

The two drafts of the prologue label the hexachords in use: A1, A3, A2, A4, followed by I1 and I3, emphasizing these complementary relationships. Each hexachord is repeated in one instrumental layer in a strict ostinato—something Ligeti has described as "a machine-like passacaglia . . . [that] tore

Example 1.18. *Istar pokoljárása*, sketch transcription, chart of combinatorial hexachords

Example 1.19. *Istar pokoljárása*, sketch transcription, Prologue, mm. 37–56

into the bass like a cogwheel"[69] and in the draft as "an authentic description of hell" (a pokol hiteles leírása). In the longer of the two drafts, excerpted in example 1.19, the six-note pitch series is paired with a four-note duration series, marking out in quarter-note values the pattern 8+8+4+4. Thus the pitch and rhythmic series will line up only after three iterations of the rhythmic series and two iterations of the pitch series, which take up eighteen measures. Subsequent entrances use progressive diminutions of the same rhythmic idea (long-long-short-short), each introduced just after the first long of a pattern. This spacing ensures that very few simultaneous attacks occur between the two complementary hexachords and that all twelve notes of the chromatic aggregate can be heard in direct succession (e.g., in mm. 39–47).

Many of the features of *Istar* reinforce the connection—present in the work of Thomas Mann—between serialism and the demonic or the Faustian. In one of the drafts, the end of which is shown in Example 1.20, the rigor of the rhythmic ostinati and methodical march through the hexachords gives way to another Schoenbergian feature: a narrator, using Sprechstimme, intones the opening lines of the poem, followed by the entire choir, with performance directions noting that "the recitation is heightened, almost like singing" (a szavalat fokozott majdnem énekszerű). Yet the work is not a one-sided caricature, either. It draws on more than just a single source of influence, and it can give voice to more than one mode of expression. If the other drafts, sketches, and works discussed in this chapter are any indication, it seems likely that Ligeti would have used more of the extensive materials he developed in order to respond to the diverse events and emotions of the story with moments of conflict, foreboding, and frustration, but also of love, triumph, and transcendence.

69. *LiC*, 48.

Example 1.20. *Istar pokoljárása*, sketch of the end of the Prologue. Reproduced with kind permission from the György Ligeti Collection of the Paul Sacher Foundation, Basel

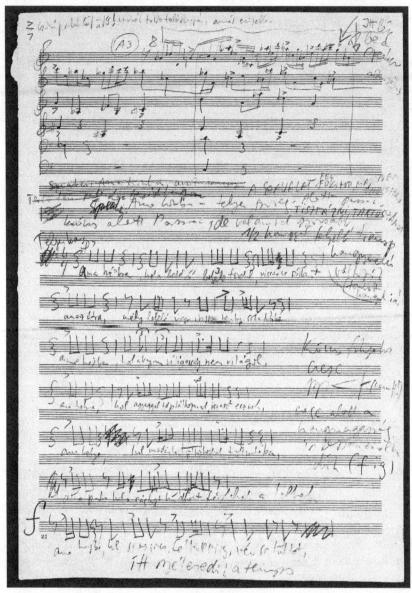

Weöres's poem contains nearly 150 lines, scarcely a dozen of which were set in the surviving sketch material, and the text contains a number of similarities to another source Ligeti held dear. The opening line sets an ominous mood, mentioning a dark homeland and a house "from which no one ever returns." As guests at this house of shadow turn inwards there is a strong suggestion that the external action of the story stands for an internal psychological drama, and as Istar unlocks a series of forbidden gates, the parallels to *Bluebeard's Castle* come through just as strongly as do those to Schoenberg's expressionism. Weöres even identifies the poem as retelling a Babylonian legend or tale, using the Hungarian word *rege*, which also marks the spoken "Bard's Prologue" from the opening of Bartók's opera.

These unfinished projects, like many of the composer's works from this time, had no chance of passing through censorship in Hungary and were consigned to "the bottom drawer." Ultimately, we can only speculate as to what shape these projects might have taken under other circumstances, but ideas first explored in these tentative experiments continue to resonate in the works he finished after leaving Hungary. This occurs not only in the concrete way that *Sötét és Világos* led to *Apparitions* (see chapter 3) but in abstract ways as well. It is in works such as *Variations Concertantes* that Ligeti began to devise a working method to systematically think through the potential of new ideas, and in works such as the Requiem and *Istar pokoljárása* that he started to craft a personal style from a mixture of influences. These are the developments that set Ligeti on his path of creative exploration and paved the way for his experiences in the West.

CHAPTER 2

Electronic Works (1957–58)

When Ligeti arrived in the West, he stepped into a completely new environment. Although there are various embellishments on the story of his escape from Hungary as the Soviets were putting down the 1956 revolution,[1] it was certainly a dramatic and life-changing event. Having crossed the border into Austria in secret, he arrived in Vienna with his wife Vera on December 13, 1956. There he met Hanns Jelinek, whose book about twelve-tone music had been his main source in Budapest, and Friedrich Cerha, a composer and conductor who would later give the premieres of his *Aventures* and *Chamber Concerto*. Unlike postwar Hungary, with its censorship, in the West information was readily at hand. And on his arrival in Cologne on February 1, 1957, Ligeti was able to avail himself not only of the recordings, scores, and resources of the Westdeutscher Rundfunk (WDR) but also of first-hand information through intensive discussions with other composers. Staying with Karlheinz Stockhausen for his first six weeks in Cologne, Ligeti soon encountered many leading figures of the avant-garde, including Gottfried Michael Koenig, Mauricio Kagel, Bruno Maderna, Herbert Brün, Henri Pousseur, and Franco Evangelisti.

Ligeti was drawn to Cologne by an interest in electronic music, sparked initially by a 1953 radio broadcast[2] and renewed by hearing the radio broadcast

1. Lucid accounts can be found in Richard Steinitz, *György Ligeti: Music of the Imagination* (Boston: Northeastern University Press, 2003). and in Richard Toop, *György Ligeti* (London: Phaidon, 1999). The overly dramatic accounts generally skip or abbreviate Ligeti's stay in Vienna and seem to take Stockhausen's recollection, transmitted through Karl Wörner, as their starting point.
2. From Ligeti's description, recounted in *Ligeti in Conversation* 35, this broadcast seems to have been one of Herbert Eimert's introductory lectures on electronic music, which he had been presenting in conjunction with Werner Meyer-Eppler since 1951, including one at the Darmstadt Summer Courses in 1953. Ligeti, however, did

of Stockhausen's *Gesang der Jünglinge* when it aired on November 7, 1956, shortly before his flight from Hungary. Now, surrounded by the personalities that had intrigued him years earlier, Ligeti was swept up in it all. He observed Stockhausen finish work on *Gruppen*, met with Hans G. Helms and others to read and discuss Joyce's *Finnegans Wake*, worked in the studio until the early hours of the morning, and began attending the Darmstadt International Summer Courses.[3] Recalling this time, Ligeti said, "In 1957 I was greatly influenced by the prevailing mood among musicians in Cologne and Darmstadt. I felt the need to work out the construction of my works with great precision."[4] Indeed, the sketches that Ligeti made during this period show just such detail.

In this brief but fruitful period of experimentation Ligeti tried out many techniques and began to develop a new approach to composition. He cited his experiences in Cologne as fundamental to the development of his compositional craft, and this is particularly true for his approach to temporal organization in terms of both rhythm and form. In conversation with Péter Várnai he recalled, "Around 1950 I could *hear* the music I imagined but I did not possess the *technique* of imagining it put on paper. The main trouble was that the possibility had never occurred to me to write music without bars and bar-lines." Only later, in Cologne, was he able to move past this issue. "Up till then," he noted, "I had not got beyond the concept of notation based on metre."[5] Ligeti's experiences with serial composition were uneven, in that he responded well to some ideas while finding others objectionable, but the exposure to the methods employed by composers in Cologne and Darmstadt made a definite impact on his composition. The idea of a "statistical" approach to serial composition, in which the distribution of different elements is precisely determined but the ordering remains free, made an especially lasting impression, and the sketches he produced thereafter bear the traces of these calculations. It was certainly a time of great upheaval and change for Ligeti, as he processed and assimilated new ideas from the avant-garde, but strands of continuity can be found as well, and the works he wrote in the electronic music studio show incremental progress toward a new style of composition.

not specify this, and said that he was only able to hear about the music, without any examples.

3. These experiences are recounted in György Ligeti, "Mein Kölner Jahr 1957," *GS*, 2:29–32, originally written in 1993 as "Meine Kölner Zeit, 1957" in *Erinnerungen: Neue Musik in Köln 1945–1971, Materials from the Exhibition* (Cologne: MusikTriennale, 1994), 16–19.

4. *LiC*, 43.

5. *LiC*, 33 (emphasis in the original).

Ligeti began working at the WDR studio in Cologne in February 1957, absorbing its technical operation by assisting Gottfried Michael Koenig and also immersing himself in the works of Anton Webern and composers who followed him, most notably Stockhausen. An examination of *Glissandi* will show that his first electronic piece, completed in August of the same year, bears the influence of exposure to new technology and to serial music and that this early work contains nascent ideas which pervade his later music.

Ligeti had a stipend for the first four months of his apprenticeship in the studio, which he described as his "second schooling."[6] He reported that he spent the first weeks listening to "hundreds of pieces" of both acoustic and electronic new music on recordings at the WDR and that it took weeks thereafter just to master the technical apparatus of the studio. Thus *Glissandi* was in part a student work that explored the machinery and equipment available in the studio. Ligeti and Koenig later described the piece as a "finger exercise," and initially the composer had a rather low opinion of the work, commenting in a discussion after a lecture by Koenig:

I don't really want to interfere with the discussion, and I believe that Mr. Koenig can say more about this, because, when I made *Glissandi*, above all, I learned from him. When he spoke of a "Finger Exercise," then that applies not to aspects of form and of musical language, but simply to the quality of the work. *Glissandi* is a weak piece, concerning both the sound and form. It has a primitive, almost schematic, form. There is a succession of sections up to a middle point and from there out, the material of the piece is doubled—there is, then, so to speak, a way of thinking in row-manipulation, "à la mode." Here there aren't really any rows, but from the middle to the end the piece goes once backwards in retrograde, and simultaneously the original shape repeats once again, in which, however, most of it is filtered out so that only traces of it are there, actually appearing on the tape. As I finished and listened to it more often, I found that the compositional standard which I set for myself was not reached. In this respect, the piece has shortcomings, and on account of this I did not want it to be publicly performed. *Artikulation* was then largely based on the experiences of what I did badly in *Glissandi*.[7]

Ligeti's criteria for self-criticism point to problems not only with the technical quality of the sounds produced (there are noticeable imperfections in the montage work, for example, abrupt level changes as material overlaps

---

6. Ligeti, "Mein Kölner Jahr," *GS*, 2:31.
7. Gottfried Michael Koenig, "Ligeti und die Elektronische Musik," in *György Ligeti: Personalstil—Avantgardismus—Popularität*, ed. Otto Kolleritsch, 11–26 (Vienna: Universal Edition, 1987), 19. This quotation from Ligeti is from the transcription of a discussion that followed Koenig's paper. All translations are the author's unless otherwise stated.

Example 2.1a. *Glissandi*, diagram of the form

A	B	C	D	E		F	
0"	40"	1'24"	1'48"	2'05"	2'38"		

RF		RE	RD	RC		RB		RA
A	B	C	D	E		F		
3'46"				5'40"				7'33"

between large sections of the piece) but also with the relationship between the global form of the work, which is quasi-serial, and the more local material, in which sections are quite independently conceived. Stockhausen, on the other hand, used the series in a more thoroughgoing fashion to derive the large-scale formal divisions, the distribution of material within each division, and the surface details of the piece.

Ligeti eventually relented and allowed the piece to be given its premiere and released on a Wergo recording in 1976. Although he did not elaborate on the reasons for this change of heart, there are, in fact, many redeeming features of this early piece and ways in which the composer's critical description is oversimplified. *Glissandi* is not strictly serial, especially in comparison to the works of Stockhausen or Koenig, and it does sound markedly sectional, but this work is also organic in that many of the details are clearly designed with the shape of the whole in mind. Furthermore, calling the structure "schematic" belies the actual perceptual complexity of the second half, which combines the original form with its retrograde. Many of the details that recur in the second half must be reinterpreted in their new context as the filtering out of material dramatically alters the resulting texture.

Glissandi runs to 7'33" and is a monaural piece, realized in only one channel;[8] the piece proceeds to a midpoint (3'46.5"), and then the original material repeats in combination with its retrograde—a feat achieved quite simply by copying and reversing the magnetic tape. This doubling of material should result in much denser textures, but the filtering of material ensures that only traces of the resultant come through, and the texture is often more sparse than it is in the first half. More significantly, the carefully planned timings of the first half's sections (labeled A–F and shown in example 2.1a) result in an arrangement wherein most of section D, a very delicate and melodic texture one-quarter of the way through the piece, maps onto its retrograde (RD) in the second half.

The work has been segmented and labeled to show the clear sequence of sections, all of which differ abruptly and substantively, and many of which are

8. Ligeti's sketches make reference to his planning a multichannel version, but there is no evidence that this was ever realized.

Example 2.1b. *Glissandi*, sketch of the first half of the piece. Reproduced with kind permission from the György Ligeti Collection of the Paul Sacher Foundation, Basel

described in prose in Ligeti's early sketches for the work.[9] The first half of the piece, however, can also be seen as progressing in three stages of growth. The first stage corresponds to section A, the second to section B, and the third, a gradual accretion of diverse materials, corresponds to sections C–F. These are arranged according to a series of durations that creates an exponential feeling of growth through these sections. In Ligeti's sketches, including the one reproduced as example 2.1b, they are labeled with roman numerals (seen across the top of the page). The steadily decreasing durations are governed by an additive series— each of the opening durations is in Stage III, for example (24″, 20″, 17″, and 15″), decreasing by a regular amount (shorter by 4 seconds, by 3, and by 2).[10] This kind of modified additive series is also used to help shape individual sections (including section B, discussed below) and emerges as an important means of controlling acceleration in both the small- and large-scale rhythmic design of the piece.

The initial material of *Glissandi* consists of 20 Hz filtered noise, moving up and down and increasing first in density, then in register. Unlike later works that eschew periodicity, the opening moves in regular pacing of about three seconds per event, achieving an effect described in the sketches as a "standing wave." This careful alignment creates the impression of one glissando fading out and back in, rather than one glissando ending and a second beginning.[11] As Ligeti increases the overall density, he aligns the peaks and troughs of ascending and descending glissandi to create a symmetrical pattern that will remain invariant when in retrograde and will sound the same when it occurs in that form toward the end of the piece. This care shows a concern for the overall form of the composition from the opening moments.

Whereas the first section uses very consistent and limited material, section B moves toward increased variety and uses a quasi-serial matrix to organize and arrange this material, along with a formalized duration scheme to determine the accretion of events. Both of these are shown in example 2.2a, along with a spectrograph showing their realization in the finished form of the piece example 2.2b.

The temporal organization of section B, seen at the bottom of the sketch in Example 2.2a, is built from an additive series of numbers, like the plan for the large-scale form of the first half. Ligeti has written out a timeline in seconds, and below it the events that occur in each second are listed individually,

9. These prose sketches are most likely from an early stage of composition, showing some variance from the final product but including notes as to whether material was continuous or intermittent, notes about whether materials were homogeneous or heterogeneous, and notes on dynamic level and density.

10. These sketches are discussed in greater depth in Benjamin R. Levy, "The Electronic Works of György Ligeti and Their Influence on His Later Style" (PhD diss., University of Maryland, 2006).

11. This technique, though more crudely constructed, resembles Shepard's Tones (described by Roger N. Shepard, "Circularity in Judgements of Relative Pitch," *Journal of the Acoustical Society of America*, 36, no. 12 [1964], 2346–2353), in which tones are carefully arranged to produce the illusion of a continually rising (or falling) sound.

Example 2.2a. *Glissandi*, sketch for section B. Reproduced with kind permission from the György Ligeti Collection of the Paul Sacher Foundation, Basel

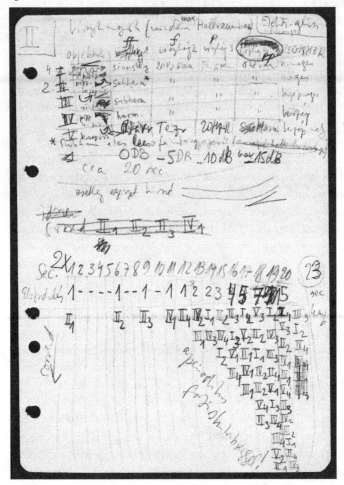

labeled as II1, II2, and so on, according to the rows and columns of the matrix. The initial pacing of these events in seconds relies on the Fibonacci series to determine the spacing of entries. The first event begins at 1″, the second at 6″, and the following at 9″, 11″, 12″, and 13″ so that they are spaced 5″, 3″, 2″, 1″, and 1″ apart, corresponding to the descending Fibonacci series. After achieving the rate of one event per second, Ligeti piles up multiple events per second and lists them in a column underneath their position in the timeline. The rate of events in the last five seconds increases by amounts also corresponding to the Fibonacci series. From the fifteenth second—containing three events—the accumulation of events in the following seconds increases in relation to the Fibbonaci sequence, adding one, one, two, three, and then five events in each of the subsequent columns. The net result of this rhythmic design is

Example 2.2b. *Glissandi*, annotated spectrograph of section B

similar to an exponential acceleration, and though the length of the timeline is doubled in the realization of the finished work, this dramatic acceleration remains the same and is readily visible in the spectrograph.

Ligeti uses a quasi-serial matrix, shown at the top of example 2.2a, to group materials into categories and assign them to the events in this rhythmic design. The roman numerals on the vertical axis of this matrix refer to the type of attack and the direction of the glissando, listed as "objects" (objektumok) on the left-hand side. On the right-hand side he lists the general registers in which these sound types occur, from very high (n. [nagyon] magas) to medium low (közép mély). Although register is interpreted loosely, this does produce a stratified texture in which different types of events are consistently associated with a particular register. For example, Type I (continuous glissandi, moving up and down) occurs in the very high register.

Each roman numeral on the vertical axis rotates through four categories of material, listed horizontally on the matrix and labeled with arabic numerals, and thus can occur with sine tones (often arranged in harmonic or subharmonic spectra) or with bands of noise filtered in three different ways: octave-filtered noise (the noisiest and most diffuse, and therefore the widest as seen in the spectrograph), third-filtered (intermediate), and 20 Hz filtered noise (the least diffuse and thinnest of the noise bands).[12] Sounds in the four upper registers proceed from the most compact to the most diffuse, so that the first three events (II-1, II-2, and II-3) are all ascending glissandi (Type II) in increasingly thick bands of noise.

As the section accelerates, Ligeti moves toward greater complexity and heterogeneity. After the initial Type II events, pizzicato glissandi alternate with their descending counterparts, Type IV. After two Type IV events, Type III is introduced (as a single gesture moving downward, then back up), and after only one Type III event, Type I enters in the highest register. The low-register events of Type V (which have characteristics similar to Type III) do not share the progression of compact to diffuse with the other types and also enter substantially later in the series, after the texture has reached a considerable density.

Although the arrangement of materials in a matrix such as the one found in section B indicates the influence of serial thought on Ligeti, there are also elements of more traditional composition in this section of *Glissandi*. Ligeti still seems to default to calculating time in seconds, rather than in centimeters, as in sketches for his later tape pieces. This suggests a connection with traditional time measurement, and in particular that of Bartók, who often timed the sections of his pieces in seconds as well as measures. Ligeti's reference

12. Following terminology developed by Robert Cogan, *New Images of Musical Sound* (Cambridge, MA: Harvard University Press, 1984), based on the phonological work of Ramon Jakobson, "compact" refers to sounds made of focused constituent spectral elements such as sine tones, whereas "diffuse" sounds are made of different noise bands.

to traditional instruments in defining his sounds, especially the label *pizzicato glissando*, found in categories II and IV of the matrix, also shows him to be thinking in terms of orchestral instruments. Finally, the choice of actual frequencies includes traditional pitches, most strikingly A 440 Hz as Event IV-1, which occurs prominently twenty seconds into the section (1′00″ into the piece as a whole).

The following sections make up the third stage of accretion in Ligeti's sketches and build up steadily to the center point. Section C is a faint echo of elements of section B. The use of such an echo section may have been inspired by Stockhausen's *Studie I* (1953), which made use of similar echo sections following each of the "structures" in this integrally serial work.[13] Stockhausen altered his echo sections by changing the speed of the tape or adding reverberation, and Ligeti alters the echo as well, but by different technical means: using a band-stop filter to remove materials in the middle register and reversing some of the materials within the section. This internal retrograde symmetry, in particular, anticipates some of the complexity of the second half and suggests that details of these sections were composed with the basic formal idea in mind.

Section D, another relatively sparse passage, keeps the rate of accretion very gradual at first. This section features only a pair of sine-tone lines with different contours. This sparse texture is a well-planned part of the whole. Since most of section D will overlap with its retrograde in the second half of the piece, the two-part counterpoint will be doubled; this effect remains audible in the thinner texture. Ligeti may be relying on his instincts for traditional counterpoint, as well; as in conventional writing, the lines are kept distinct in register and rhythm, with the upper voice generally moving at a faster rate and having a more restricted range, and the lower voice making fewer changes in direction but covering a wider range.

From the homogeneous sine tones of section D, sections E and F move to more varied materials. The most striking new features in this part of the piece are symmetrical gestures made of thinly filtered noise. These gestures are symmetrical around both the horizontal and the vertical axes, and thus are invariant in inversion and in retrograde. Since the second half of the piece involves a large-scale retrograde, these gestures will appear essentially unchanged, and they are a striking example of small-scale detail designed with the larger form in mind. They may also point to Ligeti's growing interest in Webern, who often used rows that allowed for invariant ideas under retrograde. The basic gesture

13. This process is described in more depth by Richard Toop, "Stockhausen's Electronic Works: Sketches and Work-Sheets from 1952–1967," *Interface* 10 (1981), 149–97, as well as in the composer's extensive program notes to Karlheinz Stockhausen, *Elektronische Musik 1952–60*. Stockhausen Complete Edition, vol. 3, 1991. Compact disc.

can be idealized as a diamond shape expanding outward and contracting back to the same point. This rising and falling motion, paired with a crescendo and decrescendo, creates a sound much like the Doppler effect, mimicking the sense of motion in space. The gestures are arranged around a small collection of center frequencies, octaves apart at 3200 and 6400 Hz and again at 335 and 670 Hz,[14] and their use helps Ligeti regulate a rise in register toward the center point of the piece, along with the accumulation of density all according to the accretion for Stage III, and ultimately leading to a rich and complex middle section—Ligeti's first attempt at the sound-mass compositions that he would compose in the following years.

Ligeti's schematic plan describes the second half of the piece as having doubled material—both the prime and the retrograde—but also calls for the filtering of this material. In fact, the filtering is so prevalent that the second half is in many places more sparse than the first. The resulting texture has twice the potential material available, but one only hears small snippets present in the surface of the music, often just enough to be recognizable. Almost all the material heard from this point to the end is a literal restatement or simple transformation of previous material and should be comprehensible as such, but Ligeti manages to produce an unfamiliar and unpredictable continuation by the use of filtering, the presence of invariant gestures, and other juxtapositions of materials that were separate in the first half of the piece but fall together in the second.

Ligeti's prime-plus-retrograde form necessarily establishes conflicting section boundaries and leads to more fluid stages of development. Some of the sectional changes remain strongly audible, but others are overwhelmed by the material in the other strand or are weakened by filtering out many of the striking gestures that served as landmarks in the first half. The A section's reprise, for instance, is largely overwhelmed by the retrograde of the louder, denser, and more wide ranging F section; conversely, at the end of the work, much of the F section's reprise is filtered out, and the retrograde of the A section predominates, creating a convincing ending and leaving the lasting impression of a large arch form.

Further complicating the second half is the presence of anomalies, events that cannot be ascribed to either of the strands in Ligeti's description of the piece. One such anomaly occurs between 5'24" and 5'33." Here the formal plan calls for the retrograde of sections E and D, overlapping with the return of section C. Yet bands of 20 Hz noise aligned into downward glissandi are

---

14. Given two input frequencies, ring modulation will yield the sum and difference of these frequencies, so that if the center frequency of 3200 was ring modulated with a glissando from 50 to 100 Hz, one would get mirror-image glissandi from 3250 Hz up to 3300 Hz and from 3150 Hz down to 3100 Hz. A thorough discussion of ring-modulation can be found in Charles Dodge and Thomas Jerse, *Computer Music: Synthesis, Composition, and Performance*, 2nd ed. (New York: Schirmer, 1997), 92–94.

unmistakably taken from the retrograde of section A but transposed up an octave to the range between 100 and 2400 Hz. This inclusion of out-of-place material from section A creates a richer combination of sound types and mixes them together more completely.[15]

Although Ligeti was originally quite critical of *Glissandi*, it proves to be a highly significant work in his oeuvre: the first piece composed entirely in the West, a demonstration of his understanding of serial concepts such as invariance, and the initial move toward the sound-mass compositions that would follow. There are features that look back to previous practice, including periodicity, references to traditional playing techniques (pizzicato glissandi) and traditional pitch systems (the prevalence of A 440 in section B)—but *Glissandi* has many other features that point forward. It is, in many ways, the first of the syntheses of old and new that will characterize Ligeti's style throughout his career. The degree of complexity achieved, especially in the second half of the piece, is astounding in comparison to Ligeti's Hungarian works. And though the notion of composing with independent layers can be dated to works such as the *Polyphonic Study* (1943) and *Variations Concertantes*, discussed in chapter 1, the way in which they combine into a mass of sound at the center of the piece is unprecedented until this work.

The complex center of *Glissandi* begins to suggest another kind of experiment with musical form. Since the invariant gestures sound the same in retrograde, they tend to obscure the exact center point of the piece where the large-scale retrograde begins, even though the schematic description of the form relies on this point to articulate the two-part structure. Another possible reading would take the dense, heterogeneous middle of the work as the central section of a three-part form, framed on either side by sparser sections, especially the highly recognizable A sections. This kind of formal ambiguity has been discussed in regard to many of Ligeti's later works as well.[16] Moreover, this reading evokes the symmetrical arch form, a feature that both draws on established models such as Bartók and Webern and also receives more sophisticated treatment in later works. The idea of a skewed or distorted symmetry is common in Ligeti's later works, notably the organ étude *Harmonies* (discussed in chapter 6). Thus while Ligeti may have considered *Glissandi* an imperfect product, his verdict does not do justice to its nuanced features, the boldness of its approach to form, or its significance as a stepping stone in his newly found direction.

15. See Levy, "Electronic Works," 72–82, for a more complete discussion of these anomalies in *Glissandi*.
16. See, e.g., Diane Luchese. "Levels of Infrastructure in Ligeti's *Volumina*," *Sonus* 9, no. 1 (1988), 38, and Herman Sabbe, who discusses the importance of competing asynchronized layers in what he terms the "polyrhythm of form" in his *György Ligeti: Studien zur kompositorischen Phänomenologie* (Munich: Edition Text + Kritik, 1987), 28, 57*ff*.

PIÈCE ÉLECTRONIQUE NO. 3

If *Glissandi* was a primitive attempt to engage with serial ideas, then *Pièce électronique no. 3* was an effort to do so in a more thorough way, moving beyond the mere presence of retrograde symmetry to a more integrated approach. It is the piece that is the most clearly indebted to the Cologne studio, and in particular, it shows the influence of Stockhausen's *Studie I* (1953) and *Studie II* (1954) in its choice and arrangement of materials. Ultimately, however, Ligeti used the materials and techniques of the WDR for a very different aesthetic goal. Originally conceived under the title *Atmosphères*, it was renamed after this title was used for his landmark orchestral composition of 1961, and though Ligeti emphasized that there is no explicit connection to the orchestral *Atmosphères*,[17] the composition does look forward to the innovative, texture-driven orchestral works of the 1960s, and like *Glissandi*, it must be considered an important step toward his mature style.

Most obviously related to Stockhausen's *Studien* is Ligeti's use of sine tones as the predominant material. This is, in fact, the only one of Ligeti's three tape pieces to employ sine tones so extensively, and in his assembly of tones into "groups" and groups into larger "structures," Ligeti even reflects the terminology of established serial composers in his sketches for this work. Sine tones are not themselves necessarily marks of serial composition, but many composers, including Stockhausen and Herbert Eimert,[18] saw their precision and purity—their lack of associations with traditional instruments and timbres—as being ideally complementary to this musical language.

For his *Studie II* Stockhausen composed a large network of note mixtures, or collections of sine tones. The frequencies are determined by a scale in which the twenty-fifth-root of five ($\sqrt[25]{5}$), or a ratio of approximately 1:1.066, exists between each successive step. Everything in this piece is based on fives, so each note mixture has five elements, which can be arranged in one of five different spacings determined by steps or skips in the scale. Similarly, Ligeti worked out pages upon pages of pitch material for his composition, but instead of using a constant ratio between pitches, he used constant differences, calculated in hertz, to generate harmonic series. He also inverted the resulting ratios to create subharmonic series, some representative examples of which are given in example 2.3. Thus each of the five octaves used in this piece, from 250 to

17. Ligeti makes this denial unequivocally in his interview with Paul Griffiths, *Ligeti*, 2nd ed. (London: Robson, 1997), 17. He does acknowledge an indirect influence, however, and an interesting take on this can be found in Jennifer Iverson, "The Emergence of Timbre: Ligeti's Synthesis of Electronic and Acoustic Music in *Atmosphères*," *Twentieth-Century Music* 7, no. 1 (March 2010), 61–89.
18. See Herbert Eimert, "What Is Electronic Music?" trans. Cornelius Cardew, in *Electronic Music: Die Reihe* 1 (English ed., 1958), 1–10, for an emphatic insistence on the connection between electronic music and serial technique.

Example 2.3. *Pièce électronique no. 3*, frequency charts for 1000–2000 Hz, taken from sketch materials

HARM	16	SUBHARM.	
	2000 Hz		2000
32/31	1937.5	17/16	1882.353
31/30	1875	18/17	1777.77
30/29	1812.5	19/18	1684.221
29/28	1750	20/19	1600
28/27	1687.5	21/20	1523.81
27/26	1625	22/21	1454.545
26/25	1562.5	23/22	1391.304
25/24	1500	24/23	1333.33
24/23	1437.5	25/24	1280
23/22	1375	26/25	1230.769
22/21	1312.5	27/26	1185.185
21/20	1250	28/27	1142.857
20/19	1187.5	29/28	1103.448
19/18	1125	30/29	1066.66
18/17	1062.5	31/30	1032.258
17/16	1000	32/31	1000

HARM	12	SUBHARM.	
	2000		2000
24/23	1916.66	13/12	1846.154
23/22	1833.33	14/13	1714.286
22/21	1749.99	15/14	1600
21/20	1666.66	16/15	1500
20/19	1583.33	17/16	1411.765
19/18	1499.99	18/17	1333.33
18/17	1416.66	19/18	1263.158
17/16	1333.33	20/19	1200
16/15	1249.99	21/20	1142.857
15/14	1166.66	22/21	1090.909
14/13	1083.33	23/22	1043.478
13/12	1000	24/23	1000

11			
	2000		2000
22/21	1909.091	12/11	1833.33
21/20	1818.182	13/12	1692.308
20/19	1727.273	14/13	1571.429
19/18	1636.364	15/14	1455.55
18/17	1545.455	16/15	1375
17/16	1454.545	17/16	1294.118
16/15	1363.636	18/17	1222.22
15/14	1272.727	19/18	1157.895
14/13	1181.818	20/19	1100
13/12	1090.909	21/20	1047.619
12/11	1000	22/21	1000

10			
	2000		2000
20/19	1900	11/10	1818.182
19/18	1800	12/11	1666.66
18/17	1700	13/12	1538.462
17/16	1600	14/13	1428.571
16/15	1500	15/14	1333.33
15/14	1400	16/15	1250
14/13	1300	17/16	1176.471
13/12	1200	18/17	1111.11
12/11	1100	19/18	1052.632
11/10	1000	20/19	1000

8000 Hz, could be subdivided into scales with different numbers of elements and either a harmonic or a subharmonic arrangement of these elements. The example shows only a small sampling of ways in which one octave was arranged.

The rhythmic sculpting of these sine tones resembles another aspect of Stockhausen's practice. In his electronic *Studien*, Stockhausen used "modes" or schematic entrance and exit patterns for each of his tone mixtures to determine whether the sine tones would begin together and end together, and whether there would be a pattern (e.g., low to high) for their entrances or exits.[19] The coordinated entrances and exits in Ligeti's piece, as well as the glissandi resulting from the low-to-high and high-to-low patterns, are quite similar to Stockhausen's modes. Whereas Stockhausen serialized the use of his modes, Ligeti's schemes seem roughly balanced but are not strictly serialized.

The use of harmonic arrangements and their staggered entrances suggests another decidedly nonserial use of these sine tones. As Ligeti explained in an interview, one of his goals with this piece (a goal he ultimately decided was unfeasible) was the production of difference tones. "I planned to make music out of pure sine waves with harmonic and subharmonic combinations," he said, "by introducing [these sounds] gradually, not all at once. I imagined that slowly, different composite sounds would emerge and slowly fade away again like shadows."[20] Thus an aspect of Ligeti's goal for the sine tones of the piece was not to produce precisely controlled structures like the "raindrops in the sun" illuminated "only by structural proportions"[21] that Stockhausen mentioned in reference to his *Studie I*, but rather to investigate the uncontrollable dimension of these sine tones and how they might interact with irregularities of human perception to create the illusion of low pitches not generated with the studio equipment. In fact, Ligeti had been interested in the phenomenon of difference tones since early childhood, and his ability to investigate and refine his understanding of perception was one of the most enduring results of his work in the electronic music studio.[22]

Examining the opening structure, shown in example 2.4, we see that the durations of individual sine tones depend on a series of odd numbers that also forms a connection between the large-scale and small-scale rhythmic structure of the work. In his sketches Ligeti worked with the number series 1, 7, 19, 9, 13, 11, 5, 15, 3, and 17, an arrangement of the first ten odd numbers. This series in this exact order determines the lengths of the ten structures of the piece by multiplying the original series by 100 centimeters of tape. These lengths are given, along with the original series, in example 2.5. Thus the

19. This idea of schematic patterns of entrances or exits relates to what Stockhausen has called *Struktur-Gruppenformen* in his own analysis of *Studie I* (Karlheinz Stockhausen, *Texte zur Musik*, [Cologne: M. DuMont Schauberg, 1964], 2:23–36), and to what Richard Toop refers to as "mode" in "Stockhausen's Electronic Works," following Robin Maconie's analyses of the *Konkrete Etüde* and *Klavierstücke I–IV* in *The Works of Karlheinz Stockhausen*, 2nd ed. (New York: Oxford University Press, 1990), 48–50, 63*ff*.

20. *LiC*, 37.

21. Karlheinz Stockhausen to Karel Goeyvaerts, July 20, 1953, quoted in Richard Toop, "Stockhausen and the Sine-Wave: The Story of an Ambiguous Relationship," *Musical Quarterly* 65, no. 3 (July 1979), 391.

22. Ligeti explores difference tones again in the ninth movement of his *Ten Pieces for Wind Quintet* (1968), discussed in chapter 6.

Example 2.4. *Pièce électronique no. 3*, annotated spectrograph of structure 2

Example 2.5. *Pièce électronique no. 3*, series of odd numbers

Original Series of Odd Numbers

1	7	19	9	13	11	5	15	3	17

Lengths of the 10 Structures of *Pièce électronique no. 3* in cm of tape
(equal to 100 times the original series)

100	700	1900	900	1300	1100	500	1500	300	1700

Durations which determine the internal divisions within Structure 2 (equal to 7 times the original series)

7	49	133	63	91	77	35	105	21	119

When these durations are placed in succession they define the time points below, used in Structure 2 (for reasons of tape synchronization Ligeti begins at 10 cm)

17	66	199	262	353	430	465	570	591	710

Structure 5 uses time points determined by the retrograde of the original series, multiplied by 13

221	260	455	520	663	832	949	1196	1287	1300

opening structure (which is actually structure 2) lasts 700 cm, or just under ten seconds at a tape speed of 76 cm/second.

Within this opening structure, the same series in the same ordering is used, but it is multiplied by a different constant: 7. Doing so yields the subsystem of durations also given in example 2.5. This version of the series determines several significant exit points for sine tones in the structure. When adjusted by 10 cm (a value Ligeti used to account for splicing and synchronization with other tape segments) and added in succession, these points define a timeline that determines an accelerating rate of exits, as can be seen by returning to example 2.4. Between each of the vertical gridlines, voices exit in increasing numbers: 0 voices exit between 0 and 17; 1 voice exits at 66; 2 voices exit between 66 and 199; 3 voices exit between 199 and 262, and so forth. The number of exits increases by exactly one each time until only three tones remain, in the arrangement 667 Hz, 1000 Hz, 1500 Hz, showing a constant ratio of 3:2 between the tones. Three years later, in the article "Metamorphoses of Musical Form," Ligeti would express a concern with the "compositional design of the process of change,"[23] and the rhythmic design here—overlaying a linear rate of change onto an irregular timeline—shows a definite increase in nuance and complexity of design, when compared to the additive Fibonacci-like designs seen in *Glissandi*.

23. György Ligeti, "Metamorphoses of Musical Form," trans. Cornelius Cardew, in *Form—Space: Die Reihe* 7, English ed., 5–19 (Bryn Mawr: Presser, 1965), 19.

This process also suggests a kind of connection between the use of pitch and the use of rhythm, since each parameter is treated in a similar manner. While Ligeti takes each octave and divides it into harmonic or subharmonic arrangements of sine tones, the subdivisions within the points on Ligeti's timeline exhibit similar properties. Over the first two time spans there is a harmonic arrangement of time points; the interpolated exit point at 131 provides a nearly exact 1:2:3 relationship leading to near-constant differences between the values 66:131:199 (instead of 66:132:198). Between 199 and 262, the interpolated points 216 and 237 create steadily increasing differences (+17, +21, +25) resembling subharmonic arrangements. Whereas other spans show slightly more variance, the span between 430 and 465 returns to this quasi-harmonic regularity, with constant differences of 5 and then 6 cm (430, 435, 441, 447, 453, 459, and 465).

In order to see another aspect of serial thinking in this piece, we may turn to examine structure 5. Its timeline features coordinated endings, rather than coordinated beginnings, and is based on the series of odd numbers, now in retrograde, thus linking these formal calculations to a definite serial underpinning. Just as Structure 2 used a version of the series multiplied by 7, this structure uses a version of the row multiplied by 13 to fill out the full duration of 1300 cm (see example 2.5). Groups in each channel begin according to points in the retrograde of this series, as shown in example 2.6a. Attacks occur at the beginning of the structure and at 260 and 455 cm but then cease to correspond to the multiplied retrograde, the entrance in channel 3 beginning at 700, rather than 520 or 663. At this point in the piece, however, deviations from the more ordered characteristics of the beginning are increasingly common, including entire reels labeled "transposed" in the score (a studio manipulation that could have effects on both pitch and rhythm) and the introduction of filtered noise at the end of structure 6 and impulses in structure 7 (example 2.6b).

If Ligeti is diverging from the stricter serial arrangements shown in the opening structure of the piece, then what logic now determines his choices? The effect of these decisions supports a global conception of form that Ligeti conceived of independently from the techniques he employed and, moreover, a formal scheme that he reused in the first movement of his orchestral work *Apparitions* (1958–59), albeit on a greatly expanded scale. Namely, all of the decisions that deviate from the serial idea do so in order to link structures together, blurring their boundaries and individual identities, leading to a sense of dynamic transformation rather than a succession of individually contained structures or Stockhausen-like moment forms.[24]

24. The essence of Stockhausen's idea of moment form is distant from the idea of causation; it involves appreciating each moment as a self-sufficient section. See Karlheinz Stockhausen, "Momentform" and "Erfindung und Entdeckung" in *Texte zur Musik*, ed. Dieter Schnebel, 1:189–210, 222–58 (Cologne: M. DuMont Schauberg, 1963), and also Karlheinz Stockhausen, *Stockhausen on Music*, ed. Robin Maconie (New York: Boyars,

Example 2.6a. *Pièce électronique no. 3*, structure 5. Reproduced with kind permission from the György Ligeti Collection of the Paul Sacher Foundation, Basel

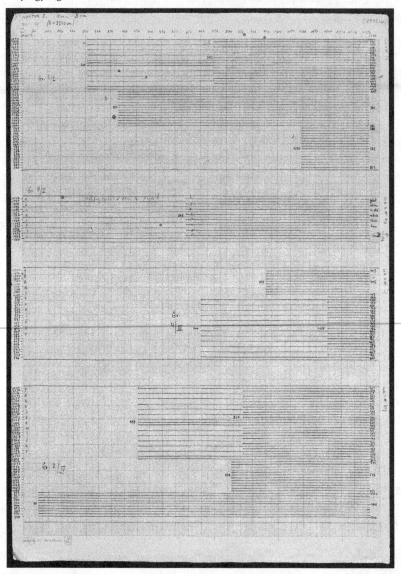

Ligeti's dynamic markings are another factor pointing to aesthetic differences with some of his contemporaries. Dynamic markings are piecemeal in the sketches, but those that exist are conspicuously nonserialized, and moreover,

1989), 63–75. He uses his works *Kontakte* (1959–60), *Carré* (1959–60), and *Momente* (1962–64) as primary examples. Jonathan Kramer also explains this concept extensively in *The Time of Music* (New York: Schirmer, 1988), 201–20.

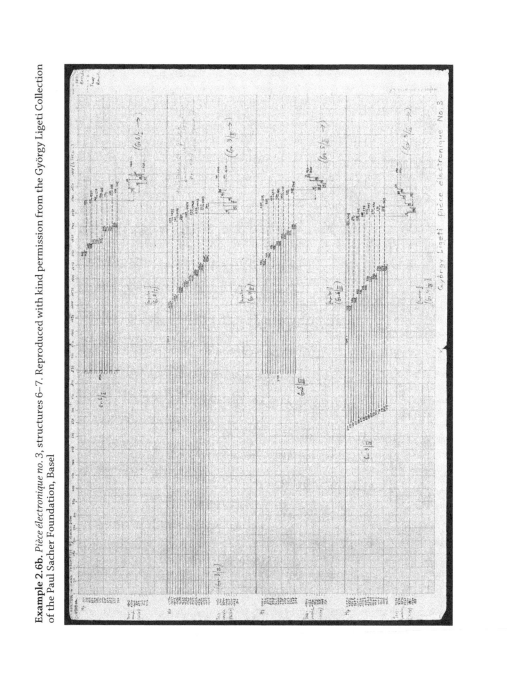

Example 2.6b. *Pièce électronique no. 3*, structures 6–7. Reproduced with kind permission from the György Ligeti Collection of the Paul Sacher Foundation, Basel

they begin to contradict, rather than support, the boundaries provided by the serial organization in the latter part of the piece. In the beginning, the dynamic indications in the sketches give distinct shapes to the larger structures, but later dynamic markings are applied to more fragmentary and often overlapping groups so that two contradictory trajectories emerge: the groups gain prominence by taking over the dynamic shapes previously reserved for structures, while the structures themselves lose their prominence, resulting in a state of dissolution in which the boundaries of structures and groups are subsumed into a greater polyphonic texture stretching amorphously through structures 8–10.

Most significant, because it represents a clear divergence from the view that serial electronic music should investigate the possibilities of microscopic sound organization, Ligeti treats the three shortest structures of the piece in an entirely different manner. Structure 1 is described in the sketches simply as "reverberation" ("Hall"), suggesting that structure 2 should emerge from this state. Structure 7 is described as "impulses" ("Impulse") and coincides with the transformation of the pitches still remaining from structure 6 into noise. And structure 9 is labeled in places as an "echo" of groups that occur in structure 8, and which go on to blur the entrance of structure 10. In fact, the boundaries of these final structures are not at all clear from the realization score; in particular, structure 9 seems more like a development within the final polyphonic texture than a self-sufficient unit.

In summary, the form of *Pièce électronique no. 3* begins with balanced structures, carefully organized and showing a steady increase in motion. At the end of structure 6, the sine tones begin to diffuse into thinly filtered bands of noise and break further with the impulses of structure 7, which seem to derail the sine tones into even wider noise bands. At this point, the low and middle registers drop out, leaving an extremely high and distorted echo of the original material.

This summary of the piece's form is quite similar to the composer's description of his *Apparitions*, involving "delicate, resonant 'textures'" of chromatic clusters at the beginning, which gain some degree of internal motion through the course of the early sections of the piece. Another type of material, marked by louder, percussive attacks, "leave[s] traces behind in the smooth noise-textures" and disrupts the opening state, which becomes more and more agitated, until, at the point of the largest attack, "the entire form is tipped over" and the register shifts dramatically from low to high.[25] Thus the general trajectory for both *Pièce électronique no. 3* and *Apparitions* is exactly the same: a balanced state increasing in activity, until impulsive disruptions tip the balance and ultimately shift the piece into the uppermost register. Moreover, in both pieces the sketches show Ligeti devising a rigorous formal plan for this

25. György Ligeti, "States, Events, Transformations," trans. Jonathan Bernard, *Perspectives of New Music* 31, no. 1 (Winter 1993), 166, written about 1960 and available in *GS*, 2:170–73.

balanced state and then diverging more and more from this plan as the piece progresses toward the tipping point—early manifestations of a trope that will be seen again and again in his music. The similarities in these pieces are quite significant; not only do they link *Pièce électronique no. 3* to other known drafts of *Apparitions* (the orchestral fragments *Víziók* [Visions, 1956] and *Sötet és Világos* [Dark and Light, 1956], discussed in chapter 3), but they also clearly set the composer apart from his contemporaries in Cologne. They suggest that, for Ligeti, compositional technique does not necessarily have an organic connection to form—a form could be conceived independently and a variety of techniques used to achieve this a priori design.

Ultimately Ligeti left *Pièce électronique no. 3* unfinished, completing the score of durations and frequencies but leaving only sketches of the dynamics and no extant tape of any of the sections. He gave various reasons for this decision.[26] The sheer work involved in synthesizing and synchronizing the number of sine tones would have been a daunting task in the Cologne studio, which at that time had only one generator. Moreover, the process of overdubbing the tape so many times would involve a loss of fidelity and an accumulation of mechanical noise that would be detrimental to the finished product. In addition, the realization that the production of difference tones would require more precision than the studio could offer, along with the nascent but growing aesthetic disagreement he had with the ideology of the Cologne studio, may have discouraged him from completing this project in favor of the allure of beginning work on *Artikulation*. Although Ligeti talked casually about returning to the piece in the 1970s (most likely encouraged by his experiences at Stanford, interacting with John Chowning and rekindling his interest in electronic music), the piece remained unrealized until 1996, when Kees Tazelaar made a realization at the Institute of Sonology in the Netherlands using the CSound computer program.[27]

ARTIKULATION

The best known of Ligeti's works in the electronic medium, and by his own account, the most thoroughly worked-out of his three tape pieces, *Artikulation* marks a critical point in his stylistic development. It is in this piece that his divergence from the prevalent serial practices of the studio of the WDR is most pronounced and that he begins to develop his own language more fully. *Artikulation* received its premiere in March 1958, shortly after it was completed, and has been highly successful since. Despite his stylistic differences with Ligeti, Stockhausen had great respect for *Artikulation*

---

26. Some of his rationale is explained in "Musik und Technik," *GS*, 1:237–61.

27. This realization is available on a CD released by the Institute of Sonology in the Hague, *His Master's Noise*, BVHAAST CD 06/0701, 2001.

and promoted the piece well into the 1960s, using it as an example in many of his lectures and radio broadcasts.[28] *Artikulation* also received continuing recognition on account of Rainer Wehinger, whose 1970 "listening score, " *Ligeti—Artikulation: Electronische Musik, eine Hörpartitur*, provides valuable information about the composition of the piece as well as a rudimentary introduction to its form.[29] The visual imagery from Wehinger's score has become an integral part of the piece's reception, even gracing the cover of a Wergo recording that presents a number of his works.[30]

Ligeti composed the piece in the early months of 1958, shortly after completing *Glissandi* and abandoning work on *Pièce électronique no. 3*. As the preceding analyses demonstrate, Ligeti had already gleaned valuable information about current developments in serialism from Stockhausen, Koenig, and others, knowledge he demonstrated later that year when he published his analysis of Pierre Boulez's *Structures Ia* in *Die Reihe*.[31] In this article as well as in his music, Ligeti demonstrated a thorough understanding of serial techniques and the rigors of this type of musical construction, but a more distanced attitude toward some of the extreme reliance on the row that had come to characterize the avant-garde. What is most striking, though, is the adventurous new techniques that he first explored in this piece—original experimentation based on the idea of a "statistical" approach to serialism, which he continued to use in his instrumental works.

Although ostensibly under the tutelage of Stockhausen, Ligeti worked more closely with Gottfried Michael Koenig in the realization of *Artikulation*, and he cited Koenig as his principal mentor in the medium. Nonetheless, Ligeti developed his own method of working with tape, one that may borrow elements from Stockhausen and Koenig but is ultimately his own. Whereas Stockhausen built his electronic compositions from the minutiae up, seeking, in his words, "to bring all the spheres of electronic music under a unified musical time, and to find one general set of laws to govern every sphere of musical time itself,"[32] Ligeti took a dramatically different approach to the composition of electronic music in *Artikulation*, embracing aleatoric

28. See, e.g., Karlheinz Stockhausen, "Elektronische Musik aus Studios in aller Welt," in *Texte zur Musik*, ed. Dieter Schnebel, 3:234–89 (Cologne: M. DuMont Schauberg, 1971), 3:249. In this collection of transcripts of radio broadcasts from between 1964 and 1966 introducing the work being done in different electronic music studios, *Artikulation* is the final example representing the WDR.

29. Rainer Wehinger, *Ligeti—Artikulation: Electronische Musik, eine Hörpartitur* (Mainz: Schott, 1970).

30. György Ligeti, *Continuum, Zehn Stücke für Bläserquintett, Artikulation, Glissandi, Etüden für Orgel, Volumina*, Wergo WER 60161-50, 1984/1988.

31. György Ligeti, "Pierre Boulez: Decision and Automatism in Structure 1a," trans. Leo Black, in *Young Composers: Die Reihe* 4 (Bryn Mawr, PA: Presser; London: Universal Edition, 1960), 36–62. German edition 1958.

32. Karlheinz Stockhausen. "The Concept of Unity in Electronic Music," trans. Elaine Barkin, *Perspectives of New Music* 1, no. 1 (1962), 48.

selection at the smallest level of sonic construction and developing rich, multilayered sounds based on variety and opposition rather than a microcosmic unity. This was a significant change from the use of pure sine tones in *Pièce électronique no. 3*, and one that more closely fit his personal aesthetic views.

Since arriving in Cologne, Ligeti had studied aspects of phonetics and in particular, according to Wehinger, "analyses of acoustic spectrum and proportion of noise in sounds; the transient process and fade-out process in plosives; and the time-proportions of consonants and vowels in spoken languages."[33] He started the composition of *Artikulation* by generating a large number of source sounds that imitated phonemes: various consonants, vowels, and their combinations. Ligeti was not alone in taking this approach to composition, either; his friend Mauricio Kagel was concurrently working on his *Anagrama*, parts of which take the Latin palindrome "in girum imus nocte et consumimur igni" and recombine the letters (or the phonemes these letters could represent) into different words in different languages.[34]

The study of phonetics at the WDR can be traced through Stockhausen to Werner Meyer-Eppler, a professor at the University of Bonn. Meyer-Eppler was trained as a physicist, but he had been working at the Institute for Phonetics in Bonn since 1947 and was at the forefront of developing communications theory; Stockhausen, who took courses from Meyer-Eppler, called him "the best teacher I ever had."[35] Stockhausen described some of the inspiration that he gained from these classes and directed into statistical composition:

In phonetics he [Meyer-Eppler] was analyzing the different sounds of language, in communications science he was engaged in studying statistics, because he wanted to know more precisely what all the different noises were, and analyzing the wave structure of noises and consonants in language led him to use statistical methods of description and analysis.[36]

Describing an exercise that may have inspired Ligeti's compositional method in *Artikulation*, Stockhausen continued:

He would give us exercises demonstrating the principles of the Markoff series; in one we were given cut-outs of individual letters from newspaper articles, and we had to put them in sequence by a chance operation and see what sort of a text came out. Then we

33. Wehinger, *Ligeti—Artikulation*, 11.
34. Björn Heile discusses *Anagrama* in greater depth in *The Music of Mauricio Kagel* (Burlington, VT: Ashgate, 2006), 21–25; see also the analysis in Matthias Kassel "Das Fundament im Turm zu Babel: Ein weiterer Versuch, *Anagrama* zu lesen," 4–26 in *Mauricio Kagel*, Musik-Konzepte 124 (Munich: Edition Text + Kritik, 2004).
35. This statement is quoted in several sources including Toop, *Ligeti*, 59, and Steinitz *Ligeti*, 80.
36. Stockhausen, *Stockhausen on Music*, 50.

would repeat the operation with individual syllables, and then with combinations of two syllables, and so forth, each time trying to discover the degree of redundancy, as we called it, of the resulting texts.[37]

According to Wehinger, Ligeti categorized the phonetically inspired sounds of *Artikulation* into forty-two types of basic materials with names describing either their means of construction (e.g., "subharmonic spectra") or more subjective associations (e.g., "barking" [*Ugató*]).[38] He then grouped the tape recordings of these short sounds together according to similarities of sonic quality and character including "combination of materials, pitch distribution, duration relationships, and intensity relationships,"[39] and he placed the similar sounds into bins. Then he began the aleatoric process of blindly selecting strips of tape containing individual sounds from the bins and splicing them together into longer segments, which, in his sketches, he calls "texts."[40] The resulting ten texts were differentiated by virtue of contrasting material as follows:

1. "coughing"
2. "coughing" and types of noise with explosion-like envelope
3. sine tones and 20 Hz noise bands—linear and glissing
4. dry impulses
5. wet impulses
6. "sandpaper"
7. mixture of "sandpaper," filtered and unfiltered impulses, and other materials
8. "completely heterogeneous materials"
9. "sandpaper," reverberated noise, and "glissando explosions"
10. harmonic and subharmonic spectra, linear and glissing[41]

37. Ibid. other information about Meyer-Eppler's role in the WDR Studio is chronicled in Elena Ungeheuer, *Wie die elektronishce Musik 'erfunden' wurde . . .: Quellensudie zu Werner Meyer-Epplers musikalischem Entwurf zwischen 1949 und 1953*. Kölner Schriften zur Neuen Musik 2 (Mainz: Schott, 1992).

38. Wehinger, *Ligeti—Artikulation*, 11–12.

39. Ibid., 17.

40. Although the use of aleatoric procedures in a composition for tape does resemble John Cage's work on *Williams Mix* (1952–53), the technique discussed here is more tightly restrained, as explained below. Ligeti would not encounter Cage directly until later in the same year, at the 1958 Darmstadt Summer Courses, where he attended Cage's infamous lectures. The effect of Cage on Ligeti and his circle is discussed further in chapter 4.

41. Wehinger, *Ligeti—Artikulation*, 18. In my investigation of the sketches, I have found similar descriptions including dry impulses (szaraz impulsok) and wet impulses (nedves impulsok) as materials occurring within multiple texts, rather than as texts themselves, suggesting a degree of overlap between the categories presented in Wehinger. Other complications recorded in the sketches for *Artikulation* are addressed below.

Example 2.7a. *Artikulation*, levels of the compositional process (after Wehinger)

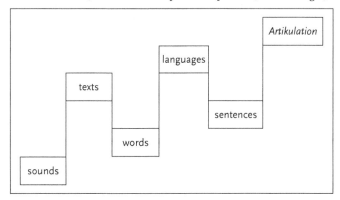

Each text runs between 11 and 43 seconds. Some were then combined, transposed, or retrograded. The evidence of serial thought in these diagrams is clear; they often show branching charts exploring every possible permutation, every transformation balanced by its inversion or opposite. What is more striking is that these branch diagrams often contain subjective comments by Ligeti, who marked some "good" while rejecting others.[42]

He then cut both the altered and the unaltered texts back into mid-length segments, termed "words." Some words were further transformed with techniques such as reverberation and ring modulation, in addition to the techniques already used to alter the texts. Ligeti then treated the words as he did the sounds. He grouped them according to their sonic characteristics, again putting similar sounds into bins. By repeating the process of splicing bits of tape together and cutting them back into smaller segments (the stages of which are shown in example 2.7a),[43] Ligeti completed the piece.

In moving from words to languages, Ligeti used categories such as type of text, duration and word density, average register, average intensity, and presence of ring modulation[44] to separate his recorded sounds into bins. Furthermore, he transformed these sounds at each level, just as he had done with the words and texts; Wehinger cites instances when the sentences were

---

42. This approach is notably different from the one Richard Taruskin suggests in the *Oxford History of Western Music*, (New York: Oxford University Press, 2005), 5.52. Although the exploration of material tends to be systematic, there is no evidence of algorithms governing the use of this material in the piece. In fact, given Ligeti's criticism of automatism in Boulez, this interpretation of Ligeti's compositional technique is quite unlikely.

43. The chart is modeled after Wehinger, *Ligeti—Artikulation*, 18.

44. Ibid., 19.

Example 2.7b. *Artikulation*, sketch showing linguistic categories. Reproduced with kind permission from the György Ligeti Collection of the Paul Sacher Foundation, Basel

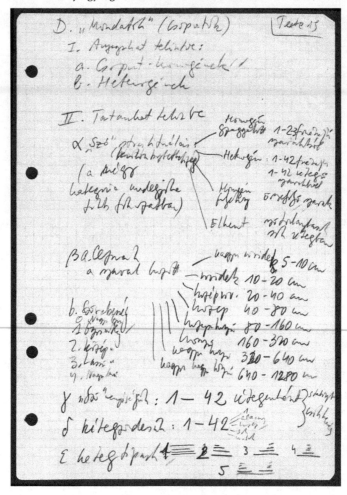

interrupted, ring-modulated in their entirety, or even synchronized with other sentences before being combined into the final piece.

The sketch reproduced in example 2.7b shows many of these features in Ligeti's own hand, but it also reveals some complexities and inconsistencies in the compositional method as Wehinger describes it. For example, material is labeled as belonging to Text 15, whereas Wehinger's list only goes up to 10; at other points in the sketches, too, Ligeti seems to switch between roman numerals, arabic numerals, and letter designations, suggesting a somewhat ad hoc treatment of material. He also equates the sentences (mondatok) with groups (csoportok), which in this example can be homogeneous or heterogeneous—suggesting a lingering use of Stockhausen's terminology and a certain interchangeability between technical and descriptive language. Roman numeral II deals with the durations, which refer to different types of "word" structuring ("szó" strukturálás) and to breaks between the words (cezúrák a szavak között). The former are subdivided into a branching diagram delineating homogeneous intermittent (homogén szaggatott), heterogeneous (heterogén), homogeneous flowing (homogén folyékony), and smeared (elkent). The bottom of the sketch refers to layer stratifications (rétegződések) and layer types (réteg-típusok), which receive schematic diagrams at the very bottom of the sketch. They closely resemble those found in Stockhausen and observed in *Pièce électronique no. 3*, and they likely indicate the coordination of material to be synchronized into larger units.

The rhythmic planning of *Artikulation* also went through several stages. The lengths of individual sounds were determined by a basic unit of 10 mm and a scale proceeding by the interval 11/10, so that the next unit would be this ratio times the previous unit. For example:

$$10 \times (11/10) = 11$$
$$11 \times (11/10) = 12.1$$
$$12.1 \times (11/10) = 13.31$$

He continued this process until it reached the fiftieth value: 1067.189553, equal to about 14 seconds. These numbers were then rounded to the nearest whole millimeter and used as the durations for events within a given type of material and eventually through the course of the piece.

It is significant that Ligeti distributed sounds of specific durations using a method that he would later employ in his orchestral work *Apparitions* and which he described briefly in "Metamorphoses of Musical Form."[45] His goal was to balance short and long durations within a given material, but not by giving all durations an equal number of occurrences, as a serial duration row would do. Ligeti explained that this process would favor the longer durations, which, given an equal number of occurrences, would make up a more substantial portion of the piece than would the shorter ones. Instead, Ligeti chose a method by which other distributions were possible—a technique he compared to a printer's case, where some letters occur more frequently according to their use in the language.[46] In Ligeti's application, the value of each duration, multiplied by the number of occurrences of that duration, would equal a constant—a specific numerical product—and thus the sum of each of the types of duration would make up an equal portion of the piece. As an example of this Wehinger cites a simple case in which "there were, for one material,

45. See Ligeti's comments in "Metamorphoses of Musical Form," 14, n. 28.
46. *LiC*, 133.

Example 2.8. *Artikulation*, material 3, product method

Length	Instances	Product	Length	Instances	Product	Material
1	30	30	8.2	3	24.6	
1.1	28	30.8	9.1	3	27.3	
1.2	26	31.2	10	3	30	
1.3	24	31.2	11	3	33	
1.4	22	30.8	12	3	36	
1.5	20	30	13	2	26	
1.7	18	30.6	14	2	28	
1.9	16	30.4	15	2	30	sin objekt, ugató
2.1	14	29.4	17	2	34	sin objekt, ugató
2.3	12	27.6	19	2	38	sin objekt, sin objekt
2.5	12	30	21	1	21	20 hz objekt
2.8	10	28	23	1	23	ugató
3.1	10	31	25	1	25	sin objekt
3.4	8	27.2	28	1	28	sin objekt
3.7	8	29.6	31	1	31	ugató
4.1	7	28.7	34	1	34	sin objekt
4.5	7	31.5	41	1	41	20 hz objekt
5	6	30	50	1	50	20 hz objekt
5.5	6	33	61	1	61	sin objekt
6.1	5	30.5	74	1	74	ugató
6.7	5	33.5	91	1	91	20 hz objekt
7.4	4	29.6	130	1	130	ugató

150 bits of tape 1 cm in length, and one bit of tape 150 cm in length."[47] At the standard tape speed of 76 cm/sec, this type of material had sounds ranging between .013 and 1.974 seconds, an indication of the meticulous level of planning involved in this piece.

According to Ligeti's sketches, he used a similar procedure to create another type of material. In the sketches labeled "Material 3," the series of durations (see example 2.8) follows an 11/10 scale, rounding at first to the millimeter and then rounding to the whole centimeter, and each time multiplying the rounded result by 11/10 to arrive at the next value. The number of instances of each duration creates a product of approximately 30. Ligeti marked off each instance by writing out the letter R, S, or U over them as they are used. These most likely stand for Rauschen (noise), Sinus (sine tones), and Ugató (barking).[48]

47. Wehinger, *Ligeti—Artikulation*, 17.
48. This is another instance of Ligeti using a mixture of languages: German—especially for technical terms, which he might have learned for use in electronic music—and Hungarian for more descriptive terms.

After the durations 31 and 34 (significant because they are the first to exceed the product, 30), Ligeti appears to find new values by adding the odd numbers 7 through 13, then skipping to 17 and 39, whose appearance cannot be explained by either system. Given the use of additive series here and elsewhere in Ligeti's work, however, one could speculate that it is equal to the sum of other odd numbers (11+13+15) or is 3×13. These longer events are given written-out descriptions as "objects" and seem to have stood outside the new technique.

By this detailed method of construction Ligeti arrives at sounds that are rich and dynamic, arguably some of the most refined and nuanced to come out of the WDR, standing alongside those of Stockhausen's *Gesang der Jünglinge* (1955–56) and *Kontakte* (1959–60). And though Ligeti's flexible method and use of chance as a determinant may seem strikingly original and even free in comparison to the strict serialism associated with the Cologne composers, it is not as divergent from Stockhausen and Koenig as it may first appear. The aleatoric method of drawing bits of tape out of a box may at first seem to undermine any idea of a planned or organized form, but at each step the pieces were organized by their common characteristics, thus limiting any randomness to the smallest scale and to the most superficial level of the piece. Moreover, it was not unprecedented at the WDR to use procedures termed "statistical" and approaching chance operations. In fact, here we see some of the influence of Koenig. While aiding Stockhausen with the realization of *Gesang der Jünglinge*, Koenig had a novel solution to the problem of creating very dense and complicated clouds of very short sounds. According to his student, Konrad Boehmer,

Koenig was convinced that it would not be at all sensible to record thousands of centimeter-long particles of sinus tones and then to measure, cut, and finally glue them together. For this reason, he proposed a quasi-aleatoric production process in which he began with tapes of short magnetic and white-taped sections and then recorded a sinus-glissando that would be automatically divided into distinct, small particles. If several such tapes are synchronized . . . one hears a "cloud" of tiny sound particles with an all-embracing global direction. Although the composer might not have absolute control over every detail, he or she can control the audible result.[49]

Koenig describes a similar method of generating material for his composition *Essay*. The instructions in this score show a process whereby certain details were left to chance, although these aleatoric elements are largely confined to specifics of frequency curves that are only schematically indicated in the

---

49. Konrad Boehmer, "Koenig—Sound Composition—*Essay*," in *Electroacoustic Music: Analytical Perspectives*, ed. Thomas Licata, 59–72 (Westport, CT: Greenwood, 2002), 62–63.

score.[50] This material is then transformed by techniques (usually serially determined) such as ring modulation, transposition, filtering, and reverberation, and finally the resulting material is divided up and recombined into sections of the finished piece. Once again, though, Ligeti differs from Stockhausen and Koenig, first, by the use of a more subjective classification of material than Koenig's classification (based entirely on the studio techniques used), and, second, by relying less on the combinatorial variety of a serial formal scheme than on an intuitive but targeted investigation of texture, fitting his a priori conception of the form of the piece.

When these materials are finally combined into the piece, they represent a new step in Ligeti's thinking about form, acting on a very innovative concept, investigating the breakdown of materials, and determining which elements blend most readily and which tend to remain distinct. In plotting the course of the piece (summarized in example 2.9a), Ligeti did not employ a serial scheme of permutations and combinations of the types of material, but, rather, he arranged the sections so as to investigate "aggregate conditions" and the "permeability" of the materials.[51] Ultimately he sought to create a large-scale form that he described as "a gradual, irreversible progress from the heterogeneous disposition at the beginning to the complete mixture and interpenetration of the contrasted characters at the end."[52] The internal diversity of material that Ligeti had worked to develop thus leads to a very complex interrelation of shared features, but instead of trying to synthesize or resolve the similar aspects of the material into recognizable categories, he emphasizes their differences.

The opening of *Artikulation* presents as clear a contrast as possible; sections A1 and A2 differ in almost every regard, yet both have a sense of growth, making an almost classical phrase pairing. Section A1 (0″–18″) is designed to imitate the effect of approaching from a distance by the use of reverberation, along with an acceleration of attacks and an expansion of register. This can be seen in example 2.9b (közel jön, "it comes near"). Section A1 mainly uses impulses—defined variously but usually considered a type of narrowly filtered noise with a relatively short duration—as its material.[53] Section A2 (18″–31″)

50. Gottfried Michael Koenig, *Essay: Komposition für elektronische Klänge, 1957. Partitur zugleich technische Arbeitsanweisung* (Vienna: Universal Edition, 1960).

51. Ligeti identified several sections of the composition, but they went through substantial alteration as he shortened the planned length of the piece from about 6′ to the current 3′45″. As a consequence, the "subsections" of A (A1–A12), which make up more than one-half of the piece, often have the length, diversity, and independence to be considered as having equal status with the entirety of later sections (B–F). See Levy, "Electronic Works," 102–4 for a full discussion of these alterations.

52. Ligeti, "Metamorphoses," 15.

53. Koenig's score for *Essay* defines an impulse as a 1 percent deviation in bandwidth from a given frequency, and a noise, by contrast, as a 5 percent deviation. Technical definitions of the term "impulse" also appear in Eimert's "What Is Electronic Music?"

Example 2.9a. *Artikulation*, synopsis of the form

A1, A2	Sections clearly separated by contrasting material coming from different channels
A3-A6	Sections move towards internal contrast using different types of material to create dialogues
A7	Consistent material moves from channel to channel
A8-A12	Diverse elements are reintroduced and begin overlapping to a higher degree
B-E	These elements accelerate and overlapping of events turns into a dense continuity
F-G	Works as a coda, mixed elements are separated into shorter events

Example 2.9b. *Artikulation*, sketch for sections A1–A5. Reproduced with kind permission from the György Ligeti Collection of the Paul Sacher Foundation, Basel

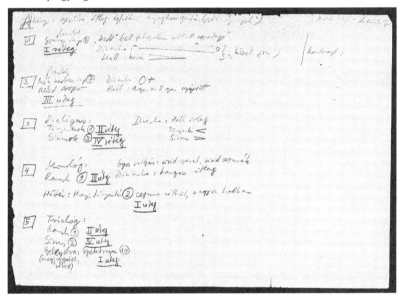

begins abruptly and has a similar pattern of growth, acceleration, and register expansion, but it contrasts with A1 in most other regards. Section A2 enters from a diametrically opposite speaker (the front answered by the back in the quadrophonic version, the right answered by the left in stereo) and features more definite pitches, in many cases held for longer durations and with slight glissandi. Thus the initial pairing of material with contrasting features emanating from different directions sets up clear distinctions that Ligeti will work to break down in the rest of the piece.

and Stockhausen's "Actualia," both in *Electronic Music: Die Reihe* 1 (1955, English ed. 1957), pages 4 and 46, respectively.

Subsequent sections present more internal contrasts, mixing pitch-based and noise-based materials, high and low registers, loud and soft dynamics, glissandi and straight pitches until polyphonic dialogues begin to emerge. By section A6 (56″–1′10″) the alternation between contrasting sections has been replaced by a polyphonic give and take within a single section. Here the contrasting sides of the polyphony are kept distinct primarily by type of material (pitch versus noise-based) and by more subtle use of spatial location (in the stereo version they all appear in the left channel, in the quadrophonic version, the left and back channels).

The following section (A7, 1′10″–1′41″) marks a major change in the piece; it presents highly consistent material beginning in the right speaker but at 1′33″ panning gradually to the left, thus asserting a single consistent sound across space. This move undercuts the use of space as the primary means of separating material and opens up the piece to further development along these lines. The section introduces the use of sine tones in nonharmonic spectra, often with slight glissandi in either direction—a new and distinctive material that aids the perception of a single type of material moving across space, contradicting the trend of the piece so far.

Once Ligeti establishes the precedent of allowing one type of material to change spatial location, the stage is set for drawing more connections between events in different speakers, and this actuality is quickly compounded by more extensive overlapping of more diverse material in different channels for the rest of the piece. The orderly dialogues of the beginning give way to a more complex conversation with multiple voices sounding at once. Simple contrasts in one or more parameters are replaced by more subtle interactions in which events echo one another in some regards while disagreeing in others. Events with glissandi or with similar dynamic envelopes may be heard across speakers and come through as related gestures, though they may differ in terms of pitch versus noise content. The piece continues its trend toward acceleration and increased overlapping, leading to complete mixture arriving in section B and lasting through section E. In these sections, the mass of diverse and overlapping sounds is sometimes differentiated only by the presence or lack of reverberation, a feature that gives the material as a whole a sense of depth or distance more than it helps define different categories within the material.

The final two sections, F and G, work as a short coda or epilogue, recasting previously introduced features anew in shorter, drier fragments. The brevity of the coda's sounds refocuses attention from issues of composite texture back to individual sounds' similarity with speech. In these sections, though, the individual sounds are not consistent; no single characteristic predominates or unites the events, but rather they are all bundles of diverse features. They mix noise and pitch, glissandi and straight tones in different registers, and any of these isolated characteristics may point back to any number of precedents scattered throughout the piece. The differences outweigh the similarities, however, and there are no recognizable repetitions, making the coda seem like a distanced commentary on the body of the piece. Expanding on the idea of the previous dialogues, we might think of the coda as an ending in disagreement: rather than each side developing or modifying a single idea, they trade in short contradictions, with only curt references to previous ideas, exchanging single loaded words as the piece fades out into silence.

This notable lack of synthesis makes *Artikulation* a complex piece that balances an organically unfolding process with subtle challenges to any thoroughgoing hierarchy, resulting in a musical structure that is quite different from any traditional form and much more in line with contemporary avant-garde ideas. The beginning of the piece presents very clear delineations of material based on type and on channel separation. Oppositions between noise and pitch and between different spatial locations are particularly important in major sectional divisions at the outset, yet once these roles are defined, Ligeti does not use these oppositions consistently throughout the piece, as one might expect from a truly hierarchical structure, but systematically undercuts their importance.

In many ways, the workings of this piece resemble the ideas of Theodor W. Adorno, whom Ligeti had met at Darmstadt during the previous year, and whose influential writings he had encountered while still in Hungary. Adorno's idea of negative dialectics has deep resonances with the structure of this piece; in explaining his grounding in Hegel, Adorno states,

As early as the Introduction to *Phenomenology of Mind*, Hegel comes close to a sense of the negativity of the dialectical logic he is expounding. That Introduction bids us purely observe each concept until it starts moving, until it becomes unidentical with itself by virtue of its own meaning—in other words, of its identity. This is a commandment to analyze, not to synthesize.[54]

Similarly, *Artikulation* presents a process with numerous oppositions, that is to say, theses and antitheses, or sides of the various dialogues. While they undergo continual recombination in the course of the piece, ultimately there is no permanent or lasting synthesis, no resolution of the disparities between them. Instead, the recombinations bring into question previous assumptions about the significance of one parameter and highlight differences in others. The materials used at the end are recognizable but are transformed from their initial appearances. Ligeti does not force any sort of contrived formal recapitulation, nor does he combine the contrasting ideas into some ultimately harmonious union, nor does he end at the extreme goal of a simple process, but instead he offers an epilogue that advances the piece while stepping back from

54. Theodor W. Adorno, *Negative Dialectics*, trans. E. B. Ashton (New York: Seabury, 1971), 156.

the climax. Observing these sound types as they engage in yet another sort of interaction—now broken back down into shorter segments, but with each segment still a bundle of constituent elements—we come to a better awareness and understanding of the dynamic facets of these complex sounds and their basis in opposition. And it is through the dialectic processes of combination and juxtaposition that make up the piece that these individual elements are better articulated, perhaps giving us a clue to its title.

Artikulation was quickly acknowledged as an important work from the WDR, and it helped secure Ligeti's reputation as a composer, rather than as a theorist. It marks one of the major turning points in his career, initiating invitations to lecture on electronic music.[55] In a remarkably short time he had gone from the "finger exercise" *Glissandi* to producing an enduring and inventive work. *Artikulation* stands, then, at the culmination of Ligeti's "second schooling" in the electronic studio—a period when he gained invaluable technical knowledge in serial and electronic composition and showed a high level of mastery in both. Despite this, Ligeti would not settle into either serial composition or the electronic medium. *Artikulation* would be his last piece for tape, although from time to time he would remark about the possibility of returning to the medium.[56] Yet it is with this work that he began to find his own voice within the avant-garde and took his first bold steps outside the world of Bartók. Ligeti's mistrust of systems, born of his experiences in Hungary, found resonance with thinkers like Adorno in his critique of the avant-garde and led to a new confidence in his own abilities as a composer and in his own unorthodox interpretation of serial composition. As Ligeti's differences with Boulez and Stockhausen continued to grow, so did his authority as an independent and original thinker in the European avant-garde.

55. An example of this is Ligeti's lecture "Erste pädagogische Erfahrungen mit elektronischer Musik: Ein Bericht von den Darmstädter Ferienkursen 1960," in *GS*, 1:117–22, originally produced for a radio program of the WDR and focusing on general developments and the works of other composers.

56. The one exception to this statement is the work *Rondeau* (1976), a theatrical piece for an actor with a tape recorder. The tape part is not very sophisticated, consisting mostly of text and sound effects to supplement the actor's role, and the same could be said of the work in general. Ligeti expressed regret that he ever wrote the work (see Steinitz, *Ligeti*, 213, citing a personal conversation with Ligeti); it was performed only a few times in Ligeti's lifetime and remains more of a curiosity than a representative work.

CHAPTER 3

Apparitions and *Atmosphères* (1958–61)

After the completion of *Artikulation* Ligeti never returned to working in the electronic medium, but the knowledge he gained from his work at the WDR proved valuable in the composition of his breakthrough orchestral works, *Apparitions* (1958–59) and *Atmosphères* (1961). These pieces show not only the composer's refined technique, developed in part through attention to detail in the electronic studio, but also an increased reliance on his own ideas and his individual craft—a confidence in his own resources that proved essential in the midst of turmoil and infighting within the Cologne avant-garde. Although these works certainly point forward to Ligeti's important innovations, they also bring to fruition the idea of composing a static, nonmotivic music that Ligeti first began to imagine while in Hungary but was unable to realize until this point. At times, Ligeti even went so far as to emphasize the Hungarian origins of this idea in a way that minimizes the dependence of *Apparitions* and *Atmosphères* on ideas of the Western European avant-garde.[1] Thus one goal of the analyses undertaken in this chapter is to uncover the extent and limits of serialism, electronic techniques, and experimental approaches to timbre in these decisive compositions and compare them with ideas present in works from the Hungarian period.

Ligeti attributed the initial motivation for such a piece of static music to a childhood nightmare related to his arachnophobia. In his commentary on *Apparitions*, specifically, he recounted the dream in detail.[2] He dreamt that

1. This trend has been noted by other scholars and treated in depth by both Charles Wilson, "György Ligeti and the Rhetoric of Autonomy," *Twentieth-Century Music* 1, no. 1 (2004), 5–28, and Rachel Beckles Willson, especially in chapter 5 of her book *Ligeti, Kurtag, and Hungarian Music during the Cold War* (New York: Cambridge University Press, 2007).
2. György Ligeti, "States, Events, Transformations," trans. Jonathan Bernard, *Perspectives of New Music* 31, no. 1 (Winter 1993), 164–71. Versions of this story also

he was unable to reach his bed because of a giant web, "finely spun but dense and extremely tangled," and as the dream continued, insects that were stuck the web struggled to free themselves, and the entire web began to vibrate and quake, shifting internally, knotting in some places and tearing in others. Ligeti concluded the account of his dream by saying, "These transformations were irreversible; no earlier state could ever recur. There was something inexpressibly sad about this process: the hopelessness of elapsing time and of the irretrievable past."[3] Much has been made of the analogy with weblike textures in Ligeti's micropolyphonic music, in which each string instrument plays its own line, weaving an incredibly dense overall texture. Other aspects of the dream, however, relate equally to characteristics of the composer's mature style, for example, the sense of a structure or system in the process of inevitable dissolution and the feeling of melancholy or nostalgia that accompanies it. Yet another important aspect of the dream is the sense of an interdependence between different parts of the whole, a disturbance in one part of the network pulling the threads of other parts into a new configuration. This is especially relevant in relation to integral serialism, in which individual parameters were treated independently, at times even indifferently, much to Ligeti's frustration. A move back toward a system in which parameters are part of an interrelated network, considered in combination with one another, was an essential step in defining Ligeti's mature compositional voice.

In discussing the creation of these internally shifting patterns and finely woven lines, however, Ligeti did cite the influence of his work in the studio, albeit often in vague, qualified, or indirect terms. In many cases he limits his remarks to leading comments about conceiving music beyond the confines of meter[4] or involving superimposed layers.[5] Talking about the innovative use of timbre and texture in *Atmosphères*, he stated, "All this really goes back to what I was doing in the electronic studios; I applied what I had learned there

exist in the GS, 2:170–73, compiled from other variants, including the original publication in *Blätter + Bilder: Eine Zeitschrift für Dichtung, Musik und Malerei* 11 (1960), 50–57, which was reprinted *Melos* 34, no. 5 (1967), 165–69. Other variants can be found in *LiC*, 25, n. 3, and in Richard Toop, *György Ligeti* (London: Phaidon, 1999), 66–67. In his interview with Várnai he downplayed what one should make of childhood experiences, and a close reading shows that it was the memory of this dream during the last years ("die Erinnerung an diesen weit zurückliegenden Traum," GS, 2:170) that was the impetus for *Apparitions*. This leaves open the questions of how long the particulars of the dream were gestating in his musical imagination, when they first started to develop musical connotations, and how the details of his memory and presentation of this dream may have shifted over time to coincide more closely with his current aesthetic ideas.

3. Ligeti, "States, Events, Transformations," 164–65.

4. See, e.g., *LiC*, 33, 90, and also Benjamin Levy, "Shades of the Studio: Electronic Influences on Ligeti's *Apparitions*," *Perspectives of New Music* 47, no. 2 (2009), 59–87, for a focused look at how Ligeti applied studio techniques to this piece.

5. See, e.g., *LiC*, 26, 90–91.

to instrumental and vocal music. More exactly, the technique of changing patterns comes from Gottfried Michael Koenig . . . . My idea was to apply to instrumental music what I had learned from Koenig in the electronic studio."[6] Indeed, encountering Koenig's work is one of the few studio experiences that Ligeti recounted—and he described that influence repeatedly.[7] Koenig's development had to do with a specific physiological fact, namely, that humans can no longer differentiate successive events when their durations are less than 50 milliseconds (1/20 of a second). Ligeti remembers that while assisting in the realization of Koenig's electronic work *Essay* (1957), there were successions of sine tones that were sped up to exceed this threshold of perception, and as this happened, "the individual tones submerged into the area below the limit of differentiation . . . and the progressions, which were originally successive, turned into a simultaneity."[8] Ligeti went on to describe the most interesting situation as successions that stay close to this threshold, so that "one finds some elements over the limit of blurring of about 50 ms and others below, so that a durational emergence and submergence takes place, then at one point rhythm changes over into tone color, and at another tone color changes to rhythm."[9] Ligeti called this phenomenon *Bewegungsfarbe* (mobile or fluctuating color) and sought to incorporate it into his instrumental works by using fast cross-rhythms, with instruments using different subdivisions, since it is impossible to get a single instrument to play fast enough to make twenty attacks per second. Thus the cross-rhythms that are common in both *Apparitions* and *Atmosphères* can be better understood as speeds than as rhythms, and in particular as speeds approaching this threshold of differentiation, blurring the line between rhythm and timbre.

Despite his admission that electronic music was an important influence, Ligeti remained resistant to the idea, which came up in early reviews, that *Apparitions* and *Atmosphères* were, "electronic music played by an orchestra,"[10] insisting that they were conceived entirely as works for acoustic instruments. He rejected the labels *Klangfarbenmelodie* and *Klangfarbenmusik* for these pieces as placing too much emphasis on timbre rather than the alteration of textures and microscopic patterns they contain.[11] At times, however, this

6. *LiC*, 39.

7. He did so first in 1968 for a lecture at the International Week for Experimental Music in Berlin, later published as "Auswirkungen der elektronischen Musik auf mein kompositorisches Schaffen," *GS*, 2:86–94, but also in an expanded version (using largely the same examples) in "Musik und Technik: Eigene Erfahrungen und subjective Betrachtungen," written in 1980 and contained in *GS*, 1:237–61.

8. Koenig's own recollections of these events are found in Gottfried Michael Koenig, "Ligeti und die elektronische Musik," in *György Ligeti: Personalstil—Avantgardisumus—Popularität*, ed. Otto Kolleritsch (Vienna: Universal Edition, 1987), 11–17.

9. Ligeti, "Auswirkungen," *GS*, 2:88.

10. *LiC*, 87; similar formulations can be found in Ligeti, "Auswirkungen," *GS*, 2:90.

11. Again, he did so in multiple sources including interviews, but perhaps most strongly in the concluding thoughts of "Auswirkungen," *GS*, 2:93.

distinction is hard to maintain, for, as in electronic music, in which the constituent partials of a collective sound must be composed individually, the colors of individual instruments in these compositions are blended together into a particular hue; as the discussion below will show, this degree of interdependence and balanced mixture between instrumental colors in different degrees and patterns remains one of the most groundbreaking developments of this period in Ligeti's work.

Ligeti's increasingly careful attempts to control the way these pieces were described in reviews was necessary because of their success and the increased critical attention they received. The highly acclaimed premieres put Ligeti in the spotlight during a turbulent period in the circle of avant-garde composers. *Apparitions* made quite a stir at its premiere at the International Society for Contemporary Music's (ISCM) World Music Days in Cologne (1960). Subsequently, he was invited to write about his own music for *Die Reihe*, rather than commenting on other composers' works; this resulted in the seminal article "Metamorphoses of Musical Form."[12] The status of *Apparitions* also helped him find a place (and, retrospectively, his first modest commissioning fee from the *Südwestrundfunk*) for *Atmosphères*, when Luciano Berio failed to complete his commission in time, leaving Heinrich Strobel looking for a last-minute replacement to include in the Donaueschingen festival in 1961. Ligeti had arrived as a leading figure in contemporary music. Yet at the 1960 ISCM festival, splits within the Cologne compositional circle began to widen. Stockhausen came increasingly into conflict with Heinz-Klaus Metzger, now a follower of John Cage, and the reception of Kagel's *Anagrama* overshadowed Stockhausen's *Kontakte* to such a degree that the two composers, competitive to begin with, were soon completely at odds.[13]

As Ligeti was coming into his own, then, the social circumstances relating to this circle of composers necessitated a tactful and careful method of promoting his works and achievements. In "Metamorphoses of Musical Form," for example, he was critical of serial practice but also positioned own works as outgrowths—albeit original ones—of the "statistical" serial methods pioneered by Stockhausen and Koenig. At other points in this article he spared the major figures direct criticism, projecting his critique onto an anonymous set of hypothetical lesser composers,[14] and thus advanced his own solutions as a type of corrective, presumably from within the school. In later commentary,

12. György Ligeti, "Metamorphoses of Musical Form," trans. Cornelius Cardew, *Form—Space: Die Reihe* 7, English ed. (Bryn Mawr: Presser, 1965), 5–19.

13. See Toop, *Ligeti*, 71–72.

14. For example, he leaves out the names in this passage: "The primitive stage to which composition is relegated by automatism will only be supported by musicians who succumb to the fetish of total integration . . . . Adorno's negative diagnosis may well apply to such musicians (but not to the elite who pursue their thoughts further)." Ligeti, "Metamorphoses," 10.

Ligeti revised this description to maintain that he was never really a part of the serial school at all and never composed serial music. The truth, of course, is somewhere in between, and the relation between his techniques and those of his contemporaries is best gauged by means of a careful examination of the compositions themselves, apart from the politicized rhetoric and diverging definitions of serial composition that different practitioners put forward in order to highlight their own contributions. In particular, though, the claims, upheld by Monika Lichtenfeld among others, that Ligeti "never passed through the serial phase of composition"[15] seem to belittle the profound importance that his exposure to serial thinking had for his technique. Whether one considers his development as a reaction against serialism or as original extensions or modifications of "orthodox" serial practice (if such a thing can actually be said to exist) is largely a matter of rhetoric rather than substance, and it is subject to retrospective interpretation in either direction. Now working in the West, and having an intimate knowledge of contemporary developments, Ligeti kept a careful balance, publicly criticizing aspects of serial practice while continuing to use the ideas he found most useful, and to certain audiences, even describing features of his compositions as indebted to serial concepts.

APPARITIONS, MOVEMENT I

Ligeti's return to orchestral composition was facilitated by the special circumstances brought about by the ISCM festival in 1960. Kagel was looking to have his work *Anagrama* programmed at this festival, but submissions were organized by national sections, and as a "stateless person"[16] he had no way to submit the work. He could arrange for an independent submission so long as there was at least one other submission by a stateless composer. Kagel, knowing that Ligeti had been at work on an orchestral piece, solicited him to put forward *Apparitions*, and both works were accepted.

What Kagel did not realize was that Ligeti had been working on an orchestral piece since well before his arrival in Cologne. Drafts and sketches for static orchestral pieces under the titles *Víziók* (Visions) and *Sötét és Világos* (Dark and Light) date from late summer and fall of 1956, respectively, predating his flight from Hungary. These pieces (discussed in depth below) show similarities in the use of low clusters and a slow, sustained tempo, but they show nowhere near the nuance or technique of the finished version. They do

15. Monika Lichtenfeld, "György Ligeti, oder das Ende der seriellen Musik," *Melos* 39, no. 2 (1972), 74: "Als einziger von denen, die der Musik dieser Dekade entscheidene Impulse und indivduelles Profil verliehen, hat Ligeti die serielle Phase des Komponierens nicht durchlaufen."

16. This description from Richard Toop, *Ligeti*, 71, is echoed in Björn Heile, *The Music of Mauricio Kagel* (Burlington, VT: Ashgate, 2006), 21.

indicate, however, that *Apparitions* was the culmination of a long project. They are part of the genealogy of this piece, as are two other versions also under the title *Apparitions*, both drafted in Cologne. The final version bears a schematic resemblance to the choral works *Éjszaka* and *Reggel* (Night and Morning, discussed in chapter 1), connected through the draft of *Sötét és Világos* to a synesthetic, yet abstract, idea: the motion from darkness or night to light or morning in a two-movement form in which slow, low-register, brooding clusters give way to faster, higher, and wilder music. Finally, there is also a similarity between *Apparitions* and *Pièce électronique no. 3*, discussed in chapter 2.

Apparitions, then, lies at the heart of what Rachel Beckles Willson refers to as the "continuity" or "rupture" narratives[17] of Ligeti's career—what he took from his experiences with serial and electronic music, what he had envisioned while still in Hungary, and the exact impact his early experiences in the West had on his first mature works. These matters are best addressed by a side-by-side comparison of the techniques used in the composition of the different versions of *Apparitions*.

Ligeti's "Metamorphoses of Musical Form" deals directly with *Apparitions*, and alongside the extensive sketch material it allows one to reconstruct much of the compositional process for this piece. In the article, features such as clusters are posited as the logical response to serialism's use of total chromaticism and the "greying" effect he describes as erasing the distinctive character of individual intervals and harmonic ideas.[18] In retrospect, then, Ligeti suggested that his use of clusters was something new and progressive, and he distanced their use from Bartók's and from his own previous instrumental music—even *Métamorphoses Nocturnes*—though clusters actually appear in drafts that pre-date his arrival in the West.

In the article's discussion of rhythmic practice, Ligeti looks at the end result of duration rows used by Boulez and others and finds that the equal distribution of durations ultimately creates an imbalance, since the longer durations make up more of the piece than do the shorter ones. To correct this imbalance, Ligeti cites his method, first developed for *Artikulation* (see chapter 2), of what

17. Rachel Beckles Willson, *Ligeti, Kurtág*, 4.
18. In many ways, Ligeti's rhetoric follows that of Anton Webern in *The Path to the New Music*, ed. Willi Reich, trans. Leo Black (Bryn Mawr, PA: Presser, 1963). Just as Webern outlines the history of tonal music as pointing toward chromaticism and the impulse for twelve-tone regulation of that chromatic world as a matter of historical necessity, Ligeti outlines the way later serial composition diminished the intervallic identity of the row, leading to a similar necessity for his cluster-based compositions, which find new ways to compose within this intervalically neutral sound world. In this way he positions his own globally balanced distributions as an outgrowth of serial manipulations and identifies his own rhythmic practice (discussed below) as one of various "tendencies that are possibly coming to the fore" within the "'freer' phase of serial composition" ("Metamorphoses," 12), even while he acknowledges that in these newer developments, serialism may hold the "seeds of its own dissolution" (ibid., 14)

he terms a "statistical basis" of distribution that "could then take the place of the fixed series."[19] Throughout "Metamorphoses of Musical Form" he refers to the idea of a "freer" or "statistical" phase of serial technique,[20] which he traces to the practice Stockhausen describes in the article ". . . how time passes . . ."[21] and to such pieces as *Gruppen, Kontakte*, and even *Gesang der Jünglinge*.[22] This rhythmic approach—epitomizing Ligeti's idea of statistical composition—is the very basis for *Apparitions*, and unlike *Artikulation*, in which the process becomes folded into different layers of mixed material types, in *Apparitions* it is more unified and can be traced from the sketches all the way to the finished score.[23]

The process of composing *Apparitions* began with this type of statistical distribution, setting up a repertoire of durations calculated in thirty-second notes, where the product of the duration value and the number of times it is used was equal to a constant value; this method is exactly what Ligeti described in his article. As noted with regard to *Artikulation*, it was not unusual for Ligeti to use a few values that were larger than the product itself and which were labeled as "objects" that stood outside the system. In the sketches for *Apparitions*, the distribution presented in example 3.1 shows a final parenthetical value of 256 thirty-second notes that is well above the product of 160, and although this value remains in subsequent planning stages of the piece, ultimately it is not used.

Ligeti then distributed the individual instances of these durations into the four sections of the first movement, labeled A, B, C, and V (example 3.2). The letter names correspond to the rehearsal letters that end a section, so "A" defines the passage from the beginning of the piece up to letter A, "B" spans from letter A to letter B, and so forth, with "V" possibly standing for the Hungarian *vége*, meaning "end," or for *világos* (light), showing that the concerns of the earlier draft of the piece (*Sötét és Világos*) remain in the finalized version.

The composer modified the initial repertoire of durations at this stage of the piece—a close examination reveals that he left out nine instances of the number 2, four 3s, two 4s, and one 10.[24] The reason for these changes appears

---

19. Ligeti, "Metamorphoses," 14.

20. Ibid., 12 and 5, respectively.

21. Karlheinz Stockhausen, ". . . how time passes . . ." *Musical Craftsmanship: Die Reihe* 3 (Bryn Mawr, PA: Presser, 1959, German ed., 1957), 10–40.

22. See Konrad Boehmer's comments about the realization of *Gesang der Jünglinge* quoted in chapter 2.

23. Many of the observations that follow were first presented in Levy, "Shades of the Studio."

24. A later sketch, which is the basis for example 3.4 below, seems to adjust the duration of section B in a different way by leaving one 6 unused, rather than by leaving three 2s unused.

Example 3.1. *Apparitions*, I, sketch of durations and products. Reproduced with kind permission from the György Ligeti Collection of the Paul Sacher Foundation, Basel

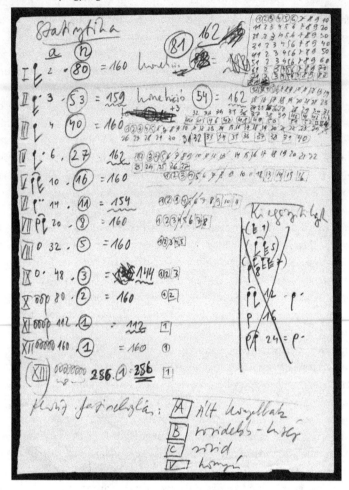

to be a concern for the proportions between large sections of the piece. In an interview Ligeti explained,

In the first movement of *Apparitions*, I applied Bartók's golden section as interpreted by Lendvai. Its first part is in a low register and the second in a high register; the relative duration of the two parts corresponds to the golden section. Subsequent shorter parts of the movement are also divided in the same proportion. The golden section is in fact the dominant formal principle of the work. Looking back on it, I must say that I could have applied any other principle of proportions just as well.[25]

25. *LiC*, 43.

Example 3.2. *Apparitions*, I, distribution of durations into four sections

Section A, sum = 585

160	80	48	32	20	14	10	6	4	3	2
			32	20	14	10	6	4	3	2
				20	14	10	6	4	3	2
					14	10	6	4	3	2
							6	4	3	2
										2

Section B, sum = 396; three instances of 2 are unused, resulting in the sum 390

32	20	14	10	6	6	4	4	4	4	3	3	3	3	2	2	2	2
	20	14	10	6	6	4	4	4	4	3	3	3	3	2	2	2	
			10	6	6	4	4	4	4	3	3	3	3	2	2	2	
			10	6	6	4	4	4	4	3	3	3	3	2	2	2	
				6	6	4	4	4	4	3	3	3	3	2	2	2	
				6	6									2	2	2	
														2	2	2	

Section C, sum = 195

20	14	10	6	4	3	3	2	2	2	2
	14	10	6	4	3	3	2	2	2	2
		10	6	4	3	3	2	2	2	
			6	4	3		2	2	2	
				4	3		2	2	2	
					3		2	2	2	
							2	2	2	

Section V, sum = 877

256	112	80	48	32	20	14	10	6	4	4	3	3	3	2	2
			48	32	20	14	10	6	4	4	3	3	3	2	2
						14	10	6	4		3	3	3	2	2
							10	6	4		3	3	3	2	2
								6	4		3	3	3	2	2
									4					2	2
														2	2
														2	2
														2	2
														2	2

This last sentence is quite intriguing, and in fact, although there is evidence that the piece started out exploring golden-section proportions and using Fibonacci numbers,[26] the final score reflects the proportion of 2:3 (or

26. See Gianmario Borio, "Komponieren um 1960," in *Die Geschichte der Musik,*

Example 3.3a. *Apparitions*, I, durations and proportions of major sections

A	B	C	V
585	390	195	877

Ratios between major sections
V:A = 3:2   A:B = 3:2   B:C = 2:1   A:C = 3:1

Example 3.3b. *Apparitions*, I, revised durations and proportions of sections

A	B	C	V
585	390	195	≈585

Ratios between major sections: 3:2:1:3
Entire Movement (A-V) to Low Register Sections (A-C), 1755:1170 = 3:2
Initial Sections A:B = 3:2

approximately 0.667) better than it does the golden section (approximately 0.618). The length of each section is shown in example 3.3a. The length of the final section, however, is not realized as such in the piece; in fact, there is some ambiguity about how to determine its length. The movement ends with two measures of rest, and if they are included in the calculations the length of the section is 637 thirty-second notes; if they are not included, then the length is 573. There appears to be another type of compromise here between the predetermined proportions and the system of durations that Ligeti devised. Within the range from 573 to 637, two meaningful durations occur. The first, 621 thirty-second notes, would be the duration of the last section without the original parenthetical duration of 256 (a value that would last precisely through the first quarter note of the last measure). The other significant value is 585—equal to the length of the first section, and a duration that creates proportions similar to what Ligeti described as the dominant formal principle. If this value is taken as the ideal length (as shown in example 3.3b), then the piece has a 3:2 relation between the entire movement and the combined first three sections (A–C), which occur in the low register, before the final section (V) abruptly shifts to a higher register. This same 3:2 proportion is also reflected in the lengths of the first two sections, A:B. The final bars of rest may then be an attempt to reconcile the difference

III: Musik der Moderne, ed. Matthias Brzoska and Michael Heinemann, 293–311 (Laaber: Laaber Verlag, 2001), for further discussion of possible derivations of these proportions based on Fibonacci numbers, including suggestions that the idealized section lengths are derived as multiples of 13 or as Fibonacci numbers plus multiples of 13. Borio also finds golden-section divisions within some of the individual sections of the piece, with varying degrees of exactitude or alteration from the ideal.

between the scheme for individual durations and the overall proportions between large sections.

In determining the ordering of durations within each section, Ligeti allowed for further adjustments to the original scheme. Before arriving at the final rhythmic design for *Apparitions*, he altered individual values for each section as shown in example 3.4a, where the top line of each system contains the original values taken from example 3.2, and the bottom line shows slight changes to them. Example 3.4b reproduces Ligeti's sketch for section V, with pairs of lines showing his modifications in different subsections. These adjustments create a more varied repertoire of durations, including values like 1 and 7, which are not generated by the original product system and which help break up potential repetitions of durations that could begin to suggest a pulse or meter. Where Ligeti adjusted the original values, he was careful to counter that action; when he added to one value, he subtracted from another, so that the durations of the large sections, and the proportions they reflect, remain the same.

Along with this allowance for adjustments, Ligeti's "statistical serial" method allows for free ordering, and minute control of individual moments, rather than the automatism of a duration series. The guiding principle of Ligeti's choices seems to be one of avoiding repetition while adhering to the a priori conception of the movement as a whole, moving from balance to disorder as the web from his dream moved ineluctably toward dissolution. Reviewing the composer's description of this movement reveals the importance of his choice in ordering the individual durations. He remarked that the beginning is "a stationary, very soft, very low, and very long sound,"[27] followed by other "planelike" sounds, which are then disturbed by more impulsive events, described in terms of "attacks" and "energy-influx." The ultimate result is that "the network is irrevocably changed; the stationary sounds heretofore only weakly stirred by internal vibrations are now crumpled. Trills and tremolos animate the sounding masses, and a continually irregular fluctuation of the dynamics hinders the retrieval of any equilibrium."[28]

To this end, the outer sections (A and V) contain a mixture of longer and shorter durations, while the inner sections (B and C) contain mostly shorter ones; these are arranged in the piece, first to effect a gradual acceleration through part A, then to create a more turbulent area through parts B and C, and finally to bring about fierce juxtapositions in the last section, where long-sustained clusters are interrupted by chaotic passages labeled "wild" in the score; the planning for some of these can be seen in example 3.4b, above. Thus, the statistical balance of longer and shorter durations is a tool for achieving an aperiodic rhythm that is essential for the locally floating, static feeling of the

27. Ligeti, "States, Events, Transformations," 166.
28. Ibid., 166–67.

Example 3.4a. *Apparitions*, I, adjustment and ordering of durations in each section

A

160	48	20	80	32	14	20	32	10	20	14	6	10	14	14
160	56	16	80	28	12	20	32	12	16	14	6	10	16	12

10	6	4	10	4	6	3	4	6	2	4	3	2	2
10	6	4	12	5	7	3	5	4	5	1	2	1	4

B

2x 4/4	20	14	6	10	4	4	2	4	6	4	2	2	4	3	2	2	2	2	2	3	2	3
Rest	20	14	6	10	4	5	1	6	4	3	1	1	5	3	2	1	2	1	2	3	1	4

4	3	2	3	2	4	3	4	6	3	4	10	6	2	6	4	6	3	32	6
5	3	3	1	5	3	4	7	4	5	3	10	4	2	6	4	6	3	32	6

															1.5	1	1	0.5
20	10	4	6	4	10	6	4	2	6	4	4	2	6	4	3	3	2	2
20	12	4	6	5	8	7	4	3	6	4	5	2	6	4	3	1	1	1

C

4	3	2	4	6	2	2	3	2	2	2	2	2	3	2	2	2	2
4	3	1	5	7	1	2	3	1	4	1	3	3	1	1	3	2	1	2

6	3	4	3	10	3	6	2	14	10	3	2	6	4	20	2	2	14
7	4	3	2	12	3	7	2	16	10	3	1	7	4	20	1	3	14	10

V

α (53):

2	3
48	

β (136):

2	2	2	3	2	3	4	3	4	6	14	10
1	1	2	3	1	4	5	1	3	7	16	10

14	10	20	32
14	8	20	36

γ (99):

2	2	2	3	2	2	3	2	3	3	4	3	4	2	3	10	3	4	6	3	2	4	3
2	1	2	3	2	1	3	1	4	2	5	4	5	1	4	12	3	4	7	2	1	5	3

δ (589):

2	1	4	3	7	10	14	20	32	48	72	108	256
1	2	3	4									

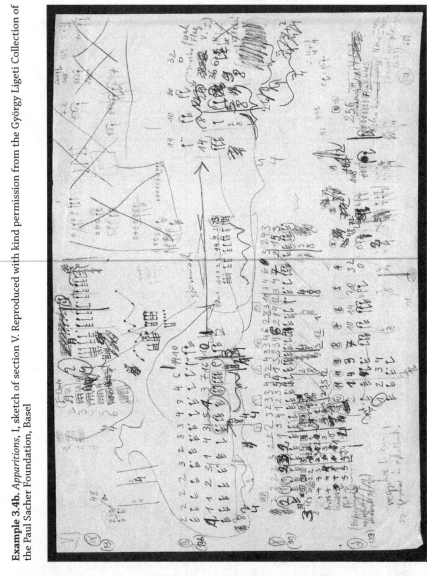

Example 3.4b. *Apparitions*, I, sketch of section V. Reproduced with kind permission from the György Ligeti Collection of the Paul Sacher Foundation, Basel

work, but the freedom of ordering within that global balance is essential for realizing the dynamic effect of the movement as a whole.

With each stage of the realization of this movement of *Apparitions*, the composer allowed himself certain freedoms. First, in calculating the product of durations and instances, Ligeti accepted a certain margin of error, which is to say that the product is not exactly a constant but instead falls within a certain acceptable deviation. Then, in defining large sections, Ligeti altered the initial distribution in order to create certain proportions, and within these sections he left open the specifics of ordering, permitting the flexibility to achieve his aesthetic goal as the work gradually disintegrates from stasis into more and more agitated forms of motion.

Although Ligeti did seem to think of his statistical rhythmic distributions as an outgrowth of serialism, providing a type of rigor to ensure that no note value would predominate, he also eliminated much of the troubling automatism of the ordered duration series, so that this rhythmic technique resulted in an underlying framework rather than a strictly deterministic ordering of a set of note values. The periodic, metric grid that frustrated Ligeti in his earlier compositions, including *Musica ricercata* and *Métamorphoses nocturnes*, was replaced with this aperiodic design, based on an irregular timeline but leaving the composer the freedom to create a musical surface that articulates points on this timeline in any number of ways. For instance, some points are marked by the entrance of a new cluster, and others by the change from sound to rest. This allows Ligeti to carry certain clusters past the duration suggested by the original scheme and to create ambiguity by leaving other suggested durations filled only in part. In the A section (see example 3.5) he does so sparingly, beginning in measure 22, where the duration of 10 thirty-second notes is marked by the interval between the entrance of the strings and the entrance of the cembalo, while the string cluster, itself, is held over as the brass articulate still other points on the timeline. The piece goes on, however, to diverge more and more from the stasis and equilibrium of the beginning, culminating in "wild" passages featuring triplets and quintuplets, which the scheme itself is incapable of deriving, over extremely long-sustained clusters.

The flexibility to articulate points in the rhythmic design in different ways is both an important means to realizing the aesthetic goal of musical disintegration and a way for Ligeti to showcase developments in his orchestration. A single duration is most often realized by a group of instruments together, and the ways in which these instruments interact takes on new intricacy. For example, to achieve tremolo effects with differing degrees of raggedness, Ligeti uses not only traditional tremolos but also effects generated by a pair of instruments trills between two notes, one starting on the upper note, the complementary instrument starting on the lower note (e.g., m. 42 in cellos I–IV)—the net effect is that of a tremolo on both pitches, although less even than if each instrument played a tremolo on one note only. Likewise, there

Example 3.5. *Apparitions*, I, rhythmic design of section A

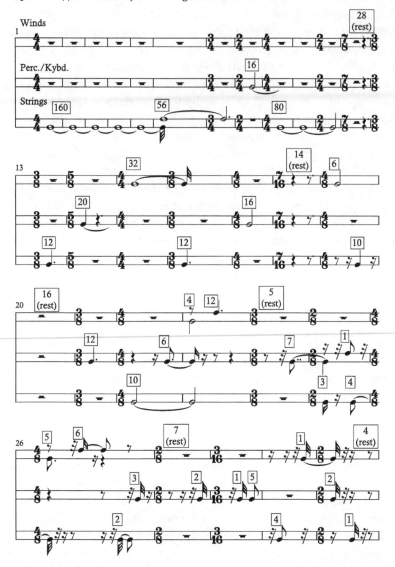

are gliding effects that also depend on the coordination of different instruments. In measures 54–57 individual string instruments all glide upwards, using staggered entrances to extend the pizzicato glissandi from the basses all the way through the violins in turn. In measures 62–63 another unique type of glissando occurs. The lowest note of the chromatic cluster jumps upwards to become the highest, and as this process replicates itself, the entire cluster shifts slowly upwards. Another innovative effect is the tremolo cluster in measure 49. A chromatic cluster from E3 to B4 in the violins and violas

Example 3.6. *Apparitions*, I, dynamic tallying for section B

pppp < *p*	14	*pppp*	8	*f* > *p*	1
pppp < *mp*	9	*ppp*	4	*f* > *pp*	1
pppp < *mf*	3	*pp*	2	*f* > *ppp*	1
pppp < *f*	1	*p*	1	*f* > *pppp*	1
		mp	1		
ppp < *mp*	6	*mf*	1	*mf* > *pp*	1
ppp < *mf*	2	*f*	1	*mf* > *ppp*	1
ppp < *f*	1			*mf* > *pppp*	2
pp < *mf*	1			*mp* > *ppp*	3
pp < *f*	1			*mp* > *pppp*	5
p < *f*	1			*p* > *pppp*	9

diminuendos, while an adjacent cluster from Eb3 to D1 in the cellos and basses crescendos. This coordination of duration, pitch, and dynamics produces a shift of focus from the high register to the low, simulating a glissando though none of the individual voices change pitch. The last two examples in particular bear a clear resemblance to precedents set in the electronic music studio— measures 62–63 relating to the glissandi seen in *Pièce électronique no. 3* and measure 49 relating to the cross-fading of different materials commonly found in *Artikulation* and elsewhere in studio pieces.[29]

Statistical distributions, tallied over the course of the movement—even when they undergo distortions, modifications, and adaptation to material— become a hallmark of Ligeti's compositional technique. Sketches show a similar method of tallying dynamic levels during this movement, although in this case, they are not intended to achieve an equal distribution, but on the contrary, to weight section B of the piece clearly towards softer dynamics, another sign that the composer was willing to adapt his technique to support the a priori image of the work. example 3.6 presents a transcription of a chart tallying the dynamic values for this section B. The numbers in this example were originally dots in the sketch, employing the same type of tallying used for the durations. As with the realization of the rhythmic design, the dynamics in the score exhibit a small degree of modification from this original plan. The distribution here decisively favors softer dynamic levels instead of louder and

29. See Levy, "Shades of the Studio," for a more detailed discussion of these connections.

Example 3.7. *Apparitions*, I, sketch transcription (detail), composite rhythm, mm. 61–62

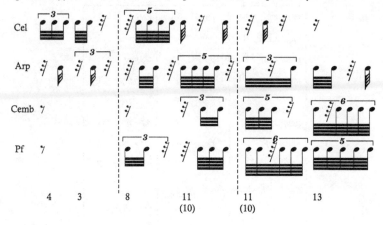

also favors mobile dynamics (crescendos and decrescendos) rather than static dynamics, matching perfectly the character of the second section of the piece, which gradually begins to become more active and turbulent but does not yet reach the tipping point.

The most extreme kind of deformation of Ligeti's original statistical distribution comes in the form of the wild passages, which begin to use an entirely different logic—one that starts to realize the cross-rhythms and *Bewegungsfarbe* effect of Koenig's experiments, previewing their more extensive use in the second movement. The wild sections, beginning softly at letter B (m. 61), make use of conflicting divisions of the beat, and a sketch excerpt (example 3.7) shows that Ligeti was interested in the composite number of attacks in a given time span. The example, which corresponds to measures 61 and 62 of the finished score, shows Ligeti working out the total number of attacks per sixteenth note across all of the keyboard instruments and writing this number below the staff. Under the fourth column, which has eleven attacks, he included the value 10 in parentheses, possibly accounting for the fact that the last note of the piano part and last note of the celesta part coincide exactly. Similarly, in the fifth column he adjusted the value from 11 to 10. There appears to be some inconsistency in these two adjustments, but the general concern with the number of attacks in a given time frame—a concern that began with his observation of Koenig's work—is quite evident.

APPARITIONS, MOVEMENT II

The second movement of *Apparitions*, in its final version, makes a brief (2′20″) three-part form whose outer sections (Agitato and Tempo Primo) are the most explicitly concerned with Koenig's idea of speeds near the threshold of

Example 3.8. *Apparitions*, II, synopsis of the form

Agitato	Wild	Tempo Primo
mm. 1–24	mm. 25–37	mm. 38–55
$\frac{2}{2}$ ($\frac{6}{4}$)	mixed	mixed
70"	26"	45"

blurring and whose middle section (Wild) is notable as Ligeti's first experiment with micropolyphony. The central section falls directly in the middle
of the work, and the return of the opening texture divides the second half
of the piece roughly according to the inverse of the golden section (as shown
in example 3.8) The rhythmic structures of the movement are derived from
dividing the large beats into multiple conflicting subdivisions, rather than
using a reservoir of minute particles, and in this top-down approach it is quite
different from the first movement.

In the opening of the movement Ligeti divides measures simultaneously
into both $\frac{2}{2}$ and $\frac{6}{4}$, assigning different instruments to different meters, so that
each half-measure could be divided into two or three parts at the slow tempo
marking of $\quarternote$ = 40 ($\dottedhalfnote$ = 40 in $\frac{6}{4}$). This basic metric-level polyrhythm is then
subdivided further, creating different speeds—the opening features speeds of
12, 16, 18, and 20 notes per half measure. In addition, certain speeds, such as
18 attacks per half-measure and 20 per-half measure, can be reached in different ways, with the possibility of subtly shifting emphasis or accent within the
measure. If all of these divisions were to occur together, one would hear 26
uncoordinated attacks per quarter note, or a bewildering average composite
speed of 34.667 impulses per second.

Ligeti, however, marshals the appearance of different speeds into a mosaic
(a kind of texture he would develop more formally in *Atmosphères*) that moves
with an irregular ebb and flow. The composite rhythm of the opening (see
example 3.9) shows this mosaic: the presence of sound is nearly consistent,
but it shifts between different instruments, all playing notes of a chromatic
cluster between B♭3 and F4. The different speeds gradually build to the last
beat, combining thirty-second notes, sextuplets in $\frac{6}{4}$ (the equivalent speed of
nonuplets in $\frac{2}{2}$), and subdivided quintuplets, combining speeds of 8, 9, and
10 per quarter note in $\frac{2}{2}$. Eliminating the theoretically shared attacks on the
quarter-note beat (in all strands) and eighth-note division (between 8 and
10), the composite speed averages to 24 per quarter note or 32 impulses per
second. This result is far beyond the threshold of differentiation that Ligeti
learned by observing Koenig's experiments. The peak of activity in this first
section falls in measures 16–19, with extended passages of 9 against 10.

The end of the movement also features very explicit combination of these
divisions of the beat, evidence of a top-down rhythmic organization that

Example 3.9. *Apparitions*, II, composite rhythm, mm. 1–3

Example 3.10. *Apparitions*, II, mm. 52–53, basses

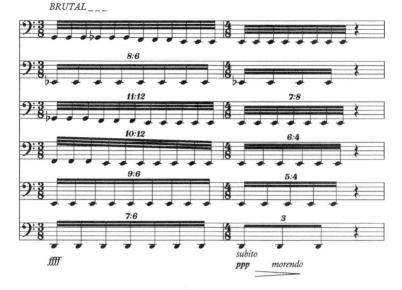

remained a part of Ligeti's compositional technique through the decade. The passage from measures 52–53 is particularly significant in light of similar procedures found in *Aventures* (1962). Here, in the space of 5 eighth notes, the double basses die away, using the entire gamut of subdivisions between three and twelve (example 3.10). Divisions seven through twelve happen over the course of a $\frac{3}{8}$ measure, while divisions 3 through 8 happen in 2 eighth-notes' time. Even while dealing with different time spans, Ligeti allocates the rhythmic strands carefully, using adjacent-numbered subdivisions and not repeating any number within a measure, thus ensuring an uncoordinated and chaotic texture. Not only will this produce the *Bewegungsfarbe* effect, but owing to the low register, intervals of a semitone, and high dynamic level, it will really produce a blanket of noise, only conveying the effect of slowing down and dying away without perceptible pitches.

The second movement of *Apparitions* is also noteworthy as the birthplace of Ligeti's idea of micropolyphony, although once again, *Atmosphères* presents a substantial refinement of this technique. The micropolyphonic section at letter D begins almost exactly at the midpoint of the movement and is marked by a new, faster tempo and the indication Wild. In addition, this section uses a more complex polyrhythm at the metric level; instead of $\frac{2}{2}$ versus $\frac{6}{4}$, as in the opening section, different instruments divide the initial measure (m. 25) into 2, 3, or 4 beats. Within these beats, each individual instrument mixes subdivisions of 2, 3, 4, and 5 freely to create an intensely chaotic texture.

Within this chaos, though, there is micropolyphonic structure; each instrument plays the same melody irregularly offset in canon. Along with the rhythm and the *fortissimo* dynamic level, the large leaps and jagged melodic contour of this passage obscure the underlying order in this micropolyphonic experiment. Each instrumental family (violins, violas, cellos, and basses) has its own melody, all starting on G but quickly diverging. The violin melody, in general, moves the most quickly and is the most chromatic; after the first three notes (the major seventh, G–F♯–G),[30] the pitch classes come from a descending chromatic scale starting on E, although all the parts routinely displace notes to create wide leaps rather than steps. This sort of melody was seen in String Quartet no. 1, albeit in a slower presentation, and will be featured again in *Aventures* (chapter 4), the Cello Concerto (chapter 5), and later pieces including the String Quartet no. 2 (chapter 6). The violas are generally more slowly paced and less thoroughly chromatic, incorporating more whole steps (again, often in wide leaps) in alternation with half steps. Their opening intervallic pattern alternates a whole step and two half steps (much like Messiaen's Mode 3), and a later passage features a long stretch of whole-tone motion. For example, in measures 33–37 viola I plays the complete whole tone scale, F♯–G♯–A♯–C–D–E, before breaking to F♮. The basses have a corresponding whole-tone stretch embedded within the same passage (bass I plays G–A–B–C♯–D♯–E♯ from the end of m. 35 through m. 37). Finally, the interjection by the flutes and clarinets in measure 32 divides the chromatic line in another interesting way: each individual instrument has a complete diatonic collection, but these collections are related by half-step (G, A, and B major collections in the flutes, C, B♭, and A♭ major in the clarinets), so that they have the net effect of a chromatic blur.

EARLY DRAFTS OF *APPARITIONS*

Sötét és Világos

One way of estimating the impact of Ligeti's experiences in the electronic music studio is to compare the published version of *Apparitions* to the orchestral drafts that he had begun before fleeing Hungary. The surviving remnants of a work titled *Víziók* (Visions or even Apparitions) are scant—they consist of two pages showing mostly the spacing and distribution of clusters, with little continuity. Another draft, titled *Sötét és Világos* (Dark and Light), is more informative, showing that Ligeti had indeed envisioned a static, cluster-based orchestral work before reaching the West. The details of rhythmic planning and ways of giving internal animation to the clusters were nowhere near as

---

30. It is possible that the sequence intended here was G–F♯–F, continuing chromatically to E, but that the limit of the violin's range required the substitution of a second G, preserving the desired contour while disturbing the pitch sequence.

Example 3.11a. *Sötét és Világos*, sketch of the formal proportions. Reproduced with kind permission from the György Ligeti Collection of the Paul Sacher Foundation, Basel

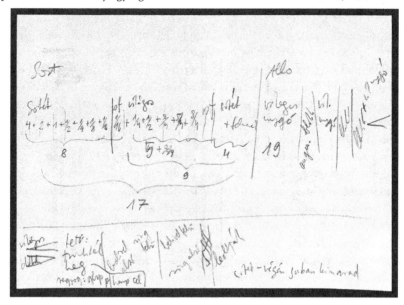

Example 3.11b. *Sötét és Világos*, reduced score, mm. 1–8

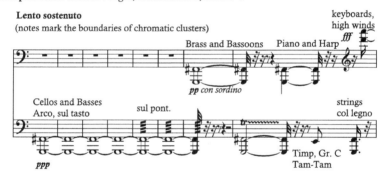

refined as they would be after his experiences in the studio, and thus make a revealing comparison to the finished version.

Sketches show that the piece is carefully proportioned in the earliest drafts, taking the measure as its basic unit (example 3.11a). The essential idea, similar to that in Lendvai's analyses of Bartók, establishes proportions of the major divisions of the piece—although Ligeti uses the twin primes seventeen and nineteen rather than the golden ratio—and then smaller divisions within each section. The initial seventeen-measure section is subdivided into units of eight and nine measures. The initial eight-measure section is proportioned harmonically, starting with a four-measure unit and dividing successive durations in half. The nine-measure section that follows uses Fibonacci numbers as it grows in units of 1, 2, 3, 5, and 8 quarter notes.[31]

The draft of the score that remains follows this scheme closely; the first eight measures are transcribed in example 3.11b.[32] The initial twelve-tone cluster in the basses and cellos moves from sul tasto to sul ponticello and tremolo, marking the first division, after four measures. After two measures of tremolo, the same cluster is transferred to the muted brass and low winds for one measure before accelerating through trilling strings, keyboard instruments, and eventually the winds and upper strings. The Sostenuto section moves from dark to light and back; the initial clusters remain in the low register with sustained sounds through the *sötét* section, switching to the upper register, a loud dynamic level, and more activity as we approach the first hint of *világos* material but quickly returning to the same cluster in the last four measures. In this draft there are relatively few timbre changes compared to the final version—only those created by a change of bow position, simple trills, and tremolos. Later, when the strings implement glissandi, they are quite literal, and work as an anticipatory gesture marked "fenyegetően" (threateningly) in the score. A second glissando is answered immediately by the beginning of the Allegro section. There are none of the complex orchestrational effects or in-between states found in the final version of *Apparitions*—no coordinated trills or degrees of variation or nuance to the combination of bow position and type of articulation (static, tremolo, or trilled), no ebb and flow to the progression, and little variation in the width of the cluster, and consequently (though also as a result of the simpler formal planning) the ultimate idea of stasis is undercut by this linear direction toward the Allegro section.

The Allegro represents the idea of *világos* using higher, faster, and brighter sounds; with its mixed rhythmic subdivisions and heavy use of the keyboards, percussion, and high winds, one can discern the beginnings of the wild outbursts of the completed *Apparitions*. This section may also bear the mark of an unlikely and previously unremarked upon influence—that of Olivier Messiaen. Moreover, once this precedent has been observed, we might see the micropolyphonic melodies in the violas, basses, and flutes of the final version of *Apparitions* (noted above) as a lingering manifestation of this influence. Messiaen and Yvonne Loriod had visited Budapest and given a series of lectures and concerts at the Liszt Conservatory at the beginning of

31. Ligeti's sketch seems to contain an inconsistency at this point. The value he calculates as being nine measures actually comes one quarter note short. The score draft does seem to follow the values of the sketch, at least through 8/4, before diverging at the end of the Sostenuto section.
32. This draft is housed at the Paul Sacher Foundation, but a reproduction (albeit greatly reduced in size) can be found in Ove Nordwall, *György Ligeti: Sketches and Unpublished Scores, 1938–1958* (Stockholm: Royal Swedish Academy of Music, 1976).

1948. According to Rachel Beckles Willson,[33] the lectures concerned Debussy and organ playing, and some of Messiaen's music was performed, but the degree to which Ligeti would have been able to absorb information about the composer's techniques, either at the time of his visit or in the intervening eight years, is unclear. Nevertheless, there are several details in *Sötét és Világos* that strongly suggest at least a cursory knowledge of Messiaen's practice. In the sketches there are several mentions of a "gamelan carillon," which can be taken to refer to the section from measure 18 on, featuring xylophone, celesta, and high woodwinds.[34] The texture is a composite in which not all instruments play the whole line; individual instruments drop notes here and there, creating a type of hocket texture within the ostinato, not far from the model of Messiaen's *Turangalîla Symphony*, which he would have been finishing at the time of the Budapest visit. The twin primes of seventeen and nineteen, which define the section lengths, also have a particular prominence in Messiaen's piece.

As in *Éjszáka*, Ligeti uses the diatonic and pentatonic collections in this section, though here they sound simultaneously rather than in succession; the piccolos and xylophone use the two-flat diatonic collection, and the celesta and E♭ clarinets use the complementary pentatonic collection, E–F♯–G♯–B–C♯ (see example 3.12). In a draft of this section Ligeti numbers the introduction of new pitches, as he did with his twelve-tone studies, showing a conscious regulation of the total chromatic. The pitches are fixed in register, and Ligeti first introduces only a tetrachord, then adds the remaining notes in the successive gestures, another feature more similar to works such as *Variations Concertantes* and *Chromatische Phantasie* than to the finished *Apparitions*. He gradually completes the full chromatic collection at the end of the third measure. In harmonic terms, there is a tightly controlled focus on seconds and sevenths (interval classes 1 and 2) with the occasional tritone but a strict avoidance of thirds or perfect consonances.

Also reminiscent of Messiaen (and of *Turangalîla* in particular) is the unpitched percussion in this section: two independent parts forming ostinatos of 44 sixteenth notes each but offset from one another and subdivided differently. The upper percussion part in example 3.12 occurs after a quarter rest and is then articulated every 14, 10, and 20 sixteenths, while the lower

---

33. This trip is documented in Rachel Beckles Willson, *György Kurtág, The Sayings of Péter Bornemisza, op. 7: A "concerto" for Soprano and Piano* (Burlington, VT: Ashgate, 2004), 15.

34. This interest in Eastern musical traditions can be found in some of Ligeti's earlier works, including *Tavaszi Virág* (Spring Flower), inspired by hearing Beijing opera. See Richard Steinitz, *György Ligeti: Music of the Imagination* (Boston: Northeastern University Press, 2003), 46–48. This interest may have also been kindled by his acquaintance with the poet Sándor Weöres, who was similarly interested in Eastern art (see Beckles Willson, *Ligeti, Kurtág*, 64–73, and also Steinitz, *Ligeti*, 40–42).

Example 3.12. *Sötét és Világos*, reduced score, mm. 18–22

part uses the duration of 13 sixteenths before settling into an alternation of 11 and 33. Once established, though, they proceed systematically through the 19 extant measures of this section.

The surviving sketches for *Sötét és Világos* cannot, however, be considered a complete composition or a finished artistic statement. It is intriguing that whereas the sketch of formal proportions seems like a complete form, the draft score seems like a fragment. The music continues just over the downbeat of the thirty-seventh bar onto a new page of staff paper that is then left blank—slurs pointing forward to an empty page, with no final bar line. *Sötét és Világos* cannot be considered a real draft of *Apparitions*, but it is nevertheless a fascinating document and a study that tells us much about Ligeti's path toward his first orchestral work in the West. In particular, it provides concrete evidence of the development of his repertoire of techniques, including which tools he had developed before contact with the Western European avant-garde and which came into place after his arrival in Cologne. The predisposition toward formal experimentation is quite clear in the draft, as well as from his twelve-tone studies, but the degree of planning is quite scant in comparison to the stages of planning found in the first movement of *Apparitions*. Moreover, by taking the measure as his basic unit in the earlier piece, he does not truly escape from the idea of meter; bars are grouped together or divided in halves, successively, much as in traditional music.

In addition, each of the timbre changes is either an instrumental change (strings to brass and back) or a change in playing technique in which all of the instruments act together (low strings moving to sul ponticello, tremolo). This

early draft, then, shows a strong connection to relatively traditional instrumental techniques and does not venture into the coordinated effects that are
seen in the final version of the first movement of *Apparitions*, effects which
require composing within the sound in a delicate and precise way, rather
than switching between predefined instrumental timbres. This is perhaps the
greatest difference in Ligeti's work after his time in the electronic music studio: the sense that one can compose *within* the sound. Instruments do not
define the possible sounds—there is no one-to-one correspondence between
instrument (or playing technique) and sound—but, rather, they are tools for
bringing to life any imaginable sound, and when creatively combined, they
can work together as constituents of a greater, more complicated whole. If
we look at how Ligeti extended the opening seventeen measures of *Sötét és
Világos* into the six-minute-long first movement of *Apparitions*, this attention
to microscopic detail and to nuanced and coordinated instrumental writing
stands alongside his increased understanding of perception (through his play
with dynamic, rhythmic, and registral extremes) as the factors that enabled
this critical step in his compositional technique.

Apparitions, Movement II, Original Version

The original version of the second movement of *Apparitions* is conceptually
simpler than the final version, yet they share many common concerns. They
both deal with speeds pushing the limits of perception, forming a dense web
of individual lines, and controlling the resulting texture to simulate a dynamic
response to external events. The original second movement, however, also
shows a stronger connection to Ligeti's earlier twelve-tone sketches in its
pitch material, as well as a degree of experimentation with indeterminacy in
performance not yet seen in his other works.

Ligeti drafted the original second movement in 1957, but it was never
given a premiere and was only published in *Musica* in 1968. The work appears
along with an introduction by Ove Nordwall, who presents it as a historical
curiosity, an example of the type of aleatoric counterpoint that Lutosławski
would develop in the 1960s,[35] and also as the earliest example of Ligeti's building such a massive polyphonic web.

Each instrument has a chromatic cell, presented in various wedge-shaped gestures, immediately reminiscent of the wedge-shaped rows that Ligeti used in his

---

35. Ove Nordwall's article "Der Komponist, György Ligeti," *Musica* 22 (1968),
173–77, is followed immediately by Ligeti's "Spielanweisungen zur Erstfassung des
zweiten Satzes der 'Apparitions,'" 177–79. For more on this fleeting connection with
Lutosławski, see also Steven Stucky, *Lutosławski and His Music* (New York: Cambridge
University Press, 1981), 109.

Example 3.13. *Apparitions*, II, original version, violin VI

Example 3.14. *Apparitions*, II, original version, diagram of the form

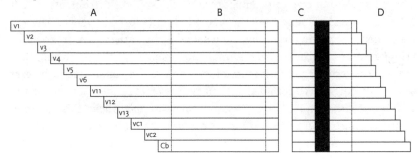

twelve-tone experiments of 1956. Here, however, each of the twelve instruments (six violins, three violas, two celli, and one bass) has a different number of notes. They increase from two in violin I to twelve in cello II twelve plus an octave repetition in the bass. The cells also overlap in register, so that the lowest note of the violin I part is the highest note of the violin II part and so forth down the line, eventually filling a chromatic cluster from G♭7 down to C1. Each instrumental part is divided into several motives, always arranged as serial transformations of the chromatic cell and always proceeding in the same order: Prime (starting from the lowest note and wedging inwards), Inversion, Retrograde, and Retrograde Inversion. Violin VI, shown in example 3.13, is a representative example.

Ligeti divides the movement into sections A–D (see example 3.14), which flow directly from one to the next through its brief duration of less than three minutes. The director cues each of these sections, as well as individual entries and exits, but much of the run of the movement is left to individual performers. In section A the director cues the instruments to enter in order over the course of about one minute, and they play these figures. Once the director cues an entrance, each player proceeds independently, using irregular durations and gaps between statements of the motives. As the instruments enter in order, a registral spread from high to low occurs. Once all have entered, the director gives the cue for section B. For thirty seconds to sixty seconds the players gradually accelerate, first reducing the gaps between motives, and continuing to push the tempo even faster, developing a dense, but still soft, web. Section C features what Ligeti called two *actions gratuites*—a sudden, brief, general pause and, about five seconds later, a sudden change to *ffff* for about one second. The movement then tapers off as it began, with instruments exiting somewhat more quickly, but again from high to low at the cue of the director.

Ligeti's description of the performance directions contains several insights into his compositional concerns that are relevant to the later version of *Apparitions*. In his instructions for section B he acknowledges that the extremity of the acceleration (which he describes as "from 'as fast as possible' to 'even faster than possible'")[36] is to the detriment of pure intonation, obscuring the actual pitches (especially in the lower voices) and aiming only for the contour. In light of this, it seems quite deliberate that the most agile and virtuosic parts are written not for the violins but for the lowest-sounding and least nimble instruments. Nevertheless, remarking on the interconnection of different parameters—that speed may affect pitch, in both performance and perception—reflects similar statements by the composer in other sources. His objection to the treatment of dynamics and accent in Boulez's *Structures*,[37] for example, is an acknowledgement that these two parameters are closely connected and cannot be treated as completely independent.

More concrete events in this early version reflect aspects of the later version of the work as well. The distinction of *actions gratuites* in section C implies an external influence on the music—an abrupt response that is not motivated from within. Ligeti's discussion of the first movement of *Apparitions* in "States, Events, Transformations" talks of a pseudo-syntax caused by the explosive "events" seeming to alter the network of the underlying "states." These two actions, similarly, can be seen as dramatic and sudden changes rather than more organic evolution. Finally, they can be seen as the root of more specific features of the final version of the second movement, the general pause being the source of abrupt cuts in the mosaic textures, and the *ffff* outburst being expanded into the wild *fff* micropolyphony that comprises the middle section. These external actions, however carefully developed in the drafts of *Apparitions*, are precisely the features left out of *Atmosphères*, as Ligeti turned his attention and growing orchestrational abilities to crafting a more continuous musical evolution.

ATMOSPHÈRES

After the initial success of *Apparitions*, which displayed his newly invented techniques for creating static music, Ligeti began to refine and expand these

36. Ligeti, "Spielanweisungen zu 'Apparitions,'" 179: "So beschleunigt sich das Tempo 'so rasch wie möglich' zu 'noch rascher wie möglich.' Das bedeutet eine allmähliche Beschleunigung des Tempos bis zum äussersten, zum Nachteil der sauberen Intonation (vor allem in den tieferen Instrumenten), bis die exakten Tonhöhen verschwinden und von den Motiven nur eine ungefähre Kontur bleibt."
37. György Ligeti, "Pierre Boulez: Decision and Automatism in Structure 1a," trans. Leo Black, in *Young Composers: Die Reihe* 4 (Bryn Mawr, PA: Presser; London: Universal Edition, 1960, German edition 1958), 36–62.

techniques in his next work, *Atmosphères*. This masterpiece for orchestra, notably without percussion, is a study in continuity and the gradual transformation of texture and timbre, and with its sublime orchestration, it has come to be not only one of Ligeti's best-known works but a landmark composition of the twentieth century. As Ligeti described the aesthetic concerns of *Atmosphères*:

The formal characteristic of this music is that it seems static. The music appears to stand still, but that is merely an illusion: within this standing still, this static quality, there are gradual changes: I would think here of a surface of water in which an image is reflected; then this surface of water is gradually disturbed, and the image disappears, but very, very gradually. Subsequently the water calms down again, and we see a different image. That is, of course, merely a metaphor or association, but one can see metaphorical elements even in the titles of these works. Typical of this is *Atmosphères*, where the word 'atmosphere' itself has a dual meaning: atmosphere in the literal sense of the word and also in the figurative sense.[38]

He was careful to position his composition on the edge of abstraction—evocative and expressive, but still ambiguous, and certainly not programmatic. Ligeti's rhetoric concerning *Atmosphères* strikes a delicate balance between other conflicting interpretations as well. At times he described it as "a composition in tone-colours par excellence,"[39] revealing that timbre has form-defining importance, yet at other times he stated that "it is a rather superficial view to lay too much emphasis on timbre." Likewise, discussing the work's connection to the avant-garde music of the 1950s, at times he identified parts of the composition as indebted to the type of constructivist planning he learned in Cologne, but at other times he criticized the entire school and even posited *Atmosphères* as a reaction against it.[40] Finally, with regard to electronic music, as discussed in the introduction to this chapter, Ligeti freely acknowledged that much of what he learned from Koenig went into the piece yet still objected when certain reviews made too much of this connection. With an understanding of Ligeti's technique in pieces like *Artikulation* and *Apparitions*, we can now investigate the details of these seemingly contradictory positions by means of a similarly probing analysis of the composition of *Atmosphères*.

Work on *Atmosphères* began with verbal descriptions of the various states through which the piece would move, followed by a progressive refinement of detail into the finished score—often passing through a form of graphic

38. *LiC*, 84.

39. *LiC*, 86, 39.

40. For example in *LiC*, 43–44, Ligeti describes the proportioning of small formal units in *Atmosphères* as "the manifestation of the constructionist phase I went through in Cologne." In contrast *LiC*, 38 states: "With *Atmosphères* I was consciously reacting against the refinement of serialism."

representation in between. This general process from the verbal through the graphic to the score became a standard working method for Ligeti.[41] He originally developed a list of twenty-four states divided into four categories, and it seems that the analogy to a reflection in a watery surface is present even in this early stage:

A) static surface (with disturbances spreading like waves in the static voices) [Álló felület (zavarokkal, melyek mint hullámok terjednek az álló szolámokban)]
B) vibrating surface [Vibráló felület]
C) mosaics without gaps [Mozaik szünetek nélkül]
D) ending type (perhaps): Very fast web, breaking off, dissipating, traces, vanishing (beaten-out measures of rest) [Zárótipus (esetleg): Nagyon gyors szövevény, abba-abbamarad, szétfoszlik, nyomok, eltünik (Kiütött szünet - taktusok)][42]

Within each of these categories there are subtypes—twelve for category A, five for B, six for C, and one for D—each of which is slightly different from the others. Ligeti chooses twenty-one from this list and reorders them into the sections of the piece, some with slight variations, yet the basic descriptions of textures in the sketches describe moments in the finished piece quite well.

Moreover, Ligeti defined different types of transitional motion between sections of material. He lists sixteen types of transition between a hypothetical material A and material B, ranging from complete contrast—"A breaks off, B enters (straightforward, one after the other, contrast)" [A abbamarad, B elkezdödik (egyszerü egymásután, kontraszt)]—to much more poetic and elaborate descriptions: "within A, B begins to raise its head, emerging like islands, B proliferates, A suddenly breaks off as B remains alone" [A-n belül B mar felüti fejét szigetszerüen, B elszaporodik, A hirtelen abbamarad, B marad egyedül] and also "A continues, while B floats up, unperceived, becomes more

41. Jonathan Bernard, in his "Rules and Regulation: Lessons from Ligeti's Compositional Sketches," in *György Ligeti: Of Foreign Lands and Strange Sounds*, ed. Louise Duchesneau and Wolfgang Marx (Woodbridge, UK: Boydell, 2011), 149–67, claims that "one cannot necessarily infer from such an order the actual, chronological order of creation for any single work" (151), and while I concur that in individual cases Ligeti may have gone back and forth between these types, I also find ample evidence to propose this as at least a general working method—for example, many of the verbal sketches contain numbered lists, categorizations, or descriptions of material that are then used in sketches and charts, even when the material has been reordered. See, for example, the analysis of *Aventures* in chapter 4.
42. This transcription comes from a typewritten sketch in which Ligeti, most likely working on a German machine without the proper diacritical marks, often uses a simple umlaut in place of the long Hungarian one (e.g., those found in eltünik, elkezdődik, and egyszerű). I have left these uncorrected.

dominant, A suddenly stops and B remains alone" [A még tart, mikor B ész-
revétlenül beuszik, elhatalmasodik, A hirtelen abbamarad, B m.e. (= marad
egyedül).] It is difficult to attribute specific transitions in the piece to every
one of the listed descriptions, but the finished composition features a subtle
variety of transitions, many of which resemble the general descriptions in
the sketch. In light of these, one might interpret letter Q, for example, as
a type of island predicting the final texture (letter T), while the intervening
sections (letters R and S) have more sustained material like previously used
textures.[43]

From these earliest sketches one can observe a clear interest in the creation of an evolving continuity. True to his experimental impulse, however,
Ligeti tested the limits of how continuity can be perceived in spite of progressively greater challenges to the literal continuity of individual voices. At the
top of sketch of the form of the piece in example 3.15, he lists five variables
(változók) that are in play over the course of the piece, and below them, he
develops two of them (dynamics and activity) into a multivalent expression
of form.[44]

1) Dynamics (Dynamika)
2) Tone Color (Hangszín)
3) Activity (Mozgékonyság)
4) Width (Szélesség)
5) Register (Regiszter)

Each state through which the piece moves involves a unique combination
of these five elements and different degrees of connection with the previous
section, based on which and how many of these variables change. This arrangement of unique states led Ligeti to write a description of the form below this
chart: "Form: alterations of the states and proportions (very strict) of the
states. Serial in the sense of a series of states and a series of proportions, but

43. Angela Ida de Benedictis and Pascal Decroupet discuss these transition types
and posit more correspondences to moments in the piece in their article "Die
Wechselwirkung von Skizzenforschung und spektromorphologischer Höranalyse
als Grundlage für das ästhetische Verständnis: Zu György Ligetis *Atmosphères*,"
Musiktheorie 27, no. 4 (2012), 322–35. They reproduce and examine other sketches in
their article, including several discussed here.
44. The idea of a multivalent form in Ligeti's music is indebted to Hermann Sabbe,
György Ligeti: Studien zur kompositorischen Phanömenologie (Munich: Edition Text +
Kritik, 1987), esp. 28–29, who describes Ligeti's approach to form as "polyrhythmic,"
involving variables such as register, timbre, and interval contour that each change at
their own tempo. My use of "multivalent" also follows James Webster (in turn following Harold Powers) in William Caplin, James Hepokoski, and James Webster,
Musical Form, Forms, and Formenlehre: Three Methodological Reflections, ed. Pieter Bergé
(Leuven: Leuven University Press, 2009), 128.

Example 3.15. *Atmosphères*, sketch of the formal parameters. Reproduced with kind permission from the György Ligeti Collection of the Paul Sacher Foundation, Basel

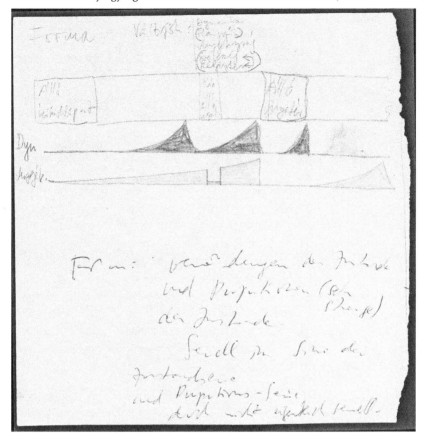

not actually serial."[45] Thus the idea of nonrepetition associated with serialism seems to remain relevant and desirable for Ligeti, and also a justification for an original and decidedly nontraditional form. The uniqueness of the proportion scheme is that no relationship is reproduced, and so no large-scale hierarchical divisions or quasi-metrical repeated time spans are produced. This is also quite different from Ligeti's use of proportional schemes in *Apparitions* and earlier works, which consciously reused the same proportion, either harmonic or golden-section proportions, between different sections. In a letter to Stockhausen dated December 19, 1961, Ligeti explains:

45. The sketch in question reads, "Form: Veränderungen der Zustände und Proportionen (sehr strenge) der Zustände. Seriell im Sinne der Zustandserie und Proportionsserie, doch nicht eigentlich seriell." The fact that this is written in German, however, whereas the majority of the sketches are in Hungarian, may indicate that this was intended as a statement to be shared rather than a private thought.

Example 3.16. *Atmosphères*, dynamic fluctuations, letter B

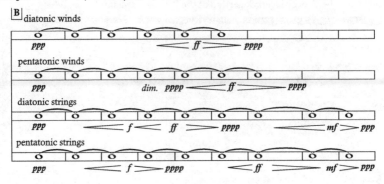

The durations of the individual sections, measured in seconds are:

48" 29" 55" 37" 6" 23" 33" 14" 21" 18" 5" 8" 10" 26" 43" 16" 9" 12" 4" 7" 71" 19"
(21 + 1 = 22 Sections)

In this way, not only are symmetries avoided, but also any similarity in the proportions of neighboring sections: the series of durations was so chosen, that the same proportion is never repeated in two successive sections. So, briefly described, the succession of duration values seems to be arbitrary. It is not, however, since the selection of a particular duration value for a particular section was made along with the "content" of the respective section, i.e. along with the type of tone color, intensity, width, and motion.[46]

The beginning of the work focuses on static surfaces with disturbances, which, quite innovatively, are created by dynamic fluctuation, and only later by other means. The giant chromatic cluster (from E♭2 to C♯7) attenuates slowly, until only the violas and cellos are left at letter A (E3 to B4). Voices reenter at letter B and begin to refocus the dynamics within parts of the cluster. Different groups within the winds and strings use either the white-note diatonic or black-note pentatonic collections and have different dynamic indications, as shown in example 3.16. From the full orchestra and total chromatic, the strings begin to predominate and then become more weighted toward the diatonic. This diatonic state becomes more wind-colored, then more pentatonic.

---

46. This letter is contained in the György Ligeti Collection of the Paul Sacher Foundation, Text Manuscripts, *Atmosphères*. "Nicht nur Symmetrien wurden auf diese Weise vermieden, sondern sogar Ähnlichkeiten in den Proportionen der Nachbarabschnitte: die Reihenfolge der Dauern wurde so gewählt, dass dieselbe Proportion von zwei aufeinanderfolgenden Abschnitten niemals wiederkehrt. So kurz geschildert, scheint die Folge der Dauernwerte arbiträr zu sein. Sie ist es aber nicht, denn die Wahl eines bestimmten Dauernwertes für einen bestimmten Abschnitt wurde im Zusammenhang mit dem "Inhalt" des jeweiligen Abschnittes, d.h. mit dem Klangfarben-, Intensität-, Ambituswert und dem Bewegungtyp getroffen."

The pentatonic state is then transferred back to the strings; finally the strings swell together as a full chromatic cluster before fading again.

In this passage we have the same diatonic-pentatonic divide that was present in *Éjszáka* and in the Allegro section of *Sötét és Világos*, now taken to a new level of refinement and finesse. Instead of being used as separate harmonic blocks defining separate sections, or as material separated by instrument to define different contrapuntal strands, the pentatonic and the diatonic are both continually present, but the balance between them shifts back and forth, along with the balance between string and wind timbres. Each of the four combinations receives its fleeting moment of emphasis in a very fluid progression in which the only sense of rhythm is the nebulous coordination of dynamic peaks and troughs. Ligeti makes further use of this technique at letter M, where a chromatic cluster from B2 to A3 is split between the brass instruments, each group entering, exiting, swelling, and abating with its own dynamic markings: horns with the diatonic/whole-tone subset, B, Db, Eb, trombones with an interlocking diatonic set, C, D, E, F, and trumpets with the adjacent chromatic set Gb, G, Ab, A.

As the piece progresses there are disturbance types involving speed or internal motion as well. For example, in section C, without moving any of the individual voices in pitch, each of the strings accelerates progressively, but out of phase—offset by one beat in a rhythmic canon in which triplets are followed by sixteenths, quintuplets, and so on all the way up to twenty divisions of the beat. This creates the *Bewegungsfarbe* effect that Ligeti described in relation to the electronic works and in *Apparitions* by ensuring that there will always be cross-rhythms creating an irregular, chaotic conflict of attack points, often exceeding the threshold of differentiation. This technique also generates an increase in surface noise and is one of the first times that Ligeti introduces noise into the texture without the use of percussion. It prepares the way for extended techniques that occur later: blowing through the brass instruments at letter P, col legno and flageolet textures in the strings, and brushed piano strings in the final section of the piece.

After exploring a number of types of internal motion, animating clusters only by means of rhythm and dynamics, Ligeti begins to compose clusters that move through pitch space as well. In order to accomplish this motion, he first arranges the texture graphically and then transfers this graphic notation into very precise traditional notation for the players (as shown in examples 3.17a and 3.17b).[47] The type of creeping glissando shown here was first carried out in *Pièce électronique no. 3* and then in *Apparitions* at measure 62 in the cellos (discussed above); at letter E of *Atmosphères* it becomes

47. Other authors have shown this, including Steinitz, *Ligeti*, 109, and Jennifer Iverson, "Shared Compositional Techniques between György Ligeti's *Pièce électronique No. 3* and *Atmosphères*," *Mitteilungen der Paul Sacher Stiftung* 22 (April 2009), 29–33.

Example 3.17a. *Atmosphères*, sketch including a graphic of registral expansion, letter E. Reproduced with kind permission from the György Ligeti Collection of the Paul Sacher Foundation, Basel

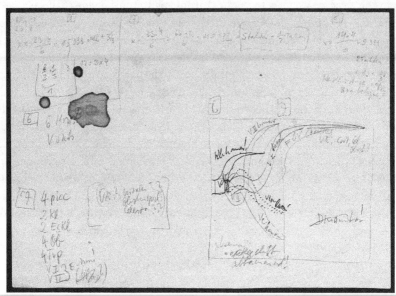

Example 3.17b. *Atmosphères*, sketch transcription translating the expansion to violin II parts

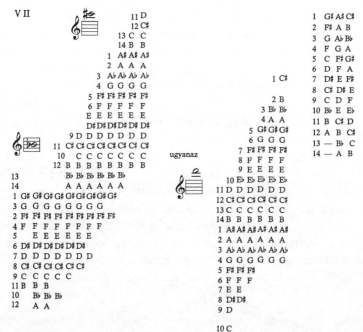

the dominant form of motion in the orchestra, with all instrumental families working to expand clusters in different directions. The net result of the whole is an expansion from a central register to the extremities, finally leaving only the uppermost notes of the violins and piccolos. Ligeti charted out each instrumental family's part separately and he included a number of rhythmic modules in these charts—figuring out what divisions of septuplets, for example, would come before or after certain divisions into quintuplets or triplets.

Register, one of the five categories defined in Example 3.15, is an important part of the concept of the piece. Nowhere, however, is this more dramatically demonstrated than at letter G, one of its most striking moments, where a cluster consisting of F7 to G♯7 in the piccolos is transferred down more than six octaves to the basses (C♯1 to G♯1). This huge gap in registral space is clearly a challenge to continuity, but Ligeti managed to prepare even this drastic leap. Letter E began to open up the register in both directions, and while the bass register drops out by letter F, leaving the upper register alone, letter G returns to this temporarily abandoned bass register. These extreme registers also complement each other acoustically. The piccolos will produce the psychoacoustic effect of difference tones (which Ligeti attempted to use consciously in *Pièce électronique no. 3*), rumbling in the lower register. And conversely, the basses, playing at maximum volume, will produce higher-pitched harmonics and surface noise filling the middle register. Multiple factors, then, help bridge this gap from high to low: the extremity of the sounds in both register and volume, the auditory effects involved, and the recent memory of the low register, even while the higher register is emphasized. A spatial or visual analogy may be most apt: it is as if the low register, temporarily obscured from view, comes back into perception through a sudden change in perspective. It is possible, then, to hear the abrupt shift in register at letter G more as a rebalancing of the audible space than a categorical change of material.

Once this wide registral space has been opened, Ligeti fills it with yet another type of motion: his new micropolyphony. The microployphony at letter H is a refinement of what we saw in *Apparitions*, one of the most meaningful developments for Ligeti's subsequent compositions, and a source of great pride for him. The violins use one melody in a closely offset canon, while the violas and cellos use another. Examining the basic melodies (shown in Example 3.18), we can see that the tetrachordal units are chromatic cells related by serial operations. In the violin melody the progression begins with an ascending semitone, followed by a descending whole tone and a semitone; the next statement begins down a whole tone from the last note for a full interval sequence of (+1–2–1, –2). The lower melody (used by the violas and cellos) has the retrograde of this tetrachordal pattern, rising a semitone and a whole tone, then descending a semitone (+1+2–1, +2). After

Example 3.18. *Atmosphères*, micropolyphonic melody

two repetitions of these patterns, each melody completes its own aggregate, and Ligeti alters the pattern for the second aggregate, rotating the intervallic sequence so that the lower melody uses +2–1+2, with the subsequent statement beginning +1. The upper voice has an inversion of this pattern, rather than the retrograde (–2+1–2, –1). The clear relation to serial practice is in contradistinction to the more irregular micropolyphony in the final version of *Apparitions*, but it does resemble the original version of *Apparitions* II in the serial transformation of chromatic cells.

The individual instruments in the texture begin on different notes of the canon, so the violin I, player 1 begins on the first note, F♯; violin I, player 2 begins on the second note, G, and so forth. Some of the instruments share starting notes so that two octaves are split among the twenty-eight instruments. The register left empty in the jump from letter F to letter G is filled immediately at letter H, although the instruments are instructed to enter imperceptibly. Near letter I, Ligeti has the violins continue with only the first half of the pattern, also moving down to the lower register and beginning to accelerate.

The newest, if not the most famous, feature of *Atmosphères* is the development of what Ligeti called "mosaics" in his sketches. These, once again, are worked out graphically and then given a detailed realization in the score. The simplest mosaic texture is found at letter K, where it governs the overlapping entrances and exits of instruments in the semitone C–D♭4—the narrowest register of the piece, in one of the shortest sections, lasting only eight seconds. This texture is, nonetheless, worked out with great care, first as a sketch (example 3.19a) and then realized with only the slightest adjustments in the score (example 3.19b, where each second of the sketch becomes one quarter-note beat in the score).

In the sketch we can see Ligeti monitoring not only the durations of each instrumental group but also, on the y axis, the calculation of how many voices are sounding at once, and on the x axis, how this instrumental density changes over time. The violin I harmonics were clearly added at a later stage; they appear in a darker writing and explain the alterations to the chart of instrumental density. The addition helps smooth out the flow of instrumental density, which does not change abruptly but rather by small increments.

Example 3.19a. *Atmosphères*, sketch of the mosaic texture, letter K. Reproduced with kind permission from the György Ligeti Collection of the Paul Sacher Foundation, Basel

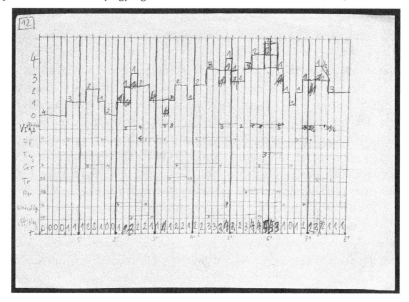

Example 3.19b. *Atmosphères*, reduced score of letter K, mm. 55–56

The final notes in the strings lead into Letter L

Moreover, this density grows in waves, increasing to successively higher peaks: three instrumental groups appear in the third second, four in the fifth, and five at the end of the sixth second.

The ending texture at letter T is the most extensive and elaborate mosaic of the piece; this time, however, Ligeti introduces some gaps in the texture as the piece fades away. The graphic stage of planning was very similar to that at letter K. Here, however, he seems to have calculated the balance between the number of instrumental groups sounding at any one time more intuitively, or visually, without the precise numerical calculations seen in the top half of example 3.19a. The texture is divided into seven basic groups, and blocks of sound are assigned to each instrumental group roughly, on graph paper (example 3.20a). The basic distribution is seen most simply in example 3.20b, a reduction of the finished score showing the most representative instruments of each group through the first four measures of this section.

Within each group, however, other instruments follow the basic pattern of durations but subdivide it into conflicting rhythmic patterns (example 3.21). Moreover, there is less in the way of precise pitch content for this section; different instruments begin gliding through artificial harmonics on different strings and in different patterns. The conflicting subdivisions will create surface noise, as will the practical consideration of technique: by playing through artificial harmonics so rapidly, one is likely to hit many of the gray areas between these harmonics, ensuring a delicate mixture of pitch and noise as the piece seems to dissolve and evaporate away.

So how does *Atmosphères* work, and what is its relation to serialism, electronic music, and *Klangfarbenmelodie*? The preceding analysis has revealed two areas where the influence of serialism is notable. The first area involves an emphasis on nonrepetition and aperiodicity in the formal proportions for sections of the piece; this is in keeping with the composer's stance in "Metamorphoses of Musical Form," where he advocates a serially conceived and highly structured form, but a freer approach in the detail work, especially concerning the ordering of individual events. The second area of serial influence is in the construction of individual micropolyphonic melodies. In both of these areas, however, Ligeti undercuts the importance of serial precision. In the timing of global sections, he allows tempo variation to distort those carefully constructed proportions. In the micropolyphonic melodies, the serially related cells are ultimately insignificant because they are rendered inaudible by the density and complete chromatic saturation of the entire section. At most they are perceptible indirectly, providing a mixture of ascending and descending contours to individual fragments that may come through momentarily, slipping in and out of audibility.

The techniques of electronic music are not as clearly present as in *Apparitions*, but again, the indirect concerns with blurring direction, composing with the full range of noise and pitch, and working with individual instruments as constituent

Example 3.20a. *Atmosphères*, sketch of the mosaic texture, letter T (excerpt showing mm. 88–96). Reproduced with kind permission from the György Ligeti Collection of the Paul Sacher Foundation, Basel

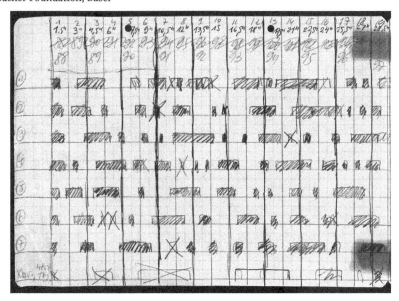

Example 3.20b. *Atmosphères*, rhythmic design at letter T, mm. 88–91

Example 3.21. *Atmosphères*, rhythmic stratification of Group 1, mm. 88–89

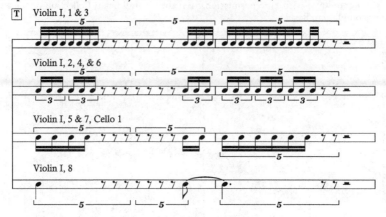

"partials" of the whole are very much present. Ligeti's assertion, then, that these works are "pure instrumental music"[48] can be taken quite literally, as directed against the misconception that the orchestra was playing with a tape part or that the orchestral recording was manipulated by studio effects. But it can also be taken as an assertion that, while the experiences in the studio opened up the sound world of electronic music to Ligeti's imagination, the composer was not trying merely to translate the use of sine tones and noise generators to orchestral instruments; he aimed, rather, to use the instruments more idiomatically, with all of the colors that they could bring. The return to chromatic writing (after the non-equal-tempered pitches of *Pièce électronique no. 3*) is one indication of this goal, as is the production of different colors by relatively standard playing techniques.

Ligeti's concerns about descriptions of *Atmosphères* as a piece of *Klangfarbenmusik* are, perhaps, more complicated. Most of his objections, as voiced in the interviews, go on to mention being "put into the same pigeon-hole with [Krzysztof] Penderecki."[49] These comments often continue by emphasizing the piece's use of changing textures and patterns over the use of individual instrumental timbres. For anyone who had worked with the idea of additive synthesis in the electronic studio—of building a composite sound from its individual constituent parts—this distinction between texture and timbre is a tenuous one at best. Much of Ligeti's objection may, then, be directed at differentiating his devices from the use of extended instrumental techniques like those Penderecki uses to produce exotic timbres (bowing

---

48. See Ligeti, "Auswirkungen," *GS*, 2:90: "Sie sind keine elektronische Musik, sondern reine Instrumentalstücke." And in "Musik und Technik," *GS*, 1:252, he states: "*Apparitions* und *Atmosphères* sind jedoch reine Instrumentalmusik, *selbst* verfremdete Instrumentaleffekte gibt es darin kaum."
49. For example, *LiC*, 39.

behind the bridge or on the tailpiece, and so forth). Ligeti's own music, on the other hand, makes very sparing use of these techniques, which (as often happened in Penderecki's experience) could scare off potential performers.[50] Similarly, the lack of percussion in *Atmosphères* is a conscious statement, written into the subtitle ("for large orchestra without percussion") and aimed at distinguishing his work from that of his contemporaries, many of whom were following Edgard Varèse in their percussion-heavy instrumentation.[51] Ligeti's objection to the label *Klangfarbenmusik*, then, is another way in which he was very conscious of his reception. It allowed him to point out the degree to which his novel-sounding orchestration depended not on individual sound-producing techniques or exotic instruments but on the careful balance and coordination of individual elements to produce something new. This is what most of the sketches attest to in their use of dynamic rebalancing, mosaic structures, and rhythmic layering. This subtle orchestration, informed by work in the studio but designed with acoustic instruments in mind, was the composer's prized invention; *Atmosphères* surpassed any of his previous works in realizing the dream of a static music and helped Ligeti carve out a place among his contemporaries at the forefront of the avant-garde.

50. See, e.g., Danuta Mirka, "To Cut the Gordian Knot: The Timbre System of Krzysztof Penderecki," *Journal of Music Theory* 45, no. 2 (Autumn 2001), 440.

51. In a draft of his introductory text, "*Atmosphères*," held at the Paul Sacher Foundation, Ligeti holds nothing back: "Serielle Musik ist gescheit. Die 'aleatorische' unterhaltsam. Viel Schlagzeug klingt modern. Musikalische Grafiken sind hübsch und die Veränderung (Änderung) der Sitzordung im Orchestrer beeindrucksvoll (eindrucksvoll)." In the published version (*GS*, 2:180) this sentiment is softened considerably: "Strenge serielle Organisation einerseits und aufgelockerte, variable oder aleatorische Formen anderseits gelten gewöhnlich als die beiden möglichen Extreme des heutigen Komponierens, zwischen denen man alle übrigen Erscheinungen einordnet." In this version he also leaves out any derogatory sentiments about the overuse of percussion, merely mentioning the absence of percussion as a feature of the work.

CHAPTER 4

Fluxus and the Absurd (1961–62)

THE FUTURE OF MUSIC

In August 1961, a year after the premiere of *Apparitions* and shortly after finishing the score for *Atmosphères*, Ligeti took the stage at the European Forum in Alpbach, Austria, having been invited to speak to an assembly of leading academics and artists gathered to address the future of their fields. As he later explained, Ligeti felt that he had nothing to say about the future that could possibly be accurate. When he expressed his doubts to the conference organizer, however, he was hastily assured, "It doesn't matter what you say . . . anything will be acceptable."[1] And so, at the end of the conference, Ligeti stood at the podium and remained silent until the crowd grew restless and noisy, and he was dragged off the stage some eight minutes later. This was the first of what would be several public scandals in the early 1960s, and he later documented the incident as a piece for the avant-garde journal *Dé-coll/age*.[2]

Interest in performance art—or, at least, a mixture of theater and sound, challenging audience expectations and often societal expectations at large—had been growing in Europe since the arrival of John Cage at Darmstadt in 1958. Many of Ligeti's associates and new acquaintances came under the influence of Cage at this time, and Ligeti attended the infamous lectures that Cage gave at the Summer Institute titled "Changes," "Indeterminacy," and "Communication."[3] Amidst the furor that these

1. Ligeti's recollection of the conversation in quoted in Richard Toop, *György Ligeti* (London: Phaidon, 1999), 80.
2. It originally appeared in *Dé-coll/age* 3 (December 1962), 5–8, reprinted in *GS*, 2:175–79.
3. Richard Steinitz, *György Ligeti: Music of the Imagination* (Boston: Northeastern University Press, 2003), 119, documents that Ligeti did, in fact, attend all three lectures.

lectures generated[4] there were also more favorable reactions and converts to Cage's way of thinking. Notable among these were two of Ligeti's close friends, Mauricio Kagel and Nam June Paik.[5] Paik, who had been living in Germany since 1957, studying with Wolfgang Fortner in Freiburg before moving to Cologne and working at the WDR, was deeply influenced by Cage. Moreover, Paik was one of the few figures to bridge the growing divide that Cage's appearance had instigated in the European avant-garde.

Paik's music took a distinctly shocking and provocative stance as he then became associated with Fluxus, a Cage-influenced avant-garde performance art group founded by George Maciunas and whose members included personalities such as Yoko Ono, Terry Riley, and La Monte Young. Paik's *Hommage à John Cage* for tape recorder and piano (1959) used numerous props and eventually involved cutting through the piano strings with a knife and warning the audience, "Stand back!" through the loudspeakers. Richard Toop recounts a private performance that Paik gave for Ligeti and Koenig in 1958 which involved putting toys on the keys of a piano, giving Ligeti and Koenig fruit to eat, and disappearing for half an hour, only to come screaming back into the room. Although Paik had clearly moved into the realm of performance art, he maintained good connections to other members of the Darmstadt group, including Stockhausen and Ligeti. In fact, Paik was one of the performers in Stockhausen's *Originale* in 1961 in Cologne and even at the September 1964 performance in New York—the one that other Fluxus members actively protested for betraying the aesthetics of their anti-art ideal. In their opinion Stockhausen remained too bound to the idea of presenting "works" at a "concert," and even his attempt to open up musical content (à la Cage) was seen as subjecting life to the rules and systems of art and technique, rather than abolishing the difference between them.[6]

Ligeti never went as far as Paik or other members of the Fluxus group. He was, however, briefly associated with their events, and during this time he undertook several projects that stand out from his other works in terms of their sketch materials, performance directions, and the working methods they

<hr/>

4. Christopher Shultis's essay "Cage and Europe," in *The Cambridge Companion to John Cage*, ed. David Nicholls, 20–40 (New York: Cambridge University Press, 2002), has a thorough account of the uproar surrounding Cage's appearance at Darmstadt, remarking that "no other event in Darmstadt's history ever generated more controversy" (38).

5. See György Ligeti, *"Träumen Sie in Farbe?" György Ligeti im Gespräch mit Eckhard Roelcke* (Vienna: Paul Zsolnay Verlag, 2003), 100, where Ligeti describes his relationship with Paik as "eng befreundet."

6. Maciunas and Henry Flynt, in particular, expressed the view that Stockhausen was an authoritarian figure during this period. See Eric Drott's summary in "Ligeti in Fluxus," *Journal of Musicology* 21, no. 2 (Spring 2004), 201–40, esp. 229–30. This sentiment was echoed by Cornelius Cardew, "Stockhausen Serves Imperialism," in *Stockhausen Serves Imperialism and Other Articles*, 46–55 (London: Latimer New Dimensions, 1974).

reflect, as well as in their more explicitly theatrical and satirical effects. At different times Ligeti gave various accounts of his reaction to Cage, but all feature a degree of skeptical distance. He admired some of Cage's ideas or innovations but was put off by his attitude or his penchant for controversy—and Cage's Darmstadt lectures were some of his most confrontational.[7] Moreover, as Eric Drott has pointed out, Ligeti never really accepted the underlying project of many of the Cage-inspired movements to break down the divide between art and life.[8] Ligeti was similarly skeptical of the pretentions of "serious" music, but his aim was more at subversive satire than revolution. In addition, Ligeti's satire took new directions as he began to realize that those dedicated to eroding the barriers between art and everyday experience took themselves just as seriously as those on the other side.

Ligeti's description of his silent lecture in Alpbach took the form of a score, now called *The Future of Music*, and was subtitled either "a Collective Composition" or a "Musical Provocation for Lecturer and Audience."[9] While amusing, his silent lecture is also revealing; it is not only a documentation of the audience's reaction but also an analysis of the result in self-consciously musical terms. Ligeti recorded the events in 20-second increments, beginning with the expectation and wonderment, dissolving into disquiet by the end of the first minute. He divided the audience into four groups:

Group 1: The disciplined or indifferent . . .
Group 2: Those who seem mildly amused . . .
Group 3: Those who probably take me for a fool . . .
Group 4: Those who probably believe that I take them for fools.[10]

About two minutes into the performance, Ligeti began to provoke the audience, writing the title "The Future of Music" on a chalkboard and evoking laughter, shouts, and the stomping of feet. He then wrote, "Please no laughing and stomping," and when that backfired, he wrote, "Crescendo," which received a more appropriate response. This is the first of the explicitly musical

7. To Pierre Michel (*György Ligeti: Compositeur d'aujourd'hui*. Paris: Minerve, 1985, 142, also quoted in Steinitz, *Ligeti*, 119), Ligeti described exactly this reaction: interested in Cage's ideas but put off by his attitude. To Péter Várnai in 1978 and Josef Häusler in 1968–69 (*Ligeti in Conversation*, 38, 40, and 87–88) he mentioned innovations like graphic notation and playing inside the piano with reference to Cage, but is careful to distinguish his use of these techniques from Cage's. To Eckhard Roelcke in 2001–02 his attitude was much colder: "Ich war von ihm absolut nicht beeindruckt." ("*Träumen Sie in Farbe?*" 99).
8. Drott, "Ligeti in Fluxus."
9. Different subtitles—"Eine kollektive Komposition" and as "Die 'musikalische Provokation für einen Sprecher und Auditorium' (auch 'Schweigevortrag' genannt)" — are given in *GS*, 2:175 and 178, respectively.
10. *GS*, 2:176.

terms that increasingly come up in Ligeti's account of the event. As he stopped writing on the board and the audience's energy began to wane, he labeled that moment the "Adagio Section," and as the renewed outrage reached a peak, he designated it as the "Opera Finale," with lively interplay between "soloists" (different recognizable members of the crowd) and chorus.

Other aspects of Ligeti's description of the event verge on self-satire, aping the language he used to describe his composition *Apparitions*. Six minutes into the lecture, a "particularly outraged university professor" suddenly left with a thunderous slam of the door. Ligeti continued:

This action works like a catalyst: it causes the overturning of the previous (relative) self-restraint of the members of Groups 3 and 4. This is the moment in which they completely lose their composure, and this change of state is irreversible. From now on those who were previously agitated (even if at times more or less so), yet on the whole of an entirely self-controlled voice, transform into a most eruptive one; static energy is converted to kinetic.[11]

The echoes of Ligeti's completely serious description of *Apparitions* in his "States, Events, Transformations" are uncanny. The "changes of state" in this piece, too, are "irreversible." Percussive or impulsive events are described in terms of the flow of energy, leading to a point where "the entire form is tipped over."[12] Ligeti's language also draws on that of Stockhausen, Eimert, and others in the Cologne group taking on a scientific tone, and so Ligeti's parody leaves very few parties untouched.

Dieter Schnebel, a colleague of Ligeti's and Kagel's who shared billing on many of the same Fluxus concerts, pursued similar compositional experiments at around the same time. Schnebel's early *Abfälle* works resemble Ligeti's lecture. *Abfälle I, 1: réactions* (1960–61, given its premiere on April 29, 1961, by Sylvano Bussotti) is also called a "Concerto for One Instrumentalist and Audience," and *Abfälle I, 2: visible music I* (1960–62, given its premiere on July 7, 1962) is a "Musical Performance for One Conductor and One Instrumentalist." Taken together with Schnebel's contributions, Ligeti's work for a lecturer (as a type of director) and audience completes a cycle of provocative works investigating the dynamics of the traditional concert experience. Schnebel's and Ligeti's works also fall alongside the Cagean project where incidental sounds become the music, although here they are less incidental

11. *GS*, 2:177.

12. I am closely following Jonathan Bernard's translation of "States, Events, Transformations," in *Perspectives of New Music* 31, no. 1 (Winter 1993), 164–71, but the similarity of language is even more striking in the German, where the descriptive words "Zustandsänderung," "unumkehrbar," and "umkippen" are repeated in descriptions of each piece. Compare *GS*, 2:170–73, 2:177.

and more the result of direct provocation or manipulation. Schnebel's *réactions*, too, has an element of commentary not simply on the traditional audience-performer interactions (or non-interactions) but also on contemporary avant-garde practice. The score for *réactions* also has similarities with some of Stockhausen's open works from the 1960s, for example 1963's *Plus-Minus*, in its complex use of abbreviations and mathematical symbols (=, ≈, ≠) to create an open work in which the performer must ultimately decide how these signs are interpreted. Schnebel, however, includes the complicating factor that the performer must also place the unwitting audience's reactions into basic categories of interaction defined by the score, and at times elicit these reactions as needed.

TROIS BAGATELLES

On one hand, Ligeti's *Trois Bagatelles* seem to move even more decisively into Cagean territory, but on the other, the aesthetic difference between Ligeti's humor and parody and Cage's serious reevaluation of art and society become more pronounced with this piece. Written for piano, the work consists of a single *dolcissimo* whole note as the first bagatelle, followed by two individual bars of rest as the other two movements; there is an optional encore consisting of a sixteenth rest. Although Ligeti, perhaps incredibly, claimed that he did not know of Cage's *4'33"* (1952) at the time, the comparison to three movements of tacet written for solo piano is readily apparent. Ligeti's work, however, gives more specific indications for performance, suggesting a somewhat shorter duration. Each movement is a single notated measure, rather than an open-ended tacet marking. The first whole note is given a metronome marking of ♪ = 40–48, yielding an approximate duration of 12 seconds. Movement two is marked L'istesso tempo (molto espressivo), implying approximately the same duration, and the third, Più lento. With total performance times (including the pauses between movements) tending to be under two minutes, these shorter durations make the work more a lighthearted joke than an extended meditation on the sounds we take for granted, and thus point to Ligeti's satire of the concert-going establishment rather than a desire to open up the definition of music to chance and to any available sound. When Ligeti does use everyday objects as musical instruments—for example, sandpaper in *Aventures*—it tends to be in strictly composed, highly organized ways.

Trois Bagatelles was given its premiere by Karl-Erik Welin, one of a group of Swedish musicians with whom Ligeti had become acquainted after the premiere of *Apparitions* and who would become increasingly involved with his career in the following years. The work was first performed on September 2, 1962, at the Fluxus Internationale Festspiele Neuester Musik in Wiesbaden, along with Stockhausen's *Klavierstück IV*, Schnebel's *réactions* and *visible music*, and works by Koenig, Konrad Boehmer, and other Europeans. Other concerts in the month-long festival included such American experimental composers as Cage, Alvin Lucier, and Frederic Rzewski and more committed Fluxus members. They included the movement's founder, George Maciunas and regular contributors George Brecht, Philip Corner, Dick Higgins, Toshi Ichiyanagi, Terry Jennings, Jackson Mac Low, and Emmett Williams, along with Paik, Riley, and Young. Other programs were devoted to happenings, tape music from the United States, French *musique concrète*, and Japanese music. Soon, however, the Fluxus events became more focused on the radical element, and the European composers were gradually left off the programs.[13]

Although Ligeti's *Trois Bagatelles* remained on the programs for longer than other works, eventually he was also dropped from Fluxus, in part because of aesthetic disagreements but also because of more practical matters involving publishing. Competing with Wolf Vostell's *Dé-coll/age*, Maciunas was actively recruiting composers, including Ligeti, to publish with him. Ligeti was frustrated with his own publisher, Universal Edition, as his next venture in musical satire shows, but he chose to stay with a major publishing house, switching to H. Litolff Verlag and C.F. Peters for the publication of *Volumina*. Once again he challenged the establishment from within, rather than pursuing the more radical route of publishing with Maciunas.

FRAGMENT

Ligeti's *Fragment* (1961) is a curious composition that derives much of its satirical value from the circumstances of its creation. It works as a parody of *Apparitions*, however, and is one of his most tongue-in-cheek compositions. The piece was written for the sixtieth birthday of Ligeti's publisher at Universal Editions, Alfred Schlee. Their relationship was not the most constructive, and that was a major reason why Ligeti would abandon Universal with his very next work. He felt slighted by the fact that Schlee did not attend the premiere of either *Apparitions* or *Atmosphères* and thought that the latter piece was only published because, having been accepted at Donaueschingen, there was an immediate need for materials for the festival.[14] There are certainly elements of *Fragment* that make it an odd birthday dedication. Not only does it poke fun at the very work of Ligeti's that Schlee chose to publish, but also the ensemble is heavily weighted toward the low register (using three

---

13. Again, more specifics can be found in Drott, "Ligeti in Fluxus," 215–19.
14. This is reported in Steinitz, *Ligeti*, 123.

contrabasses, contrabassoon, bass trombone, contrabass tuba, bass drum, and tam-tam, along with harp, harpsichord, and piano) and as Richard Toop describes it, "sepulchral."[15]

The parody of *Apparitions*, though, extends farther than just the occasion of its premiere. The orchestration recalls the low-register opening of the first movement of *Apparitions*, and the keyboard instruments resemble the wild sections of the work. The low clusters of *Fragment* were built from the letters of Schlee's name (E♭–C–B–E, or eS–C–H–E in the German system), which conveniently provide two sets of semitones and a substantial overlap with the opening cluster of *Apparitions* (D♯–E). The chord in *Fragment*, however, never shifts or changes register, as the clusters of *Apparitions* did. The instrumental forces reprise their typical roles from the earlier piece but in greatly exaggerated ways; the opening clusters are *overly* static, and the wild excursions are even more abrupt and chaotic. There are none of the ways of animating clusters or gradually moving from stasis to motion, and with the exception of the basses gradually moving between sul ponticello and sul tasto, there is very little of the nuance in timbre. Likewise, the careful proportional planning of the first movement is completely absent in *Fragment*; it is simply a caricature of the most obvious features of *Apparitions*.[16]

VOLUMINA

The organ work *Volumina*, composed from December 1961 to January 1962, though challenging and experimental, is less openly provocative than his more purely Fluxus-influenced works. It returns to a more standard conception of a free-standing work of art, not dependent on satire for its effect, but still infused with the sense of daring and theatricality that pervades this period. The work was commissioned by Hans Otte, an organist and composer who was the head of music for Radio Bremen. Another impetus for writing an organ work may have been his acquaintance with a number of younger composers who were also talented organists. Ligeti was trained as a pianist and had experience on the organ, but his friend Mauricio Kagel, and especially the Swedes Bengt Hambraeus and Karl-Erik Welin, were adept organists. In particular, Welin, who gave the premiere of *Volumina* as well as the *Trois*

15. Toop, *Ligeti*, 83.
16. Depending on the timing of measure 2 (*senza tempo*, holding the note as long as the wind players can) and measure 3 (given the wide range of 2 to 4 minutes) it is possible that the golden section of *Fragment* could arrive near the *fff* outburst of measure 7, but with such wide latitude given to individual measures this seems too approximate to consider part of a conscious plan, and the extant sketches show no evidence of the detailed planning seen in *Apparitions*.

Bagatelles, helped Ligeti work out some of the instructions for various organ techniques and shares its dedication with Otte.

By 1961 Ligeti had developed strong connections to the Royal Swedish Academy of Music in Stockholm; much of this connection came originally through Ligeti's countryman Mátyás Seiber (1905–60), who had taught Ingvar Lidholm (b. 1921) and in 1959 recommended Ligeti for a position teaching solfège there. Ligeti did not win the job, but his lectures at the Royal Academy made an impression, and other members of the conservatory were equally impressed with Ligeti's radio lectures on Webern,[17] as well as the premiere of *Apparitions*, which was attended by Karl-Birger Blomdahl (1916–68) and Lidholm. Soon after this Ligeti was invited to lecture in Stockholm on the subject of orchestration and later to teach more regular composition seminars.[18]

Welin's premiere of *Volumina* lent an almost legendary aura of controversy to the composition. It was to be on a concert including Hambraeus's *Interferenzen*, Kagel's *Improvisation ajoutée*, and Otte's *Alpha Omega*, but the work met with numerous complications before its premiere could occur.[19] As Welin was rehearsing *Volumina* in Gothenburg, the opening of the work, in which all the stops are drawn at once, overpowered the electrical circuit of the organ (which had evidently been repaired with a needle), causing a lot of smoke as insulation began to melt.[20] Whereas some reports cite this incident, and exaggerations of it, as the reason for the cancelation of the concert, others cite Otte's plan to use dancers in the cathedral, which did not meet with the approval of church authorities. For whatever reason, the Bremen premiere was replaced with a broadcast of a recording, but this recording also had its difficulties—the tape was too short to accommodate the full work, and so it was broadcast incomplete. Shortly after these incidents, Welin successfully gave a full premiere at the Westerkerk in Amsterdam, but by this time news

17. Many of these lectures, which started at the WDR in 1958 but continued through the early 1960s at the Bayerischer Rundfunk (Munich) and SWDR (Baden-Baden), are reproduced in *GS*, 1:325–410.

18. Ligeti's method of teaching in some of these composition seminars is the subject of his "Neue Wege im Kompositionsunterricht," in *GS*, 1:131–56.

19. See Zsigmond Szathmáry, "Die Orgelwerke von György Ligeti," in *György Ligeti: Personalstil—Avantgardismus—Popularität*, ed. Otto Kolleritsch, 213–21 (Vienna: Universal Edition, 1987). Szathmáry does not include Otte's work, which is mentioned in Toop, *Ligeti*, 92.

20. There is disagreement as to whether this organ was in Gothenburg Cathedral (reported in Toop, *Ligeti*, 92, and Steinitz, *Ligeti*, 126) or the Gothenburg Concert Hall (reported by Hambraeus *Aspects of Twentieth-Century Performance Practice: Memories and Reflections* [Uppsala: Royal Swedish Academy of Music, 1997], 129–30, who also notes the role of Otte's dancers in the concert's cancellation). Kimberly Marshall provides a thorough account of these events in her chapter on György Ligeti in *Twentieth-Century Organ Music*, ed. Christopher S. Anderson, 262–85 (New York: Routledge, 2012), esp. 275–76, quoting Hambraeus's recollection.

of the short circuit had given the work an infamous association with danger and scandal.

Volumina employs a type of graphic notation unique in Ligeti's oeuvre; in fact, the composer was fairly skeptical about musical graphics, though several of his colleagues in Vienna, where he was now based, used such notation extensively. Roman Haubenstock-Ramati and Anestis Logothetis were deeply impressed by John Cage and David Tudor at Darmstadt in 1958, and together with Sylvano Bussotti, they followed Cage and Earle Brown. Ligeti stated his views concerning this trend in a 1964 lecture at Darmstadt, differentiating between musical graphics and notation, and insisting that the latter requires a consistent means of communicating musical relationships by a system of signs, and the former relies on freer associative connections between the visual element and the resulting musical or performative features or events.[21]

Ligeti allowed for gray areas and types of mixture between the two, but it is clear that he privileged this idea of notation as a system of signs over pure graphics and that the notation he used for *Volumina* falls well within this definition. Although some indeterminacy in performance remains in timing and exact pitch, each page is defined with pitch and time on their respective vertical and horizontal axes, and the relative shape of every musical gesture remains fixed in relation to these axes. When desired, Ligeti could use his notation to achieve very precise effects, as shown in example 4.1a, where the cluster is defined as the minor third from B2 to D3 and different timbres are achieved by changing between the manuals. Clusters predominate as harmonies and thus individual pitches and precise intervals are less meaningful than registral gestures, textural changes, and timbral effects. Ligeti distinguishes between chromatic, diatonic (white-key) and pentatonic (black-key) clusters, as well as between static clusters and those with internal motion example 4.1b.

The material and effects used in *Volumina* resemble those found in *Atmosphères*, and, in fact, the notation resembles some of the graphic sketches of the earlier piece. Rather than seeming unfinished, however, the notation for *Volumina* is actually more efficient and duly precise for the musical idiom, since there are no issues of ensemble coordination in this solo work. Even the coordination of assistants (two are recommended) to help with registration and pulling or half-pulling various stops—a technique borrowed from Hambraeus's *Constellations I–III* and used extensively—can be done quite precisely from the score.

The comparison to *Atmosphères* goes beyond the simple use of material; in many ways *Volumina* is comparable to an organ reduction of the

---

21. This lecture is reproduced as "Neue Notation—Kommunikationsmittel oder Selbstzweck?" in *GS*, 1:170–84. Ligeti does not use an example from *Volumina*, but he does discuss Kagel's *Improvisation ajoutée*, the work Kagel had programmed on the same Bremen concert.

Example 4.1a. *Volumina*, rehearsal nos. 33–34. Copyright © 1973 by Henri Litolff's Verlag. Used by permission of C.F. Peters Corporation. All Rights Reserved

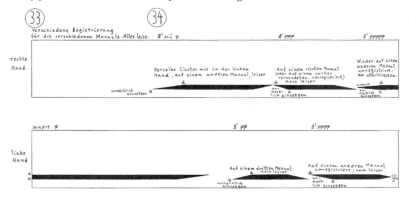

Example 4.1b. *Volumina*, rehearsal nos. 35–36. Copyright © 1973 by Henri Litolff's Verlag. Used by permission of C.F. Peters Corporation. All Rights Reserved

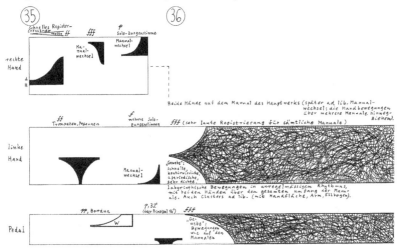

orchestral work, or as Richard Toop has put it, the "photographic negative."[22] Throughout the 1960s Ligeti would develop techniques in one piece and then in subsequent pieces explore a wider range of expression that he found in each technique. The pieces have the same general shape, moving from static clusters to more developed types of internal motion and eventually dissolving, and within this shape, many specific parts of *Volumina* parallel or complement moments of *Atmosphères*. In addition to playing with the diatonic-pentatonic division of the chromatic collection, both pieces use timbral changes within the same cluster, done artfully in *Volumina* by

22. Toop, *Ligeti*, 91.

transferring between manuals (as seen in example 4.1a, above), with the gradual exchange of notes between the manuals leading to a gradual change parallel to the use of dynamic fades in the opening of *Atmosphères*. Both works also open with an extremely wide cluster, which filters down to a central register; whereas *Atmosphères* does this entirely within the softer dynamic levels, *Volumina* has a massive *ffff* opening with all of the organ's stops pulled, but attenuates the dynamic by having the assistants gradually cancel the stops. Rehearsal number 15 of *Volumina*[23] enacts a massive and abrupt register transfer from the highest register to the lowest, closely resembling letter G in *Atmosphères*, although here, too, the quiet dynamic level is the inverse of the *ffff* found in *Atmosphères*.

In contrast to *Atmosphères*, however, *Volumina*'s more active moments begin to move away from the concept of a completely static music, or from the idea of fluctuating internal motion within a single sound, and become mobile, even gestural. Perhaps the influence of Kagel's *Improvisation ajoutée* can be seen in the graphic directions for increasingly detached staccato gestures. During their 1978 interview Péter Várnai suggested to Ligeti that one could construe the form along the lines of an alternation between these types of texture, saying, "I think that in *Volumina* we find both basic types of your music, the static and the wildly gesticulating . . . . Am I right in thinking that the way you combine the two types corresponds more or less to a fairly conventional A-B-A-B-A form?"[24]

Ligeti's response is quite interesting, in that it acknowledges this as one formal conception coexisting with at least two other possibilities:

Looking at it in this way, yes it does. If you are just listening for the alternation of the static and the gesticulating type of music, you can easily make out an A-B-A form. But if you look at it from the point of view of pitch you see an entirely different formal structure: the piece has two culminating high points in high register. My idea was a form uninterruptedly rolling forward, in which different kinds of musical motion appear either through gradual transformation or with abrupt switches. But I agree that it is possible to reduce it to an A-B-A formula. And that is nothing to be ashamed of. My formulation would not be so very different, since somewhere in the background a passacaglia is reflected in *Volumina*. Take the exposition, for instance. It is a big mass of sound, which starts very loud, then gradually diminishes and is followed by variations of the original mass.[25]

---

23. Here and throughout I am following the numbering of the score for György Ligeti, *Volumina*, rev. ed. with English translation by Eugene Hartzell (New York: Litolff/C.F. Peters, 1973), which adds several rehearsal numbers not present in the original edition.
24. *LiC*, 41.
25. *LiC*, 41–42.

Example 4.2. *Volumina*, synopsis of the form

Rehearsal No.	Material		
[1]–[12]	Static Clusters	A	a
[13]	(Motion)		b
[14]	Static		a
[15]–[22]	Transition to…		
[23]–[32]	Rapid Motion	B	b
[33]–[34]	(Static)		a
[35]–[36]	Motion		b
[37]–[39]	Transition to…		
[40]	Static Cluster	A	a

Ligeti's ABA form is easy to conceptualize along these lines (example 4.2). The piece consists of mostly static material from the opening through rehearsal number 15. A gradual transition starts at 16 and arrives at more extensive internal motion by 23; this motion goes through legato and staccato episodes through rehearsal 36. The final section slows dramatically at 37 and settles back to stasis for the end. A later proponent of the piece, Zsigmond Szathmáry, follows this basic division in his analysis but terms the final A section a "cadenza" and "coda."[26] In this basic concept, the initial static A section has a significant episode of motion at rehearsals 12–13, and the active B section has an episode of stasis around rehearsals 33–34 that may account for some of Várnai's additional sections.

The conception of the work as a passacaglia is more tenuous, but it is notable that there are recurring features or gestures that do come back, though always in varied form.[27] If register, rather than internal motion, is taken as the primary form-defining feature, then the piece can be seen as two large ascents, the first culminating at rehearsal 14 and the second picking up shortly after the precipitous drop at rehearsal 15 and culminating at rehearsal 40. Each of these ascents reprises other subsidiary gestures, textures, and characteristic treatments of material, giving the piece a sense of continually evolving variation and transformation, if not a strict passacaglia form. The characteristic "voluminous" opening is echoed, for example, by the grandioso cluster at rehearsal 36, and although the first instance is static, the second has "dense, continual, labyrinthine" internal motion.[28] Each of the two major ascents can,

26. Szathmáry, "Die Orgelwerke," 217.
27. Diane Luchese investigates different formal interpretations of *Volumina*, including the conception of the work as a passacaglia, in her article "Levels of Infrastructure in Ligeti's *Volumina*," *Sonus* 9, no. 1 (1988), 38–58.
28. Quoting from the score for Ligeti, *Volumina*, 18.

moreover, be subdivided into subsidiary ascents and returns, perhaps a kind of variation on this theme. In the first part there is an initial rise from rehearsals 8–9 before the pedal enters at 10 and starts a second ascent. In the second half, there is a suggestion of an ascent at rehearsals 21–22, and then a return to the lower register with the static clusters of 32–33 and then 37, which couples the Cymbel III ranks with the pedal, activating the high and low registers at once and leaving the middle register hollow and empty. Many of these subsidiary ascents and returns create similar textures in which the extreme registers, low and high, are used together or in rapid succession, an observation which could link rehearsals 10–11, 14–15, 26–27, 32, and 37.

The formal complexity of *Volumina* is one of several factors that contribute to its enduring appeal and inclusion on concerts and recordings. Equally appealing is the mismatch between the solemn and lofty reputation of the king of instruments and the very corporeal nature of the piece, whose sounds, in their extreme registers and extreme dynamics, often border on vulgarity and provoke a visceral reaction in the audience—to say nothing of the physical demands placed on the organist. This subversive use of the instrument, backed up by a probing and sophisticated exploration of the sonic potential of the medium and formal potential of Ligeti's cluster-based musical language, moves beyond the satire and provocation of *The Future of Music* and *Trois Bagatelles* and begins to show the constructive possibilities Ligeti found by rebelling against musical conventions and embracing the absurd.

POÈME SYMPHONIQUE

As unlikely as it may seem from the instrumentation, Ligeti's *Poème symphonique*, for one hundred metronomes, has come to be appreciated for its musical value as much as for its novelty, and has come to have an enduring place in the literature. Ligeti seems to have recognized this musical value retrospectively; as Eric Drott has pointed out, the shock value of the premiere is emphasized in the early version of the score but is downplayed in the later version in favor of more purely musical criteria.[29]

The premiere of the work was a scandal as great as that of *The Future of Music* a year earlier. Ligeti had been invited to the Gaudeamus Music Week in September 1963, and his performance was scheduled for the reception closing the event. Alongside the assembled dignitaries and the official speeches

---

29. Drott, "Ligeti in Fluxus," 232–35, reproduces the text of the original version of the score as published by Maciunas in *ccV TRE* no. 1. The revised version was published by Schott in 1996, although it listed 1982 as the copyright date. The text of the revised version is also found in *GS*, 2:195–96, which dates the revision to a 1990 performance at a Ligeti festival in Gütersloh.

of the ceremonious affair, the satirical details of Ligeti's performance directions must have had their full effect. The early version of the score is written in intentionally grandiloquent language with a marvelous attention to irrelevant detail (e.g., specifying that in case the metronomes for the performance are borrowed, their owners' names should be written on an attached piece of paper—ballpoint or fountain pen is recommended), and his account of the premiere went even farther in cultivating this air of overceremonious formality. The performers processed onstage in formal dress, hiding the metronomes from view to enhance the surprise.[30] In the original version of the score the lengthy act of winding up the metronomes and setting them to different speeds was to be carried out as part of the performance, after which there was to be an extended, motionless pause (between two and six minutes!), and only then would the metronomes be released, at which point the performers would march off the stage.

The use of metronomes as instruments was a dramatic effect in Ligeti's piece, although he was not the first or the only composer associated with Fluxus to employ them. The metronome is the quintessential tool for musical practice and is thus rather symbolic of the discipline and routine that go into any musical performance, but it is always relegated to the preparation phase of the work and hidden from the audience. Here, however, in another playful inversion of the norm, Ligeti presents the metronome as the performer and minimizes the human element.

Toshi Ichiyanagi's *Music for Electric Metronome* (1960) is a very different work. It was performed at the same Fluxus Festival as was Ligeti's *Trois Bagatelles*; however, since Ligeti did not attend the concert it is unclear whether he knew of the piece. In Ichiyanagi's work performers trace a path through a graphic score with indications to change the setting of the metronome by following lines connecting different numbers.[31] Different types of lines may also indicate more theatrical actions such as moving or making sounds with or without other objects. Maciunas himself used a metronome in his *In Memoriam to Adriano Olivetti*, in which the device is used, along with the numbers from an old adding-machine tape, to indicate beats on which different people perform a prescribed action or sound.

These other Fluxus scores, then, do not downplay the human element but, rather, they use the presence of the metronome as a nonhuman agent mysteriously organizing or controlling the actions of the performers. In Ligeti's work, on the other hand, the metronomes are set in motion by the performers

30. These details—hiding the metronomes as the performers process in and the concert dress—are not specified in either version of the score but have become such a common part of Ligeti's description of the premiere that they are often taken as being obligatory (see, e.g., Toop, *Ligeti*, 84).

31. Ichiyanagi's piece is contained in La Monte Young and Jackson Mac Low, eds., *An Anthology*, 2nd ed. (N.p.: Heiner Friedrich), 1970.

and then left to run their own course in what comes to sound like an almost naturalistic process.

Focusing on the purely musical characteristics of the work, Ligeti turned to terminology from the natural sciences. He described the rhythmic networks as "Moiré patterns" created by the interference of different grids and compares the process to elements of entropy found in both information theory and thermodynamics.[32] Ligeti addresses the work as a texture created by numerous individual elements, creating composite speeds that push the threshold of perception, something that has clear precedent in the *Bewegungsfarbe* effects from the electronic studio and their application to his orchestral pieces. The metronomes are surprisingly musical in the way they create temporary composite patterns which seem to shift and even swirl, dissolving and reforming fluidly as individual metronomes stop.

The expression of this textural idea in *Poème Symphonique* also helped make way for later developments. The idea of constructing a mesh of conflicting tempi stayed with Ligeti throughout his career, as seen in such works as the *Magyar Etüdök* (1983) and the Études for Piano (1985–2001), to name just a few that postdate scope of the present book. Moreover, the mechanical ticking of individual machines has extramusical associations, which are explored in greater detail in *Aventures* (discussed below) and also present in the "meccanico" sections of both the Chamber Concerto and Second String Quartet (both discussed in chapter 6). The *Poème*'s expression of the meccanico idea, however, is slightly unusual; whereas most of Ligeti's works in this style progress from order to chaos, *Poème Symphonique* moves from initial chaos to increasing order as the metronomes wind down.

AVENTURES AND NOUVELLES AVENTURES

Compared to the other compositions from this period, *Aventures* and *Nouvelles Aventures* are clearly major works. They approach the intricacy, complexity, and emotional range of an opera but are condensed into a shorter form and written for only three singers and chamber ensemble. Both works combined last less than a half-hour. Ligeti had grown up listening to the opera in Cluj— some of his early musical memories are centered around attending performances with his older cousin[33]—and the deep-seated desire to write an opera of his own began to take shape during this time. Although Ligeti would not compose *Le Grand Macabre*, his only full-length work in the genre, for another decade, *Aventures* was an important step in this direction. This surreal and disorienting work was Ligeti's first true expression of absurdist themes in

32. Ligeti, "Zum *Poème Symphonique*," *GS*, 2:194.
33. See comments in the biographies by Steinitz, *Ligeti*, 9, and Toop, *Ligeti*, 14.

an extended serious work. It also served as a precursor to the opera, which was based on a play by Michel de Ghelderode (1898–1962), a Belgian author known for depictions of the unsettling and the grotesque.

Aventures, at times, parodies the conventions of opera, but it does not attempt to break them down or cause a spectacle; it remains a work for the stage. And though Ligeti created the text for the work, which consists entirely of nonsense syllables and other vocal sounds, grunts, exhalations, sighs, and so on, he found precedent in literature as well as music, stating,

> I also had literary sources of inspiration in Vienna, but mainly in Cologne; *Sonate mit Urlauten* by Schwitters, Hugo Ball's first Dadaist poems dating back to World War I, the letterist movement in Paris—Dufrêne, Henri Chopin, Isou. Around 1960 came several compositions influencing me along the same lines; Stockhausen's *Carré*, Kagel's *Anagrama* and some works by Berio and Haubenstock-Ramati. The difference with these—with the exception of *Carré*—is that they all contain intelligible speech. I wrote my own text, which is semantically meaningless and has only emotional content.[34]

In addition, one can clearly see the influence of the plays of Alfred Jarry (1873–1907), Samuel Beckett (1906–89), and Eugène Ionesco (1909–94), all of which deal with the apparent meaninglessness of the human condition, mixing a raw look at the human psyche with a heavy dose of dark humor. Berio's electronic works *Thema (Omaggio a Joyce*, 1958) and *Visage* (1961) come to mind, along with Ligeti's own *Artikulation*, for their play with vocal and pseudo-linguistic sounds. Both Ligeti and Berio moved this idea of an artificial language from the electronic studio to vocal and instrumental composition, but *Aventures* predates Berio's *Sequenza III* for voice (1965–66) in this endeavor.

Moving artificial language back into acoustic composition meant reintroducing a human and performative element to the music and thus a change of effect from that found in *Artikulation*. The sudden and seemingly unprovoked changes of emotion result in a heightened state of suspense and activity and at times suggest an even more schizophrenic perspective. Ligeti came to call this combination of frantic activity and ironic distance a "cooled" or "deep-frozen expressionism" in discussions of *Aventures* and of later pieces in the same style, the Dies irae section of the Requiem and *Le Grand Macabre*.[35] Owing in part to the demands on human performers and the need to sustain a high degree of concentration in the audience, Ligeti was apprehensive about the length of the work as he progressed in the realization of his original plan. He eventually split the work into *Aventures* and *Nouvelles Aventures*, which he completed after the Requiem. He realized *Nouvelles Aventures* in

---

34. *LiC*, 44–45.
35. See, e.g., *LiC*, 17–20.

two movements, the first including newly composed material and the second containing what he originally intended as the continuation and conclusion of *Aventures*.[36]

Along with their concern with the creation of an artificial language, *Artikulation* and *Aventures* share elements of compositional technique, especially in creating layers of material, interspersing them through the course of the piece, and quickly changing back and forth between these contrasting elements. With the stage directions and theatrical elements of *Aventures*, however, another possible influence may be the quick cuts between scenes in film. Managing the associative content of his material, Ligeti names five emotional layers, like the different "texts" or "languages" of the electronic piece. These layers are widely cited according to Ligeti's own description of them in an interview:

Music in *Aventures* moves on two distinct levels. One level is constructive; for instance a section may consist only of vowels, or only of liquid consonants . . . . The other level is the emotional level. I put together a kind of "scenario" by joining five areas of emotions; humor, ghostly horror, sentimental, mystical-funereal, and erotic. All five areas or processes are present, all through the music, and they switch from one to the other so abruptly and quickly that there is a virtual simultaneity. Each of the three singers plays five roles at the same time. *Aventures* is a very complex piece.[37]

36. Another change in Ligeti's original conception of the work was the addition of a libretto to the two works, consisting of stage and lighting directions and actions for a group of mimes and dancers added to the singers on stage. In his talk "Über szenische Möglichkeiten von *Aventures*," first given in Darmstadt in 1966 (reproduced in *GS*, 2:198–201), Ligeti discussed the libretto. He admitted that the music was conceived first and that strictly speaking the libretto is superfluous, but he went on to state that the "conception of the libretto . . . arose associatively in composing" and argues for its legitimacy. He also warns against seeking any deeper moral or allegory in the libretto, saying that it is merely a collage of patterns of human behavior. For the purpose of my musical analysis I will treat the libretto as largely extraneous; although it does contain some keywords that are similar to those found in the sketches, on the whole it does not add significant insight to the analysis.

37. *LiC*, 45. See also Toop, *Ligeti*, 96, and Steinitz, *Ligeti*, 131, for similar formulations; Michel, *Ligeti*, 62, has a slightly different formulation reads, "Cinq groupes de caractères expressifs sont à l'origine d'*Aventures*. Le premier groupe comprend l'ironie, la moquerie, la raillerie, la négation[;] le deuxième groupe des caractères dépressifs: la nostalgie, la tristesse, la mélancolie, les sanglots et le manque de contact; dans le troisième groupe, nous trouvons des formules humoristiques et ricanantes; dans le quatrième des caractères érotiques, des formulations de toutes sortes de désirs, des exaltations et des agressions. Enfin, le cinquième groupe expose diverses formes de peur, d'épouvante." Erkki Salmenhaara, *Das musikalische Material und seine Behandlung in den Werken "Apparitions," "Atmosphères," "Aventures" und "Requiem" von György Ligeti* (Regensburg: Bosse, 1969), 107–8, uncovers a system similar to what I give below, taken directly from the sketches.

Example 4.3. *Aventures*, sketch of sound types and subtypes. Reproduced with kind permission from the György Ligeti Collection of the Paul Sacher Foundation, Basel

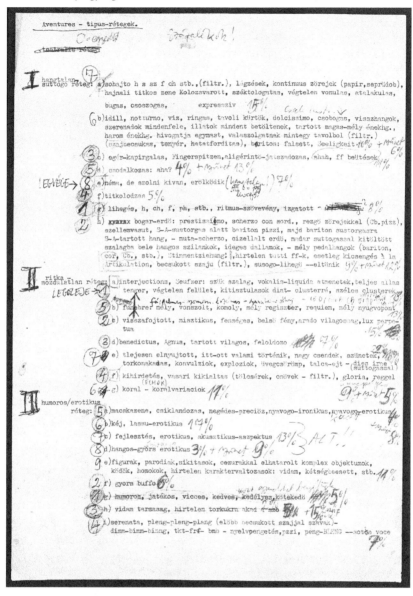

The planning stages of the piece went through several different classifications of material, and the sketches (including example 4.3) show a slightly different system of five categories, based on a mixture of emotional content with more purely musical characteristics and with each basic type having numerous subdivisions:

I. Voiceless-whispering layer [hangtalan-suttogo réteg] (8 subtypes)
II. sparse, stationary layer [ritka mozdulatlan réteg] (7 subtypes)
III. humorous/erotic layer [humoros/erotikus réteg] (9 subtypes)
IV. "speech"-layer ["beszéd"-réteg] (11 subtypes)
V. expressive layer [expressziv réteg] (7 subtypes)

Ligeti divided each of these types into multiple subtypes, listed underneath these headings. The categories from the sketches may seem to conflict with the emotional areas mentioned in the interview, but many of the subtypes reflect similar ideas. For example, while the "mystical-funereal" area mentioned in the interview does not appear directly in the sketches, Layer II (sparse, stationary) contains subtypes described as "funebre" and "mystical" (misztikus), as well as subtypes that refer to a requiem and to many of the specific sections of a requiem including "lux perpetua," "benedictus," "Agnus," "dies irae," and "gloria."

The subtypes undergo significant reordering in the sketches. Ligeti first simply listed subtypes below each heading, giving each a lower-case letter designation. In another set of pages, however, he wrote them out in a different order, listed and numbered in terms of their general speed and dynamic level. And at yet another stage, the composer renumbered the subtypes along the left-hand margin of the first sketch (see example 4.3), this time using numbers alongside the letter designations; it is this register of roman-numeral designations for the layers and arabic numerals for the subdivisions that corresponds most closely to later stages of the sketches. The subtypes were also given percentages, which add up to 100 percent for each layer and include a projected amount of rest or silence for each. Because Ligeti split the piece up into *Aventures* and *Nouvelles Aventures*, and composed new material in the process, it is hard to identify these percentages in the score. The use of rests—often termed "windows" (ablakok) in the sketches—is essential for the general character of the piece, which is full of abrupt silences, general pauses, and instructions to "stop suddenly as if torn off."

Finally Ligeti arrived at a continuity sketch made up of numerous pages taped together lengthwise that depicts the course of the piece, which at this point consisted of *Aventures* and the second movement of *Nouvelles Aventures* (example 4.4 shows an excerpt). He gave the continuity sketch timings in seconds along the lower side of the page, although these timings are freely adjusted, marked longer in some places, shorter in others. The bulk of the

---

38. As in other typed sketches, Ligeti left out certain unavailable diacritical marks (accents over a, i, o, and u—e.g., típus, suttogó) and long umlauts are printed as short ones. These are left uncorrected in the transcription here and other references to it, below.

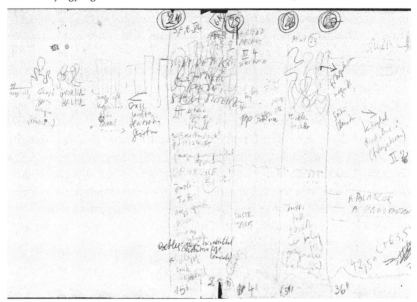

sketch is a list of "material segments," which are short passages of a particular character and construction, now given a numerical designation according to the order of their occurrence within the whole. These segment numbers recur throughout the sketches, often circled twice, as Ligeti worked out details of the composition of individual passages belonging to each segment. Material segments 1 through 43 occur in *Aventures*, and the second movement of *Nouvelles Aventures* picks up with segments 44 through 66.

Along with the numbered segments, the continuity sketch also contains prose annotations, graphically depicted contours or registral placements of material, and references back to the system of roman and arabic numerals used to describe the layers and subtypes above. The original descriptions of different subtypes, however, are often complex, and individual segments may draw on only part of the original description. Subtypes may also return in more than one segment, either in a consistent way or with a degree of variation or development from one instance to the next, investigating different aspects of the original prose description. Some segments also list multiple types of material, either freely mixed or assigned to different instrumental or vocal parts polyphonically.

The exact method of determining the order and combination of subtypes in the piece is unclear, and perhaps was intuitive. The record of layers and subtypes remains incomplete in the continuity sketch; nevertheless, they can be matched to the finished score in enough detail to provide valuable information about both the large-scale organization and, especially, about compositional methods employed for individual sections. For the purpose of general orientation, I have provided a brief outline of the form of these two pieces in example 4.5. The grouping of material segments into larger sections is my own, but the correspondence between individual material segments and measures of the finished score can be discerned reliably by matching the descriptions in the continuity sketch (cross-referenced with the list of layers and subtypes) to the events of the piece as depicted in the musical notation and performance directions of the score.

The Senza tempo and Sostenuto sections of *Aventures* (mm. 89–98 and 99–107), which are particularly rich in changes of type and affect, illustrate how Ligeti turns these prose descriptions into musical notation and performance directions. Measures 90 and 96 draw from type IV6, which Ligeti describes as "fast, soft, differentiated monotone" (gyors, halk, differencialt egyhang). This is reflected in the stage directions in the finished score: "monotonously rattling on." Interrupting this is Type III5 in measure 93, labeled in the sketches as "caterwauling, tickling, demure/precious, ironic meowing, erotic meowing" (macskazene,

Example 4.5. *Aventures* and *Nouvelles Aventures*, synopsis of the forms

Aventures

1. Agitato (mm.1-19; material segments 1-12)
2. Presto (mm. 20-37; segements 13-20)
3. "Conversation" and baritone solo (mm. 38-46 and 47-48; segments 21-23)
4. Allegro appassionato (mm. 49-88; segments 24-27)
5. Senza tempo and sostenuto grandioso (mm. 89-98, 99-107; segments 28-36, 37-39)
6. "Action dramatique" (mm. 108-115; segments 40-43)

Nouvelles Aventures I

1. Sostenuto, più mosso, sostenunto (mm. 1-14, 15-20, 21-27)
2. "Hoquetus" and molto espressivo "miming and gestures" (mm. 28-29, 30-39)
3. Più mosso (mm. 40-57)
4. "Commérages" [Gossiping] (58-74) and sostenuto/senza tempo (75-82)
5. "Communication" (83-91)

Nouvelles Aventures II

1. Agitato molto "Grand Hysterical Scene of the Soprano" (mm. 1-13; segments 44-46)
2. Sostenuto misterioso "recitation" (m. 14; segment 47)
3. Agitato molto "Grand Hysterical Scene of the Soprano" (mm. 15-18; segments 48-49)
4. "Chorale" (mm. 19-21; segment 50)
5. Agitato molto "Grand Hysterical Scene of the Soprano" (mm. 22-28; segment 51)
6. Alto solo and G.P. (mm. 29-30; segments 52-53)
7. "Les Horloges Démoniaques" (31-35; material segments 54-57)
8. Prestissimo "chase" (mm. 36-40; segment 58-59)
9. Subito a tempo and senza tempo (mm. 41-43; segments 60-61)
10. "Coda" (mm. 44-57; segments 62-66)

csiklandozas, negédes-preciöz, nyavogo-ironikus, nyavogo-erotikus); again, these are very similar to the written direction for the alto in this measure (which also appear for the soprano through this passage): "coquettish, sensual, feline— yet always restrained." [39] As the section moves on it visits material from Type I3, "mouse scratchings, fingertips, playing while hardly touching" (egér-kapirgalas, Fingerspitzen, aligérintö-jatszadozas), realized in measure 98 by having the cello and bass players slowly and aperiodically run their fingernails up and down the length of the strings; the piano and harpsichord players do the same on the strings of the piano. This is immediately juxtaposed with Type II4 (m. 99), described in the sketch as a "proclamation" and a "Gloria" (kihirdetés . . . gloria) and realized in the score by having the singers use megaphones in a grand tutti with the instruments, all *tutta la forza* and *ffff*. Type II5 follows (m. 103), described in the sketch as "funebre: deep, lugubrious, grave, deep register, requiem, deep resting point" (funebre: mély, vonszolt, komoly, mély regiszter, requiem, mély nyugvopont), and is realized as an echo effect in the low alto and baritone, followed by a low piano and harpsichord cluster also marked *solemne, funebre* in the score.

As we saw in sketches for *Artikulation*, Ligeti freely mixes technical descriptions of his material with more associative, subjective, and colorful descriptions. This balance between abstraction and reference is an extremely important and distinctive feature of his work, one enabled by the particulars of his compositional method. Through the verbal stage of planning material Ligeti taps into a vast range of referential ideas, drawing on everyday sounds and experiences, alluding to previous musical works, genres, or traditions, and even referencing concepts from visual art, literature, and the sciences. This accumulated network of associations is then pared down into isolated musical gestures, so that an event like the single low, soft cluster on the keyboard instruments in measure 103, mentioned above, can be marked simply *funebre* and yet seems to carry the entire weight of a requiem. This method of developing a rich world of associations and then concentrating this world into a single representative musical gesture allows Ligeti to remain abstract enough to avoid overly literal tone painting or cheap programmatic effects, while still creating sounds that are engaging and that interact with the imagination outside the closed world of pre-defined musical relationships.

The instrumental parts of the coda of *Nouvelles Aventures* (movement II, mm. 44–57) provide another well-planned example, this time of Type I7—an intriguing point of reference that reads in part, "the secret music of Kolozsvár at dawn, shuffling chairs, infinite progression, metamorphosis" (hajnali titkos zene Kolozsvarott, széktologatas, végtelen vonulas, atalakulas). One possible meaning of this enigmatic description may put a new light on these works and their synthesis of different influences. Ligeti discussed his early childhood in

---

39. The translations are by Cornelius Cardew and are taken from the supplemental comments to the score of *Aventures* (New York: C.F. Peters, 1964), 22–23.

Kolozsvár (Cluj) and how he used to imagine music attached to different daily chores and routines.[40] This may help explain some of the household items used in the percussion parts for both *Aventures* and *Nouvelles Aventures*, especially in this section, which includes shuffling feet on the floor, a wooden bowl filled with small balls, tissue paper, newspapers, and metal foil. Earlier in the pieces a heavy rug and carpet beater, tin cans, wooden furniture, plastic cups, and balloons are used. These everyday items make for unusual instruments, and as much as the subversive act of using tools as musical instruments has echoes of Cage, Dadaism, and the theatrically absurd, the ones used in these works may relate as much to this idea of a secret, private childhood music of household objects.

Such an innocent take on the idea of music in everyday life is particularly poignant, placed as it is at the end of the piece and juxtaposed with the virtuosic and highly trained singers, who are using material described as "mute but wanting to call out, struggling" (Type I8, néma, de szolni kivan, erölködik)—material that, according to the sketches, was designated for the end of the work, even from an early stage of sketching.[41]

The section of *Nouvelles Aventures* labeled "Les Horloges Démoniaques" (movement II, mm. 31–35) has also received much attention owing to its associative context as a literary reference and its status (along with *Poème Symphonique*) as the precedent for the meccanico style of music prevalent later in Ligeti's career. This material type (Hungarian "gonosz órák" [literally, evil clocks]) appears in these early sketches as well. Although the Ionesco play *The Bald Soprano* (1950) also features a malfunctioning clock, Ligeti identified his specific inspiration here as the works of Gyula Krúdy (1878–1933), in which

you find again and again a character, a widow whose husband was either a botanist or a meteorologist and has been dead for years. The widow lives alone . . . . She would have a house among the dunes which is full of clocks, barometers, hygrometers. I don't know if you [to Várnai] can remember this figure, who appears in several of his works and is the subject of one of his short stories . . . . One of the stories was about the widow living in a house full of clocks ticking away all the time. The meccanico-type music really originates from reading that story as a five-year-old, on a hot summer afternoon.[42]

40. Various biographies, relying on conversations with the composer, report this: "As for the young György Ligeti, music—his own music—was part of his inner world from the start. At the age of three, he remembers, he already had an imaginary music for getting up and going to bed . . . . It never occurred to him that this was anything unusual: for many years he assumed that everyone heard their own music!" (Toop, *Ligeti*, 13). And: "But, even as a small child, Gyuri imagined music in his head. To his daily routines he attached different musical ceremonies, a tune to brush his teeth to, a march for going to bed" (Steinitz, *Ligeti*, 6).
41. Materials for both the beginning of the piece (II1) and the end (I8) are labeled in the sketches (see the margins of example 4.3) as such: "legeleje" and "legvége," respectively.
42. *LiC*, 17.

In fact, Ligeti's connection to Krúdy may be another feat of imagination and condensation. Characters in Krúdy's works may come and go, making brief cameos and then reappearing with little announcement after numerous intervening pages. Ligeti's music has strong affinities with Krúdy's work; both tend toward a mixture of nostalgia, absurdity, and the macabre. Krúdy's Sindbad muses at one point, "It was as if Hungarian village life had remained unchanged over the centuries. The people had changed but they had been replaced by others precisely like them. As if birth, death and marriage were all part of some curious joke. Even now it was the ancestral dead sitting around the table."[43] The type of stock character that Ligeti recalled, indeed, seems to be his own conflation of different references from several of Krúdy's works. The brief references to such characters in these novels seem to be greatly expanded in Ligeti's imagination.[44]

At times Ligeti's management of different layers of material is quite straightforward, but at other times it becomes extremely complex. The "Conversation" section of *Aventures* (mm. 38–46), which is described in early notes as the "Polyphonic Trio," contains a great variety of material types, all shared by the three voices. The material types are derived from the original categories IV3, V3, and II1 (and seemingly from other categories, as well). Features taken from these basic material types and subtypes are extracted and then reorganized into five different categories, assigned letters from A to E, and given additional subtypes, described as "characters," labeled with arabic numerals as shown in example 4.6.

These characters are clearly observable in the finished piece as well, with only the slightest alterations from the sketch. The A group of short isolated syllables is clearly recognizable, often punctuated with exclamation marks. A1 generally uses unpitched sounds, and A2 is generally given pitches; the same distinction

---

43. Gyula Krúdy, *The Adventures of Sindbad*, trans. George Szirtes (New York: Central European University Press, 1998), 45.

44. Sindbad spends most of his adventures either about to die or already dead (often the progression of time is deliberately unclear in the stories), remembering or appearing as a ghost to his former lovers, among them numerous widows. One is identified as Mrs Banáti, whom Sindbad visits: "It was at this time, one autumn night . . . . when clocks that no one could remember working began to move their hands, and when doors on unoccupied floors of occupied houses started creaking as if in pain because someone behind them dared not cross the threshold—it was then that Sindbad rose from the dead" (Krúdy, *Sindbad*, 81). Clocks often appear in these stories as symbols of time passing and the approach of death. A similar figure also occurs in Krúdy's novel *Sunflower*. Risoulette is not a widow but is married to a rather disinterested or preoccupied man who lives in "a clean and cloistered environment, redolent with the scent of innocence and resonant with the chimes of a musical clockwork. Risoulette's husband, a retired captain, suffered from gout, and surrounded his aching limbs with barometers and weatherglasses. For him the two questions in life were: what's the weather like, and what's for dinner. He cared not a whit about anything else." Gyula Krúdy, *Sunflower*, trans. John Bátki (New York: New York Review of Books, 1997), 125.

Example 4.6. *Aventures*, sketch transcription and translation of material segment 21

21 - material

A) Short [xx] isolated

1) supported[?], intensive, *between [?] und coughing (not naturalistic!)**

2) hocket – different syllables, intensive *but not loud*

B) Medium long, isolated

1) ah – wondering (medium soft)

2) ohó – dismissing (medium soft)

C) Long, isolated
(soft)

1) Φ   2) f-v°   3) θ   4) s-z°   5) ʃ — ʒ

6) ç   7) h   8) l°   9) r°   10) Vowels, o e,

ten types in gradual changes, also by flowing one to another: see the baritone's G in the previous section. (rarely, occasionally voiced, also)**

D) Groups of short elements
(soft)

1) whispering – as a carryover from the previous section (fast)

2) mumbling groups—Barracqué [sic] (fast)

3) evil clocks– rigid (medium fast—slow)

4) stammering groups (fast)

5) jabbering groups (fast)

capriccioso

E) Groups of varied elements
(medium fast and slow)

1) theatrical—pathetic— rappresentativo—fantastical embellished—mannered expressions (*generally soft*) declarations *knightly—elegant*

2) shaking ones head, aj-aj

3) satirical, ej-ej

4) satirical, saying na-ne

5) affected—satirical apology, with support [?]

6) authentic apology, with support [?]

7) disparaging, cö-cö

8) explanatory pompousness [crossed out in red]

CONVERSATIONAL TONE

9) nasal

10) huffed

11) murmuring ("aside")

Notes to the example:

[?] In several places Ligeti writes "stöd" the meaning of which is unclear. Given that Ligeti was spending time in Stockholm, this could be related to a Swedish word meaning support. However, the translations in these places are uncertain.

* Italics indicate additional handwritten text over the typed sketch some of which was illegible or crossed out. Diacritical markings in the typed text are sometimes missing or altered but have been preserved as typed (e.g. short umlauts rather than long ones).

**In Group C, the ° indicates a circle above the letter. Ligeti uses circle either above or below to indicate unvoiced consonants. The baritone's G refers to measure 26 of the finished score.

Example 4.6. Continued

21 - anyag

A) Rövid xxxx izolált:

1) stöd, intensiv, *zwischen [?] und Husten (nicht naturalistisch!)*

2) hoquetus – verschiedene syllaben, intensiv *de nem hangos*

B) Középhosszu izolált

1) ah – csodálkozó (középhalk)

2) ohó – elhárító (középhalk)

C) Hosszu izolált
(halk)

1) Φ   2) f-v°   3) θ   4) s-z°   5) ∫ — ʒ

6) ç   7) h   8) l°   9) r°   10) Vokalisok o

e tiz tipus fokozatos változásban is egymásba átfolynak: lásd
bariton-G-t elöbbi szekcióban). (Ritkán néhol zöngés is).

D) Csoportok rövid elemekböl
(halk)

1) suttogás – mint átvitel az elöbbi szekcióból (gyors)

2) makogó csoportok—Barracqué (gyors)

3) gonosz órák – merev (középgyors-lassu)

4) dadogó csoportok (gyors)

5) hadaró csoportok (gyors)

capriccioso

E) Csoportok vegyes elemekböl
(Középgyors és lassu)
(halk átlag)

1) teatrális-patetikus-rappresentativo-fantasztikus-
verschnörkelt-maniriert expressziok,
kinyilatkoztatások *ritterisch-elegant*

2) fejcsóváló aj-aj

3) gunyos ej-ej

4) gunyos na-ne-mondja

5) affektált-gunyos sajnálkozás stöddel

6) igazi sajnálkozás stöddel

7) lekicsinylö cö-cö

8) *magyarázó fontoskodás*

TÁRSAGLÓ TÓNUS

9) nazális

10) verschnupft

11) mormolás ("félre")

can be observed between longer notes of B1 and B2. The C group sticks to the syllables listed in the sketch very closely, though several different members of the C group are often presented in succession, smoothly changing from one syllable to another. The D group uses repeated notes with special syllable content and performance directions, D1 (whispering) using fricative and sibilant syllables, D2 labeled as *stammelnd*, D3 as *uhrwerkartig*, and D5 as *plappernd*. The E group shows the most variety, consistently reflecting the content of the original sketch in performance indications like *Elegant bis manieriert* for E1 and *murmelnd* for E11. The sequence of characters is not the same for each voice, but is worked out (see the sketch reproduction, example 4.7a) to use each character

Example 4.7a. *Aventures*, sketch for the sequence of characters in the polyphonic trio. Reproduced with kind permission from the György Ligeti Collection of the Paul Sacher Foundation, Basel

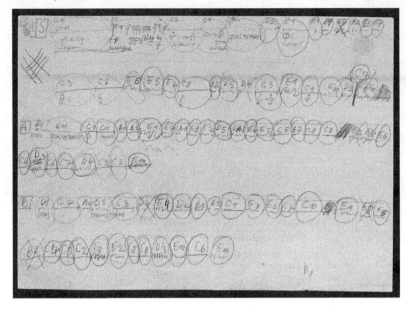

Example 4.7b. *Aventures*, "Conversation," mm. 38–39, annotated. Copyright © 1961 by Henri Litolff's Verlag. Used by permission of C.F. Peters Corporation. All Rights Reserved

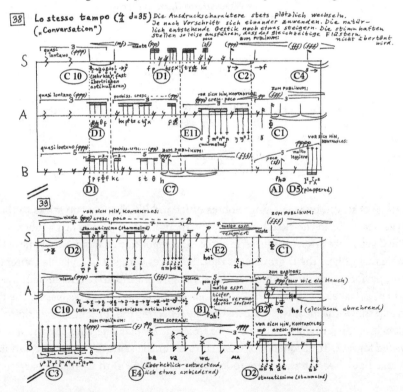

Example 4.8. *Aventures*, sketch transcription, material segment 1

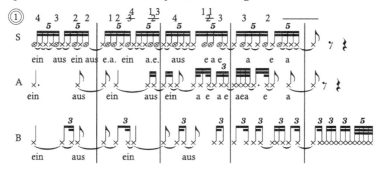

exactly once. Many of these can be seen in example 4.7b, my annotation of the published score, showing correspondences with the material of the sketch.

In the process of realization from sketch to score, Ligeti makes several changes to the sequence of characters. He eliminates E8 entirely; he also omits D4 from the soprano and baritone, realizing it only in the alto, and in a way very similar to the texture of D5. The alto part also omits E2, although this character is present in the other voices. Ligeti has described the "Conversation" section as "virtually a strict Bach three-part invention whose subjects appear in each voice in different permutations."[45] Through the sketches one can see how this structure was composed. It is significant, in this regard, that D1 is presented in all three voices at or near the beginning of the passage, and the sequence allows other points of close imitation with material B1 (mm. 39–40) and with material D3—the "demonic clocks" material that will receive more extensive treatment in *Nouvelles Aventures*—which occurs in all voices toward the end of the passage (mm. 44–45).

In his realization of the material segments, Ligeti develops different approaches to rhythm and pitch, some of which become important for his later practice. He deals with a full range of pitched and unpitched vocal sounds, and the relative prevalence of non-pitched sounds in *Aventures* in particular leads him to an increased focus on rhythmic technique in many of the sketches. The initial section, described in the sketches as "interjections and sighs" (Type II1), materializes as the measured inhaling and exhaling of all three vocalists, all without notated pitch (example 4.8). The soprano part, which is structured quite carefully in the sketches to balance durations, provides a clear example of this feature of Ligeti's rhythmic practice.

The quintuplets are written out with all five notes in each beat, and then tied together in the durational sequence 4–3–2–2–1–2–4–1–3 4 1 1 3 3 2 . Other numbers, crossed out in the example, show alterations in this sequence, indicating that these groupings were a matter of concern for the composer. A closer examination shows that the durations between one sixteenth note and

45. *LiC*, 45.

four sixteenth notes are balanced. Each duration between one and three is used exactly four times in this sequence; the duration of four is used three times. This can be seen as an extension of the tallying system for durations seen in *Apparitions* and *Artikulation*. Here, however, Ligeti is working across a very small segment of music and using a smaller repertoire of durations, and he uses equal distribution of durations, rather than the product-technique discussed in relation to the earlier works. The other voices, however, seem to be composed in a freer counterpoint to the soprano, the alto accelerating and then holding back, making room for the baritone, who ultimately accelerates into his first solo in measure 6—the second material segment of the piece, switching to the expressive layer (Type V) and culminating in the devilish laugh (labeled "teuflisch" in the original continuity sketch, changed to "drohend" in the finished score).

Rhythm in these pieces seems to be composed section by section according to the texture and affect required by the scenario, yet some consistent features are found throughout. The rhythm uses mixed subdivisions, both horizontal and vertical, often using at least one pair of conflicting subdivisions in the voice parts simultaneously. It also changes the type of subdivisions used in the same voice frequently, often doing so on every beat. In *Aventures* and in subsequent works such as the String Quartet no. 2, it is also typical for Ligeti to use "neighboring" subdivisions—for example, quintuplets and sextuplets—in pairs of voices to help regulate the cross-rhythms of the parts and heighten the conflict between them. Some of these are simple as those in measures 7–8, using progressively slower rhythmic subdivisions to create a deceleration in the women's voices (example 4.9), or in measure 28, where a similar acceleration is formed across all three voice parts.

The episode in *Nouvelles Aventures* II marked "Les Horloges Démoniaques" (mm. 31–35), one of the most famous passages in the piece, provides an excellent example of another of Ligeti's common rhythmic techniques. This section corresponds to material segment 54, and in sketches for this segment there are two systems of tallying, both approximating equal distribution. As with his other tallying systems, there is some room for deviation from the ideal balance; Ligeti remains more concerned with preventing any particular value from dominating the texture than with a precise equality of values. The first tally is for the subdivisions used: quintuplets, sextuplets, septuplets, sixteenth notes, or nonuplets (labeled as values 5 through 9); these are distributed to the voices in the bottom system of example 4.10a and tallied in the right-hand side of example 4.10b, where the rhythmic values are given in notation and each dash extending to the right marks one use of that type of subdivision. This distribution is adjusted in the sketch, and ultimately, in the score we find the near-equal distribution of 5–4–4–6–5, slightly favoring the more common sixteenth notes over the other divisions. Along with this concern is the careful planning along the principles seen above, ensuring that the same subdivision is never used in two voices simultaneously or in the same voice for two beats in a row.

Example 4.9. *Aventures*, mm. 7–9. Copyright © 1961 by Henri Litolff's Verlag. Used by permission of C.F. Peters Corporation. All Rights Reserved

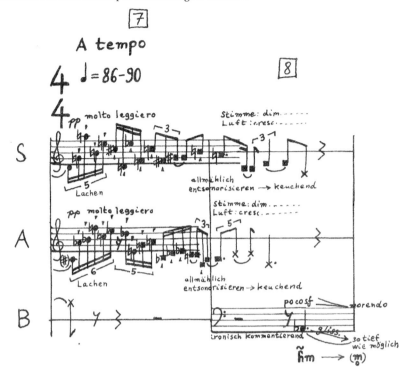

The second tally keeps track of the number of repeated notes before a singer changes pitch and syllable. Ligeti allows between one and five notes in a row, and all values are used either seven or eight times. These are distributed to individual voices in the top system of example 4.10a and tallied on the left-hand side of example 4.10b. As with the subdivisions, Ligeti avoids the direct repetition of any value in a single voice through this passage. If repeated notes cross over a beat, they may entail multiple subdivisions (see the score, excerpted in example 4.10c), so what starts as a series of quintuplets might finish as sextuplets. Whereas in the sketch Ligeti generated the material as a unified whole, in the piece he splits it up with a general pause in measure 33. When the voices resume, they have changed from strictly pitched material to unpitched syllables in measure 34. In the sketch, one value is circled in the soprano, indicating this split. Ligeti does not alter his technique to take this interruption into account, but rather lets the abrupt interruption find its full force by having it cut across technique.

Other sections seem to be generated in a similar manner—and if not in the same painstaking detail as this passage, at least in accordance with the same principles. The Presto section of *Aventures* (starting at m. 20), for instance, uses

Example 4.10a. *Nouvelles Aventures*, sketch transcription, rhythmic planning for material segment 54

Example 4.10b. *Nouvelles Aventures*, sketch transcription, further rhythmic planning for material segment 54

Example 4.10c. *Nouvelles Aventures*, II, mm. 31–32. Copyright © 1966 by Henri Litolff's Verlag. Used by permission of C.F. Peters Corporation. All Rights Reserved

more consistent subdivisions of the beat in each voice but avoids repeating or overusing any number of repeated notes. The voice parts at the beginning of the coda of *Nouvelles Aventures* II (mm. 44–45) appear to be constructed along very similar principles. In each of these cases, though, the material is split up to a greater degree and is less thoroughly documented in the sketches, making a complete reconstruction difficult. Along with these interruptions, the coda also begins a gradual deceleration, which will bring the work to a close and may entail either more modifications of any underlying system or a freely composed approach within these basic rhythmic precepts.

Pitch organization in *Aventures* plays a decidedly secondary role in the piece, yet at times it also reveals consistent principles. The continual reference to chromatic clusters, for example, provides some degree of cohesion. The instrumental parts feature recurring harmonic clusters around middle C at points throughout the work, including the opening (C, C♯, D), gradually drifting and expanding through the first 19 measures. Clusters are spread through wider registers, in the bass at measure 30 and the soprano at measure 36, returning to the middle register as the goal of a dramatic narrowing process from measure 49 to measure 80.

The voices also tend to have strongly chromatic parts, featuring wild jumping lines in individual parts and semitone relationships between the voices. Along with the rhythmic aspects discussed above, example 4.9 shows the typical pitch usage for *Aventures*, including wide leaps emphasizing seconds, sevenths, ninths (mostly interval class 1), and tritones between the pair of voices. This style of writing, formalized to a higher degree in sketches for the De die judicii section of the Requiem, and is discussed in greater depth in chapter 5.

Another texture later applied to the Requiem originates in the Allegro appassionato section of *Aventures* (m. 49 and following). Here the voice parts use large leaps, emphasizing dissonant intervals and oscillating back and forth between two different registers. The instrumental parts use the same pitch material, but it is segmented differently, drawing on different registral strands of the voices. For example (as shown in example 4.11a), the flute takes the upper pitches of the soprano and alto, the horn takes the lower notes of the soprano and the upper notes of the baritone, and the cello takes the lower notes of the alto and baritone. Each instrument then presents these notes in the same register as the voices, but in a different rhythmic pattern, and all together divide the chromatic aggregate in different ways (example 4.11b).

Another characteristic texture involves more precise pitch organization, projecting a musical line across different voices—often indicated with dotted lines showing the chain of succession. This first appears with straightforward chromatic motion in the Action dramatique section at the end of *Aventures* (starting in m. 108), in which the voices share the notes of a descending chromatic scale. In *Nouvelles Aventures* I, Ligeti designates a similar texture as the Hoquetus section (m. 28). This wording appears in the sketches as well. The

Example 4.11a. *Aventures*, doubling between voices and instruments, m. 49

Soprano	B5	D6	E♭6	D♭6	Upper Flute
		D♭4	C4	B3	Lower Horn
Alto		F5	F#5	E5	Lower Flute
	A3	E3	D3		Upper Cello/Bass
Baritone	B♭4	A♭4	F4		Upper Horn
		G2	A2	B♭2	Lower Cello

hocket techniques of earlier music are not literally in play here, but the individual voices do work together to create a composite pattern; in this section of *Nouvelles Aventures* the parts are unmetered, but each voice follows as quickly as he or she can after the preceding one.

Generally speaking, *Nouvelles Aventures* pays more attention to pitch structure than does its predecessor. This is especially true of the first movement of *Nouvelles Aventures*, which was composed later than the second and may reflect the reemergence of interval structures in Ligeti's writing in the intervening years.[46] The opening of *Nouvelles Aventures* uses a fixed repertoire of pitch-vowel pairs: D (a), E (ɛ), E♭ (ʏ), and G (œ) in the voices while the instruments sustain these pitches as echoes, responses, or subtle shifts in timbre, occasionally punctuating them with a wider cluster. These pitch-vowel pairs are consistent for large parts of the movement, including the return of the original Sostenuto texture in measure 21, as well as the Hoquetus section in measure 28, along with supplemental or partial returns elsewhere in the movement.[47]

Other referential sets featuring chromatic content or emphasizing tritones provide a degree of consistency across the work, and may relate to the emerging "interval signals" found in the Requiem. The first three pitches of *Nouvelles Aventures* make the chromatic trichord D–E♭–E, although the voicing typically displaces E♭ an octave lower than the other notes. The horn solo in measure 14, the first extended instrumental solo in either work, picks up on this beginning using the chromatic tetrachord E♭–D–E–C♯ and continuing through the aggregate with another chromatic tetrachord, G–A♭–B♭–A, followed by a (0167), F–B–C–F♯, thus emphasizing chromatic tetrachords and tritones, in the form of

46. The introduction of Jonathan Bernard, "Ligeti's Restoration Interval and Its Significance for His Later Works," *Music Theory Spectrum* 21, no. 1 (Spring 1999), 1–31, sketches out the chronology from Ligeti's work on the Requiem to the works of the 1970s.

47. For more on these "pitch-vowel couples" and pitch structure in the work more generally, see Istvan Anhalt, "Ligeti's *Nouvelles Aventures*: A Small Group as a Model for Composition," in his *Alternative Voices: Essays on Contemporary Vocal and Choral Composition* (Toronto: University of Toronto Press, 1984), 41*ff.*

Example 4.11b. *Aventures*, mm. 49–53. Copyright © 1961 by Henri Litolff's Verlag. Used by permission of C.F. Peters Corporation. All Rights Reserved

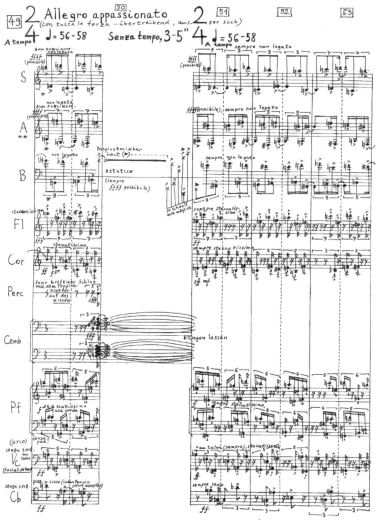

a Bartókian Z-cell (see chapter 1). The continuation of the horn solo and the vocal melismas that follow in measure 15 also tend to emphasize major and minor seconds and tritones, although these are less regular in the way they complete aggregates.

Compared to *Aventures, Nouvelles Aventures* contains more set pieces, which satirize conventional musical genres with their titles but also tend to use these characteristic interval sets. The Hoquetus (m. 28) begins with the same tetrachordal division as that used in the horn solo's first aggregate (m. 14), although it reorders the tetrachords and rearranges pitch content within each tetrachord: D–E–Eb–C#, F–B–C–F#, and Ab–A–G–Bb. As with the horn solo, the continuation is less regular, but the initial pitch material does have further consequence. If one takes the hexachords of the Hoquetus, rather than the tetrachords, there is a connection to another set piece in the work, the second movement's Chorale (mm. 19–21). The Chorale's upper part uses Db–Eb–E–F–Gb–G, and the lower uses D–C–B–Bb–A–Ab to create two inversionally combinatorial (012346) hexachords. The hexachords occur in very close position with a literal pitch axis around C#/D4, and so they express a cluster from Ab3 up to G4. There is no serial ordering of the hexachords, but the harmonic language of the Chorale is carefully regulated, strictly excluding thirds but allowing fifths and fourths along with the seconds and tritones familiar from the rest of the piece.

Nouvelles Aventures II (mm. 36–39) is also noteworthy, because the pitch system Ligeti uses in these four measures is a direct precursor to his handling of pitch in the Chamber Concerto (1969–70). Sketches link this passage to subtype V6, reading "panic, terror, chase (but soft)—many octaves heaped up, organ like, *pppp* possibile, tutti, swift motion" (panic, rémület, hajsza [de halk]—sokoktavas orgonaszerü felrakas, pppp possibile, tutti, gyorsan mozog). Here each instrumental part voices a chromatic hexachord through running figures in fast, rhythmic unison and parallel semitones in multiple octaves. Ligeti carefully designed the basic pattern to avoid repeated tone successions, so that, for example, if F goes to F# first, Ligeti will not use that succession (F–F#) until all of the other possible continuations from F have been exhausted (i.e., F–G, F–G#, F–A, and F–Bb). The same applies to all of the individual pitches, so that F#–F, F#–G, F#–G#, F#–A, and F#–Bb will each be used before any of these successions are repeated.

Although *Aventures* and *Nouvelles Aventures* can be seen as results of Ligeti's engagement with Fluxus and the absurdist inclinations of that milieu, they are also the works that begin to channel these tendencies into different creative outlets, including those that would become regular features of his later compositions. Perhaps because of their fragmentary nature, Ligeti felt free to use an ad hoc approach to working out individual sections, and in doing so to try out a number of different compositional techniques, investigating and experimenting with varied approaches to rhythm, pitch, and timbre. While this pluralism was a perfect fit for the scattered, ironic collage of reference points that made up the works' background, these pieces became a cache of ideas that Ligeti would draw on for years to come. The techniques first investigated here return as the basis of the more formally defined approach to melody in the Requiem, of repeated-note meccanico ideas and pitch-succession melodies that appear in the Second String Quartet and the Chamber Concerto, and of satirical and dramatic effects that lead to the opera. These works stand at the critical point of defining Ligeti's style and technique, his use of irony and humor, and his relationship to his peers and his past.

CHAPTER 5

Synthesis of Technique (1962–67)

THE REQUIEM

With a string of successful compositions and attention-grabbing premieres extending from *Artikulation* through *Apparitions* and from *Atmosphères* to *Aventures*, Ligeti had achieved a reputation, a degree of fame, and a number of important connections, even as he was splitting time between different locations. In Vienna he had established a good relationship with the composer and conductor Friedrich Cerha, who gave the premiere of *Aventures* with his ensemble "die reihe" in 1963. In Cologne and Darmstadt he got to know Stockhausen, Kagel, and Bruno Maderna, an avid supporter who would also conduct many of Ligeti's works. At the Royal Swedish Academy, where Ligeti was invited to return and teach more extensively throughout the 1960s, his connections and collaborations were starting to lead to more substantial projects. In particular it was through these Stockholm connections that Ligeti received his first major commission, for a work celebrating the tenth anniversary of Swedish Radio's "Nutida Musik" concert series. This resulted in the Requiem (1962–65). Although he was still living a somewhat itinerant life, these factors gave him enough income, stability, and time to focus on composition and refine his technique, and he described the extended time he could devote to the Kyrie of the Requiem in particular as a "utopian indulgence."[1]

Even with the luxury of time, however, Ligeti shortened the overall plan of the Requiem from seven movements including the Offertorium, Sanctus, Agnus Dei, and Communio (Lux aeterna) to four (Introitus, Kyrie, Sequentia,

---

1. Both Richard Toop, *György Ligeti* (London: Phaidon, 1999), 101–2, and Richard Steinitz, *György Ligeti: Music of the Imagination* (Boston: Northeastern University Press, 2003), 143, cite the composer as using this wording, although they disagree about the exact length of time it took. Toop states that it took six months during 1964, and Steinitz says nine.

and Lacrimosa), breaking the Lacrimosa off from the Sequentia and treating it in a separate movement as a type of epilogue. The instrumentation remained grand, involving two choirs, vocal soloists, and a full orchestra with celesta, harpsichord, harp, and three percussionists; sketches show that at one point Ligeti was also considering a children's choir in the Sanctus. There may have also been purely musical reasons for shortening the original scope of the Requiem. A typewritten sheet describing the original seven-movement plan called for the work to completely dissolve at the end of the Communio movement (Lux aeterna) (végén teljes feloldódás), but handwritten above it is a comment rethinking this ending because it was already present in the Lacrimosa (nem, mert lacrimosában volt), which stands as the final movement of the work.

Why Ligeti, a secular Jewish composer, would choose a Requiem setting for his first major commission is a puzzle to which there are different possible solutions, each with some validity. One commonly stated line of thinking was that in coming to terms with the aftermath of World War II and the Holocaust, the requiem genre somehow crossed over religious divisions in the wake of universal tragedy. Indeed, Ligeti's earlier drafts of a requiem (including the 1956 draft discussed in chapter 1 and elements present in *Aventures*) suggest a long-standing need for this type of expression in the years after the war. Another line of thinking recalls Ligeti's early instruction in strict counterpoint as a conservatory student in Budapest and upholds Renaissance contrapuntal masses as the apotheosis of technique, a proving ground for an emerging composer to show his abilities in a large form.[2] The more frequent references to earlier composers in the sketches for this work may lend support to this interpretation, too. Ultimately, Ligeti's Requiem serves both ends: it is a riveting work, driven by the highest emotions, and also a codification of his micropolyphonic techniques. With its divergent textures, the Requiem also begins a process of synthesis between the static style seen in *Atmosphères* and the frantically active ("wild gesticulating") style seen in *Aventures*.[3] Of the works that follow, *Lux aeterna* and *Lontano* develop and codify features of the static style, while the Cello Concerto continues the synthesis of divergent techniques and styles.

2. For a sampling of interpretations of the Requiem, see Steinitz, *Ligeti*, 140–46; Wolfgang Marx, "'Make Room for the Grand Macabre!' The Concept of Death in György Ligeti's Oeuvre," in *György Ligeti: Of Foreign Lands and Strange Sounds*, ed. Louise Duchesneau and Wolfgang Marx, 71–84 (Woodbridge, UK: Boydell, 2011); Harald Kaufmann, "Betreffend Ligetis Requiem" in *Von innen und aussen*, ed. Werner Grünzweig and Gottfried Krieger (Hofheim: Wolke Verlag, 1993), 134–48; and Jennifer Iverson, "Ligeti's Dodecaphonic Requiem," *Tempo* 68, no. 270 (October 2014), 31–47.

3. These types, or poles, are defined in Erkki Salmenhaara, *Das musikalische Material und seine Behandlung in den Werken "Apparitions," "Atmosphères," "Aventures" und "Requiem" von György Ligeti* (Regensburg: Bosse, 1969), 171ff. and also taken up by Péter Várnai, *LiC*, 24.

Introitus

The Kyrie and Sequentia are the most substantial movements of the Requiem, but the Introitus sets the general mood and shape of the work. Erkki Salmenhaara has noted that the fundamental motion of the Requiem as a whole is from low to high and that this motion is prefigured in the first movement.[4] This carries with it certain connections with the text of the Requiem— especially considering the precedents in earlier pieces (*Éjszaka, Reggel* [Night, Morning], *Sötét és Világos* [Dark and Light], and *Apparitions*) of associating low-register, nearly static clusters with darkness, and more activity in the higher registers with light. A verbal sketch outlining the seven-movement scheme makes this explicit, with a contrast between the deep ending lines of the Offertorium (mély quam olim) and the start of the Sanctus, described as "black ➞ suddenly surging light" (fekete ➞ hirtelen áradó fény). Though these movements were never composed, verbal sketches describe the Sanctus as high and radiant (magas, ragyogó) and specify instruments appropriate to that character, including harp, celeste, glockenspiel, and children's choir. The more understated motion from low to high set up by the Introitus and ending with the Lacrimosa stands in place of this more sudden and complete shift, but the overall plan, and its symbolic motion toward the eternal light mentioned throughout the text, remain an essential gesture of the work.

In planning the important registral motion of the Introitus, Ligeti moved from these verbal associations to graphic representation and then to more precise definition—a general progression that becomes increasingly common in this period. An early sketch lays the form out graphically, but without reference to specific pitch levels, dividing it into sections based on the text and instrumental interludes, which reach upwards and become brighter during the course of the movement. For each section Ligeti made notes on the choral and instrumental forces, many of which carry over into the score, including all the vocal indications, as well as the muted trombones at the beginning, the contrabass harmonics following, and clarinets at the end. This registral diagram is then translated into staff notation in the upper half of another sketch, shown in example 5.1. In it Ligeti has plotted out the range of each vocal block, at both its entrance point (the small staff labeled "Ausgangspunkte" in the sketch) and the exit points, which are on the large grand staff. Thus the passage at measure 65, which is worked out in greater detail in the bottom half of the sketch, begins on F♯3 (as shown in the second-to-last note of the small staff) and expands upwards to fill the range of B3 to A4 shown in the grand staff.

---

4. Salmenhaara, *Das musikalische Material*, 145–46.

Example 5.1. Requiem, Introitus, sketch for mm. 65–69. Reproduced with kind permission from the György Ligeti Collection of the Paul Sacher Foundation, Basel

The different sections are then realized in more detail with the aid of block diagrams like that seen in the bottom part of example 5.1. These sketches plan out the way each voice moves in order to effect the register change required, without deviating too far from the cluster harmonies that characterize the work. The note names are aligned by syllable in the sketches, but in the final score these syllables are stretched and skewed to different beats according to a different plan. The numbers above and below the sketch deal with the rhythmic aspect of the section; they calculate the number of attacks (note changes or rearticulated notes) in any given beat. There are several attempts to arrange the sequence of attacks, which range from 9 to 14 attacks per beat. The sequence seen in this sketch, written above the grand staff—13,

12, 11, 14, 13, 11, [10]—occurs in measures 65–69 of the Introitus, with the bracketed 10 altered to 9 attacks in the score (the second half of m. 68). The branching diagrams to the left are used to make sure that no succession is repeated. The first time Ligeti uses 13 attacks in a beat, he follows it with 12; the next time he follows it with 11. This kind of detailed control is typical of the Requiem, as both a demonstration of his focus on refining technique and an insight into the types of compositional decisions with which he was occupied. In this process, the use of a fixed range of values for attacks stipulates a general level of activity, but the meticulous avoidance of repetition ensures unpredictability within that level. These are the first stages of a more developed method that the composer systematized in *Lux aeterna* (analyzed below). Other calculations in this early version of the system keep track of the number of times a different rhythmic module (e.g., placing an attack on the second quintuplet rather than the third or fourth) is used; again, Ligeti aimed for an approximately balanced distribution, something achieved more fully and systematically in later works.[5]

Kyrie

The Kyrie was the movement that occupied Ligeti for such a long time and in which he developed his micropolyphony to such a high degree. The organic growth and decay which Ligeti worked out in this movement serves as a finely constructed bridge from the static, suspenseful Introitus to the frantic emotions of the following movement. It also represents the composer's first attempt at shifting between these two poles smoothly, within a continuous flowing polyphony, rather than the abrupt juxtapositions between extremes seen in earlier works. The movement uses a twenty-part ensemble consisting of the five voice types (SMATB), each divided into four parts, and it is structured as an intricately contrapuntal "fugue" intertwining and overlapping the Kyrie and Christe strands in a dense mesh of gradually shifting textures. Each melodic entrance expands from a unison beginning and generally calmer rhythms to a dense, palpitating mass, eventually tapering back into a more tranquil state. Doing so allows the Kyrie to move gradually and confidently between extremes from compact stepwise motion to disjunct leaps, from sparse to dense textures, from narrow to wide registers, and from soft

---

5. In the first part of this section (mm. 65–69, setting "et lux perpetua") the balance of rhythmic modules is fairly even, especially for quintuplet and sextuplet divisions. The following distributions can be compared to those of *Lux aeterna*, discussed below: abcd = 10, 7, 10, 0; mnop = 7, 6, 7, 8; wxyz = 6, 7, 7, 8. In the second part (mm. 70–74, setting "luceat eis") the balance is slightly more skewed: 9, 6, 7, 0 / 6, 6, 5, 5 / 8, 4, 5, 5. The second part is also interrupted by a "window" of rest, similar to the windows that were featured in sections of *Aventures*.

to overpowering dynamics. Ligeti described the Kyrie as a "web" (szövevény) composition, and it is a marvel of intricate construction in which the composer was finally able to reconcile serial and nonserial influences to form a unique amalgam and a personalized technique, demonstrated in a large-scale tour de force.

Ligeti referred to early masters including Ockeghem and Bach for the idea behind his endlessly flowing polyphony, in combination with concepts taken from serial music. The composer hinted at this mix of influences as he described the genesis of the movement to Péter Várnai:

In this movement I wanted to combine Flemish polyphony with my own new micropolyphony. I took Ockeghem as my model, and adopted his "varietas" principle, where the voices are similar without being identical . . . . The canonic parts are identical in their notes but their rhythmic articulations are always different and no rhythmic pattern is ever repeated in a canon. I think here that I succeeded in realizing Ockeghem's "varietas" principle. I had worked out for myself beforehand a set of rules both for the melodic lines and for the harmonic structure, rules that are almost as strict as those of the Flemish composers or Palestrina's. For instance, the permutation of the rhythmic patterns, which is reminiscent of methods employed in serialism although the Kyrie-fugue is not serial music. Working on the composition was rather like weaving a carpet, some parts ready, some threads still hanging loose: and then I would go on weaving according to the rules I prescribed for myself. At any given point there were several possibilities of how to go on; I chose one and went on weaving the smaller patterns of the canons and the larger ones of the fugue.[6]

In addition to Ockeghem, Bach's motet "Singet dem Herrn ein neues Lied" seems to have been another inspiration.[7] This motet, admired by composers from Mozart to Wagner, is often held up as a superlative example of contrapuntal construction,[8] and it was therefore a logical model for a work that Ligeti would consider a statement piece of his new micropolyphony. Bach's work shows not only an intricate contrapuntal interplay between the two choruses but also a level of rhythmic complexity that pushes toward density—something Richard Wagner compared to the buzzing of insects—an effect that Ligeti magnifies in his micropolyphony.[9]

6. *LiC*, 49–50.
7. Salmenhaara mentions this (*Das musikalische Material*, 136, 139, and 151), citing both his conversations with the composer and also a lecture that Ligeti gave in Jyväskylä in 1965.
8. This motet and comments attributed to Mozart and Wagner are discussed in Martin Geck, *Johann Sebastian Bach: Life and Work*, trans. John Hargraves (Orlando: Harcourt, 2006), 453–58.
9. Martin Geck, "Richard Wagner und die ältere Musik," in *Die Ausbreitung des Historismus über die Musik*, ed. Walter Wiora, 123–46 (Regensburg: Bosse, 1969), 129, referenced in Geck, *Bach*, 455.

From the quotation above we can also begin to discern that there are serial elements in the work, and indeed, the analysis below will show that they go far beyond what the composer mentions. In particular, much of the movement can be derived from a twelve-tone row that has been called the "Grundtypus" by Jonathan Bernard; this row is directly related to the Christe melodies and the overall form of the work and is indirectly related to the Kyrie melodies.[10] The Kyrie and Christe texts are interwoven from the beginning, and each type of melody exhibits distinct features, described below. Each voice type (SMATB) carries only one text at a time and presents it starting from a unison—supported by a sustained note in the instrumental forces, giving the singers their starting note and helping articulate the large-scale form of the entrances—before expanding outwards in imitative polyphony. Each individual voice within the block proceeds in canon, with a unique rhythmic sequence.

Although the Kyrie is not an integral-serial work, the degree of influence that this row has on almost every aspect of the work, from the individual melodic lines to the larger form, is surprising. In fact, many of the work's features can be seen as a kind of response to the practices Boulez used in *Structures Ia*—as Ligeti had first critiqued the work in print, he then responded to the idea of thoroughly serialized structure with a piece of his own. The basic architecture of the work echoes Ligeti's reading of Boulez in another way, as well. The voice types work as blocks or "bundles of voices" (Stimmbündel), as Monika Lichtenfeld (a close associate of Ligeti's) has described them, which all use the same text and melody but do so in canon. This idea of bundles suggests a comparison to the "bundles" made of "threads" of individual rows (Bündel and Fäden) mentioned in Ligeti's analysis of Boulez's *Structures Ia*, and as in Boulez's work, both the individual threads and the greater structures derive from an underlying serial conception.[11]

In the sketches Ligeti went through several iterations of a basic form for the piece, and the sketch presented in example 5.2a shows much of his working method, which involves increasingly familiar techniques for avoiding repetition and for balancing the statistical distribution of musical parameters, as well as traces of more explicitly dodecaphonic organization. The charts across the top of the page demonstrate several of Ligeti's concerns. The crosses and dashes on the top left are a type of tallying system, helping to balance the number of times each voice type uses the Kyrie and Christe text. The branching diagrams toward the top center arrange the succession of voice entrances,

10. Jonathan Bernard, "A Key to the Structure of the Kyrie of György Ligeti's Requiem," *Mitteilungen der Paul Sacher Stiftung* 16 (March 2003), 42–47, calls this row the Grundtypus, citing the label in Ligeti's sketches. Iverson, "Ligeti's Dodecaphonic Requiem," follows this terminology.

11. For the language used to describe each piece, see Monika Lichtenfeld, "'Requiem' von György Ligeti: Einleitung und Kommentar," *Wort und Wahrheit* 23, no. 4 (1968), 308–13, esp. 312, and compare to Ligeti's "Entscheidung und Automatik in der *Structure Ia* von Pierre Boulez," *GS*, 1:413–46, esp. 423.

Example 5.2a. Requiem, Kyrie, sketch planning the movement. Reproduced with kind permission from the György Ligeti Collection of the Paul Sacher Foundation, Basel

Example 5.2b. Requiem, Kyrie, transcription of a detail from a later sketch

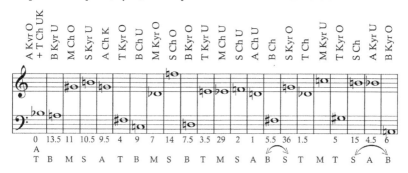

and the table just to the right of this, concerns the balance of the original form (O) and inversion (U [Umkehrung]) of the Christe melody in the different voice types. In the final version of the piece the number of entrances is reduced from 30 to 28, as shown in this sketch, and then to 23, a system that requires only one instance of the original and the inverted Kyrie per voice.[12] With these changes, the importance of managing the voice successions seems to have given way to balancing the number of times each voice has the Kyrie and the Christe text and how many times they occur in the prime and the inverted versions. This can be observed with a high degree of regularity in the first ten entrances of the composition, where two entrances occur in each voice part in regular succession, representing the prime and the inversion of the Kyrie and all of the different serial transformations of the Christe, which, unlike the Kyrie, also occurs in retrograde (K [Krebs]) and retrograde inversion (UK).

The lower half of the sketch presents a chronological overview of the movement showing how and where the voices enter and (added in red pen in the original sketch) the note names for the unison starting points of each vocal block. These entrances follow the initial sequence Bb–A–G#–B–G–F#–C–Db, which would continue with F–D–E–Eb to complete the Grundtypus row. The numbers in the lower left, written in red pen and circled, are rhythmic calculations. Ligeti began with the sequence consisting of every half-number from 1 to 15 and reordered them into a sequence starting 13.5, 11, 10.5, 9.5, 4, 9, 7, 14, 7.5, 3.5. These numbers describe the interonset interval between vocal entrances, measured in beats (half notes), and the sequence is completed (with a few modifications and omissions, most likely made as he reduced the original number of entrances) below the staff in example 5.2b. Following this pattern, the first entrance of the tenors and altos lasts for 13.5 half notes before the bass entrance in measure 7; the bass entrance lasts for 11 half notes

12. The boxed text reading "rövidíteni minden szolamban Kyrie O+U, nem többször[?]" (abbreviate in each voice Kyrie O+U, not further) makes this decision explicit.

before the mezzos enter in measure 13, and so forth, to the end of the piece. This chart shows a later stage of composition completes and summarizes the information given in example 5.2a, including some of the rationale for reducing the number of entrances.[13] In this form Ligeti uses the complete original Grundtypus row (P10, starting on B♭), followed by the retrograde inversion starting on E (RI9), and so dovetailing the last two notes of the first row with the first two notes of the second. Two further rearrangements complete the progression from sketch to score, both indicated with arrows in the sketch. Ligeti switched the bass entrance on F♯ and soprano entrance on G and has moved the soprano entrance on B later, to become the final entrance of the movement.

In example 5.2a there are other subjective descriptions of the musical texture that may help explain some of the reordering. The sketch contains segments labeled "csak férfikar" (only male choir) and "tiszta nőikar" (purely female choir), and the reordering of the bass and soprano entrances helps prolong the female-choir section. This change also breaks the strict alternation of Kyrie and Christe entrances by creating repeated Kyrie sections in the male voices, followed by repeated Christe blocks in the female choir. This shift to the high voices, along with a thinning-out of the overall texture (circa mm. 60–61 in the finished score), perhaps points to the three-part division of the traditional mass setting. The following segments, labeled sűrű (dense), and "coda," show attention to the dramatic flow of the movement. The peaks of density, registral width, and dynamics (circa m. 40 and again around m. 86 of the finished score) also help frame a three-part design. One other alteration present at the end of the movement helps reconcile parts of the formal plan. The sopranos' final entrance is delayed from what the original twelve-tone sequence called for, but this Christe statement is also kept very brief, so that the basses, singing a longer Kyrie block, still bring the work to a close. As Eric Drott and others have observed, there are several possible interpretations of the overall form of the movement.[14] In contrast to the echo of the traditional three-part form, the P + RI order of the entrances suggests a two-part conception, although here, too, the exact boundaries are never articulated as clear sections but, rather, they overlap, flowing smoothly from one into another.

13. This sketch is reproduced in Iverson, "Ligeti's Dodecaphonic Requiem," as well as in Jonathan Bernard, "Rules and Regulation: Lessons from Ligeti's Compositional Sketches," in *György Ligeti: Of Foreign Lands and Strange Sounds*, ed. Louise Duchesneau and Wolfgang Marx, 149–67 (see color plate 7) (Woodbridge, UK: Boydell, 2011), which expands on observations about this sketch in his "Key to the Structure." The interonset intervals as found in the score largely follow the alterations in pitch shown in the sketch, but also lengthen some of the values, continuing after the value of 3.5 as 29, 2, 1, 36, 5.5, 1.5, 7 (not shown in the sketch), 5, 4.5, 6.5 (instead of 6), 15.

14. Eric Drott, "Lines, Masses, Micropolyphony: Ligeti's Kyrie and the 'Crisis of the Figure,'" *Perspectives of New Music* 49, no. 1 (Winter 2011), 4–46.

Example 5.3. Requiem, basic Kyrie melody, alto I, mm. 1–21

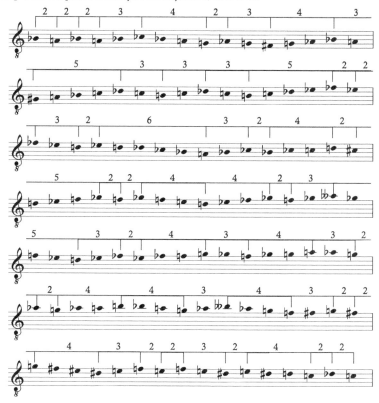

The Kyrie melody (example 5.3) is a long and highly chromatic line spreading outwards to move through the twelve pitch classes. As with the form of the piece, the construction of melodic detail went through many stages of careful planning. Jennifer Iverson has discussed the possible evolution of the melody as it moved through several sketch drafts, eventually settling on the wedge-like expansion of the final draft. Similarly, Jonathan Bernard has discussed the construction of this melody and its development from a draft using strictly chromatic motion to the version used in the finished piece, which breaks up this chromatic flow with carefully placed whole tones.[15] In one sketch Ligeti monitors the contour segments, plotting out how many notes occur between changes of direction; Bernard transcribes this sketch and notes that the contour remains the same between this version and the final melody. This seems to indicate the relative priority of contour and register over exact pitch content. As another way of diminishing the importance of exact pitches,

15. Iverson, "Ligeti's Dodecaphonic Requiem;" Bernard, "Rules and Regulations," esp. 159–67.

Example 5.4. Requiem, rows for the Christe and Kyrie

Ligeti added lines in the score indicating points where the singers of these thorny melodies are no longer held to a strict intonational standard.[16]

Although the exact pitch content of these melodies may not prove to be as salient or perceptible a feature as the mass of texture they produce or the cumulative register they occupy, they are, like almost every aspect of this work, carefully constructed according to discernable principles, or rules of construction, which can be summarized as follows:[17]

1. Contour segments (i.e., the number of notes between changes of direction, including the starting and ending notes) are between 2 and 6 notes in length. Repeated notes are not used.
2. Smaller contour segments are used more frequently than larger ones.[18]
3. Contour segments of the same length may be repeated, but only to a total of three instances in a row.
4. Segments that are longer than three notes use a whole tone to break up the chromatic motion. This whole tone always occurs between the third and fourth notes of the segment.

This gradual expansion of contour segments helps Ligeti guide the melody through all twelve pitch classes, completing the aggregate at the fifty-first note, F♮. The order of introduction of these pitches is as significant as in other parts of the piece. Example 5.4 presents this as a kind of twelve-tone

16. See the introduction to György Ligeti, *Requiem*, vocal score by Zsigmond Szathmáry, revised ed. (New York: Peters, 2006) where he states, "Choral passages marked by a continuous black line. . . need not be sung in exact intonation. As far as possible, however, effort should be made to keep to the correct pitches" (n.p.).

17. Bernard, "Rules and Regulation," 166–67, also provides a set of hypothetical rules governing these lines. My formulation is indebted to his, although mine also condenses Bernard's rules 2 through 5 into my rule 4. I believe this is a more concise yet equally accurate description.

18. There is some suggestion of a product method for regulating their use (along the lines of that used for durations in *Artikulation* and *Apparitions*—see chapters 2 and 3). The three-note segments are used 16 times and the four-note segments 12 times; both have a product of 48. The two-note segments are used 22 times, coming close to this figure with a product of 44. The other values (4 five-note segments, and 1 six-note segment), however, do not have similar products.

row and compares it to the more strictly defined row used in the Christe segments. These rows have many similarities: the two hexachords are invariant, and, moreover, the hexachords of each row keep many of the order positions in place. The first hexachord involves a rotation in order positions 3–5; the second involves a retrograde of positions 9–12.[19]

In rhythmic terms, the Kyrie melody uses mixed divisions within each voice part, slowly accelerating and decelerating through simple eighth-note divisions of the half-note beat all the way up to nonuplets. The voices rarely hold to the same division for more than two beats in a row, and there is a continual mix of conflicting subdivisions between the voices, reaching a maximum point of complexity in measure 13. Since the Kyrie melodies are all 21 measures long, this position is a significant way of structuring the dramatic arch of the Kyrie blocks using Fibonacci numbers and an approximate golden section to place the climax of rhythmic activity.

Inversion occurs in the Kyrie strands with blocks of texture as well as with the melody. A comparison of the alto entrance and subsequent bass entrance demonstrates this relationship. Not only is the melodic line inverted (beginning with an upper neighbor rather than a lower neighbor and continuing as an exact inversion), but the rhythmic roles of the voices are inverted as well. Starting in the second half of measure 8, the rhythm of bass 4 is based on that of alto 1, the rhythm of bass 3 on alto 2, and the rhythm of basses 2 and 1 on altos 3 and 4, respectively. These parts are compared in examples 5.5a and 5.5b.

The Christe melodies are more directly related to serial technique but undergo an unorthodox adaptation. They are all derived from the Grundtypus row that defines the form of the work and which occurs explicitly in the soprano part in measures 40–52 (example 5.6a). Other instances of these melodies include not only transpositions and inversions, as in the Kyrie melodies, but all of the standard serial transformations including retrogrades and retrograde inversions as seen above in example 5.2b. Ligeti also uses idiosyncratic internal retrogrades of these forms, which at times complicate and obscure the underlying row. Some of these are very simple, for example, the basses in measures 29–41 using I0 followed by a retrograde of the entire row. Others, however, are more involved. The initial entry in the tenors, for example, is based on a retrograde inversion of the fundamental row (RI3) but uses internal retrogrades, moving through order positions 12, 11, 10, and 9, then progressing back to order position 12, as annotated in example 5.6b. Another internal retrograde around order position 5 (F♯) leads to the repetition of order positions 6 through 8, as Ligeti traces a back-and-forth

19. Iverson, "Ligeti's Dodecaphonic Requiem," 41–42, also points out similarities to the row constructions in Webern's Symphonie, op. 21.

Example 5.5a. Requiem, Kyrie, altos, mm. 1–3. Copyright © 1965 by Henri Litolff's Verlag. © Revised Edition 2006 by Henri Litolff's Verlag. Used by permission of C.F. Peters Corporation. All Rights Reserved

Example 5.5b. Requiem, Kyrie, basses, mm. 7–9. Copyright © 1965 by Henri Litolff's Verlag. © Revised Edition 2006 by Henri Litolff's Verlag. Used by permission of C.F. Peters Corporation. All Rights Reserved

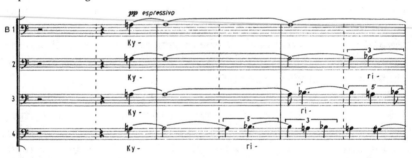

Example 5.6a. Requiem, complete row for the Christe, soprano I, mm. 40–52

Example 5.6b. Requiem, Christe melody, tenor I, mm. 1–23

path through the order positions of the row. In this statement as well as the mezzo-soprano statement (P8, mm.13–28) and the alto statement (R2, mm. 23–55) the row statement is incomplete, using only 9 or 10 of the pitch classes.

Though they are more directly derived from the Grundtypus row, the Christe melodies are treated with more freedom than are the Kyries. Sometimes (as with the bass entrance on C, m. 29, and the final soprano entrance on B, m. 102) Ligeti begins the row with leaps rather than steps, inverting the more standard contour of the other statements. At other times he heavily favors certain pitches by settling on specific order positions by the use of internal retrogrades. For example, near letter K (m. 79 and following), the mezzo-sopranos, using I3, come to focus on the last four notes of the row, emphasizing large leaps between A♭4, B3, A4, and B♭3. Meanwhile, in the same passage, the altos are using a different row, I2, but they also settle on the last four notes, creating a similar pattern with the notes G4, B♭3, A♭4, and A3. Individually these voice parts seem to split into compound lines,[20] but together the voices create trichordal clusters in different registers: A–B♭–B3 and G–A♭–A4. In works such as *Aventures* (and again in the Dies irae of the Requiem), textures built from closely spaced clusters and those built from frantic wide leaps are constructed by very different means, but here in the dense web of the Kyrie, Ligeti's contrapuntal technique manages to move gradually and smoothly between sustained clusters and agile leaps and to create structures that harness the tension between these extremes with great expressive power.

Rhythm in the Christe melodies is also quite different from that in the Kyries. Here each voice stays with one type of subdivision, as in the Introitus and in the later work *Lux aeterna*, where a more fully developed technique emerges. As in these works, Ligeti uses only a limited set of rhythmic modules, but he seems to use them freely, without tallying the individual instances of their use. In fact, in a draft of the score Ligeti appears to be more concerned with monitoring the durations of notes of the Christe melodies (which he measures in eighth notes separately within each type of subdivision) and limiting repetitions of durations rather than tallying the individual modules.

Ligeti allows himself more liberty in the Christes than in the more uniform Kyries—and in doing so takes a step away from the automatism he found in Boulez's *Structures Ia*. The use of internal retrogrades can change the length of individual entrances and can change the focus to different registers or pitch classes. The control of rhythm can also affect the density of the overall texture. All of these tools give Ligeti the ability to shape the movement in a more moment-by-moment way, creating variety between blocks, in addition to dynamic motion within them. Whereas both the Kyrie and *Structures Ia* use a single row to determine both the individual melodic lines and their formal organization, Ligeti assured himself of a certain freedom to avoid the mechanistic determinism

20. Drott, "Lines, Masses, Micropolyphony," discusses the internal retrogrades of the Christe melodies and their perceptual effects (esp. 23–24).

he found so objectionable in Boulez. In particular, the flexible handling of the Christe sections allows him to avoid the blocklike sections of Boulez's work and create a flowing and organic whole. In the Kyrie movement, then, Ligeti seems to be demonstrating not just the individuality and broad-reaching capabilities of his micropolyphonic technique but also making another kind of statement: that a piece with thorough serial underpinnings can still respond to a composer's vision for both the large-scale design and the small-scale details, and that a different kind of system of rules can allow for both flexibility and rigor.

De die judicii sequentia

If the Kyrie is the pinnacle of technical construction and micropolyphony in the Requiem, the "De die judicii sequentia," or Dies irae section, is the epitome of its expressive content, verging on the absurd and the macabre, drawing on *Aventures* both in spirit and in more technical ways. After the Kyrie, with its smooth flow between extremes of relative calm and turmoil, the abrupt contrasts of the Dies irae are particularly effective. It stops and starts, shifts suddenly between different types of material, and bursts forth with impulsive energy not seen in the other movements. Ligeti's sketches draw on both musical and nonmusical sources of inspiration for the turbulent character of this movement. Extensive verbal sketches make frequent reference to the visual arts. One short page is translated in example 5.7.

The references to the visual arts in the Dies irae tend toward works from the medieval and Renaissance periods and their particular union of religious sentiment and the horrifying aspects of tragic experience. Ligeti explicitly mentions Hieronymus Bosch (ca. 1450/60–1515), who was known for his portrayal of divine scenes of sin and damnation in such paintings as *The Garden of Earthly Delights* and *The Last Judgment*. In other verbal sketches for this movement Bosch is associated with the terms "visionary," "expressive," and "sinister" (baljóslatú). El Greco (ca. 1541–1614) is described as being "twisted" or "wrung out" (kifacsart), presumably in reference to the stretched or elongated figures in such works as his *Crucifixion*. Pieter Bruegel (the elder, ca. 1525/30–1569) is mentioned alongside Bosch in interviews,[21] but not in the sketches. One modern point of reference is Swedish artist Öyvind Fahlström (1928–76), whose "swarming" (nyüzsgés) is seen in the busy and intricate character of his drawings on paper. The musical and artistic references all point to a charged state of activity, a frantic environment of distortions, exaggerations, and multiple perspectives, both religious and secular. The De die judicii sequentia draws on all of these, channeling the existential terror of a previous period through a more modern means of expression.

21. See, e.g., *LiC*, 46, 59.

Example 5.7. Requiem, sketch transcription and translation describing the Dies irae

<u>DIES IRAE</u>　　　　　　+ *"Utrecht-chorus"*　　+ *A Cappella*

<u>Character (expression):</u>

Complex, interlaced, dramatic, expressive, visionary, exaggerated, characteristic of Bosch, mannerist, baroque, wrung out like [El] Greco, hellish vortexes, sudden contrasts, mosaic-like character, lots of layers, pulverized, strongly fragmented, with *fff* and *ppp* contrasts, without transitions, rushing, racing, concentrated (wide regions in some places, breaking up the rushing), troubled. Sudden tempo- and meter-changes. Swirling, then sudden still surfaces, then breaking out again. "Mahler"-transparency—layers may be heard from behind one another. Meticulous "Fahlström"-swarming.

Vine-like, intricate. On the inside: objects, swirling knotted balls. Sudden standstills.

<u>DIES IRAE</u>　　　　　　*"Utrecht-kórus"*　　+ *A CAPPELLA*

<u>Jellege (kifejezése):</u>

complex, szövevényes, drámai, expressziv, vizionárus, túlzó, <u>Bosch</u>-jellegü, manirista, barokk, Greco-szerüen kifacsart, pokolszerü forgatagok, hirtelen kontrasztok, mozaikszerü jelleg, sok réteg, pulverizált, igen széttöredezett, fff és ppp kontrasztálnak, átmenet nkül, Siet, hajszolt, koncentrált (széles régiók egyes helyeken megbontják e sietést), zaklatott.

Hirtelen tempo- és metrum-változások. Gomolyagok, majd hirtelen nyugodt felületek, ismét megbontás. "Mahler"-átlátszóság – egymás mögötti rétegek áthallatszanak. Aprólékos "Fahlström"-nyüzsgés.

Folyondáros, bonyolult. Benne objektumok, gomolyagok. Hirtelen megtorpanások.

> Notes to the example:
> * In this example and other transcriptions, italics indicate additional handwritten text over the typed sketch. Diacritical markings in the typed text are sometimes missing or altered but have been preserved as typed.

Musical sources of inspiration are also documented in the sketches, including the mention of the "Utrecht korus," a possible reference to Handel's *Utrecht Te Deum* and *Jubilate* and to a "transparency" found in the layered counterpoint of Mahler. This association with Mahler is developed into a more refined technique in later works such as the Chamber Concerto.[22] The connection to the *Utrecht Te Deum*, though somewhat more speculative, is plausible. Handel's work was written to celebrate the Peace of Utrecht in 1713, and Ligeti's can be seen as a response to World War II. Ligeti also cited a Baroque precedent for the Kyrie, in the form of Bach's motet, and there is biographical evidence that he was familiar with works by Handel including the *Dettingen Te Deum* as a student in Budapest.[23] Both works include choral textures ranging

22. See Ligeti's remarks in "Zur Collagetechnik bei Mahler und Ives," *GS*, 1:285–90, and also the discussion of what Ligeti's sketches term the "Mahler technique" in chapter 6.
23. See Steinitz, *Ligeti*, 46.

from brief solos to large antiphonal sections, and both move between these varied textures, often abruptly, through a succession of short sections that frequently run together.

Other verbal sketches for the movement define it as having a main layer—using the two choirs and soloists and described as "wild, extreme, gesticulating, and threatening" (vad, túlzó, hadonászó, fenyegető)—as well as two contrasting layers, and finally "isolated objects," which are often instrumental effects. The depictions of the contrasting layers seem to belong to a brainstorming period, and it is difficult to connect the entirety of any one sketch to the finished score, yet parts of these descriptions prove quite recognizable. The first contrasting layer is explained, in part, as a "sotto-voce layer (almost whispering, but with pitch-levels) (perhaps not exact)" (sotto voce [majdnem suttogò, de hangma-gasságokkal] [esetleg pontatlan] réteg) and the second layer (again, in part) as a "tranquil surface" (Nyugodt felületek) and "like windows, in any case, sudden *ppp*, sostenuto, *a cappella*," including a reference to Machaut (ugyis mint ablakok, hirtelen ppp, sostenuto, a cappella = Machaut.). Much of the planning for the two contrasting layers was mixed together, and there is repeated wording in descriptions of each. And though some aspects of these characterizations were changed or abandoned, other features clearly remain. Erkki Salmenhaara's analysis divides the material of this movement into five different types (Typschichten), which one can relate to these layers.[24] For example, the whispering sotto-voce choir appears in Salmenhaara's Type III, and the tranquil, *a cappella* sostenuto texture appears in his Type IV; both of of these types have two episodes within the movement. The analysis that follows shows how Salmenhaara's Types I, II, and V can be understood in relation to the set of compositional rules for the main layer and how Types III and IV relate to the contrasting layers, are more significantly divergent, and operate by different means.

The chaos of the main layer is strictly organized by compositional rules, some of which survive in the sketches. In fact, one page lays out the principles of voice leading and harmony for the main choral and solo textures of the Requiem's Dies irae with a degree of specificity unusual for his sketches. This sheet reads like the text of a counterpoint treatise, showing the influence of Ligeti's exposure to Jeppesen in his counterpoint training in Budapest. The page is translated as example 5.8.[25]

24. Salmenhaara, *Das musikalische Material*, 158–62, and appendix 3, 187–88, translates some of these sketches into German, but, perhaps because the descriptions overlap and shift, he does not connect them directly to his five types.

25. I address this sketch in my article "'Rules as Strict as Palestrina's': The Regulation of Pitch and Rhythm in Ligeti's Requiem and *Lux aeterna*," *Twentieth-Century Music* 10, no. 2 (2013), 203–30, discussing the hard and soft rules of this sketch and Ligeti's approach to compositional rulemaking in comparison to his peers. I also go into greater depth regarding the origin and transmission of alternate versions of these rules found in Salmenhaara, *Das musikalische Material*, 139–41, and in Bernard, "Rules and Regulation," esp. 164–65.

Example 5.8. Requiem, sketch transcription and translation of the rule sheet for the main layer of the Dies irae

<u>DIES IRAE</u>   *"MICROPOLYPHONY"*

<u>Main Layer</u>:   VOICE LEADING: mostly leaps, with steps mixed in.

Leaps: every interval is allowed, from the minor third up to the major ninth, excluding the octave.

Large leaps (both sevenths and both ninths) are the most common.

Very occasionally minor and major 10ths are permitted.

(In solo voices, larger leaps are possible).

Leaps in succession: two jumps in the same direction are forbidden.

jumps in changing directions are possible without restriction

Steps: Minor and major seconds

Steps in succession: forbidden in the same direction, but in changing directions two different seconds are allowed, after this it is necessary to have a leap

Leaps + Steps: Allowed both in the same direction and in changing directions, In one direction, leap + step or step + leap requires a change in direction afterwards (i.e. jump + step + jump or step + jump + step are forbidden in the same direction)

This does not apply to "dead" intervals*

"Dead" intervals are free (except the octave)

Note repetition is forbidden

The same pitch (or octave transposition) should not occur in the same voice too soon. There must be a minimum of three (as a rare exception, two) other notes in between before reappearing in the same voice.

Repeating the same interval is prohibited

Returning to the same interval after 1 other intervening interval is to be avoided

Returning to the same interval after 2 other intervening intervals is permitted

TEXT SETTING: SYLLABIC

"HARMONY" a minimum of one second (minor or major), vertically, is required

Exception: perfect unison (for "nodal points")

Minor second/tritone (making a fourth/fifth) is desirable at "stationary points."

Octaves must be "hidden" (= Aventures m. 49-technique)**

Explicit octaves are forbidden.

12-TONE MANAGEMENT: a) option: reservoir-technique

b) option: voice-distribution technique

(the a)-option predominates)

(continued)

Example 5.8. Continued

<u>DIES IRAE</u>   *"MIKROPOLYPHONIE"*

<u>Fö réteg</u>: SZOLAMVEZETES: ugrások túltengnek, köztük lépések.

ugrások: minden intervallum lehetséges kisterctöl

nagynónig, oktáv kivételével.

Nagy ugrások (a két szept és két nón) túltengnek.

Egészen kivételesen kis és nagy decimal lehetséges.

(Soli számára nagyobb ugrások is lehetségesek).

ugrások egymásutánja: két egyirányu ugrás tilos.

iránytváltoztató ugrások korlátlanul

lehetségesek

lépések: kis és nagy szekund

lépések egymásutánja: egyirányban tilos, irányváltoztatással

két különbözö szekund lehetséges, utána

ugrani kell

ugrások+lépések: mind egyirányban, mind irányváltoztatással

lehetségesek.

Egyirányu ugr.+lép vagy lép.+ugr. után irány-

változtatás kötelezö (azaz ugrás+lép+ugr.

vagy lép.+ugr.+lép. egyirányban tilos)

"holt" intervallumokra mindez nem vonatkozik.

"holt" intervallumok (oktáv kivételével) szabadok

hangismétlés tilos

ugyanazon hangmagasság (vagy oktávtranszp.) lehetöleg ne

térjen egyazon szólamban hamar vissza.

Minimum 3 (egészen kivételesen 2)

más hang kell a visszatérö hang

között feküdjön.

ugyanazon intervallum egymásutánja tilos

ugyanazon intervallum visszatérése 1 közbeiktatott más inter-

vallum után elkerülendö

ugyanazon intervallum visszatérése 2 közbeiktatott más inter-

vallum után megengedett

SZOVEGKEZELES: SZILLABIKUS

"HARMONIA": minimum egy szekund (kis–lehet nagy is) vertikálisan kötelezö,

kivétel: teljes unisono ("csomópontoknál")

kisszek-tritonus (qua-qui-vel) "állóhelyeknél" kivánatos.

oktávák "elrejtendök" (=Avent. 49T- technika)

nyilt oktáva tilos

Example 5.8. Continued

12-HANG-GAZDÁLKODAS: a) lehetöség: reservoir-technika

b) lehetöség: szólam-elosztás-technika.

(az a) lehetöség túlteng).

Notes to the example:

Italics indicate additional handwritten text over the typed sketch

* see Knud Jeppesen, *Counterpoint: The Polyphonic Vocal Style of the Sixteenth Century*, trans. Glen Haydon (New York: Dover Publications, 1992), 160: "In the case of 'dead' intervals (intervals which are found between the final note in one melodic phrase and the initial tone of the next and which are made clear by textual separation), occasionally forbidden intervals can be used, such as the descending sixth, the major sixth, and the sevenths."

** This refers to a method of doubling pitches between the voices and instruments as in the *Allegro appasionata* (mm. 49ff.) of *Aventures* (see chapter 4 and below).

These rules apply most directly to the main choral material in the Dies irae section, Salmenhaara's Type I. The opening vocal parts of this movement, shown in example 5.9, demonstrate almost all the intricacies of these rules in effect. The opening measures demonstrate the handling of steps and leaps, as well as the use and nonrepetition of pitches and intervals. Not only do large leaps predominate, but moreover, while ninths, sevenths, and even sixths occur freely, the tenths, which the rules identify as rare occurrences, do not. In addition, when consecutive seconds occur (e.g., in the opening of the tenor line, and again in the bass at the end of m. 3) they are, in fact, in alternating directions and of different sizes, creating chromatic (012) cells rather than neighboring or scalar patterns. The rules concerning the combination of steps and leaps in various directions are also evident in the opening bars, ensuring a jagged contour to lines by forbidding more than two moves in the same direction.

The rules for consecutive seconds, along with the prohibition of repeated intervals and of leaps in the same direction, work together to prevent most cases in which the same pitch class might occur after one intervening note.[26] Ligeti, however, overprotects against this eventuality, prescribing that ideally there should be at least three intervening notes in a single voice before a return to the same pitch class. The opening measures show a strict observance of this

---

26. Only two allowable formations (a seventh plus a step in the same direction or a ninth plus a step in opposite directions) would be likely to return to the original pitch class after one intervening note. Other formations (a third plus a tenth in opposite directions or a similar combination) would be technically allowable but unlikely, since they involve intervals that are specifically indicated as less common. Any other neighboring or returning figure would have to involve the repetition of an interval or two consecutive leaps in the same direction, both of which are explicitly forbidden.

Example 5.9. Requiem, De die judicii sequentia, mm. 1–7, Copyright © 1965 by Henri Litolff's Verlag. © Revised Edition 2006 by Henri Litolff's Verlag. Used by permission of C.F. Peters Corporation. All Rights Reserved

rule as well. It is common to find the minimum distance of three intervening notes between a pitch and its octave transposition; this occurs at least once in every voice in the first seven measures (see, e.g., m. 4, E♭–D♯ in the bass and C♯–C♯ in the alto). The exceptional distance of two intervening notes occurs only once in this passage (C♯–C♯ in the bass, mm. 4–5). Within a single phrase, though, this rule is never violated, and proximate pitch-class repetitions are consistently deemphasized by using the octave transposition rather than a return at the exact pitch level.

Ligeti's rules for harmony are clearly observable in the opening passage, as well. Example 5.9 shows consistent use of harmonic seconds, an important vestige of Ligeti's cluster-based harmonic language, which he describes here as obligatory or mandatory. The exception is an allowance for unisons at "nodal" points, which can be taken as the beginning of the movement and at points where Type I material returns (e.g., at m. 74, m. 102, and m. 143) or where other significant material types enter (e.g., Type V material in m. 111 and the Type IV chorale entrances in m. 94 and m. 148).[27] One can also observe the preference for seconds and tritones, especially the (016) trichord, embedded in various ways. Harmonic seconds and tritones are evident when the soprano and mezzo move in unison rhythms at the opening. The more specific (016) harmony—one of the first instances of "signal" harmonies[28]—is evident at both of the static points in Example 5.9: it appears in the A–G♯–D♯ and A–G♯–D harmonies in measure 2, and is worked into the harmonies of measures 6–7 as B–B♭–F. A striking melodic instance comes in the mezzo-soprano solo Salva me on C–G♭–F in measure 105.

Ligeti signals are important part of his language, providing consistency to the intervallic profile and general sound within and across works, but in general they are created opportunistically, as a preference rule within the stricter rules of melodic construction of individual voices. This option can be discerned in the wording of Ligeti's rule sheet: the harmonic second is *obligatory* (kötelező), whereas the tritone-and-minor second is *desirable* (kivánatos). The signals, then, are not the main result that the more extensive rules were designed to achieve, but are a sought-after stylistic effect. In the Requiem the (016) works alongside more purely chromatic harmonies and other configurations that the rules permit.

27. Unisons are also used in support of solo passages such as that in the mezzo-soprano, mm. 13–14 (see example 5.10) and again in mm. 24 and 28.

28. The idea of characteristic "Ligeti signals"—recognizable or recurring interval combinations, especially those based on the sets (016) and (025)—goes back to his interviews with Péter Várnai and Josef Häusler (both interviews in *LiC*, 28–31 and 95–98, respectively). This idea is taken up by Jonathan Bernard, with particular reference to *Lux aeterna*, in "Inaudible Structures, Audible Music: Ligeti's Problem, and His Solution," *Music Analysis* 6, no. 3 (1987), 222–28, and especially in his "Voice Leading as a Spatial Function in the Music of Ligeti," *Music Analysis* 13, nos. 2–3 (1994), 227–53, and also by Jane Piper Clendinning, "Contrapuntal Techniques in the Music of György Ligeti" (PhD diss., Yale University, 1989), 20–21, 91–95, 140–42, and 146–51. Miguel Roig-Francolí briefly addresses Ligeti signals in his "Harmonic and Formal Processes in Ligeti's Net-Structure Compositions," *Music Theory Spectrum* 17, no. 2 (Fall 1995), 249–50, n. 20, emphasizing that in Ligeti's music as a whole, "their role should not be overestimated or overstated"—a sentiment with which I generally concur, and find to be in agreement with their introduction in the rules of example 5.8.

The "twelve-tone management" of the sketch is essentially concerned with the completion of aggregates, either by voices collectively (the "reservoir" technique) or in individual voices. This aspect of the composition is also less systematic, as Ligeti clearly prioritizes the rules for individual voices over a preference for equal pitch-class distribution. The tenor's G♯ in measure 2 completes the first aggregate, coinciding exactly with the sustained (016) harmony. This aggregate, however, does not use a completely equal distribution of pitch classes, repeating E between the soprano and tenor and C♯ between the alto and mezzo. Later aggregates have similar repetitions. Ligeti made charts with the notes of the chromatic scale written out vertically, with what appears to be a tallying system stretching out horizontally from each pitch class. These charts, however, often appear to have been reused, marked in different types of pencil or ink, and are hard to match to individual passages. They also appear to allow limited repetitions within aggregates, and thus slightly uneven distributions, so long as no single pitch class is favored.

The solo voices (Salmenhaara's Type II) are permitted more leniency than the choral parts but can still be understood in relation to rules sketched for the main layer. The rule sheet states that solos are permitted larger leaps, and it appears that in practice they are also allowed more license in other ways. The mezzo-soprano solo at measures 12–16 (example 5.10) demonstrates many exceptional features, including consecutive jumps in the same direction, as well as the use of tenths and larger intervals. At times the large leaps exceed the range of one voice, and notes of the melody are traded off between different voices; for example, the text "coget omnes ante thronum" (mm. 36–47) is split between soloists and members of the choir, as marked in the score with connecting lines. This stretches the solo passages to yet more powerful effects, projecting a single line across extreme ranges in a way that begins to transcend any individual voice.

Some of the unisons that support solo passages when they come to rest on a specific pitch (e.g., the instrumental and then choral G♭s in example 5.10 above) have a similarly dramatic effect. These changes in timbre during a single note are a particularly haunting feature of this movement—not only providing an anchor for the soloist's pitch and an opportunity to breathe, but also amplifying the soloist's power, playing with ideas of distance and presence.

Example 5.10. Requiem, De die judicii sequentia, mezzo-soprano solo, mm. 12–16

Example 5.11. Requiem, De die judicii sequentia, soprano and mezzo-soprano duet, mm. 111–15

Along with the melodies that are split between voices, these effects expand the soloist's already demanding line to the territory beyond the capabilities of any individual, in way that is perfectly suited to the terrifying and supernatural character of the text.

The rules from Example 5.8 also apply to passages of Salmenhaara's Type V, with only slight liberties, similar to those seen in the solo parts. One such passage is the duet Ingemisco tamquam reus, mm. 111–15 (Example 5.11), which is continued in different combinations and with numerous interruptions through m. 146.[29] The voice parts here feature the same intervallic repertoire, heavily emphasizing tritones, sixths, sevenths, and ninths in changing directions. The first passage begins at a unison nodal point and then uses these intervals exclusively, never using tenths, but occasionally moving with two leaps in the same direction. Later passages add the option of seconds, including consecutive seconds in changing directions, as in the main layer's choral parts (m. 120 contains several examples in both the female solos and choral bass part). The duet parts, however, tend to adhere more strictly to the larger intervals, with less frequent use of seconds, fourths, and fifths.

If the two-part texture of many of these vocal duets is more sparse—and therefore less consistent in completing aggregates and providing the obligatory harmonic second—the accompanimental figures tend to make up for it with more activity. Throughout the main layer the instruments usually double the vocal parts, although they may split the notes of one vocal line among several instruments, or a single instrument may sometimes combine notes from several vocal parts. This type of accompaniment was featured prominently in

29. With the end point of m. 146, I am including the tenor and bass passage ("confutatis maledictis"). Salmenhaara, *Das musikalische Material*, 161, labels this passage as Type I, presumably on the basis of the participation of both choirs, but the music here, using the combined basses and tenors singing as a two-part texture, resembles the soli duet passages (with occasional participation from choir I) that are labeled as Type V. This similarity also includes the more angular nature of their lines and the accompanimental figures discussed here.

the Allegro Appassionata section of *Aventures* (mm. 49*ff.*), which is referenced directly in Ligeti's rule sheet. In many of the Type I passages, the accompaniment follows the rhythm of the vocal lines precisely (or as precisely as possible, given the difficulties of execution), in accented staccato figures. The harp and cembalo are exceptions; they draw together notes from multiple voice parts and replay them in different rhythms. The Type V passages increase the complexity of the texture by adding legato lines, usually in the flutes and clarinets. For example, the accompaniment for the passage above, the first clarinet draws notes from the soprano solo (B♭–G–E♭–E–D–A♭) and sustains them, creating a legato line with significantly smaller intervals. These lines, then, stand out both from the leaps of the voice parts and the staccato figures in other instruments, creating a different type of counterpoint from the same underlying technique.

Salmenhaara's Type III, derived from ideas found in sketches for the contrasting layers, is a more radically different choral texture, seen in the passages setting Mors stupebit (mm. 35–38, 43–45) and Rex tremendae (mm. 80–92). Here the choir proceeds in unison rhythms, using short notes separated by unpredictable durations and an entirely different kind of voice leading. Both passages feature unusual singing techniques; in the Mors stupebit passage, the choir is sotto voce in an unvoiced half-whisper, which crescendos to full voice. The Rex tremendae passage reverses this direction; the choir begins practically screaming at *ffff*, though still in singing voice, and decrescendos back to a sotto voce whisper.

The voice leading for both passages is deliberately awkward; it features regular voice overlaps from one chord to the next and no sense of holding tones in common. The first section features ten-note chords with no doubled pitches; the second builds from smaller chords including doubled pitches to the same kind of ten-note chord found in the first. Ligeti planned these sections from a more regular state, which he then worked to destabilize. Example 5.12 is a transcription of the uppermost voice in these two passages, where the most regularity can be found. The original sketch works out all of the vocal parts on separate staves and groups the passage into fours, reflecting the rhyme scheme and two-footed trochaic meter of the original Latin text. The upper voices reinforce this with a regular four-note pattern. Mors stupebit repeats a note and then ascends

Example 5.12. Requiem, De die judicii sequentia, melody lines for the Type III passages

twice by semitone, repeating the pattern up a whole step in the next two bars, and finally accelerates the pattern to pure chromatic motion in bar 4. The Rex tremendae passage is an inversion of this pattern resembling the descending Lamento motif found frequently in Ligeti's works. The reference to this stock bass line may reinforce the connection to earlier musical traditions, in particular the speculative connection to Handel's *Utrecht Te Deum*. The Utrecht Chorus is mentioned in sketches for the contrasting layers, connecting it to the *a cappella*, almost-whispering vocal style seen here. Moreover, the Lamento topic occurs quite conspicuously in one brief section of the *Utrecht Te Deum* (movement III, m. 15), which features a shift to an *a cappella* texture with prevalent dissonances, a highly chromatic bass line descending from tonic to dominant, and the à propos words "when thou hadst overcome the sharpness of death."

In the score the regular metric groupings are greatly distorted by a rhythmic technique similar to the one Ligeti used in arranging the vocal entrances of the Kyrie movement. In a sketch for the Rex tremendae, Ligeti writes out a series of numbers (i.e., 1, 1.16, 1.33, 1.5, 1.66, 2, continuing up to 5) standing for approximate durations (.5 = an eighth-note duration, .33 = a triplet, 1.16 = two triplets plus an eighth, and so on). He then reorders this list into the interonset intervals between the syllables in the text. Starting with the syllable "-men," after the fermata and return to tempo in measure 85, these follow as 3.33, 1.16, 2.5, 1, 2.33, 2, 4.16, .5, 2.66, 1.33, 5, 3.33, and 1.66. By this process, which once again emphasizes nonrepetition, what was developed as a highly regular pattern becomes irregular, unpredictable, and well suited to the chaotic nature of the movement.

Ligeti's other contrasting layer, which Salmenhaara assigns to Type IV, has its origins in a softer, smoother *a cappella* texture, described in part as an "'infinite' space" ("végtelen" tér) and an animated, many-voiced counterpoint (Mozgalmas, sokszólamu kontrapunktika). Later in the sketches Ligeti depicts this as "tranquil surfaces" (nyugodt felületek) and a "choral web" (Korusszövevény) expressing "pleading, complete despair" (kérlelés, teljes elkeseredés). These descriptions match the texts and musical characters of the two instances of Type IV: the Salva me section (mm. 94–100) and the Oro supplex section that closes the movement (148–58). These are both sustained chorale textures, exclusively in women's voices, and written in a kind of free counterpoint, where voices contribute to cluster-based harmonies. They all feature the mandatory second, as seen in other sections of the Requiem, but without the imitative relationships between individual voices found in the Kyrie or later in *Lux aeterna*.

The chorales' organization in terms of rhythm and pitch resembles that of the Introitus—a variety of free counterpoint that is a feature of many of Ligeti's later works, as well, including movements of the *Ten Pieces for Wind Quintet* (1968). Sketches for the blocks of the Introitus suggest a compositional progression from registral motion to more definite pitch relationships (especially the entrance and exit points), and then to a working out of specific progressions in individual voices, in order to maneuver from point A to point B, while keeping a dense cluster present in the texture. Both of the chorales have similarly distinct registral profiles, begining in unison and expanding outwards, as can be seen in examples 5.13a and 5.13b, which present range graphs of the sections. Each chorale adds pitches below and above the starting point in rough alternation. Initially the new pitches do not stray more than a whole tone away from previous pitches, though this practice becomes less regular as the chorale progresses. Salva me is more loosely constructed, with more gaps in the cluster, allowing for wider spacing as long as there is at least one vertical second present in the sonority. Oro supplex is more consistent; there is almost never a gap of more than a major second anywhere in the

Example 5.13a. Requiem, De die judicii sequentia, range graph of the chorale Salva me

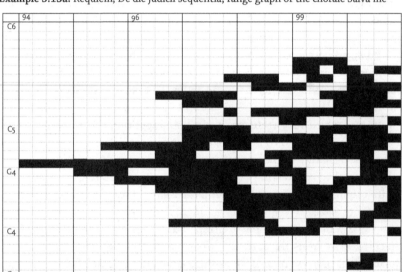

Example 5.13b. Requiem, De die judicii sequentia, range graph of the chorale Oro supplex

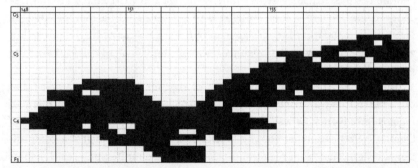

mass of voices. Oro supplex is also remarkable in the way individual voices replace one another within the same beat to ensure the near-constant presence of individual pitches and the possibility of directing the contour into a more intricate shape, spiraling down and then up. For example, soprano 3 is the first voice to introduce F♯ at the very end of m. 148, beat 4, and as soon as soprano 3 leaves this note, in m. 149, beat 2, sopranos 2 and 4 each move to cover this note within a fraction of the beat. Although the registral expansion of these passages resembles the polyphony of the Kyrie and Christe melodies, this free counterpoint has a very different effect. Within the gradual motion of the registral block, the more tenuous connections between these independent melodies, passing notes between different voices, produce a kind of internal flickering of the individual note changes—something that captures a sense of fragility, in contrast to the powerful tumult of the main layer.

Lacrimosa

Compared to the other movements of the Requiem, the Lacrimosa is brief and somewhat austere. Ligeti described this final movement as a type of epilogue, "like a look back at the previous musical events, distantly removed in time and space."[30] The Lacrimosa seems to complete both the registral motion from low to high and the sense of dissolving into traces that Ligeti envisioned for the longer version of the Requiem. The reduced means of this movement, featuring treble instruments and using only a small ensemble with the soprano and mezzo soloists, contributes to this sense of dissolution, but the reduction in complexity also helps uncover structural features of the previous movements.

Ligeti provides some clues to the relationship between the pitch material of the Kyrie and the Lacrimosa, stating that "moreover, the same arrangement of intervals—although frustrated in one or another ordering and in transformed variations—shapes the foundation for the harmony of the 'Lacrimosa' movement."[31] In fact, the opening wind parts unfold a chromatic cluster, expanding outward to fill a tritone in a vaguely familiar way. The order of pitches introduced in the flute and piccolos follows an exact transposition of the start of the Christe row: F♯–F–E–G–E♭–D–A♭. The following passage, adding the oboes, follows the pattern G♯–A–G–B–B♭–C. This rearrangement corresponds to an inversion of the Kyrie row's first hexachord. Moreover, the pervasive

---

30. *GS*, 2:231: "Der 'Lacrimosa'-Satz ist wie ein in Zeit und Raum weit entfernter Rückblick auf das vorherige musikalische Geschehen."

31. Ibid.: "Zudem bildet dieselbe Intervallanordnung, allerdings in einer von anderen Ordnungen durchkreuzten und umgewandelten Variante, die Grundlage für die Harmonik des 'Lacrimosa'-Satzes."

chromatic motion and boundary interval of a tritone recall the primary intervallic features of the Sequentia movement.

From this starting point the movement can be seen as a series of variations, each spreading out from isolated F♯s: first in the flutes in measure 2, and then in the voices in measures 20, 36, and 47. The first vocal entrance follows the pattern of the flutes, but with more internal repetition of pitches, and ultimately settling on the tritone B–F rather than D–A♭. Each of the subsequent entrances expands outward in a slightly different way, having the sense of a return to the beginning, even while losing touch with the initial presentation—the type of dissolution indicated in the verbal sketch. With internal repetitions and reorderings the specifics of the original version become more and more vague, and yet the essential features emerge more clearly. Ligeti described this as a "'deciphering' of the harmony of the previous movements: intervallic and harmonic constellations, which to some extent were present underground—embedded in the musical structure—become apparent in the 'Lacrimosa.'"[32] Each variation crystallizes one of the aspects of the original interval signal, using highly chromatic motion to come to rest on tritones (B–F in m. 28, A–E♭ in m. 42), perfect fifths (G–D in m. 41, D–A in m. 51), or octaves (A♭ in m. 43, B♭ in m. 55). A sustained major second (E♭–F in m. 31) is the only significantly emphasized interval not found in the (016) signal, but this is still consistent with the more general harmonic language of the piece.

After the chaos and complexity of the preceding movements, the transfigured material here does not suggest a perfect resolution or triumph over death, but rather the relief of a distanced perspective. No longer are we in the midst of the tumoil, swept up in the flow of the Kyrie or caught in the wild, unpredictable upheaval of the Dies irae; the slow tempo and sparse texture place us at an objective distance, watching from outside and turning over the previous events critically in our minds. Given the multiple purposes that the Requiem served for Ligeti, as a turning point in his life and career, an overly simple or unambiguous resolution would never satisfy, and if the resulting Lacrimosa is austere, at times bleak, it is also, in its own way, transcendent.

LUX AETERNA

Lux aeterna, composed just a year after the completion of the Requiem, is a free-standing piece but in many ways also a continuation of the project,

32. *GS*, 2: 231–32: "Vor allem aber durch die 'Entschlüsselung' der Harmonik der vorhergehenden Sätze: Intervallische und harmonische Konstellationen, die vorher gewissermassen unterirdisch—eingebettet in die musikalische Struktur—vorhanden waren, werden im 'Lacrimosa' offenbar.

stemming from the original seven-movement plan for the Requiem. The work develops the canonic pitch techniques from the Kyrie movement of the Requiem but does so with greater deference to the interval signals found in the Dies irae and the Lacrimosa. It also initiates a more precise control of rhythmic regularity, ensuring a smooth and seamless surface ideally suited to the movement's text. In fact, the opening of this movement, pairing *a cappella* women's voices with this rhythmic calm, seems perfectly in line with the registral plan of the Requiem itself, associating a move from low to high with the conceptual progression from darkness to eternal light.

This well-known work consists of three "microcanons"[33] linked by two brief passages in the basses (both on the word "*domine*"). These canonic "melodies" fulfill the requirement to include harmonic seconds, as seen in movements of the Requiem, but they allow for more use of the major second, resulting in moments of diatonic emphasis and a focus on the (025) interval signal, rather than the (016) of the Requiem.[34] The melodies (shown in examples 5.14a–c) do not generally introduce notes farther than a major second away from the previous notes of the canon, notes likely to be sustained in other voices, thus ensuring the presence of a harmonic second. The only exception is in the short canon using the *Requiem aeternam* text. While the sopranos introduce B♭—a major third away from D, the closest note already introduced—the altos provide the second by sustaining C as part of the trichord G–B♭–C, a (025) trichord that they keep in play throughout the section, apart from any canonic material. As in the Requiem, this kind of interval signal is emphasized in various ways through the course of the composition, including moments in both the linking passages (e.g., the first bass entrance in m. 37, on F♯–A–B) and within

33. The use of this term follows Clendinning, "Contrapuntal Techniques," and Jane Piper Clendinning, "Structural Factors in the Microcanonic Compositions of György Ligeti," in *Concert Music, Rock, and Jazz since 1945: Essays and Analytical Studies*, ed. Elizabeth West Marvin and Richard Hermann, 229–56 (Rochester NY: University of Rochester Press, 1995). Other analytical literature discussing the work includes Jan Jarvlepp, "Pitch and Texture Analysis of Ligeti's Lux Aeterna," *ex tempore* 2, no. 1 (1982), 16–32, accessed through http://www.ex-tempore.org/jarvlepp/jarvlepp.htm, March 12, 2012; Herman Sabbe, "Techniques médiévales en musique contemporaine: Histoire de la musique et sens culturel," *Revue belge de Musicologie* 34–35 (1980–81), 220–33; Clytus Gottwald, "*Lux aeterna*: Ein Beitrag zur Kompositionstechnik György Ligetis," *Musica* 25, no. 1 (1971), 12–17; and Jonathan Bernard, "Voice Leading as a Spatial Function."

34. The importance of diatonic moments in both *Lux aeterna* and *Lontano* has given rise to many interesting interpretations, among them the mathematical approach to *Lux aeterna* found in Ian Quinn, "A Unified Theory of Chord Quality in Equal Temperaments" (PhD diss., Eastman School of Music, 2004), 100*ff.*, and Amy Bauer, who posits in *Ligeti's Laments: Nostalgia, Exoticism, and the Absolute* (Burlington, VT: Ashgate, 2011), 96, that "the essential paradigm consonance-dissonance-consonance is re-written [in *Lontano*] as diatonic-chromatic-diatonic."

Example 5.14a. *Lux aeterna*, canon 1, "Lux aeterna," sopranos and altos, mm. 1–37

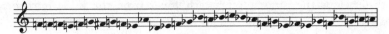

Example 5.14b. *Lux aeterna*, canon 2a, "Cum sanctis tuis," tenors, mm. 39–46 (basses join at m. 46); canon 2b, "Requiem aeternam," sopranos, mm. 61–79

Example 5.14c. *Lux aeterna*, canon 3, "Et lux perpetua," altos, mm. 90–119

the canons. Melodic statements can be found, for example, in the progressions F–E♭–A♭, B♭–A♭–F, and F–B♭–G, notes 9–11, 20–22, and 28–30, respectively, of canon 1, but also come from nonconsecutive notes, as in the final section's B–A–F♯/G♭, where notes 6, 10, and 15 from the third alto's melodic statement are reinforced by coordinated and sustained entrances in the sopranos and tenors (mm. 94–100).

Much of Ligeti's sketch work had to do with the rhythmic organization of this piece, which systematizes principles of nonrepetition and variety that began to emerge in the Requiem. As in earlier movements, each voice part uses one of three rhythmic strands (sextuplets, quintuplets, and sixteenth notes), which are rotated through the voice parts in a regular and symmetrical pattern. Other analyses of *Lux aeterna* have noted as much but generally relegate any further discussion of rhythm to the idea of an "elastic talea"[35] or to an analogy with Ockeghem's *Missa Prolationum*. The talea principle, however, turns out to be a very loose ideal, and the strict rules that Ligeti uses in this piece are of a very different sort.

Example 5.15a shows a page in the sketches where the composer has planned out the opening section of the piece. His sketch includes the text, the note names connected with each syllable, and a list of letter names that stand for rhythmic ideas. Specifically, each letter name refers to the exact

---

35. See Gottwald, "*Lux aeterna*," Jarvlepp, "Pitch and Texture Analysis," and Sabbe, "Techniques médiévales,"who all use this wording. See also Levy, "Rules as Strict as Palestrina's," for discussion of how Ligeti's own words may have led analysts to seek out a duration-based talea, rather than the time-point modules that are evident from the sketches.

point within the quarter-note beat at which a note will change. Example 5.15b is derived from another page of the sketches (omitting several scratched-out drafts and extraneous material), which associates these letter names with specific rhythmic modules.[36] These show Ligeti's preference for using retrograde-symmetrical pairings of beat divisions (e.g., ♪. + ♪, reversed to ♪ + ♪.) and his care in avoiding the duplication of any individual time point in different strands (which could have occurred in the sixteenth-note and sextuplet strands, for example, on the beat or halfway through it).

The circles, triangles, and boxes around these letters are a refined system of tallying the number of times each letter is used, as explained in example 5.15c.[37] We have seen Ligeti use simple hash-mark tallying, starting with *Artikulation* and *Apparitions*. Here, however, the tallying system is applied to time points rather than durations, and instead of a product-based distribution, Ligeti clearly favors an equal distribution of these divisions of the beat.[38]

Throughout the opening section, then, these modules are distributed as evenly as possible. In the sextuplet divisions (labeled wxyz; see example 5.15b) each letter occurs 7 to 9 times in the voices S1, S4, and A3, and each letter occurs 24 times total in the section, with the exception of w, which occurs 25 times. The quintuplet divisions (mnop) have a similar distribution, occurring 7 to 9 times in each voice (S2, A1, A4) and 25 times each in the total, with the exception of n, which occurs 24 times. The sixteenth-note divisions (abcd, in S3 and A2) are less regular, as Ligeti seems reluctant to use d—a note change that would fall on the conductor's beat—as often as the others. These totals are given in example 5.16, along with the distributions for the remaining canons of the piece.

These rhythmic modules show more evidence of statistical-serial thought in their preference for symmetry and equal distribution, but they are not

36. Pierre Michel, *György Ligeti: Compositeur d'aujourd'hui* (Paris: Minerve, 1985), 205, shows these modules, although he omits module "d" and does not specify details of their use. Similarly, Herman Sabbe's *György Ligeti: Studien zur kompositorischen Phänomenologie*, (Munich: Edition Text + Kritik, 1987), 22, briefly mentions the quintuplet divisions (identified as 1+4, 2+3, 3+2, 4+1), noting their balance but none of the more systematic treatment that follows.

37. Example 5.15c is not a transcription of sketch materials but, rather, a key devised by the author to explain the symbols.

38. It is intriguing that this shift to thinking about time points occurred in about the summer of 1964, when Ligeti and Milton Babbitt were both instructors at Darmstadt, and to consider that this shift might have been the result of hearing (or hearing about) Babbitt's lectures "The Structure of Musical Systems." See Amy Beal, *New Music, New Allies: American Experimental Music in West Germany from the Zero Hour to Reunification* (Berkeley: University of California Press, 2006), 138ff., for more on Babbitt's presence at Darmstadt. Given Ligeti's secrecy about his working methods and his antagonism to Babbitt's strict serial methods, it is hard to substantiate this speculation with any statements by the composer himself, and the method of working with time points that Ligeti developed is, of course, quite different from Babbitt's use of time-point rows.

Example 5.15a. *Lux aeterna*, sketch of canon 1. Reproduced with kind permission from the György Ligeti Collection of the Paul Sacher Foundation, Basel

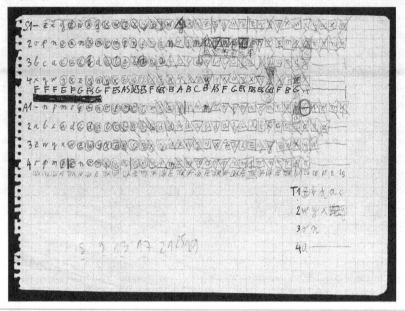

Example 5.15b. *Lux aeterna*, rhythmic modules

Example 5.15c. *Lux aeterna*, graphic tallying system

      1) First time a module is used: simple letter name,

      2) Second time: circled letter

      3) Third time: circled twice

      4) Fourth time: circled twice with a slash

      5) Fifth time: triangle pointing upwards

      6) Sixth time: triangle pointing downwards

      7) Seventh time: square

      8) Eighth time: square with a slash

      9) Ninth time: square with an X

serially arranged; there are no systematic permutations or ordering schemes. Rather than retrogrades or inversions of basic orderings of these modules, their arrangement seems to reflect the "varietas" principle Ligeti found in Ockeghem and emulated in the Kyrie of the Requiem. The principle of variety is an important driving force, from the initial investigation of a wide number

Example 5.16. *Lux aeterna*, distribution of rhythmic modules

Canon 1 (Soprano and Alto, "Lux aeterna," mm. 1–37)

	a	b	c	d	m	n	o	p	w	x	y	z
S1									9	8	8	9
S2					9	8	9	9				
S3	9	9	9	4								
S4									7	8	9	7
A1					8	9	8	8				
A2	9	7	9	8								
A3									9	8	7	8
A4					8	7	8	8				

Sums:

18	16	18	12	25	24	25	25	25	24	24	24

With Tenors:

20	17	19	13	25	25	26	25	26	25	26	25

Canon 2 (Tenors, "Cum sanctis tuis," mm. 39–88)

	a	b	c	d	m	n	o	p	w	x	y	Z
T1	8	9	10	6								
T2									8	8	8	9
T3					8	8	9	8				
T4	8	10	9	5								

Sums:

16	19	19	11	8	8	9	8	8	8	8	9

With other voices including Basses (joining the canon at m. 46), Sopranos (Canon 2b, mm. 61–79), and Altos (using non-canonic material, mm. 61-79):

28	28	32	17	20	20	21	21	29	23	25	27

Canon 3 (Altos, "Et lux perpetua," mm. 90–119)

	a	b	c	d	m	n	o	p	w	X	y	z
A1					6	6	7	6				
A2	7	6	7	5								
A3									7	4	6	7
A4					6	5	5	6				

Sums:

7	6	7	5	12	11	12	12	7	4	6	7

With other voices, emphasizing the (025) interval signal:

7	7	7	6	12	11	12	12	7	5	7	7

Total of all independent entries

Including all of the above along with linking phrases (Basses, "Domine," mm. 37-39, 87-90):

a	b	c	d	m	n	o	p	w	x	y	z
55	54	58	38	57	56	59	58	62	54	58	59

Example 5.17. *Lux aeterna*, draft of the score showing rhythmic calculations. Reproduced with kind permission from the György Ligeti Collection of the Paul Sacher Foundation, Basel

of rhythmic modules in *Atmosphères* and *Aventures* to their refined use in parts of the Requiem (in particular, the Christe melodies and the Type IV chorales of the Sequentia). In the Requiem, varietas seems to have been based on the nonrepetition of durations, usually calculated as eighth notes or tuplets within each rhythmic strand; in *Lux aeterna*, it is based on the time-point modules and involves elements of limited repetition and the higher demand of equal distribution. In this new system we can begin to uncover more stringent rules in use: modules are not used by different voices in the same beat— that is to say, different voices do not change together—and though modules may be repeated, there rarely are more than two consecutive occurrences in the same voice.[39]

This method also allowed Ligeti to work directly on the score as shown in example 5.17, which comes from a manuscript draft.[40] We can see Ligeti employ the same system of tallying. The letters and symbols, which were written in green ink over the notes of the draft, would have given him the flexibility to make detailed adjustments to the musical surface that might not be foreseeable in the abstract plan, while still keeping track of the tally to ensure an equal distribution.

Besides adhering to the rules governing the use of rhythmic modules, Ligeti was also concerned with another type of constraint: the rate of change from

39. Levy, "Rules as Strict as Palestrina's," discusses some of the exceptions found in the piece in greater depth.

40. In my 2013 article (ibid.), I reported that the draft of the score with these markings was incomplete, but the missing pages have since been recovered and reunited with the rest of the draft housed at the Paul Sacher Foundation in Basel.

beat to beat, which he calculated in red ink at the bottom of each system of the score. He counted the number of modules used in each beat (i.e., the number of note changes including syllable changes on the same pitch), and throughout *Lux aeterna* the rate of change is consistently within the range of plus or minus one from beat to beat. So if there are three note changes in one beat, the next can have two, three, or four, but not one or five. This is a way of ensuring a smooth surface without any sudden changes or bursts of activity, and something we can take as another important compositional principle, crystallizing in the counterpoint of this piece. Moreover, no more than four note changes occur in any one beat, setting a maximum level of activity for the work. By balancing this concern for rate of change with his distributional scheme for avoiding periodicity and mixing beat divisions, Ligeti arrived at the essential features of rhythm in the mature form of this style of counterpoint. Balancing the vertical harmonic constraint of clusterlike, secundally weighted sonorities there is a horizontal constraint: a certain number of voices can and must change from one beat to the next, but those voices must do so with respect for a global balance of time points, and also with respect for the harmonic criteria.

Lux aeterna marks an important point in the development of Ligeti's rhythmic technique, but its significance is not merely one of compositional craft. Ligeti often scorned what he, joining Adorno, labeled as a fetish of technique, and he despised the logical-positivist attitudes that celebrated compositional system-making for its own sake.[41] Though Ligeti reused ideas from *Lux aeterna* in later pieces, and references to the "Lux technique" (Lux-technika) occur in sketches for later pieces including the Cello Concerto, String Quartet no. 2, and *Ramifications*, these methods had their origins in expressive goals, realizing compositional structures that he felt other contemporary techniques could not. In his articles for *Die Reihe* he advocated a type of composition that moved away from both the reliance on chance found

41. See György Ligeti, "Pierre Boulez: Decision and Automatism in Structure 1a," trans. Leo Black, in *Young Composers: Die Reihe* 4, English ed., 36–62. Bryn Mawr, PA: Presser; London: Universal Edition, 1960), 39–40: "What is unorganic is this pointless transplantation of a system; note-qualities labelled with numbers, the dematerialised numbers organised into tables, and the tables finally used like a fetish;" and György Ligeti, "Metamorphoses of Musical Form," trans. Cornelius Cardew. *Form—Space: Die Reihe* 7, English ed., 5–19, (Bryn Mawr, PA: Presser, 1965), 10: "The primitive stage to which composition is relegated by the automatism will only be supported by musicians who succumb to the fetish of total integration . . . . Adorno's negative diagnosis may well apply to such musicians (but not to the elite who pursue their thoughts further)." Ligeti cites Adorno's "Das Altern der Neuen Musik;" see *Dissonanzen; Einleitung in die Musiksoziologie*, Gesammelte Schriften 14, ed. Rolf Tiedemann, 143–67 (Frankfurt: Suhrkamp, 1973); translated as "The Aging of the New Music" in Theodor W. Adorno, *Essays on Music*, ed. Richard Leppert, trans. by Susan H. Gillespie, et al., 181–202 (Berkeley: University of California Press, 2002).

in Cage, and the "decision and automatism" of *Structures Ia*, noting that both of these methods tended to result in structures Ligeti described as "event—pause—event—pause, etc."[42] Instead he advocated an approach to composition in which the "serial preformation of the global determining factors" is followed by "filling out by detailed decisions the network of possibilities that is the result of the first phase."[43] By doing so, he felt, the composer could limit automatic predetermination while having rigorous control of moment-by-moment events, which in turn helped the purposeful deployment of different musical characters. Ligeti's concern for statistical balancing left the ordering of modules free and resulted in a seamless musical texture—a consistent musical character that fit the expression of eternity implied by the text and also demonstrated an undeniable contrast to the stop-and-start textures of many of his contemporaries. By composing with primary attention on the rate of change and balance of rhythmic strands and time points, Ligeti worked with perceptible criteria, corresponding to features such as density, smoothness, and freely ametric flow of time. If the Kyrie was a response to *Structures Ia* at the level of form, then *Lux aeterna* was a response at the level of the musical surface.

LONTANO

Lontano is an instrumental variant, or expansion, of the basic techniques developed in *Lux aeterna*; Ligeti even called the two "sister compositions."[44] He further stated that "the harmonic and polyphonic technique harkens back partly to the Lacrimosa movement of the Requiem and to *Lux aeterna*, yet the compositional questions and answers here are completely different: the quality of tone color switches over to the quality of harmony, and harmonic-polyphonic metamorphoses gain the appearance of tone-color transformations."[45]

Indeed, the technical workings and structure of the pieces are nearly identical. Both consist of three micropolyphonic canons with interposed linking phrases. Moreover, as Richard Steinitz has observed,[46] the canons

42. Ligeti, "Metamorphoses," 10.
43. Ibid., 11.
44. Ligeti, "Auf dem Weg zu *Lux aeterna*," originally in *Österreichische Musikzeitschrift* 24, no. 2 (1969), 82–88, reprinted in *GS*, 2:239: "einem Schwesterwerk von *Lux aeterna*."
45. *GS*, 2:245: "Die harmonische und polyphone Technik greift teilweise auf den 'Lacrimosa'-Satz aus dem *Requiem* und auf *Lux aeterna* zurück, doch sind die kompositorischen Fragestellungen und Lösungen hier ganz anders: Die Qualität Klangfarbe schlägt um in die Qualität Harmonik, harmonisch-polyphone Verwandlungen erhalten den Anschein von Klangfarbentransformationen."
46. See Steinitz, *Ligeti*, 154–58, building on observations from Michel, *Ligeti*, 84ff. The additional observation on the origin of the first ten notes of Canon 2 is my own.

Example 5.18a. *Lontano,* canon 1, mm. 1–41

Example 5.18b. *Lontano,* canon 2, mm. 57–111

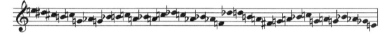

Example 5.18c. *Lontano,* canons 3a and 3b, mm. 122–45

of *Lontano,* shown in examples 5.18a–c, are adapted from those of *Lux aeterna.* The first canon of *Lontano* corresponds to the first of *Lux aeterna* transposed up a minor third. The first ten notes of *Lontano'*s second canon correspond to the prior work's canon 2b, transposed down a minor third; the continuation, notes 10–20 and 24–36, correspond to *Lux aeterna'*s canon 3, transposed up a minor ninth. The final canon of the orchestral piece is based on the earlier work's canon 2a. Here, however, the last few notes are left off (although in one sketch the parallel continuation, C♯–E–D♯–B–C♯, is left in, and some of these notes are, indeed, prominent at the end of the piece; see below). Moreover, like *Lux aeterna'*s canon 2a and 2b, *Lontano'*s canon 3 is split into two parts, the second carried by the upper voices starting at letter Y (m. 127). This upper-voice canon is the inversion of the beginning of the lower-voice canon, and sketch material originally worked out the complete inversion of the melody, which was then excerpted to create the final version.

These melodies, however, are only the basic framework for *Lontano,* and the expanded resources of the orchestra, which rest on this technical construction, allow the effects that Ligeti described above: blurring the lines of these melodies into a sense of harmony, texture, and timbre, and pointing to a different sort of expressive effect. The instrumental forces of *Lontano* behave quite differently from the *a cappella* voices of *Lux aeterna.* Most notably, the

The separation of the first ten notes of this canon is also significant in the layout of other sketches for *Lontano* (see below).

melodic strands in *Lontano* are no longer identical with instrumental voices. Some instruments join in for only part of the melody, to color particular segments of the line. For example, the flutes, who take the lead in the opening of the piece, sustain the first 9 notes of the melody in measures 1–13. The oboes then take notes 10 and 11 in measures 13–14, before the flutes pick up with note 12 and the following notes at letter B (m. 14). When the flutes return they are an octave higher and double the cellos, who play sul tasto tremolos, adding noise to the sound mass. Meanwhile, horns 1–3 start notes 15–19 before the flutes, who formerly led the canon, have reached these notes. Other instrumental groups operate similarly, adding octave doublings or tremolos and from time to time splitting the canonic line into segments, skewing the order of which instruments lead and follow. These ways of recasting the line make the basic melody significantly less clear than in *Lux aeterna*, adding a sense of plasticity to the temporal flow of the work such that an individual moment could be heard as an echo of an idea already stated or as a premonition of one about to occur.[47]

Sometimes instruments from different families are coordinated in rhythm and in pitch, either in unison or octaves, as a way of changing the tone color of the line, making it seem at times brighter or more subdued, blended or more individuated, and not only stratifying the individual canonic melodies but giving an internal diversity, life, and shape to the voices themselves. In each canon, the different timbres and registers grow through different peaks of brightness (created by octave doublings and the registration of individual instruments), peaks of noise content (created by tremolos, or surface noise in speedier attacks), and peaks of dynamic levels and density. Each section has a similar overall shape, swelling and receding, increasing complexity in each of these independent parameters. The particulars of how each canon unfolds in these areas, however—as in the multivalent forms of *Atmosphères* and *Volumina*—are coordinated differently, making the shapes intuitively similar yet nebulously varied in their details.

The approach to rhythm is also very important to producing these effects, and again, is similar to the system developed in *Lux aeterna*, with a few slight changes that make use of the expanded resources of the orchestra. Sketches, including charts similar to example 5.15a, above, exist for all three of the canons of *Lontano*, and they show the same use of rhythmic modules, abcd, mnop, and wxyz, as well as the same system of circles and other shapes for

47. Many of these complications account for differences in the way I represent the basic melody and similar representations in Bruce Reiprich, "Transformation of Coloration and Density in György Ligeti's *Lontano*," *Perspectives of New Music* 16, no. 2 (Spring–Summer 1978), 167–80, esp. 169; Clendinning, "Contrapuntal Techniques," 2:28, and Steinitz, *Ligeti*, 156–57. My melodies are synthesized from sketch materials, including pages of charts (similar to those for *Lux aeterna* in example 5.15a) and also notation in the margin of a draft of the score.

Example 5.19. *Lontano*, rate of change across instrumental groups, mm. 11–12, 133–36

m. 11

Flutes	2	1	1	2	1	1	1	0
Clar/Ob	0	1	1	0	1	0	0	0
Violins	0	0	0	0	0	1	1	2
Basses	0	0	1	2	2	1	0	1
Sum	2	2	3	4	4	3	2	3

m. 133

Violins	2	1	2	3	2	2	2	1	1	1	1	2	1	0	0	1
Violas	1	1	0	0	0	1	0	1	1	1	0	0	1	1	1	0
Sum	3	2	2	3	2	3	2	2	2	2	1	2	2	1	1	1

tabulating their near-equal use.[48] Drafts of the score also show Ligeti monitoring the number of modules used in each beat, to ensure a regular rate of change.

Lontano uses the same approach to rhythmic organization found in *Lux aeterna*, but the particulars of the opening are different; though the pitch sequence is borrowed directly, the rhythm is composed anew. There is evidence from both the score and sketches that Ligeti was calculating the rate of change separately at first, within instrumental groups, and then summed together across the whole orchestra. At letter A, where the texture becomes more complex, each individual strand obeys the same succession rules used in *Lux aeterna*, but moreover, when the sums are calculated the whole texture also obeys the same principles, as shown in example 5.19, which tabulates the number of note changes per beat in each instrumental part separately, then totals them. In a draft (similar to the draft of *Lux aeterna*, reproduced as example 5.17 above) for part of the third canon (around m. 133), Ligeti shows calculations for rate of change in both the violins (carrying the upper canon) and violas (carrying the lower canon) separately and then sums them in a similar way.

One can see how this expansion of technique allows Ligeti to compose smooth transitions from one timbre to another by shifting activity from one

---

48. The calculations on which I base my claim of near-equal use are based on the charts, scanned in the Sacher Collection as Images 11 (corresponding to canon 2, note 10 and following); Image 12 (canon 1 plus the first ten notes of canon 2); and Image 13 (canons 3a and 3b). The totals for each sheet (abcd/mnop/wxyz) are as follows. Image 12: 36, 38, 32, 33 / 41, 41, 43, 41 / 40, 42, 42, 42. Image 13: 23, 24, 20, 18 / 16, 16, 17, 17 / 17, 17, 18, 18. There are a few modifications in the score, but its basis in these sketches is also quite clear. Moreover, the sketch for the final canon shows the clear conception of canon 3a as four-part polyphony and canon 3b as an eight-part canon, both of which are given diverse instrumentations, whereas other canons are mixed into specific instrumental blocks from an earlier stage in the sketching.

instrumental group to another within the texture, and without creating dramatic changes in the rhythmic density of the overall texture. Measure 74, for example, concentrates activity in the more distinct timbres of the brass instruments, allowing them to carry the fragment Bb–Ab–F—a (025) interval signal—in a way that is slightly foregrounded, coming through as a brighter, less blended, and so a more purely melodic statement starting to emerge from the texture.[49]

The linking phrases are also expansions of those found in *Lux aeterna*, showing more complexity, as well as the tendency to blend together with the main canons more organically than those in the choral work. As in *Lux aeterna*, they are generally in the low register, but the orchestra has more available resources and more extremes in this register than does the choir. The orchestral sections also have more motion and go through a greater variety of configurations. In addition to the (025) signals, however, *Lontano* also employs the tritone and (016), as in the Requiem, and other sets as well. The first linking phrase expands from a sustained unison C (the last note of canon 1), moving through the entire aggregate before settling on the tritone E–Bb. The E then holds over to start the next canon, while the lower voices creep down from Bb through A and G to rejoin the main canonic melody mid-stream (shortly after letter K), weaving both notes of the interval signal into the subsequent canonic melody. The second linking phrase blends even more seamlessly into canon 3, moving from a three-note chromatic cluster to a (025) signal (D–F–G) at letter W. This signal is sustained into canons 3a and 3b, which take the signal's D and G as their respective starting notes. This upper canon eventually settles on a bare D♯ in the highest register (ca. bar 137), which Ligeti has compared to a beam of light breaking through distant clouds in a painting by Altdorfer (*The Battle of Alexander*).[50] As both canons take their starting notes from the deep register of the original linking phrase and proceed to this high focal point, the integration of linking phrases and canonic material, along with the expanded resources of the orchestra, produces a marvelous play with register, time, imaginary perspective, and spatial effect.

Lontano also integrates canonic and noncanonic material in other ways, leading to a more unified whole. The passage in the brass mentioned above prefigures the use of (025)s in the linking sections by bringing them out more melodically. Conversely, at other moments canonic notes are articulated together as a chord, more in the manner of signal harmonies. On the second beat of measure 77, for example, several instruments begin a fragment on C (as note 15 of canon 2); along with this, however, the flutes play sustained Es and the third trumpet adds an A, subtly introducing a minor triad into the texture, although this is more likely to be heard as lending a kind of acoustic resonance to the sound mass than as having tonal associations. A similar event

49. Ligeti discusses this passage with Häusler in *LiC*, 98.
50. *LiC*, 92–93.

occurs just five measures later, with the notes C–E–F, (015). The ending also provides an example of the integration of canonic and noncanonic material. Sketches originally listed canon 3 as continuing after the final D to include the notes C♯–E–D♯–B–C♯, which trace the rest of the *Lux aeterna* melody on which it is based. Many of these notes are compressed into signal-like chords in the low register that end the work in a manner similar to the linking phrases: the C♯s are sustained from before, E occurs in the basses in measure 158, supported by G and C in the manner of a signal harmony, this time making a rare major triad. D♯ and B follow in measure 160, and the clarinets add C♯ to notes previously sustained to form the final B–C♯–D (013) trichord, which ends the piece.

Ligeti suggested that despite their similarities in technique, *Lontano* and *Lux aeterna* involved different kinds of compositional exploration. Moving out of the religious context of the Requiem text and the expression of spiritual eternity, *Lontano*'s title implies a concern with the effects of distance—a preoccupation that is manifest in several ways. There are effects that evoke physical distance, connoting nearness or farness by shifts of dynamics, as well as by the focus on individuated instruments or timbres against the backdrop of blurred or muted sounds. Ligeti discussed timbre and instrumentation in Mahler and other romantic composers as exactly this kind of distancing effect.[51] Register, particularly the moments when the more dramatic extremes of the orchestra are present, can call attention to the vastness of space, and in doing so implicate another type of distance. More probing in this piece, however, is the evocation of temporal distance. The fragmentary treatment of individual lines leads to a temporal confusion, in which the leading and following voices exchange roles and other instruments participate only in isolated figures of the melody, all of which emerge and resound at different rates. Finally, there is a more conceptual presentation of a temporal distance; the lush orchestration along with individual signal harmonies that are diatonic or even triadic recall the orchestra of the romantic era, heard here from an ironic or critical distance, as it is presented through Ligeti's novel method of handling rhythm and pitch. Indeed, all of these distancing effects take the syntax of microcanons and rhythmic smoothness as a backdrop but rely on the particulars of Ligeti's realization through orchestration and implementation of the system to create the brilliant effects of distance implied by the work's title.

CELLO CONCERTO

Ligeti's Concerto for Cello and Orchestra begins to combine the archetypes seen in *Lux aeterna* and *Aventures*, reconciling polar opposites of style within

---

51. Ligeti, "Raumwirkungen in der Musik Gustav Mahlers," *GS*, 1:279–84.

the same piece, and in doing so, starting to move out of a period of invention into one of synthesis. Ligeti had been juggling different projects throughout the mid-1960s, putting off the completion of *Nouvelles Aventures* until after the Requiem was finished. Similarly, the completion of the Cello Concerto was delayed until the commission for *Lux aeterna* was filled.[52] The concerto bears the traces of many of these projects. On one hand, the sketches include a reference to the "lux" idea of "hidden chordal-areas" (rejtett akkord-felületekkel ["lux"]) being relevant to the network of opening sections. On the other, Ligeti described later sections of the work as being a kind of instrumental *Aventures*, with several explicit passages cited as the basis for different "characters" that the cellist takes on through the course of the second movement.[53] These characters are written out on different sheets of paper and then linked into an order that will become the final progression of the piece, in a collage-like assemblage that draws on the composer's practice in *Artikulation* and *Aventures*.

The concerto is structured in two movements, one moving attacca into the other. Both parts have a similar shape, and Ligeti saw the two movements as variations on the same structure, as can be seen in his sketch of the form of the piece, example 5.20. In it Ligeti highlights specific correspondences with arrows pointing to the narrow beginnings and sparse endings, and also with the circled regions of density in the middle. Meanwhile, the first movement is described in its broadest form as "static" (Statisch) and the second, in contrast, as "motion in color," branching into both "wild" and "mechanical" directions (in Farben Bewegung, wild, mechanisch).[54]

As with *Lux aeterna* and *Lontano*, the first movement begins with different presentations of a single note, in this case E4, articulating the narrow starting point shown in the sketch. The soloist begins alone almost inaudibly, making a gradual crescendo before being joined by the other strings, entering as softly as possible. All move between sul tasto, ordinary, and sul ponticello positions, gradually adding vibrato and crescendoing. For more than 16 measures of a very slow tempo ($\downarrow$ = 40, $\frac{4}{4}$), these variations in sound color are the primary means of development. This single note is heard on different strings, with different bow positions, and in harmonics before moving

52. The chronology is gathered from Steinitz, *Ligeti*, 130, 150.

53. A page in the sketches describes the concerto in French as "*Aventures* sans paroles." Ligeti himself placed this wording in quotation marks, aware, no doubt, of the irony that *Aventures* did not contain any actual words. A passage in GS, 2:244, also brings out the connection to *Aventures*.

54. The German wording of this sketch is somewhat atypical for Ligeti's diagrams, and given that some of the same correspondences are discussed in the Einführungstext (the first one dating from the 1967 premiere and reproduced in GS, 2:243–44), it is possible that some of this sketch was done as an after-the-fact explanation for others, and not sketched during the early process of composition.

Example 5.20. Cello Concerto, sketch of the form. Reproduced with kind permission from the György Ligeti Collection of the Paul Sacher Foundation, Basel

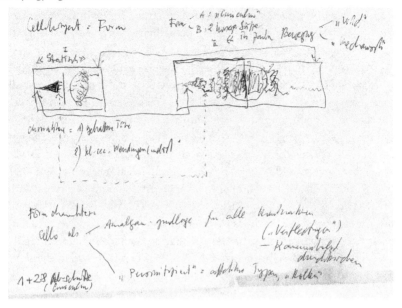

to tremolos. The expansion in pitch begins in the most gradual way, with a nearly inaudible trill to F♯ in the clarinet (end of m. 17), and for another 9 measures (just before m. 27) it remains confined to this semitone. From this point, however, the pitch expansion moves quickly to fill the fifth between D4 and A4, shifting between string and wind timbres, before switching to octave B♭s in measure 36—a tritone away from the opening of the piece, and presented now in extreme registers. The sketch marks this point with a dotted line and an arrow pointing to the clear lines at the end of the initial expansion. Moreover, as the sketch indicates, the remainder of the movement dissolves into traces as the B♭s in different octaves spread and dissipate, completing the aggregate (B♭–B–C♯–C–D–E♭–A–F). A dramatic moment occurs in measures 53–54, where the soft dynamics suddenly grow to *fff* but then cut off, like one of the impulsive events of *Apparitions*. This move leaves only the solo cello in the highest register and the contrabass (later joined by the trombone) in the lowest, highlighting the vast empty space between these extremes.

The second movement parallels the first, starting with a narrow opening and then expanding, in pitch and in other parameters, developing the character types mentioned in the sketch and eventually branching into an alternation of wild and mechanical types of motion. It starts by defining a three-note diatonic or whole-tone cluster, D♭–E♭–F, and expands more quickly than in the first movement, adding D, G♭, and G in the second measure. This creates another reference back to the opening of the first movement, developing a tri-tone cluster, C♯–G, but omitting the center point, E4—the starting note of the previous movement. The C♯–G tritone, along with the E–B♭ tritone, articulated in the first movement, suggests a symmetrical division of the octave as a pitch scheme uniting the two movements.

As the second movement progresses, Ligeti achieves greater internal motion by having instruments oscillate between two notes of the cluster, like slower versions of the paired trills and tremolos seen in *Apparitions*, and as the second movement begins to expand, these grow into melodic gestures. Often these gestures highlight the expansions in pitch; for instance, the horn in measure 7 expands the active space from D♭ to G by a melodic gesture, C to A♭, a semitone to each side. The solo cello then adds A and B, similarly, in measure 8–9, and measure 10 completes the aggregate, adding as the last notes the E–B♭ tritone that was a significant signal in the first movement. After this point, the texture abruptly shifts to different registers, starting with the low-register floor arriving in measure 11, articulating the second point of similarity with the first movement (octave B♭s in m. 36). This is shown in the sketch with a dotted line. The upper registers come in shortly thereafter and quickly progress to other musical types, or characters, for the bulk of the movement.

The melodic types Ligeti develops have strong connections to the melodies of *Aventures* and the Requiem and constitute much of the dense middle section, the third point of correspondence between the movements (circled in the sketch). The melodic types also contribute to the alternation between mechanical and wild categories of activity mentioned in the sketch. Led by the solo cello in pick-up notes to measure 16, the instrumental melodies cultivate a particular intervallic profile including an emphasis on large leaps similar to that of the melodies of the Requiem's Dies irae. Here, too, sevenths are prominent along with sixths, tritones, and ninths, but seconds are generally excluded and perfect fourths and fifths are avoided. The inclusion of sixths, occasional tenths, and consecutive leaps in the same direction echo the solo vocal melodies of the Dies irae. Later melodies develop these basic features into more specific characters by modifying some of the intervallic constraints, changing directions, and shifting the frequency of returns to specific pitches. These more subtle changes in construction are often highlighted by more obvious changes in articulation, instrumentation, and register—resources Ligeti draws on all the more in the works that follow the concerto. In measures 23–24, for example, sleek melismatic figures occur in the winds similar to the passages in *Aventures* starting at measure 17. These passages allow seconds and more consecutive intervals in the same direction, leading to smoother contours, which complement their legato character. In contrast, passages from measures 44–46, 62, 67–68, and 70, are marked *cappricioso, virtuoso, prestissimo possible* and "*staccato, molto leggiero*," and have some precedent in the *molto leggiero* passages of *Aventures* (e.g., m. 7). These unmetered passages use seconds, but retain the frequent direction changes and more angular contours of the original melodies.

In addition to these general melodic types, with intervallic profiles connected to *Aventures*, the second movement borrows several more specific types. Some of the more closely spaced melodic lines (e.g., mm. 27–29 and 41–42) seem to follow the principle of limiting repeated note successions in a manner similar to the "chase" episode of *Nouvelles Aventures* (movement II, mm. 36–39). They do so in a way that the Chamber Concerto and later works develop quite explicitly. The use of a displaced chromatic scale, as seen in measures 51–54, dates back to the *Chromatische Phantasie* and the first String Quartet, but is also present in the Action dramatique section of *Aventures*. The Mechanisch-Präzis sections, beginning at measure 57, refer directly to Horloges Démoniaques (*Nouvelles Aventures* II, mm. 31–34). And finally, the section at measure 63 clearly resembles the Hoquetus passage (*Nouvelles Aventures* I, mm. 28–29). All these are combined in the Cello Concerto to create an alternation of mechanical and wild passages. Along with the alternation of soloist and ensemble, they suggest an incomprehensible drama invoking the drama of the concerto genre, but alienating it from traditional romantic virtuosity in the same way *Aventures* played with the expectations of the operatic stage.

As the final passage of the concerto, labeled the Flüster-Kadenz (whispering cadenza), dissolves into silence, we may see how elements from earlier experiments have come together into something different and new. In this instance, Ligeti is once again drawing on *Aventures*, paralleling its ending, with characters who are "mute but struggling to speak." The effect of the solo cellist laboring intensively to produce almost no sound encapsulates this perfectly. Ligeti is also channeling Mauricio Kagel's idea of instrumental theater with this dramatic effect. Particularly relevant is Kagel's work *Sonant*, written in 1960. In two sections of this piece—the movements *Pièce touchée, pièce jouée* and *Marquez le jeu (à trois)*—Kagel allows for a "virtual" interpretation, in which some of the performers may mime their parts, reproducing the movements involved in performance as closely as possible, without producing any sound. The inaudible dynamics of Ligeti's work have much the same effect. Whereas the Kagel has an element of caustic satire and anti-authoritarian rebellion, deconstructing the concert experience in order to dismantle it, with Ligeti things are somewhat different. He integrated many of these satirical elements back into more traditional settings as a type of joke or tongue-in-cheek commentary from within, rather than a true call to question the validity of high art. Here, in particular, the heroics of the romantic virtuosity are spoofed, but from within the context of the concerto. While drawing on his Fluxus-inspired works and on the work of Kagel, Ligeti has put them together, once again, into a curious and individual amalgam of drama and humor.

CHAPTER 6

Compositional Flourishing (1967–70)

Having gone through experimental phases in the late 1950s and early 1960s and developed his micropolyphonic style in *Apparitions* and *Atmosphères*, the cooled-expressionist style of *Aventures*, and the synthesis of these in the Requiem, *Lux aeterna, Lontano*, and the Cello Concerto, Ligeti began to explore the fruits of his compositional metamorphosis at the end of the 1960s. The works written from 1967 to 1970 include keyboard, chamber, and ensemble pieces in which Ligeti made full use of all the innovations of the previous decade, while developing an interest in microtones, adding subtle refinements in his use of melody, harmony, and orchestration, and arranging passages featuring these techniques in new and kaleidoscopic combinations.[1] After completing the Requiem Ligeti had offers of teaching positions, commissions, and opportunities to put these compositional devices into play. In addition to Stockholm and Vienna, Ligeti was lecturing regularly at Darmstadt and was invited to give courses in Finland, the Netherlands, and Spain. A grant from the Deutscher Akademischer Austauschdienst allowed him to spend most of 1969 in Berlin and led to further performances and commissions.[2]

One reason for this flourishing could simply have been the need to keep up with these requests, but another can be found in the degree of comfort Ligeti had with his refined compositional craft and honed power of expression. The

1. Ligeti mentions the kaleidoscopic principle in his compositions, including the *Ten Pieces*, Second String Quartet, and Chamber Concerto in his self-interview (*LiC*, 135). He also connects the combination of a repertory of diverse elements to earlier statistical thinking seen in his "letter-case" method. Richard Steinitz, *György Ligeti: Music of the Imagination* (Boston: Northeastern University Press, 2003), 137ff., also makes a significant analogy to kaleidoscopic methods in Ligeti's works.

2. See Steinitz, *Ligeti*, 188–91, for more on the chronology of these appointments and commissions.

sketches he made during these years typically have fewer pages than those for works such as *Artikulation, Atmosphères*, and the Requiem, but they are fascinating documents that point inward—to Ligeti's growing repertoire of techniques, addressed in this chapter—and also to external influences and expressive goals, taken up more fully in the conclusion. In particular, the sketches that contain significant verbal planning, such as those for the String Quartet no. 2, the *Ten Pieces for Wind Quintet*, and *Ramifications*, refer back to ideas and techniques developed in previous works and mention the works of earlier composers and other extramusical inspirations more frequently than did sketches for previous compositions, suggesting an increased engagement with historical models and self-conscious consideration of his place within a compositional tradition.

The synthesis found in the Cello Concerto set the stage for some of the driving technical concerns in this period. Although several of the second movement's melodic types rely on techniques developed in *Aventures*, they are given pointedly different presentations, often achieved by changes of articulation, dynamics, or timbre. Thus, we see in this work the impulse toward more diverse expression and differentiation of character within a single compositional technique—something that the pieces discussed in this chapter explore extensively. In other moments the concerto also begins to combine different techniques and fashion transitions between them. In his previous works Ligeti often developed techniques for either widely spaced melodies—like those of the Dies irae, relying on a repertoire of allowable intervals, direction changes, and concern for aggregate completion—or for closely spaced clusters such as those that take the mandatory second as an organizing principle. In the works from the decade's end, the challenge of mediating between these extremes became a major preoccupation.

Stepping back from the large orchestra and choir pieces of the previous years, Ligeti focused on instrumentations ranging from solo keyboard pieces to chamber music and small ensembles. A chronological overview of works discussed in this chapter is given in example 6.1. The keyboard works contain the clearest demonstrations of some of Ligeti's technical innovations. The organ étude *Harmonies* (1967), given its premiere by Gerd Zacher, develops a new type of harmonic network, taking a bold step away from cluster-based language. The harpsichord work *Continuum* (1968), commissioned by Antoinette Vischer, marks a significant new development in Ligeti's style—the "pattern meccanico" pieces.[3] The second organ étude,

<hr />

3. Jane Piper Clendinning coins the term "pattern meccanico" in her "Contrapuntal Techniques in the Music of György Ligeti" (PhD diss., Yale University, 1989) and "The Pattern-Meccanico Compositions of György Ligeti," *Perspectives of New Music* 31, no. 1 (Winter 1993): 192–234. Miguel Roig-Francolí also discusses these techniques in his "Harmonic and Formal Process in Ligeti's Net-Structure Compositions," *Music*

Example 6.1. Chronological overview of works discussed

1967	*Harmonies* (Étude no. 1 for Organ)
1968 (Jan.)	*Continuum* (Harpsichord)
1968 (Feb.–Aug.)	String Quartet no. 2
1968 (Aug.–Dec.)	*Ten Pieces for Wind Quintet*
1968–69 (Winter)	*Ramifications*
1969	*Coulée* (Étude no. 2 for Organ)
1969–70	Chamber Concerto
1971	*Melodien*
1972	Double Concerto
1972–73	*Clocks and Clouds*
1973–74	*San Francisco Polyphony*
1976	*Three Pieces for Two Pianos (Monument, Selbstportrait, Bewegung)*
1976	*Rondeau*
1974–77	*Le Grand Macabre*

Coulée (1969), follows in this style, as do movements from many other of Ligeti's works.[4]

The year 1968 also saw the creation of two major works of chamber music: the *Ten Pieces for Wind Quintet* and the String Quartet no. 2. This invites the speculation that Ligeti, feeling that he had, in some sense, arrived at a new level of compositional ability, was grappling with the past in yet another way and that he had gone back to rewrite his major works of the Hungarian period, the first String Quartet (*Métamorphoses nocturnes*) and the *Six Bagatelles for Wind Quintet* (arranged from *Musica ricercata*). These works showcase all of Ligeti's compositional developments in the intervening years. The String Quartet no. 2 contains five movements, each exhibiting stylistic changes exemplifying the kaleidoscopic style with juxtapositions of fragmentary material from different techniques, and yet showing a measure of internal coherence through transitions and underlying connections between styles. The short movements of the *Ten Pieces*, which alternate between ensemble works and "miniconcertos" for the five instruments, are concentrated studies in

Theory Spectrum 17, no. 2 (Fall 1995), 242–67. This led to Clendinning's response in "Review/Article of Miguel A. Roig-Francoli's Article 'Harmonic and Formal Processes in Ligeti's Net-Structure Compositions,'" *Music Theory Online* 2, no. 5 (1996). I will follow Clendinning's more widespread terminology, but I also want to make clear (in the analyses below) their connection to underlying harmonic networks—hence my discussion of these works after a section on harmonic networks more generally. I also wish to distinguish these pattern-meccanico compositions from other works that invoke the meccanico prototype through simple repeated notes—along the lines of the "Horloges Démoniaques" section of *Nouvelles Aventures*.

4. *Coulée* was also given its premiere by Zacher, and Ligeti had planned two other works for organ, "Le son royal" and "Zéro," but he did not realize them. *Continuum* has also been arranged in versions for barrel organ and for two harps.

technique, expression, and form. The chamber ensemble pieces that immediately followed—*Ramifications* (1968–69) and the Chamber Concerto (1969–70)—expand the possibilities first explored in the smaller works, and so pave the way for larger orchestral works in the early 1970s and eventually the opera, *Le Grande Macabre* (1974–77). The Chamber Concerto, in particular, influenced these later works, revealing innovations in both melody and harmony.

Each of Ligeti's previous compositions seemed to break new ground in compositional technique; at the end of his musical metamorphosis, different works capitalize on similar methods. Rather than analyzing each work individually, as in previous chapters, the discussion that follows is designed to bring out the development and transformation of individual techniques in the service of the diverse expressive goals of these pieces. First I take up contrapuntal structures and then harmonic structures, acknowledging, however, that this is somewhat of a false dichotomy because one type may bleed over into the other. Material developed contrapuntally still takes harmonic considerations into account from an early stage of development; an analysis of the first movement of the Chamber Concerto demonstrates the depth of this interdependence. Conversely, structures developed harmonically may be expressed melodically and put into dense canonic polyphony. This is particularly evident with the pattern-meccanico works, which often are developed from harmonic cells but are deployed in numerous ways. These become so characteristic of Ligeti's work that they are discussed in a separate section of this chapter.

CONTRAPUNTAL STRUCTURES

Throughout this period Ligeti continued to employ and expand on his previous methods, including the contrapuntal techniques that had been an essential part of his language from *Apparitions* through *Lux aeterna* and *Lontano*. These techniques were primarily designed to give linear expression to the chromatic and diatonic clusters or to preserve the mandatory second that was a consistent part of Ligeti's harmonic palette. These same techniques, however, operate in increasingly diverse ways. The microcanons of *Lux aeterna* can be seen in a pure and extended form in the ninth movement of the wind quintet, using the melody shown in example 6.2a. The piccolo plays this entire melody before jumping up to a high A♭7. The oboe plays in canon only through G♭; the clarinet continues through G♮ before skipping to A♭6, an octave below the piccolo. The melody begins as a strict chromatic wedge out from E♭, until G♭, then G♮ and C create familiar (016) trichords (D♭–G♭–G and G♭–G–C). The interval of a second is preserved throughout the texture, just as in *Lux aeterna*. The rhythm is also constructed as in *Lux aeterna*, with a relatively even rate of change in which each instrument plays one type of subdivision (sixteenths, quintuplets, and

Example 6.2a. *Ten Pieces for Wind Quintet*, no. 9, piccolo melody (sounds 8ᵛᵃ)

Example 6.2b. *Ten Pieces for Wind Quintet*, no. 9, distribution of rhythmic modules

Piccolo				Oboe				Clarinet			
a	b	c	d	m	n	o	p	w	x	y	z
4	4	4	4	4	3	3	3	3	3	4	4

sextuplets, in the piccolo, oboe, and clarinet, respectively), and with the same repertoire of rhythmic modules used with near-equal distribution, as shown in example 6.2b.[5]

What is strikingly different between this movement and *Lux aeterna* or *Lontano* is the style of presentation. The earlier works employed soft, gentle, and unnoticeable entrances, whereas the wind quintet is performed at a constant *ff* dynamic level, *sempre con tutta la forza*, in a piercingly high register and with the special instruction that "breathing can be clearly audible."[6] Moreover, these high, loud, closely spaced sonorities are likely to produce low, rumbling difference tones like those projected to be produced in *Pièce électronique no. 3* (see chapter 2). Just as *Volumina* reversed certain aspects of *Atmosphères* and the Cello Concerto developed different characters from similar melodic principles, many of the works of the late 1960s push earlier techniques into new expressive models, exploring the full range of affect that Ligeti could find in each. Having developed this seamless technique as an expression of eternity in *Lux aeterna* and of echoing distance in *Lontano*, here the harsh and abrasive sound of the high winds is the polar opposite—immediate, visceral, and hyper-present—and yet it is achieved by the same technique.

In other works from this period, Ligeti uses *Lux aeterna*–style microcanons in a looser or less thoroughgoing manner, in transitions or alongside other new techniques. In movement II of the String Quartet no. 2, Ligeti begins with imitative entrances of each instrument in reiterations of the starting note—inflected eight times with continually changing timbres—and initial neighboring motion, common to the other canonic melodies in this style. The exact imitation eventually begins to diverge in the different

---

5. Given the limited instrumentation, the rate of change is more difficult to manage, and there are three instances when it decelerates in a slightly more abrupt way, from two changes in one beat to zero changes in the next.

6. György Ligeti, *Zehn Stücke für Bläserquintet* (Mainz: B. Schott's Sohne, 1969), 32.

Example 6.3. String Quartet no. 2, II, basic melody, violin I, mm. 1–12

1. G♯ is reiterated 8 times with different timbres.
2. The viola and cello diverge from the melody.
3. Violin II diverges from the melody.

instruments. All four instruments are in canon up to the third A. After that the viola and cello branch off, and the second violin stays with this sequence for two more notes, including microtonal inflections of G♯ and A♮, before branching off (as marked in example 6.3). Thus, as the intonation begins to deviate from the equal-tempered system, the canonic organization (already obfuscated by the repeated notes and neighboring motion) also gets fuzzier. Rhythm in this work is also more loosely constructed; it uses the established repertoire of rhythmic modules, but allows instruments to change subdivisions and switch freely between rhythmic strands—perhaps taking advantage of the increased flexibility of a small ensemble. In *Ramifications* a brief interlude (mm. 35–44) reduces this canonic technique to the bare minimum—a single note change from E♭ to E, performed in imitation across the voices.

In addition to microcanonic techniques following *Lux aeterna*, Ligeti continues to use the free contrapuntal style seen in chorale sections of the Requiem such as the Oro supplex chorale discussed in chapter 5. These works also use the common principle of expanding from a single note or other narrowly spaced starting point to a wider range, while still maintaining the mandatory second in their vertical harmonies. Since these works are not canonic, there is more versatility in the way they move through space, but individual voices always work together to expand or shift the sound mass up and down, filling in holes that other voices leave.

As the ninth of the *Ten Pieces* brought a substantially different character to the counterpoint of *Lux aeterna*, the free contrapuntal pieces also explore a creative recombination of familiar elements into new forms. The first movement of the quintet (see the range graph in example 6.4a)[7] begins with a diatonic collection, E–F–G–A–B—decidedly different from the chromatic character of the Requiem—and slowly adds pitch classes from this starting point. Ligeti first fills in the spaces of the diatonic cluster in measures 3–4; then he expands the range in a quasi-symmetrical fashion, with D♯ below, C above, and D below in measures 5–7. At this point only C♯ is missing. The

7. The range graphs in example 6.4 show semitones on the vertical axis and beats and measures on the horizontal axis. They do not take tempo changes into account. The graph for movement 3 omits an isolated melodic passage in measures 10–12 to focus on the underlying clusters.

Example 6.4a. *Ten Pieces for Wind Quintet*, no. 1, range graph

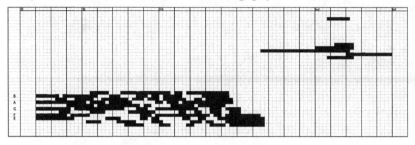

Example 6.4b. *Ten Pieces for Wind Quintet*, no. 3, range graph

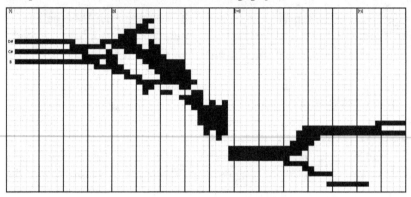

rhythm accelerates through measures 8–16, but stays within the minor seventh from D3 to C4, focusing on the lower part of this range in measures 15–16. The introduction of the final pitch class, C♯, occurs at the golden section of the piece, halfway through measure 16. This moment is also a dramatic change in register and dynamics from a focused, animated cluster from D3 to F3 in the clarinet, horn, and bassoon, swelling and dying away between *pp* and *mf* in the different instruments, to the sudden introduction of C♯5 as a unison attack in the alto flute and English horn, subito *fff*. The other instruments then rejoin with C♯5 at the end of measure 17 and begin spreading chromatically before finally settling on C♯5.

This miniature resembles the first movement of *Apparitions* with its acceleration to a tipping point and sudden shift to a higher register at the approximate golden section of the work, but it is also a prototype for other movements of the quintet. The third movement is similar in concept, but differently directed. As shown in example 6.4b, the movement begins with a diatonic/whole-tone subset (B–C♯–D♯) before filling in the missing chromatic notes. The acceleration then moves toward a texture change at the golden section, gradually shifting this chromatic cluster downward rather than suddenly shifting it up.

This movement begins to toy with the idea of reestablishing fleeting tonal centers. At significant points, the pitch class B is the lower boundary of the piece. The first chromatic shift changes D♯ to D♮, perhaps playing with a reference to B major and minor, and later, in measures 12–15, the horn recapitulates the opening cluster, now in descending melodic form, E♭ (D♯), D, C♯, B. The pitch B also reappears as the upper note of the final dyad, now held by the clarinet against the flute's A, which undercuts the ultimate stability of B. These references to B are ephemeral at best, but worth noting as precedents for Ligeti's later works, which include stronger tonal allusions.[8] Here, however, the tonal references are neutralized. At the golden section, in measure 10, a unison melody emphasizes the set (014), which can have tonal associations involving the major third and the minor third but in this case follows more strictly intervallic logic. Ultimately, register, dynamics, and internal speed are still the major means of formal articulation.

Repeated-Note Meccanico Treatments of Contrapuntal Structures

In several works from this period, both free and imitative counterpoint are given a special kind of treatment using a stream of fast repeated notes rather than sustained pitches—another instance of Ligeti emphasizing the diverse means of expression he can achieve. The Type IV chorales were islands of relative calm in the frantic Dies irae section of the Requiem; this treatment imparts a driving energy to the movements. The often-accented or staccato nature of these repeated notes also harkens back to the meccanico idea as expressed in *Poème Symphonique* and the "Horloges Démoniaques" section of *Nouvelles Aventures*. The fifth of the *Ten Pieces* epitomizes this change of character and reassembly of elements; its melodic organization remains the most similar to the model of the Requiem's Oro supplex and Salva me, yet its sharp accents and hurried streams of repeated notes played as quickly as possible by each instrument, do not. The movement begins from a single pitch (D4) and expands outward in a quasi-symmetrical wedge. Each instrument uses a different melodic succession, but they hold true to the mandatory harmonic second in their coordination for the first eight measures. At this point—as with other ensemble movements of the quintet, the approximate golden section of

8. See Michael Searby, *Ligeti's Stylistic Crisis: Transformation in His Musical Style, 1974–1985* (Lanham, MD: Scarecrow, 2010), especially chap. 1, "Ligeti's Music and Its Relationship to Tonality," for an introduction to some of these issues in the composer's later works.

Example 6.5. String Quartet no. 2, III, range graph, mm. 3–12

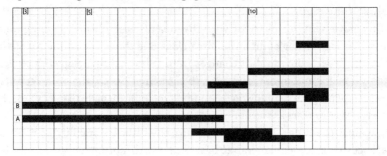

the work—they break into a completely different style with more pointillistic texture, wider register differences, more consistently loud dynamics, and sudden tempo changes.

The relation to the meccanico prototype is all the more clear in the third movements of the Second String Quartet and the Chamber Concerto, both of which feature more percussive sounds. The pizzicato movement of the quartet is a novel use of this technique, yet in part an homage to similar movements from the tradition: the second movements of the Debussy and Ravel quartets, not to mention the Allegro-pizzicato fourth movement of Bartók's String Quartet no. 4. Ligeti's movement opens with a free polyphonic expansion of a whole tone A5–B5 outward for the first twelve measures as shown in example 6.5, while also changing the subdivisions used by each instrument from eighths to quintuplets and progressively accelerating to reach twelve divisions per quarter-note beat. At this point the instruments move to a more central range, and they begin a more extreme expansion and acceleration incorporating microtonal glissandi, before finally (in m. 30) breaking out into a texture more closely reminiscent of *Nouvelles Aventures*.

The third movement of the Chamber Concerto begins a chromatic expansion from E4—a reference to the dedicatee of this movement, Friedrich Cerha and his work *Fasce* (1959, revised 1974), which ends by having all the instruments slowly converge on this same pitch. This movement uses a canonic polyphony but splits up the sustained pitches with fast repeated notes, which become the source of rhythmic innovation. The instruments' entrances are staggered, but from the initial E they all expand through a chromatic wedge, E–F–E♭–D–F♯–E–C♯.[9] The F♯ introduces nonuplets, and the following E septuplets, as each instrument arrives on these notes in turn. The instruments, however, use different numbers of note repetitions and rests so that the timbres of individual instruments come through in a patchwork, like the mosaic patterns

---

9. The oboe omits the E♭, D, and C♯ of this melody but plays the others in the same order, and other instruments do not bring the melody to full completion.

of *Atmosphères*. In a draft of the score Ligeti seems to have been monitoring the number of repeated notes from the very opening, and as we have seen with other works, the guiding principle seems to be that of balancing and limiting repetitions. In the passage before the split to different subdivisions, Ligeti uses groups of four to twenty repeated notes, and in this span no individual value is repeated within a single instrument. Among the wind instruments that open the movement, most values are used twice, and none are used more than three times.[10]

The keyboard instruments help transition to a similar passage in the strings, who play a variant of the opening canon. In this version, the tuplets are introduced earlier in the canon, accelerating and decelerating in steps, going through patterns of 6, 5, 6, 7, 6, 5, 4, and 3 notes per beat and changing subdivisions on each successive note. Here, too, most of the repetition values appear two times, but longer strings of repeated notes are added to the end that generally are unique values. The first violin exemplifies this construction, using groups of between 6 and 13 repeated notes exactly once each. This exposition carefully builds from a patchwork of instrumental streams at a regular tempo to a state of multiple conflicting speeds, but the next section of the movement moves toward even further complexity. A Senza tempo section at letter C allows all the instruments to play repeated notes, ad libitum, so that "the density of tone repetitions will be different in each instrument."[11] Soon after this metric freedom is introduced, Ligeti loosens the pitch structure as well. The passage begins on octave A♭s, but glissandi begin to expand this nodal point into a chromatic cluster.

The Chamber Concerto also adds a new technique for organizing counterpoint in these different speeds. In his sketches Ligeti calls this move the "Mahler Technique," referring to moments like the end of the development section of the Third Symphony, I (rehearsal number 54), where the snare drum reenters with the original march tempo, preparing the recapitulation, while the cellos and basses are instructed to remain in the existing tempo for the completion of their phrase. Each group is instructed in the score to proceed without regard (ohne Rücksicht) for the other's tempo.[12] Other

10. In the winds, streams of 8, 12, and 16 repeated notes occur three times each; streams of 17, 18, and 20 are used only once; all other values between 4 and 20 are used twice. In the string passage that follows the value 10 is used four times; 12 and 13 are used three times; 4, 8, 14, and values above 16 are used only once. All other values are used twice.

11. György Ligeti, *Kammerkonzert für 13 Instrumentalisten* (Mainz: B. Schott's Söhne, 1974), 67.

12. In Gustav Mahler, *Symphonies nos. 3 and 4 in Full Score* (New York: Dover, 1989, reprint of Universal Edition, [n.d.]), 75, the indication for the snare drum (kleine Trommel) is "Im alten Marschtempo (Allegro Moderato) ohne Rücksicht auf Celli und Basse [*sic*]," and the indication for the cellos and basses reads, "Celli und Bässe im Tempo fort ohne Rücksicht auf die Kl. Tommeln, welche das erste gemässigte Marschtempo beginnen." Ligeti mentioned the example from the Third Symphony in

brief moments in Mahler have similar indications, for example, a short violin solo just before rehearsal number 20 of the Eighth Symphony, I, which is marked, "veloce, accel. ohne Rücksicht auf das Tempo."[13] Ligeti's use of this technique goes a step farther in the Chamber Concerto, not just dovetailing the end of a passage in one tempo with the start of one in the new, but having these divergent tempi coexist for longer stretches. From letter E of the third movement through letter G, the conductor brings in different instruments at different tempi, while the score instructs instruments already playing to disregard these changes, continuing in the old tempo. The wording in the score clearly reflects the precedent in Mahler; each instrument continuing in an older tempo is instructed to stay at that tempo, regardless of the beat (ohne Rücksicht auf den Taktschlag). The remarkable synthesis of rhythmic techniques in this movement of the Chamber Concerto advances the canonic micropolyphony of *Lux aeterna* and *Lontano* but also draws on techniques for the statistical balancing of repeated notes, develops a concern with different instrumental speeds dating back to *Atmosphères*, and revisits the meccanico character of *Poème Symphonique* and *Nouvelles Aventures*. Most striking, however, is that by connecting his individual techniques back to Mahler, Ligeti finds a traditional precedent for complex polyphonic textures built from different rhythmic strands.

Melodic Construction in the Chamber Concerto, Movement I

The free and imitative contrapuntal structures discussed above are never far removed from harmonic concerns and are most often tied to the mandatory second and cluster-like harmonies so characteristic of the composer. The canonic melodies are often wedge-like, gradually expanding outward from a unison beginning and creating secundal harmonies with previously introduced notes. The free contrapuntal movements have more varied melodic designs, but they move through registral space in similar ways and bind voices together with at least one vertical second sounding as a near-constant

interviews (e.g., *LiC*, 25, with a related example, 62) and in his essay "Zur Collagetechnik bei Mahler und Ives," *GS*, 1:285–90. The most explicit identification of this as the "Mahler Technique" comes from sketches for the unfinished *Labyrinth* pieces (listed as *Labirintus* in the Sacher Foundations holdings under the category Werkprojekte, Fragmente), which originated about 1970. A page from these unfinished sketches reads, "'Mahler-Technique:' instruments remain in the old tempo, the others change tempo with the conductor. Several such tempo-layers are possible simultaneously." ("Mahler-Technik": hangszer marad régi tempóban, a többiek dirigenssel tempót váltanak. Több ilyen tempó-réteg leheséges szimultán.)

13. Gustav Mahler, *Symphonies, no. 8* (New York: Dover, 1989, reprint of Izdatel'stvo "Muzyka," Moscow, 1976), 25.

Example 6.6. Chamber Concerto, I, basic melody of the opening

harmonic identity. Other melodic designs, however, express clusters individually within instrumental lines. These melodies generally employ faster rhythms to move through the chromatic pitch cell more quickly, and they are often combined in canon with different rhythmic variants of one another. One of the most characteristic of these is the melodic prototype—first found as an isolated section of *Nouvelles Aventures* (the "chase" episode, movement II, mm. 36–39)—which limits the repetition of pitch successions within a specific cluster. The first movement of the Chamber Concerto develops this type of melodic construction in new ways, creating polyphonic textures out of similar melodies, and varying them in order to effect a large-scale harmonic change through the course of the movement.[14] The opening of the piece expresses a cluster from F♯4 to B♭4 with canonically intertwined melodic lines in different rhythms. The basic melody is shown in example 6.6.[15]

As with the micropolyphonic melody from letter H of *Atmosphères*, the instruments enter simultaneously, but on successive notes of the basic melody: bass clarinet on the first note, cello on the second, flute on the third, and clarinet on the fourth. From the fourth note (B♭) on, the melody follows strict rules limiting pitch successions, which are considered as the move from one specific pitch to another (i.e., B♭ to G is a different pitch succession than G to B♭). No pitch succession is repeated until all possible pitch successions between notes of the cluster have been exhausted. This principle maximizes the internal melodic variety of note successions, while leaving the cluster they

14. The Chamber Concerto has been discussed by several authors including Pierre Michel, *György Ligeti: Compositeur d'aujourd'hui* (Paris: Minerve, 1985); Clendinning, "Contrapuntal Techniques;" Roig-Francolí, "Ligeti's Net-Structure Compositions;" and Michael Searby, "Ligeti's Chamber Concerto: Summation or Turning Point?" *Tempo* 168 (1989), 30–34. These all contain observations about the canonic organization of the work but do not turn to the details of melodic construction and sketch study discussed here. One source that does approach an explanation of the melodic structure is Robert Piencikowski, "Les points sur les 1: Le Concerto de Chambre de Ligeti," *InHarmoniques* 2 (1978), 211–16.

15. Clendinning "Contrapuntal Techniques" gives 46 notes as the basic melody, adding A–G–A♭–B♭–A♭–G to the end. This pattern is held by the flutes in m. 11, but can be seen as an elaboration, an internal retrograde of notes 39 to 31 of the basic melody, omitting G♭/F♯. The following analysis shows the significance of Ligeti's omission of the lowest note of the cluster and the use of internal retrogrades not only here but in the course of the movement as a whole.

represent unchanged. The passage from note 4 to note 24 makes one complete cycle of all twenty possible successions between these five pitches. The span from note 24 to note 41 also contains no repeated successions, and, if taken with the introductory notes 1-4, completes another exact cycle of all possible successions.

Throughout the sketches for this piece are charts in which Ligeti tallies these note successions, often using semicircular diagrams as shown in example 6.7a, my theoretical reconstruction reflecting the opening passage. Each line connecting the central pitch to one of the exterior pitches marks one use of that note succession, and hash marks (here shown across the first line, but sometimes occurring beside the exterior note name) represent a subsequent use of the same. These diagrams exist in all different states of completion or exactitude, including states in which the register shifts and new notes—often clearly added after the initial part of the diagram was sketched—are accommodated inexactly. The reproduction of one such sketch in example 6.7b shows both a chromatic cluster from D to G and a similar expression of the interlocking diatonic and pentatonic clusters D–E–F–G and D♭–E♭–G♭–A♭.

Once the strict melodic prototype is established, it immediately becomes the source of variations. Starting with the horn (transferred to violin II) and oboe in measures 4 and 5 respectively, instruments soon begin using the retrograde of portions of this basic melody, like the internal retrogrades seen in the Christe lines of the Requiem. With the string entrances at letter B (m. 9) Ligeti begins to use melodies that are derived from the basic melody, but which accommodate a large-scale register shift in the continuation of the movement. From letter B to letter E the register shifts slightly higher, abandoning F♯ in measure 11 and adding B, and then C in measures 15 and 16. In order to bring about this shift, the basic melody is altered in the string instruments. The individual string melodies are all based on the retrograde of the basic melody. The violin I melody is shown in example 6.8.

This pitch succession is a retrograde of the basic melody with a few simple changes to accommodate the shift in register and changing content of the cluster. The melody includes the first F♯ but omits subsequent occurrences of this pitch class (notes 35, 27, 21, 18, and 13). The retrograde also combines the two A♮s (notes 8 and 10) that would produce a note repetition when the F♯ occurring as note 9 is omitted. When the retrograde melody arrives on note 3, this G♭ is not omitted, but rather replaced as Ligeti begins a new process, proceeding in the original direction and substituting B (or C♭) for this G♭ and for all subsequent G♭s, as shown in the annotations of Example 6.8. In this way the lowest note of the original cluster falls out and a note a semitone higher than the original is introduced in its place. Ligeti continues this registral expansion in a similar manner. When C enters, it substitutes first for A in note 15, then for A♭ in notes

Example 6.7a. Chamber Concerto, I, tallying of note successions

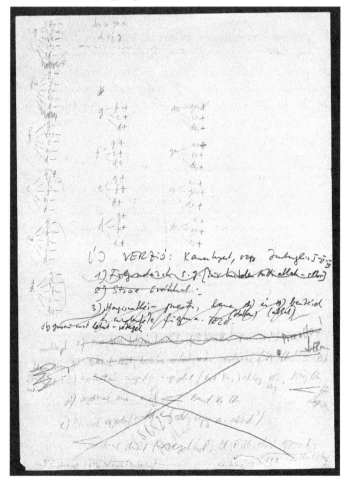

Example 6.7b. Chamber Concerto, I, sketch tallying note successions. Reproduced with kind permission from the György Ligeti Collection of the Paul Sacher Foundation, Basel

Example 6.8. Chamber Concerto, I, derived melody of violin I

*B substitutes for F♯ in the original melody.
**C substitutes for A in the original melody.
***C substitutes for A♭ in the original melody.

30 and 33. Ligeti derives melodies for the other strings in a similar fashion. Violin II begins in retrograde on note 29 continuing to note 4, the viola in retrograde from note 39, and the cello in the original direction starting on note 35, before reversing direction at note 40. Each melody goes through the same modifications in the same order: first removing F♯, then using B in its place, and finally introducing C in place of A and then A♭. Thus, in the first part of the movement, the active collection shifts slightly higher and then begins to thin, gradually shifting from F♯–G–A♭–A–B♭ to G–A–B♭–B–C. From this point, the melodies in the keyboard instruments (what Jane Clendinning calls Block C)[16] pick up with the same pitch content in measures 19–23, the strings (Clendinning's Block D, mm. 22–27) reduce this to a diatonic subset, G–A–B♭–C, and the winds and keyboards (Block E, mm. 26–29) shift this to G–A♭–B♭–C, before beginning to fill chromatic pitches back in to end the first half of the piece.

The second half of the work uses similar techniques of combining pitch-succession melodies with internal retrogrades. Keyboard melodies that transition out of the chordal section (Block G, mm. 46–50) split the cluster into diatonic and pentatonic segments, but each is controlled in the same way. In fact the collections D–E–F–G and D♭–E♭–G♭–A♭ are exactly those shown in the sketch reproduced as example 6.7b above; notes 1–15 of the diatonic melody (celesta, right hand) and 2–16 of the pentatonic melody (celesta, left hand) complete an exact cycle of pitch successions, shown in example 6.9a. The next melodic block, which returns to more chromatic material in the winds,

16. Clendinning "Contrapuntal Techniques," 1:249*ff*. and examples 4.6 and 4.8 (2:140–50, 155).

Example 6.9a. Chamber Concerto, I, celesta, m. 47. Ligeti Kammerkonzert für 13 Instrumentalisten, 1974, Edition Schott 6323. Copyright © 1974 by Schott Music, Mainz, Germany. Copyright © renewed. All Rights Reserved. Used by permission of European American Music Distributors Company, sole U.S. and Canadian agent for Schott Music, Mainz, Germany

Example 6.9b. Chamber Concerto, I, cello, mm. 48–49. Ligeti Kammerkonzert für 13 Instrumentalisten, 1974, Edition Schott 6323. Copyright © 1974 by Schott Music, Mainz, Germany. Copyright © renewed. All Rights Reserved. Used by permission of European American Music Distributors Company, sole U.S. and Canadian agent for Schott Music, Mainz, Germany

keyboards, and strings (Block H, mm. 50–56), has a similar melody using the cluster that is written down the left-hand margin of example 6.7b. A core 30-note interval succession melody extends from note 9 through note 38 (cello, example 6.9b), and the remaining notes can be seen as completing internal retrogrades (notes 1–7 are retrograded by notes 7–13, and notes 14–38 are retrograded by notes 38–62).

As with the third movement, the first movement of the Chamber Concerto draws together developments from Ligeti's earlier works and combines them into something new. The pitch-succession melody originated as an isolated occurrence in *Nouvelles Aventures*, where all the instruments play transposed versions of the same melody together in the same rhythm; another instance of this type of melody occurs in the fourth movement of the Second String Quartet (mm. 37–40) as a brief contrasting passage from the brutal vertical cluster chords that form the bulk of this movement. In the later part of the Cello Concerto, some of the melodies show the general principle of limiting repeated pitch successions, but again as characters within a whole. With the Chamber Concerto, however, these melodies are more organically at the heart of the movement and are the basis for its melodic variation. In addition to the melodies themselves, other techniques also draw on previous works. The canonic entrances, in which each instrument starts on successive notes of the same melody, harken back to *Atmosphères* but with significantly more rhythmic differentiation between the lines. The use of internal retrogrades has precedent in the Christe melodies of the Requiem, where they helped introduce a level of freedom into the serially derived form of the work. The Chamber Concerto combines these techniques and elevates the result to a new level: a system in which the composer can animate the musical surface with different combinations of rhythmic and melodic density, and still coordinate these complex textures with the harmonic structure of the work, effecting changes in register and pitch content to shape the movement as a whole.

HARMONIC STRUCTURES

As the preceding analyses show, Ligeti often conceived of his melodic and contrapuntal structures with a harmonic underpinning in mind—especially the chromatic, diatonic, and pentatonic clusters that defined his harmonic palate from the mid-to-late 1950s and the interval signals that included major and minor seconds, such as (016) and (025), which began to emerge in the mid-1960s. Underlying all of these is the mandatory second, an idea that endured in Ligeti's thought, as reflected in the sketches, well into the 1970s. Sketches from *San Francisco Polyphony* (1973–74) included regulations for one of its hypothetical sections projecting vertical intervals that were "complexes of microtonal, minor, and major seconds, with gaps also, but a *minimum* of one second in each place" (hyperkis szek, kis sek, nagy sek, komplexumok. Lyukak is, de MINIMUM egy szek[u]nd egy helyen). Ligeti investigated some of the possibilities that stem from this rule, modifying or crossing out different ideas as he went (microtonal clusters, for instance, are not to be found), but the origin of much of what follows remains grounded in this harmonic constraint.

Beginning with *Harmonies*, chronologically the earliest work addressed in this chapter, Ligeti's pieces start to develop structures using more widely spaced intervals, which push past the familiar harmonic palate and its limitation of a harmonic second. Just as the contrapuntal structures were never far removed from harmonic ideas, the harmonic structures that originate in this period also have melodic manifestations and often give rise to contrapuntal textures. As such, these harmonically conceived networks provide the means to transition from more closely spaced clusters to more widely ranging configurations, both harmonic and melodic—a feature on which Ligeti capitalized in many of his subsequent pieces.

Sketches for *Ramifications* also cover many of these developments; early ideas for a piece with that title date to 1967, but it did not begin to take its present shape until the winter of 1968–69, and the sketches contain an interesting record of the composer's concerns at the time.[17] In one set of notes

17. See Steinitz, *Ligeti*, 179, for information about the commission of *Ramifications* and its chronology. Along with the prose examples discussed here, the sketches include a draft of an early version of this piece. The opening measures are not

for the work Ligeti ponders the use of harmonic regions as a background (harmónikus régiók mint háttér), which could be either composed out as a network (harm. háttér auskomponiert ["szövevény"]) or expressed virtually, arising from the lines (harm. háttér virtuális, vonalakbol adódik). And the works from 1967–70 do show new harmonic networks that are expressed explicitly and those which are hidden below the surface, as well as those that are arpeggiated melodically—in whole or in part—by individual instruments and those which rely on the coordination of multiple instruments for their expression. These sketches also propose a harmonic technique for these structures involving clear and confused moments, as in *Lontano* and *Lux aeterna*, with transitions, and possibly also including seventh, ninth, or eleventh chords (harm. technika: tiszta és zavart momentumok, = Lontano, Lux—átmenetekkel. [7, 9, 11-akkordok?]). The mention of tertian harmonic structures is significant, not so much for their tonal associations but for their abandonment of the limitations of a mandatory harmonic second, indicating an openness to the broader harmonic repertoire that the pieces from this period employ.

Harmonies, Étude no. 1 for Organ

Ligeti's first organ étude, *Harmonies*, is the clearest prototype for this new direction, and an understanding of it can form the basis for understanding much of Ligeti's working method in other works from this period, including the second movement of the Chamber Concerto, and beyond. Moreover, a clear understanding of *Harmonies* will facilitate a comparison to the pattern-meccanico style seen in the second organ étude *Coulée*, analyzed below.

Harmonies begins with a ten-note symmetrical harmony that alternates minor thirds and major seconds; the piece expands slowly outward and returns, forming a perfectly symmetrical structure, as can be seen in example 6.10.[18] Since all of the harmonies contain ten notes, each hand uses all five fingers constantly. In this new harmonic language, voice leading is strictly by semitone, with one note moving in each measure; the player an individual finger either up or down a note on the keyboard. The harmonies, constrained by the limits of the hand, generally go no farther than a major third between fingers, occasionally a perfect fourth or, between thumb and

carried to completion, and the meandering direction and non-imitative counterpoint actually bear a greater resemblance to ideas in the Chamber Concerto than to the finished score.

18. The symmetries of *Harmonies* are discussed in Pozzi Escot, "'Charm'd Magic Casements,' Mathematical Models in Ligeti," *Sonus* 9, no. 1 (1988), 17–37. The range graph excludes the final pedal tone.

Example 6.10. *Harmonies*, range graph

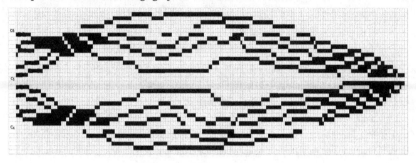

index finger, up to a minor sixth. Each move in one hand is balanced by a move in the opposite direction by the same finger in the other, so that the result is symmetrical. At first the hands alternate regularly, one note change in the right hand answered by the corresponding move in the left, but as the piece goes on multiple changes begin to occur in one hand before the other is allowed to catch up, creating momentary disturbances in the symmetry.

By this method, Ligeti begins with familiar territory, using secundally weighted sonorities as he did in previous works—the opening sonority can be taken as stacked (025) signals—but he slowly breaks out of those sonorities into more widely spaced harmonies. In measure 71, in fact, Ligeti arrives on stacked minor thirds in each hand, sharing the fully diminished seventh chord, E–G– B♭–D♭, and the next twenty measures (until m. 92) contain different configurations of major and minor thirds along with an occasional perfect fourth to aid the expansion of the cell. In this passage, then, each hand goes through any number of configurations resembling extended tertian harmonies, but all are governed by their symmetrical construction and the parsimonious, semitonal voice leading typical of this new development, rather than any implication of tonal function.

Looking beyond the voice leading and harmonic innovations of the work, the symmetries throughout *Harmonies* are greatly distorted by the means of their presentation. Whereas the note changes are notated in even bars, the duration of each is determined freely, and according to the composer's extensive performance notes, "Nowhere in the piece should the chord succession create an impression of metre or periodicity."[19] Moreover, Ligeti asks the performer and assistants to "denature" the sound by preparing the organ so that "pale, strange, 'vitiated' tone colours must predominate."[20] This is to be done by reducing the wind pressure. Another result of these preparations is that:

half-drawn stops, half-depressed keys, and pipes (especially reeds) that do not speak properly due to too little wind pressure all cause fluctuations of dynamics and

19. Ligeti, *Zwei Etüden für Orgel* (Mainz: Schotts Söhne, 1969), 4.
20. Ibid.

intonation (micro-intervals, glissandos, etc.). "Impurities" of this kind are welcome in realizing the piece; they contribute further to denaturing the tone colors. The notated pitches in the musical text, then, refer only to the keys to be depressed or held; the succession of pitches that actually results can fluctuate freely; the "harmonies" are "tainted" and more or less diverge from the written text.[21]

The microtonal deviations from pitch and the free rhythms that distort the in time are, in some ways, more immediately characteristic of the work than the balanced symmetries that support them. The development of an intricately conceived model or system, followed by the gradual abandonment, distortion, or destruction of the model through the course of the work, has been a common rhetorical device in Ligeti's music. This trope goes back to the prime-plus-retrograde form of *Glissandi*, which was altered by filtering techniques, and the intricate rhythmic balance of *Apparitions*, which underwent progressively more dramatic distortions. Parallel to this formal conceit is Ligeti's attitude toward the rules that he develops in his compositions: they are there in the background helping build the scaffolding for the musical works, but they are ultimately secondary to the acoustic effect of the music.

Chamber Concerto, Movement II

The second movement of the Chamber Concerto is based on a very similar harmonic skeleton featuring entirely semitonal voice leading, although it is less symmetrical in its pattern of contraction and expansion. Ligeti's method of construction is shown in example 6.11a, a reproduction of a page of a sketch that shows the semitonal moves through slurs. Ligeti also rewrote the full harmony periodically for reference or to switch to enharmonic equivalents of the notes. I have also provided a transcription (example 6.11b) in which the full harmonies are written out in a manner resembling the score for the organ étude, with one note change per measure of the example; I have also added boxed measure numbers for reference and to aid with following the finished score.[22]

The initial harmony is a not-quite-symmetrical construction, spaced from low to high as [2-3-4-2-4-3-4]; as in *Harmonies*, this mixture of major seconds with minor and major thirds is not far removed from the interval signals Ligeti

---

21. Ibid.

22. Some accidentals in the score are different from (but enharmonically equivalent to) those in the sketch and transcription. There is also extensive material at the end of the sketch that is not used in this movement and not included in the transcription. From measure 15 on, marked with an asterisk in the transcription, harmonies are expressed melodically in at different rates in different instruments; the clarinet is used as the main instrument for measure designations in the example and from measures 28–29 a combination of the clarinet and keyboard instruments is used.

Example 6.11a. Chamber Concerto, II, sketch of the harmonic skeleton. Reproduced with kind permission from the György Ligeti Collection of the Paul Sacher Foundation, Basel

Example 6.11b. Chamber Concerto, II, transcription of the harmonic skeleton, mm. 1–39 (note changes 1–94)

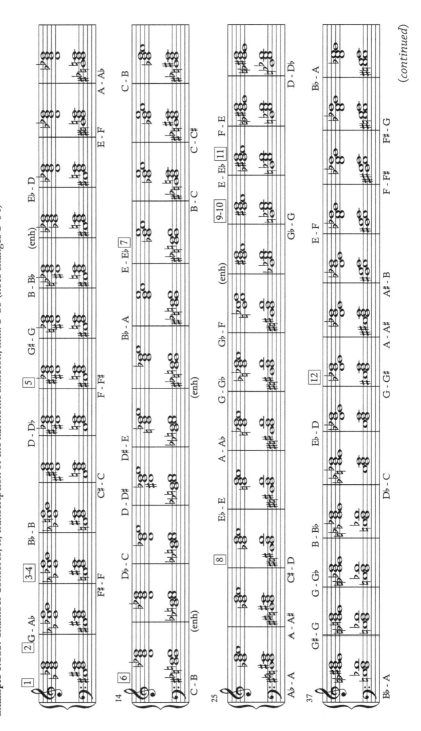

(continued)

Example 6.11b. Continued

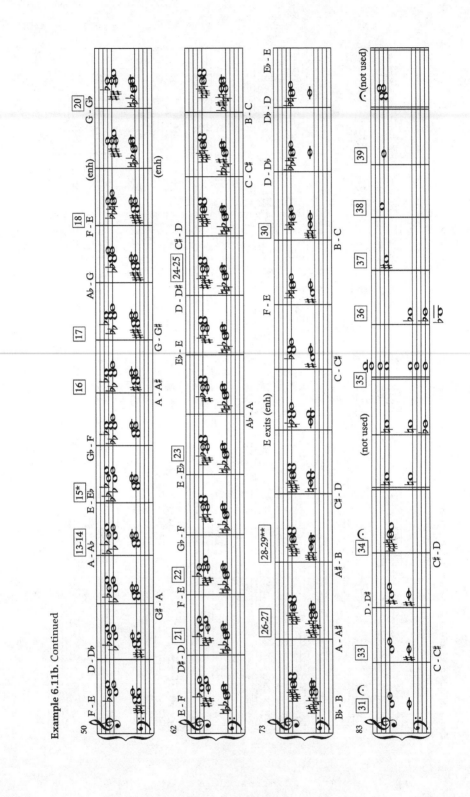

used in previous pieces. In this movement, however, he begins with a contraction to even more closely spaced, clusterlike harmonies before moving
outward, saving the registral expansion for the end of the movement. Over
the course of the first 26 measures, Ligeti works gradually and irregularly
toward a chromatic cluster (note change 74) filling the space between A♯3 and
F4. From measure 26 to measure 34 Ligeti begins narrowing this further to
the three-note cluster D4–D♯4–E4. A linking passage follows that uses the tritone B–F in multiple octaves. After this point, he resets the harmony and texture once again, resuming semitonal voice leading and pushing toward even
more open sonorities, reaching a harmony of stacked fifths in measure 77.

Some of these harmonies are obscured by the manner of their presentation, which, using the full resources of the chamber orchestra, are much more
varied than in the organ étude. Note changes are sometimes performed by
individual instruments, but more often a new note arrives while the note it
replaces is still in the process of fading out, leading to a blurred emphasis on
the harmonic semitone in each of these successions. example 6.12 shows the
string and wind parts of the opening four measures, where the first four note
changes seen in the harmonic skeleton, example 6.11b) are all introduced in
this manner: G–A♭ (violin II to viola), F♯–F (bass clarinet to trombone), B♭–B
(flute to cello), C♯–C (cello to violin II). The order of B♭–B and C♯–C is switched
from what is shown in the sketch, but otherwise there are no changes. In an
additional orchestrational nuance, the oboe d'amore takes over D from violin
I and moves it to C♯ (D♭ in the sketch) to create the fifth note change. Even
more than with *Harmonies*, the harmonic skeleton here is flexibly deployed in
order to support the continual process of color change from the different and
gradually evolving combinations of instruments.

In measure 13, the spacing of the entire eight-voice harmony has contracted
to such a degree that a single instrument can realize the whole of the cluster, and the clarinet can be seen as taking the harmonic content and realizing
it melodically. The opening melody of the clarinet, shown in example 6.13, is
derived from the harmonic block G–A–B–C–D♭–E–G♭–A♭ (see example 6.11b,
above, note change 53, mm. 13–14). The successive variations of this melody
reflect the note changes predicted by the harmonic skeleton; E moves to E♭
(written D♯) in the next figure, G♭ (F♯) moves to F, and A to B♭ in measure 16, G
moves to G♯ in measure 17, and F (from F♯ in m. 15) moves to E at the beginning
of the figure in measure 18. A comparison of example 6.11b to the first half of
the score reveals the network of semitonal shifts that define this voice leading.

Other instruments follow the clarinet's lead and begin to realize this melody in canon.[23] As with the first movement's canon, instruments begin on
different notes of the melody, and the clarinet, the first instrument to begin

---

23. Clendinning, "Contrapuntal Techniques," 1:278–80, discusses the canonic aspects
of this piece, but not the harmonic underpinnings.

Example 6.12. Chamber Concerto, II, mm. 1–4. Ligeti Kammerkonzert für 13 Instrumentalisten, 1974, Edition Schott 6323. Copyright © 1974 by Schott Music, Mainz, Germany. Copyright © renewed. All Rights Reserved. Used by permission of European American Music Distributors Company, sole U.S. and Canadian agent for Schott Music, Mainz, Germany

an active melodic line in measure 13, starts on note six of the melody carried by the flute in measure 15. All of these introductory notes, however, belong to the opening harmony of measure 13. From its gradual beginning, the lines begin to emerge from these harmonies, reflecting the underlying skeleton in displaced melodic form. The lines are more flexible and meandering than in

Example 6.13. Chamber Concerto, II, mm. 13–18, clarinet. Ligeti Kammerkonzert für 13 Instrumentalisten, 1974, Edition Schott 6323. Copyright © 1974 by Schott Music, Mainz, Germany. Copyright © renewed. All Rights Reserved. Used by permission of European American Music Distributors Company, sole U.S. and Canadian agent for Schott Music, Mainz, Germany

the concerto's other movements, and the canon progresses with significant rhythmic variety in the different instruments, mixing subdivisions and introducing new tempos in individual instruments, according to the "Mahler technique" discussed above.

The second half of the movement combines the textures seen in the first half. From measure 40 through measure 72 the three lowermost voices are realized with sustained notes, in the same manner as the opening of the movement, while concurrently, the five uppermost voices of the texture are realized melodically in the same kind of canon that the clarinet led in measure 13. Unlike the first canon, which used independent rhythms and tempos, here the instruments play in lockstep. Though they begin on different notes of the melody, they play in unison rhythms, with occasional rests or skipped notes providing some variation in the texture, and allowing the winds to breathe. This melodic texture accelerates to a rhythmic peak in measures 51–56, before slowing down to the chordal finale in measures 73–77 that emphasizes a sonority made up of stacked fifths, and the brief epilogue, 78–81, not contained in the sketches, which thins the texture and moves chromatically to settle on octave Gs.

Melodien and Later Works

The melodic expression of harmonically conceived structures is one of the last developments in Ligeti's musical metamorphosis: a nearly complete interdependence of melody and harmony. Works such as *Lux aeterna* and *Lontano* started with melodic lines, which were then blurred into harmonic and timbral combinations through slow, microcanonic presentations, and the intricately composed melodies of the first movement of the Chamber Concerto also gave way to large scale harmonic shifts. With the second movement, we have the transformation in reverse; a harmonic background structure becomes animated as melody and then returns to its chordal nature at the end. First seen in the Chamber Concerto, this technique is vital for Ligeti's subsequent compositions, including *Melodien* and *San Francisco Polyphony*. In fact, the sketches for *Melodien*, a page of which is shown in example 6.14,[24] are almost identical in format to the skeleton for the concerto movement analyzed above. The first part of the work filters out pitches from a wide chromatic collection—sketched as a cluster but expressed as the scalar passages—and eventually settling on a bare A; each note that is removed is marked with a looping symbol similar to an editor's deletion mark. The fermata in the fifth system, just before letter B, thus corresponds to measures 11-13 of the score. After this point Ligeti begins adding notes back in (shown in the sketch with a plus symbol attached to the circled note), and in the sixth system, near the passage that has been scribbled out, the slurs mark semitonal voice leading moves of the same type found in *Harmonies* and the Chamber Concerto. The different surface articulations, from the rising lines of the beginning and end to the more meandering melodies found elsewhere, from passages that express the full run of the most densely loaded parts of the harmonic skeleton to others that are thinner or that split the harmony into different parts, all derive from the same source. Even the notation on the page, sometimes stacked vertically and other times spread horizontally, suggests an irony found in the title: that its melodies and harmonies are part of the same system.

PATTERN-MECCANICO PIECES

Continuum and *Coulée*

Along with the new harmonic networks, Ligeti developed a particular way of articulating them—the so-called pattern-meccanico style, which has received much scholarly attention.[25] These works can be seen as a treatment of harmonic networks parallel to the repeated-note "meccanico" treatment of contrapuntal structures seen above. Works such as *Continuum* and *Coulée* are other

24. Jonathan Bernard's "Ligeti's Restoration of Interval and Its Significance for His Later Works," *Music Theory Spectrum* 21, no. 1 (Spring 1999), 1–31, analyzes parts of *Melodien*, with observations that support those found here. Though Richard Steinitz ("Á qui un homage? Genesis of the Piano Concerto and the Horn Trio," in *György Ligeti: Of Foreign Lands and Strange Sounds*, ed. Louise Duschesneau and Wolfgang Marks [Woodbridge, UK: Boydell, 2011], 171) remarks on the incomplete nature of sketches for this piece, some sketches for *Melodien*, often bearing the working title "Dürer" (the work was commissioned in honor of the five-hundredth anniversary of the birth of Albrecht Dürer), have subsequently been identified and reunited as part of the Sacher Foundation's collection.

25. Clendinning coined this term in "Contrapuntal Techniques." The abundant analytical literature on *Continuum, Coulée*, and other works in this style includes her "Pattern-Meccanico Compositions;" Michael Hicks, "Interval and Form in Ligeti's *Continuum* and *Coulée*," *Perspectives of New Music* 31, no. 1 (Winter 1993), 172–90; Uve Urban, "Serielle Technik und barocker Geist in Ligetis Cembalo-Stück *Continuum*," *Musik und Bildung* 5, no. 2 (1973), 63–70.

Example 6.14. *Melodien*, sketch. Reproduced with kind permission from the György Ligeti Collection of the Paul Sacher Foundation, Basel

manifestations of Ligeti's fascination with malfunctioning machinery, first seen in *Poème symphonique* and the "Horloges Démoniaques" passage from *Nouvelles Aventures*. In fact, the limitations of the mechanism of the harpsichord, which Ligeti described as being "like some strange machine,"[26] were a particular inspiration—the paradox of a plucked instrument with a typically noncontinuous sound being played fast enough to generate the impression of an imperfect continuity. *Continuum* marks the first instance of this important new development, which was refined in the organ étude *Coulée*. At a time when Ligeti was increasingly occupied with creating transitions between different compositional models, the pattern-meccanico style proved to be a particularly flexible tool; it became a typical Ligeti sound and subsequently entered the repertoire of techniques seen in parts of the Second String Quartet, the *Ten Pieces for Wind Quintet*, and numerous later works.

The defining new feature of *Continuum* and *Coulée* is the use of repeated patterns in a stream of running eighth notes, which are performed evenly, but as fast as possible, and which undergo a series of shifts and transformations. Each hand begins with the same two pitches (G and B♭ in *Continuum*, A♭ and E♭ in *Coulée*). The left hand starts with the lower note, arpeggiating upward, and the right hand starts with the upper note and arpeggiates downward on a different manual of the instrument, so that, theoretically, each note is continually present. From this common starting point, however, each hand works independently to developing the intervallic cell in different ways.

In these pieces Ligeti uses a regular repertoire of pattern transformations that closely resemble those found in the harmonic networks. Thus there is a connection between these compositional techniques, even if the pieces that employ them sound quite distinct. The most common transformations are the addition or deletion of a note from the arpeggiated cell and the shifting of a note in the cell to a note a half-step away. This chromatic shifting is exactly the type found in the semitonal voice leading of *Harmonies*. The removal of notes from the cell also has a precedent in *Harmonies*, near the end, although this type of transformation is more common in the pattern-meccanico pieces and emerges as one of the main ways of creating complex rhythmic interactions. New notes introduced into the cell are most often connected by a semitone to existing notes, although the occasional introduction of a new note a major second or a minor third away can also occur.

These operations can be seen as the primary transformations of the piece, and less common events can be seen as using compound or secondary types of transformations (see the summary in example 6.15). These include shifting a note by a whole tone, shifting two notes simultaneously, or other operations that can be seen as combining several primary transformations into a single move. In *Coulée* there are spots where two notes a major second

26. *LiC*, 22.

Example 6.15. Types of pattern transformation

Primary Pitch Changes

1) Shifting one note by one semitone

2) Adding a note

3) Removing a note

Secondary Pitch Changes (can be seen as combinations of the above)

1) Shifting by a whole tone (in rare cases, by even more)

2) Shifting two notes at once

3) Making two notes converge on a single pitch (whole-tone collapses to a unison)

4) Making one pitch diverge in multiple directions (unison expands to a whole tone)

Changes in Character (more common in the ensemble pieces)

1) Change in articulation

2) Change in direction

3) Change in rhythmic subdivisions or pulse

4) Putting patterns in canon

5) Having polyphonic patterns diverge or develop independently

apart will both shift inward, converging on the center note—another type of secondary transformation, which one could alternatively think of as the removal of one note along with a semitone shift. Conversely, notes will occasionally diverge from a unison to a whole tone. Rarely, more abrupt changes occur: an entire cell may jump to a new starting position, or the direction of arpeggiation may change. The three primary transformations, however, account for 75 percent of the individual shifts in *Continuum* and 90 percent of those in *Coulée*.[27]

The passage from *Coulée* example 6.16 shows an abundance of primary transformations. In this excerpt the rhythmic activity in the left hand is quite rapid, changing patterns frequently, with only a single statement of the pattern or a single repetition before moving on. The right hand, by comparison, repeats a five-note chromatic pattern throughout, but soon has its turn to carry the piece as it accelerates toward its end. The ascending motion of the example also signals the end of the piece, as discussed below. The transformations here are frequent but regular, showing single notes shifting by semitone in the way that was typical of the companion étude, *Harmonies*; the only secondary transformation is number 4, where two notes shift simultaneously. The small-scale inversional symmetries—seen in the interval structure of the cells, for example, from pattern 5 through pattern

---

27. In my calculation only 42 of 168 shifts in *Continuum* are secondary transformations, and only 20 of 208 in *Coulée*.

Example 6.16. *Coulée*, mm. 148–51. Ligeti Coulée from Zwei Etüden für Orgel, 1969, Edition Schott 6477. Copyright © 1969 by Schott Music, Mainz, Germany. Copyright © renewed. All Rights Reserved. Used by permission of European American Music Distributors Company, sole U.S. and Canadian agent for Schott Music, Mainz, Germany

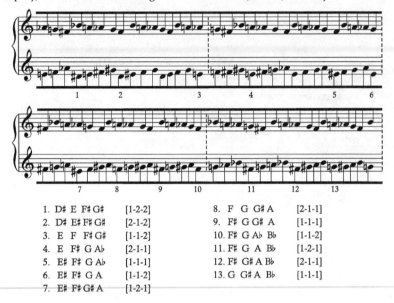

1. D♯ E F♯ G♯	[1-2-2]		8. F G G♯ A	[2-1-1]
2. D♯ E♯ F♯ G♯	[2-1-2]		9. F♯ G G♯ A	[1-1-1]
3. E F F♯ G♯	[1-1-2]		10. F♯ G A♭ B♭	[1-1-2]
4. E F♯ G A♭	[2-1-1]		11. F♯ G A B♭	[1-2-1]
5. E♯ F♯ G A♭	[1-1-1]		12. F♯ G♯ A B♭	[2-1-1]
6. E♯ F♯ G A	[1-1-2]		13. G G♯ A B♭	[1-1-1]
7. E♯ F♯ G♯ A	[1-2-1]			

13—are a result of this regular shifting but also recall the symmetries seen in *Harmonies*.[28]

Although these pieces are built from seemingly simple rhythmic material—straight running eighth notes compared to the mixture of different concurrent divisions of the beat seen in previous pieces—their workings become quite involved because the transformations have effects on the grouping and phase of the patterns in each hand and begin to produce a hypnotic complexity.[29]

28. Roig-Francolí, "Ligeti's Net-Structure Compositions," discusses symmetry in *Ramifications*; see also Jonathan Bernard, "Inaudible Structures, Audible Music: Ligeti's Problem, and His Solution," *Music Analysis* 6, no. 3 (October 1987), 207–36.

29. The similarity between Ligeti's pattern-meccanico compositions and the motoric pulse streams and additive rhythms of American minimalist composers, including Steve Reich and Philip Glass, has given rise to speculation that he may have heard or been influenced by their music around 1968. Ligeti claims not to have known their music until his visit to California in 1972 and only to have known Terry Riley briefly through his Fluxus connections in Europe. It is quite plausible that through his teaching and his increased contact with a younger generation of composers he may have learned about American minimalism while still in Europe; this claim is difficult either to prove or refute. A sketch for *Continuum* discussed by Martin Scherzinger, "György Ligeti and the Aka Pygmies Project," *Contemporary Music Review* 25, no. 3 (June 2006), 227–62, esp. 256, contains abbreviated references to later pieces, including both *San Francisco Polyphony* [SF Poly] and *Three Pieces for Two Pianos* [3 st. f 2 Kl], along with references to Reich, Riley, Glass, and Young. The titles of these works, however, clearly date the annotations to at least the mid-1970s, so while Scherzinger's intuition that Ligeti may have known about the minimalists (and possibly their African sources) earlier than he acknowledged deserves serious consideration and further research, this

Since the addition or subtraction of notes in the cell is a relatively common transformation, the number of notes in the cells varies, resulting in groupings that conflict between the hands. Metric displacements and grouping dissonances are prevalent throughout these pieces. Whereas previous works tended to favor conflicting divisions of a regular beat (e.g., triplets against sixteenth notes or sixteenths against quintuplets), these works feature grouping dissonances, which have a common pulse but not a common size (e.g., groups of four eighth notes against groups of five, or 4/5 groupings, adapting the terminology of Harald Krebs).[30] In both cases, however, Ligeti tends to use neighboring values for a maximally conflicting sense of meter. In the pattern-meccanico keyboard pieces, individual patterns are limited to a maximum of five notes, most commonly using neighboring values in simultaneous groupings of 2/3, 3/4, or 4/5. The pieces also employ different displacements of patterns of the same length; as one cell may expand and contract against another, it can arrive back at an identical grouping but be out of phase with a group of the same size in the other hand. The passages of displacement, however, tend to be shorter than the ones employing different groupings and can be seen as transitional passages allowing one hand to catch up to, and then pass, the grouping of the other. In their execution, the conflicting groupings seem to function as different speeds or tempi. No matter how carefully a performer strives for an even surface, the beginning of each pattern repetition will carry some degree of accent, which can establish a secondary level of pulse dependent on the size of the pattern, in turn establishing a close and perceptible link between pitch structure and speed and an interrelationship between musical parameters.

Other psychoacoustic illusions also arise from the interplay between parameters and their effects on perception and expectation. For example, as a player arpeggiates the harmonic cells first seen in works such as *Harmonies*, the more clusterlike cells can come off as scales, while the more widely spaced cells come off as more pure arpeggiations. As these chromatically shift from one to the other, they are stretched and skewed, often leaving the listener in the uncomfortable space between these two familiar categories. Moreover,

document is too problematic to be taken as definitive proof. The extensive German used in this sketch may also suggest that it comes from a later explanation of the piece, perhaps one given to Ove Nordwall, or in preparation for a lecture, and not from the time of its composition. Ligeti did revisit *Continuum* in 1974, arranging it for two harps (sketches for this version are contained in the Paul Sacher Foundation and dedicated to Aristid von Würtzler and his New York Harp Ensemble). The work was arranged again for barrel organ by Pierre Charial in 1988.

30. The terminology of Harald Krebs in *Fantasy Pieces: Metrical Dissonance in the Music of Robert Schumann* (New York: Oxford Universty Press, 1999) works very well for these pieces. This terminology and approach to metric dissonance may also help connect to Ligeti's rhythmic practice in the Piano Études, as discussed by authors including Steinitz, *Ligeti*, 277ff., and Stephen A. Taylor, "Chopin, Pygmies, and Tempo Fugue: Ligeti's 'Automne a Varsovie,'" *Music Theory Online* 3, no. 3 (May 1997).

as the two hands perform the same note on different manuals, often in different groupings, and therefore at different speeds, irregular repetitions of this single note result; these patterns can overshadow the consistent direction of arpeggiation in each hand—refocusing attention on the interference pattern of the combined result, rather than the separate arpeggiated strands in each hand. When combined with the speeds approaching the *Bewegungsfarbe* threshold these works remain engaging through the multiplicity of ways in which they play with listeners' perceptions.[31]

Ligeti discussed the form of *Continuum*, and in these pieces more generally, with reference to areas of "mistiness" and "clarity"—deceptively simple terms that actually rely on the interaction of different pitch and rhythmic factors.[32] In the broadest sense, form seems to be defined by large-scale registral motions, and often sections or entire pieces will establish a floor or ceiling for a time and then move past it toward extreme registers at the end. More locally, a sense of clarity is provided by pure intervals or trichordal signal harmonies that can then move toward cloudiness by adding chromatically related notes via pattern transformation. Most of the works in this style begin with pure intervals in clear presentation and use the familiar repertoire of interval signals in key moments. *Continuum* begins with a minor third, expanding it to a (025) signal in measure 10. It moves through areas of chromatic consolidation and then registral expansion, punctuated by more sudden register changes at measure 87 and most dramatically at measure 126, the golden section of the piece, which shifts suddenly to the tritones F–B–F and G–C♯–G. Tritones have been characteristic of signal harmonies before, and here, voiced in each hand and doubled by the harpsichord's stops, mark a clear disjuncture in the musical surface and thus a point of formal articulation.

Coulée starts in a manner similar to *Continuum*, moving from a pure interval (a perfect fifth) to a familiar signal harmony (016); its continuation, however, has fewer dramatic shifts and balances the use of different parameters to express its form. As discussed above, the process of adding pitches to the pattern in one hand also entails a rhythmic change, and the clarity of equal groupings in phase with one another can be disturbed by introducing grouping and displacement dissonances. The rate at which pattern transformations

31. In *LiC*, 22, Ligeti estimates that the harpsichord is capable of speeds up to fifteen or sixteen notes per second, short of the twenty needed to cross the perceptual threshold but enough to approximate the effect.
32. Ligeti's wording in *LiC*, 60, puts this as contrasting "passages of 'mistiness' with passages of 'clearing up.'" Hicks, "Interval and Form," takes an intervallic approach to defining clarity and mistiness. Ligeti's sketches also address these concepts harmonically, as "tiszta" and "zavart," for example, in passages from *Ramifications* that mention "harmony with disturbances and clearings-up" (harmonikus zavarokkal és kitisztulásokkal), as well as wording from the same sketches that appears above, in the section of this chapter introducing harmonic structures.

Example 6.17. *Coulée*, range graph

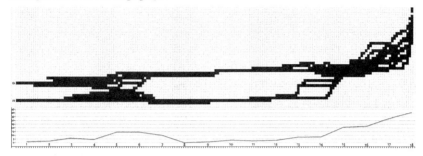

occur also has an effect on form. Although the acceleration of pattern changes is often tied to an accelerated shift in register, this is not necessarily the case—these parameters are connected but can work with or against one another as shaping forces. This surprisingly involved means of formal articulation can be compared to the multivalent interaction of different parameters to create form in *Atmosphères* and *Volumina*, where register, internal motion, and tone color combined to define different sections. As in these previous works the understanding of form is a complex negotiation between multiple, nonhierarchical parameters.

The chart presented in example 6.17 shows a range graph for *Coulée* along with a diagram charting the rate of pattern change (calculated as an average number of changes per ten-measure unit); along with the size of the cells in each hand, these help gauge the complexity of these interactions.[33] The chart shows how the parameters can work together to shape different sections. The shifting and addition of notes in the cells can help fill in existing intervals—as is seen in the first section of the work—or these same transformations can effect a more dramatic change in register, as seen at the end. Likewise, an increase in the rate of pattern change can be used to change the size of individual cells, creating more complex and varying interactions between the hands, without necessarily having an equally dramatic change in register. Alternately, an increase in the rate of pattern change could shift notes within cells while maintaining the same kind of interaction between the hands. The global form of *Coulée* can be seen, then, as having three stages: the first moves from the open fifth to a more complex state through increased rhythmic complexity (reaching 4/5 groupings in m. 36) and by filling in the intervallic space of the opening fifth, but without a dramatic shift in register. The first stage can be seen as complete by measure 65, where the rhythm settles on a 3/2 grouping between the hands and a relatively hollow space between the semitone

33. Clendinning charts many of these factors separately in "Pattern-Meccanico Compositions."

boundaries, G3–A♭3 and F♯4–G4. The second stage is defined by this relative calm and a more independent role for the pedals in the low register. The end of the second stage and the beginning of the third is more fluid and difficult to define, but the stretch from measure 130 to measure 134 provides successively clearer indications that the piece is taking a new direction: the use of three successive transformations in the left hand in measure 130 (marking a very perceptible increase in the rate of change), the move to 4/3 grouping in measure 132, and then the abandonment of the lowest pedal register in measure 134 all point towards the coming acceleration, increasing complexity, use of secondary transformations, and dramatic registral expansion that shape the end of the piece.[34] The regularity of the transformations throughout the opening of the piece, as well as the flow between sections, make the abrupt ending of the work all the more striking as it spirals higher and faster, seemingly out of control.

Pattern-Meccanico in the Chamber and Ensemble Compositions

The pattern-meccanico style, first seen in *Continuum*, takes on a long and varied life in subsequent works in which Ligeti was able to add degrees of complexity to the technique. In this process he also explored new modes of expression within the technique, including associations that contrast with the original mechanical nature of the style. The keyboard works *Continuum* and *Coulée* already show some variation in expression. *Continuum* created the paradoxical situation of a harpsichord producing continuous, almost sustained sound; *Coulée* also works against the common method of playing of the organ—rather than sustained chords (as in *Harmonies*), this étude demands a "sharp and colorful" registration "so that the striking of the keys is audible and thus the extreme speed of the piece evident."[35] These are autonomous movements composed as demonstrations of the style, challenging the sonic possibilities and limitations of different keyboard instruments. In the ensemble works that follow, the pattern-meccanico technique appears in combination with other techniques, taking advantage of the broader sound world of different instruments and the increased complexity made possible by utilizing multiple performers.

34. Clendinning, ibid., marks m. 118 as a significant point, based on the increased frequency of pattern changes starting there; Hicks, "Interval and Form," on the other hand, marks mm. 140–53 as a transitional area, abandoning the registral floor of A♭3 and beginning to shift upwards.

35. See the performance directions in the score to *Coulée*, 5; this observation is also made in Clendinning, "Pattern-Meccanico Compositions," 229, n. 10.

These pattern-shifting techniques are found in passages of many works from the late 1960s and early 1970s, although often as part of a movement, rather than a whole one written exclusively in this style. The eighth of the *Ten Pieces for Wind Quintet* (discussed further below) and the last movement of the Second String Quartet both feature pattern-shifting sections, as do *Ramifications*, the Double Concerto, *Clocks and Clouds*, and the *Three Pieces for Two Pianos*. In the works for multiple instruments, new possibilities include mixing rhythmic subdivisions in the different parts, changing the type of subdivision used within each part, and interrupting the flow of the pattern by placing irregular rests into the lines. The last is sometimes a practical consideration, allowing for breathing in vocal or wind parts, but sometimes is done as a way to offset patterns and create areas of haziness. Ligeti also puts sequences of pattern changes in canon between different instruments. Sometimes the sequence of pattern transformations is a strict canon, the same in all parts, but in other works, the canonic parts slowly start to diverge and develop independently. Some instruments are capable of incorporating microtones into this technique, something found first in *Ramifications*, where the two string ensembles are tuned a quarter-tone apart, and also in the Double Concerto and *Clocks and Clouds*, where microtones are incorporated within individual parts. All of these developments move toward greater mistiness and away from the meccanico inspiration of this technique.

The last movement of String Quartet no. 2 begins with a minor third, F♯ to D♯, arpeggiated at different speeds by all the instruments. The regular transformations of the pitch structure show a great deal of small-scale symmetry in the way they expand, as can be seen in example 6.18. The individual parts, however, move through these patterns in canon, going through the sequence of pattern changes at different points. Moreover, they move smoothly

Example 6.18. String Quartet no. 2, V, pattern changes

Pitch										G♯
									G	
	F♯	F♯	F♯	G♭	G♭	G♭	G♭	F♯		
			F	F	F	F				
		E		E	E		B♭	E	E	E
	D♯	D♯	E♭	D♯		D♭	D♭			
					D	D	D	D	D	D
Intervals	[3]	[2]	[1]	[1]	[1]	[1]	[2]	[2]	[3]	[4]
		[1]	[2]	[1]	[1]	[2]	[1]	[2]	[2]	[2]
				[1]	[2]	[1]	[1]			

between different rhythmic subdivisions, starting with a mixture of triplets, sixteenths, quintuplets, and sextuplets, and gradually building to include septuplets, thirty-second notes, and nonuplets. The conflicting subdivisions, along with the legatissimo and pianissimo performance directions, undercut the sense of the mechanical that was at the origin of this style and turn it into a cloudy, amorphous texture.

Ramifications also demonstrates the subsequent nuance found in these works. In this piece, the twelve string parts are divided into two groups tuned about a quarter-tone apart, allowing for some fluctuation as long as the two groups remain in this approximate relationship and do not fuse. They use related material, starting with major seconds (in their respective tunings) and moving through related pattern transformations. The instruments begin with different rhythmic subdivisions, introduce rests at different points in their patterns, and change individual patterns in canon with other instruments in their group. After an opening that demonstrates many small-scale symmetries, material in the two groups begins to diverge. In measure 19, both groups share the cell E–A♯–B and its quarter-tone pair.[36] At this point, however, group 2 becomes more static, while the outer notes of group 1 continue expanding by semitone, with one whole-tone shift as a secondary transformation. Thus E moves down to E♭ and D; B moves up through C, D♭, E♭, E, and F. Near measure 21, group 1 becomes relatively static, and group 2 becomes more active, shifting first upward, and then downward, the low E of the cell first traveling up to A before chromatically descending to meet group 1 on D. In previous works we have seen Ligeti set up a system and disturb or distort it over the course of the piece; here, however, the particular types of distortions are related to the ramifications of the title, where groups branch off, take different twisting paths of development of different sizes and speeds, and eventually rejoin.

Pattern-Meccanico and Harmonic Networks in Later Works

Once he has established his repertoire of compositional devices, Ligeti uses this kind of pattern-shifting technique in works from the early 1970s that are at times more mechanical and at times more fluid. Sections of the Double Concerto, *Three Pieces for Two Pianos*, and *Clocks and Clouds* make use of pattern-meccanico ideas in various ways. These works include some innovations in execution, but as discussed below, they remain fundamentally grounded in the techniques established in the pieces from the late 1960s.

Harmonic networks, in various guises, also form a significant part of the Double Concerto. The slow-fast, two-movement form of this work resembles

36. Roig-Francolí, "Ligeti's Net-Structure Compositions," analyzes aspects of this piece in greater depth.

that of the Cello Concerto, as do many of the melodic characters employed in the second movement. Yet the Double Concerto introduces several new features and more refined transitions. Although the first movement is written in a free-contrapuntal style, Ligeti sketched part of the harmonic background using the same techniques for expanding harmonic networks seen in previous pieces. Example 6.19a, a transcription of one of the sketches, shows the initial whole-tone cell (again reminiscent of the Cello Concerto) and how it is filled in chromatically, expanded, and then reduced to a diatonic segment. Each move involves one of the primary transformations seen in previous works. In this sketch the cells are written in ascending order, and the changing note is either written out before the rest of the cell or circled, with pluses and minuses indicating additions and pieces. Example 6.19b shows a harmonic plan for the second movement, gradually expanding from a minor third to a tritone by letter C, incorporating quarter-tones into the progression, and expanding toward the dramatic register shift of letter G. The majority of this harmonic skeleton is realized in a pattern-meccanico style up to the frenetic ending of the movement, which introduces wider leaps at measure 87 (letter CC), repeated-note meccanico patterns at 96–97 (letter FF), and pitch-succession melodies with expanding clusters at 117 (letter MM).

Example 6.19a. Double Concerto, I, sketch transcription, details of the opening patterns

Example 6.19b. Double Concerto, II, sketch transcription, harmonic skeleton

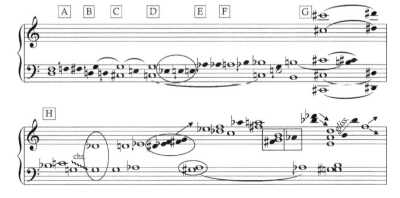

The *Three Pieces for Two Pianos*—individually titled *Monument, Selbstportrait mit Reich und Riley (und Chopin ist auch dabei)*, and *In zart fließender Bewegung*—also make use of harmonic networks.[37] This is most clear in the last movement, *Bewegung*, where the resemblance to the pattern-meccanico works is readily apparent (see example 6.20a). The descending runs of the beginning expand to arpeggiations, initially through semitone shifts in the pattern of each of the four hands. The main difference between this and the earlier pattern-meccanico keyboard works is the consistency of the three-note patterns in each hand, which is then complicated by a faster rate of change—almost continually altering the patterns—as well as by the conflicting rhythmic subdivisions in each piano part. The second movement, *Selbstportrait*, adds an interesting wrinkle to the technique. Here Ligeti uses a peculiar technique, which he employs again in the piano étude *Touches bloquées* (book 1, no. 3), whereby the pianist silently depresses keys in one hand while the other hand continues to play normally, regardless of whether the key will sound or not. The notated patterns in *Selbstportrait* follow the same repertoire of transformations, by and large, although they employ secondary transformations (multiple shifts, and moves by whole tones or larger intervals) more frequently than in the earlier keyboard works. The audible patterns, however, are quite different. The addition of a blocked note to the pattern results in an audible change in the rhythm (an added or lengthened rest) but not to the overall pitch content. This produces a rhythmic result from a basically harmonic process. It also means that even when the two pianists are playing the same pattern with their right hands, the different blocked notes in the left hand mean that these patterns sound differently.

A less straightforward path connects these harmonic networks to the first movement of this set. A sketch for *Monument* begins with a harmonic skeleton, partially transcribed in example 6.20b. The pitches are all derived from an opening (025) signal harmony (A–F♯–B), adding C and D♭ above and E♯ below, successively expanding the cell by semitone. From this point semitone shifts expand the harmony in the familiar way. The notation used in the sketch, which leaves the new note (whether added or shifted) as an open note head, recalls the score for *Harmonies*. In the realization of this harmonic plan, however, Ligeti splits the notes between the two pianos and

37. These works, composed in 1976, after Ligeti was already working on the opera, fall outside the timeframe of this book. My discussion focuses on their use of structures related to the harmonic networks of the 1960s. They introduce other techniques as well, and more thorough analytical treatment of them can be found in Steinitz, *Ligeti*, 207–10; Searby, *Ligeti's Stylistic Crisis*, 91ff.; John Cuciurean, "Aspects of Harmonic Structure, Voice Leading, and Aesthetic Function in György Ligeti's *in Zart Fliessender Bewegung*," *Contemporary Music Review* 31, nos. 2–3 (April–June 2012), 221–38; and Bernard, "Inaudible Structures" and "Restoration of Interval."

Example 6.20a. *Bewegung*, mm. 1–4. Ligeti Monument, Selbstportrait, Bewegung, Facsimile Edition, ED 6687. Copyright © 1976 by Schott Music, Mainz, Germany. Copyright © renewed. All Rights Reserved. Used by permission of European American Music Distributors Company, sole U.S. and Canadian agent for Schott Music, Mainz, Germany

Example 6.20b. *Monument*, sketch transcription, opening harmonic network

uses a different registration and doubling for each note. This is, then, one of the few instances when he deploys one of these harmonic networks as a pitch-class structure, rather than a structure purely in register. The finished piece, however, introduces exactly these notes in order: A in measure 6, G♭ in 13, B in 19, C in 23, and F in 27, which shifts to E in 40. This piece also raises questions about the interaction between harmony and melody. Rhythm is tightly controlled in a way that parallels the pitch structure; individual lines use durations that are expanded or contracted by sixteenth-note values accelerating and decelerating by the smallest available subdivision in the same way the pitch patterns expand and contract by semitone. As the piece continues, the pitch structures, as sketched, become gradually wider, but are combined with an incremental acceleration. From the imposing opening, then, where single notes resound through the hall, far removed from the following or preceding sounds, the acceleration starts to connect individual notes together more as resultant melodies, even while they become farther apart in pitch.

In particular, *Clocks and Clouds* moves fluidly between extremes, not just between the cloudlike and clocklike archetypes within the meccanico style, but also between construction based on harmonic networks and the type of polyphony seen in *Lux aeterna* and *Lontano*. The work opens with a descending whole tone, E–D, echoing through the flutes and then the clarinets. Rests not only interrupt the patterns to facilitate breathing but also help create distance between the instrumental groups, at first allowing each to sound independently, and later contracting the distance between groups so they overlap and blend. As the harmonic cell grows, rests placed at different points in the individual figures help change the direction from descending to ascending. As the surface rhythm accelerates through the different parts, Ligeti sneaks in sustained pitches in the ensemble that begin to deviate into microtones and eventually prepare the entrance of the choir at letter H.

The voices show their own refinements of technique as well. They sing a canonic line reminiscent of *Lux aeterna*, now with microtonal inflections. They begin with repeated Gs and slowly branches outward. The sopranos, mezzos, and altos begin identically for the first ten notes and syllables but then diverge. They first separate in pitch, drifting toward a B–F tritone that works as a signal harmony near letter L. More remarkably, they begin slowly diverging in their syllable content as well. The syllable changes begin subtly, skipping certain elements of the sequence, but they grow more pronounced, exhibiting the same type of branching seen in the melodic patterns of *Ramifications*, here creating a richer array of vocal timbres. Most remarkably, though, as the choral section gives way to a return of the meccanico instrumental textures, an acceleration to repeated figures and harder syllables (*b* and *d* sounds) helps make the transition very organic.

TRANSITIONS BETWEEN DIFFERENT TECHNIQUES

Although some of the works discussed above show a monolithic stylistic consistency—*Continuum* and *Coulée*, for example, never deviate from a pattern-meccanico presentation—most of Ligeti's works from this period are varied and often employ diverse techniques. And whereas earlier works such as *Artikulation* and *Aventures* relied on juxtapositions of different sections in a type of collage, more and more at the turn of the 1970s, Ligeti developed ways of smoothing out the transitions between different styles and techniques, bringing them together into a more unified flow. We have seen how *Clocks and Clouds* went back and forth between *Lux*-style microcanons and *Continuum*-style meccanico patterns, and we have seen how harmonic networks, including those in the Chamber Concerto and those with pattern-meccanico treatments, can range between more melodic and more harmonic effects, but other types of transitions are now widely available. The internal variety of expression within individual techniques—something Ligeti cultivated throughout the 1960s—resulted in a highly versatile environment, where different methods of construction can blend together in unified textures and unbroken formal sections.

Some of these connections take their starting point from the wild, gesticulating melodies of the Dies irae and *Aventures*. These angular melodies emphasized a repertoire of widely spaced melodic intervals along with rules for frequent changes of direction and rules against repeating pitches too frequently, but in subsequent pieces these stipulations were handled with more flexibility. By loosening the restrictions against note repetitions and arpeggiating back and forth between a more limited number of pitches—as occurred in parts of the Cello Concerto—these melodies can come to resemble the more widely spaced harmonic networks. In addition, the constantly changing directions and widely spaced intervals of *Aventures* and the Dies irae often resulted in a kind of compound line with groups of notes clustered together in two different registers. The instrumental accompaniments in these works began to collect notes in similar registers and connect them, taking advantage of this property. By simply abandoning one of these registers, Ligeti found another way to transition between more widely spaced musical textures and more narrowly delimited clusters, which can then be animated by one of the familiar techniques for handling closely spaced harmonies.

The pitch-succession melodies form another starting point for transitions that lie on the other extreme, most often used for clusters of various types. The rules of construction for these melodies emphasized maximal variety of note successions within the cluster, whereas the typical presentation of a pattern-meccanico texture emphasizes consistent direction of arpeggiation or scalar motion through the cell. The same underlying cluster, however, can easily be converted from one style of presentation to another. The meandering melodies seen in the clarinet part of the Chamber Concerto's second movement lie in between these extremes—neither unidirectional, nor striving for maximal variety, but with more leisurely melodic twists and turns. The concern with constraints on the typical direction of a line, then, proved to be of the utmost significance in differentiating between techniques and mediating between them.

String Quartet no. 2, Movement I

The String Quartet no. 2 is a catalog of different compositional techniques and the transitions between them. We have noted features of most of the movements already. The microcanonic writing in the beginning of the second movement gives way to wild outbursts; the meccanico repeated notes of the third movement are mixed with a section (mm. 30–37) that more closely resembles the original Les Horloges Démoniaques; the fourth movement's pitch-succession melody is set as an interlude between passages of harsh cluster chords; and the fifth movement's pattern-meccanico texture widens and contracts into different styles. It is the first movement, however, that exemplifies the smooth transitions between different models, combining them into a lively kaleidoscopic form, described in the sketches as a rhapsody ("Rhapsodia").

Ligeti has discused a lineage stretching from his own string quartets back to Bartók, whom he cited as the "point of departure" for one common contrapuntal technique. In this device, "two instrumental parts—two violins or a violoncello and a viola—are not fused but intertwine much more like twisted strands of a thread," and together form a chromatic composite.[38] In the first movement of the Second String Quartet, this type of intertwined chromatic composite accounts for much of the melodic motion and is the starting point for many transitions. The introduction is an atmospheric section featuring tremolo harmonics that expand fragmentary figures to complete the aggregate at measure 15, where the intertwined chromatic motion begins. Measures 15–19 (example 6.21) show several passages where two instruments work together to fill out chromatic spaces. In the opening beats the second violin has a diatonic line, A#–C#–D#–E, while the first violin fills out the complementary pitches, B–D–C–F. The passage continues in this way, using a two-part counterpoint alternating between the high and low strings. This type of melodic activity begins to alternate with more sustained textures. Measure 19 settles on a sustained (025) interval signal that again expands to complete an aggregate by measure 22. Measure 23 begins a three-part counterpoint in the same fashion, and the movement continues to morph in and out of this style, using different contrapuntal combinations.

The continuation of the movement shows even more skillfully executed transitions. In measures 28–32 these entwined melodies begin to settle into different registers as the second violin and the viola separate. In measure 33 both arrive on widely spaced arpeggiations, and for three measures they unfold harmonic networks with semitone shifts in their patterns. Meanwhile, the first violin plays a chromatic scale with octave displacements—a melodic type seen in the String Quartet no. 1 and in the Cello Concerto.

The most dramatic shift of this type occurs toward the end of the first movement. In measure 52 all of the instruments begin with this kind of displaced chromatic scale, and with a brief interruption in measures 64–70, continue in this manner, growing through measure 73. From here a more extensive chain of transitions occurs, ultimately bringing the movement to its conclusion. The first violin part, which is representative of the different shifts of technique, is shown in example 6.22 with annotations reflecting the following analysis. In the second beat of measure 74, Ligeti breaks up the chromatic motion by introducing whole tones (or widely spaced versions of interval class 2) into the line. These in turn become wider gaps, and the texture in measures 75–76 approaches the use of harmonic networks, with patterns shifting by semitone and occasionally by whole tone. These start to abandon the outer registers and contract toward a central range in measure

38. *LiC*, 15.

Example 6.21. String Quartet no. 2, I, mm. 15–19. Ligeti String Quartet no. 2, 1971. Copyright © 1971 by Schott Music, Mainz, Germany. Copyright © renewed. All Rights Reserved. Used by permission of European American Music Distributors Company, sole U.S. and Canadian agent for Schott Music, Mainz, Germany

76, and by measure 77, the counterpoint between the first and second violins resembles the intertwined lines heard earlier in the movement. At the end of measure 77, Ligeti has contracted the first violin's range to the chromatic cluster from B♭4 to E♭5, and presents this cluster with a complete pitch-succession melody. After this he presents more complete pitch-succession melodies, contracting the cluster to B♭–D and B–D♭, eventually settling on the trill from C–D♭ and finally a tremolo on C. The tremolo returns to the mysterious atmosphere of the opening of the work, but it arrives there smoothly after traversing through different techniques, all combined into one extended motion.

Example 6.22. String Quartet no. 2, I, violin I, mm. 74–79. Ligeti String Quartet no. 2, 1971. Copyright © 1971 by Schott Music, Mainz, Germany. Copyright © renewed. All Rights Reserved. Used by permission of European American Music Distributors Company, sole U.S. and Canadian agent for Schott Music, Mainz, Germany

1. The displaced chromatic scale begins to introduce whole tones and then wider gaps.
2. These gapped structures begin to act like harmonic networks; notes in different registers shift by semitone and occasionally by whole tone.
3. Outer registers are abandoned and activity contracts to the center.
4. Along with the second violin (not shown) the lines intertwine to fill out chromatic regions.
5. Chromatic clusters are expressed by pitch-succession melodies. Clusters from B♭ to E♭, B♭ to D, and B to D♭ are exact cycles (shown in brackets). The intervening space presenting the cluster from B to D (mm. 78-79) overlaps with the other cycles and is an inexact pitch-succession melody.

Chamber Concerto, Movement IV

The end of the Chamber Concerto uses a similarly sweeping transition encompassing the entire last section of the final movement. Ligeti begins with pitch-succession melodies, which spread out to become harmonic networks before dissolving at the end. In measure 31 the double bass begins with a chromatic cluster from E1 to A1, presented in the manner of a pitch-succession melody after 27 notes, and so before the cycle can be completed, E is heard for the last time, and Ligeti introduces B♭ into the cluster, shifting it upward. This process continues, and other instruments enter with similar lines. At measure 36 the bass has arrived on a cluster from D♭2 to G2 and begins filtering out notes, hollowing out the inner part of the cluster. First D and F♯ are removed in measure 37, then E♭, F, and E in measures 38, 39, and 40, respectively, at which point only the tritone C♯ to G remains. This tritone, taken over by the cello, becomes an interval in arpeggiating figures that begin in measure 42 and continue as harmonic networks, shifting their patterns in predominantly semitonal voice leading. From letter Y (m. 49) they become increasingly stretched and haggard, and wind instruments enter into this uneven environment with other melodic ideas. In measure 50 the string arpeggiations begin to abandon their registers and progressively narrow and compact themselves into the space of a trill by measure 52. The entirety of the second half of the movement, then, and the closing gesture of the work as a whole, is a technical tour de force, transitioning between melodic types with minimal interruption in the surface of the music or the underlying sense of form.

Conclusion

Form and Expression at the Turn of the 1970s

Throughout the analyses presented so far, interrelationships between technique, expression, and form have been central concerns. Ligeti himself addressed these issues in both "Metamorphoses of Musical Form," which he drafted as early as November and December of 1958,[1] and again in a lecture given as part of the conference "Form in New Music,"[2] held during the 1965 Darmstadt courses. In a period of compositional development and flux, certain ideas and themes resonate through Ligeti's essays with remarkable consistency, extending from the time of his first experimental works through this study and beyond. If we are to reach any lasting conclusions about the remarkable transformation of the 1950s and 1960s, we must, then, address not only the innovations of technique but also the guiding vision they supported, as manifested in his writings and sketches and in the aesthetics of his works. Ligeti's remarks make it clear that his conception of form involved strong spatial and temporal components: "musical form," he maintained, "arises only when one retrospectively views music's course in time as 'space.'"[3]

1. *GS*, 1:104, lists these dates for the early conception of this essay, although it was not published until 1960.
2. The conference, "Form in der Neuen Musik," consisted of several lectures given during the course of the festival and also featured Theodor Adorno, Pierre Boulez, Earle Brown, Carl Dahlhaus, Roman Haubenstock-Ramati, Mauricio Kagel, and Rudolf Stephan as speakers. See Gianmario Borio and Hermann Danuser, eds., *Im Zenit der Moderne: Die internationalen Ferienkurse für neue Musik, Darmstadt, 1946–66* (Freiburg: Rombach Verlag, 1997), 3:630–32.
3. György Ligeti, "Form in New Music," in *Contemplating Music*, vol. 3, *Essence*, ed. Carl Dahlhaus and Ruth Katz (New York: Pendragon, 1987), 783.

And though this retrospective positioning primarily meant the cognitive recognition and apprehension of the work's internal relationships as they unfold through time, for Ligeti, it also involved the historical conditioning that gives these moments context and meaning. The related roles of spatial analogies and historical context, in fact, are prominent in Ligeti's conception of the unique place his music held in the avant-garde. As fundamental as they are to his essays, these twin concerns are also reflected in his verbal and graphic sketches, which return to these consistent themes even as they put forward changing ways of realizing them. The following pages revisit these features as they gradually crystalize, leading to *San Francisco Polyphony*, the last major work he composed before the opera *Le Grand Macabre*, and a composition that serves as an epilogue, representative of the final conditions of Ligeti's metamorphosis. In this conclusion, we may see how the diverse techniques discussed in the preceding chapters are united in a conception of form and expression that acknowledges the roles of both past precedent and inherent shape in the audible comprehension of a work.

In his Darmstadt lecture Ligeti gave his appraisal of the state of experimental music, its origins, differences from and similarities to traditional music, and the "paradoxical situation"[4] he found in his contemporaries. He faulted John Cage for his "gesture of traditionlessness"[5] and his illusory sense of isolation and independence from history. In fact, Ligeti acknowledged that with the passage of time, many of the most radical gestures of new music, including those found in his own compositions, had unwittingly become a part of a common language, if not cliché:

Aperiodic jumps to and fro in wide intervals, followed by sudden inertia and then a resumption of the jumping movements; unbroken, fixed layers of sound usually built up like clusters; sound objects that are deposited as it were individually into the space of the form; certain colour combinations, such as tender and bustling percussion immersed in sounds of vibraphones and bells. These types have made so extensive an impression that they have become all but as familiar as a perfect cadence.[6]

More than simply lamenting the recognizability of these textures, Ligeti seemed troubled by the fact that radically different compositional methods often generated similar types of sounds, since this was an indication that compositional language had become somewhat divorced from perceptible sense. Thus one of the major faults Ligeti found in the contemporary practice of new

4. Ibid., 791.
5. Ibid., 787.
6. Ibid., 790.

music was "the loosening of the connection between compositional process and the resulting sensual appearance of music."[7] This more broadly echoes his complaint in "Metamorphoses" that the "total determinacy" of integral serial techniques "comes to be identical with total indeterminacy" in their end result.[8] Ligeti feared that this separation of audibly recognizable form and the underlying compositional technique often resulted in forms that were arbitrary or that arose automatically from the implications of technique in ways which the composer could hardly foresee. Most of all, with both integral serialism and chance composition—the most prominent postwar compositional schools of thought—it was the dogmatic value placed on technique at the expense of a listener's perspective or historical context that Ligeti found troubling. When composers place more emphasis on the purity of technique than they do on audible result, a type of loosened syntax and formal function slips in "through the back door,"[9] quite possibly unbeknownst to or unintended by the composer, through perceived similarities to other musical textures, which arise in the same historical moment and develop associations through connections to other repertoire.

Ligeti ultimately concluded that a change in attitudes toward form and technique would remedy some of the undesirable aspects of the current condition in new music. He held that "by virtue of a shift in the starting-point of compositional method, it becomes possible again to dispose over form as something intentional . . . what is primarily given is not the compositional procedure but the conception of the form's totality, the imagination of the music as sound."[10] With the formal concept taking primary importance, rigorous techniques can be designed to achieve the acoustic character demanded by the form, and these diverse techniques—as we observe in this period—can be unified by their common goals in formal articulation, rather than by sharing the same internal logic or consistent set of precepts. If audible comprehension is set up as a goal, then the unwanted or unintended side effects of the rote application of unadulterated technique will not enter the picture. In this way Ligeti worked to achieve the "individual, unconfused characters"[11] he first sought out in "Metamorphoses."

Looking at the works of a composer such as Ligeti, who was so aware of the pitfalls of widespread contemporary methods, necessitates examining his works in multiple contexts—the immediate context of the compositions themselves,

7. Ibid., 791.

8. György Ligeti, "Metamorphoses of Musical Form," trans. Cornelius Cardew. Form—Space: Die Reihe 7, English ed., 5–19 (Bryn Mawr: Presser, 1965), 10.

9. Ligeti, "Form in New Music," 790.

10. Ibid., 796. The original German (GS, 1:199) reads: "Andererseits ergibt sich, durch eine Verlagerung des Ansatzpunktes der kompositorischen Methode, die Möglichkeit, über Form als Intendiertes wieder zu verfügen . . . . Nicht das kompositorische Verfahren ist primär gegeben, sonder die Konzeption der Totalität der Form, die Imagination der erklingenden Musik."

11. Ligeti, "Metamorphoses," 11.

a mid-range context of their place in his evolving oeuvre, and the larger context of their historical position in the avant-garde movement of his time. In fact, we can understand Ligeti's entire compositional approach, as it evolved, as working to bring compositional process back into a closer accord with experienced result and into a greater awareness of its own historical context and precedents.

Throughout this book we have seen Ligeti address the themes of historical context and comprehensible formal shapes through his working method. The verbal planning stage is often laden with references to historical precedents and contemporary influences, and the graphic stage often encapsulated the spatial conception of the form in a clear, comprehensible way. With both of these concerns in mind, then, Ligeti would envision techniques geared toward the progressively more detailed working-out of musical material. Although Ligeti often moved back and forth between these different stages, mixed them together, and at times repeated part or all of this process for individual sections, this can be seen as his normative process. Sketches for *Ramifications* show this progression quite clearly. The verbal sketches include references to the idea of an accelerating chase, the film directors René Clair and Charlie Chaplin, and scenes from Kafka's *Amerika* (hajsza, lassan kezdödik, majd mind gyorsabb, végül hihetetlenül gyors—René Clair, Chaplin, Brunelda a kocsiban, Karl Rossmannt üldözik a rendörök). Alongside these are descriptions of polyphonic and harmonic features and ideas for density, tone color, and form, including some of the harmonic ideas mentioned above. Remarkably, however, at two points in these sketches Ligeti actually provides himself with a to-do list:

Compositional Process:
1) form-drawing + "script" (characters)
2) harmonic frame
3) filling out the harm. frame with voices and objects
   a) drawing b) musical notation

Komp. Vorgang:
1) forma-rajz + "forgatókönyv" (karakterek)
2) harmonikus váz
3) harm. váz kitöltése vonalakkal-objektumokkal
   a) rajz b) hangjegyek

And on another page he sets down a similar list:

Compositional Process:
1) form-drawing + *"harmonic background"*
2) transfer of those to a cumulative voice drawing
3) working out of the voices on this basis, approximate combination in the score
4) after the score: labeling indication figures for the copyist of the parts

Komp. menete:
1) forma-rajz + *"harmonikus háttér"*
2) ennek átvitele szólam-összesitö-rajzba
3) ennek alapján szólamok kidolgozása, hozzávetőleges partiturában egyesitve
4) Partitura után: tájékoztató figurákat megjelölni stimmiró számára

These lists clearly indicate that the next steps involved explicitly graphic or spatial representation of the form, along with charts or frameworks like the harmonic skeletons seen for many of the works from *Harmonies* to *Melodien*. Finally, by means of these charts, Ligeti would transfer these ideas into individual voices, writing them into the musical notation of the score. The compositional process, as explicated here, is in perfect keeping with the top-down process recommended in his essays, prioritizing a clear formal concept over the purity of technique, and the wording of these sketches even acknowledges a degree of "approximate combination" involved in the later steps so long as they help realize the original concept.

The stages of the compositional process we find in his sketches also show the importance of some of the recurring themes and concerns of his articles: the development of "individual, unconfused characters," the recognition of the work's historical context and relationships to other pieces, and the utilization of spatial analogies in conceptualizing form. In the verbal stages we find a great deal of explicit attention to the character of the work being composed, often using references to Ligeti's previous compositions and to pieces by other composers. These references typically latch onto individual details from these earlier works, which are then recontextualized in the resulting composition, but still seem to have special significance to Ligeti and frequently contain the starting points for more technical workings of the piece.

In the graphic planning stage there are often formal drawings that depict the flow of the work loosely in time (from left to right) and register (from low to high). Verbal descriptions, mentions of instrumentation, pitch levels, density, and so forth, often accompany these graphic designs. Closely associated with these form diagrams are charts for tallying different parameters, harmonic skeletons, and other mid-level calculations reflecting compositional rules. In the more detailed writing-out, these features move from loose organization to their more fixed form in the score, always realized in the spirit of the overall form, but with some flexibility in the application of individual techniques.

Despite their seemingly objective titles, the *Ten Pieces for Wind Quintet* and the String Quartet no. 2 contain numerous examples of expressive reference to both traditional music and extramusical inspirations. Ligeti said of the Second Quartet not only that it "sums up all the different kinds of music I had composed, all the various technical and expressive features,"[12] but also that

12. *LiC*, 17.

it contained "many traditional elements . . . . The entire string quartet tradition from Beethoven to Webern is there somewhere in the quartet."[13] In the sketches there are references to aspects of his own first quartet, *Apparitions*, the Requiem, *Aventures, Lux aeterna, Lontano*, and the Cello Concerto, as well as to the use of pizzicato in Debussy, Bartók, and Cerha, and to mosaic textures in Webern (op. 9, no. 6). In early ideas for movement V, Ligeti mentions "enigmatic Schubertian harmonies" (Titokzatos Schuberti harmóniák) alongside references to the first movement of Mahler's Sixth Symphony and later to the "mystical, luminous, harmonic light" and "quiet, ecstatic" atmosphere of the Adagio from Bruckner's Eighth Symphony, although adding the qualification that the quartet movement should always remain active (misztikus-világitó-harm. fényre, puha, eksztatikus, Bruckner VIII adagio. [de mindig mozog]). These reference points often take the same approach seen in *Aventures*—concentrating on a single aspect of older music and using it as a symbol of tradition—although the use in these later pieces tends to be more sympathetically integrated, rather than satirically referenced.

The sketches for the *Ten Pieces for Wind Quintet* are also full of expressive references—especially the "mini-concerto" movements, which already refer to the traditional genre. Like the fifth movement of the quintet, an ensemble piece discussed in chapter 6, the sixth movement, the mini-concerto for oboe, features a light stacatissimo presentation of repeated notes. In this movement, however, the repeated notes begin to take on a new character, one with a particular point of reference. Sketches for this piece describe it thus:

> "Oboe Concerto" short, medium-fast. Note repetitions—staccato—clockwork, precision mechanism, polyrhythm-polymeter, internally otherwise elegant legato-staccato, alternation, mannerist oboe solos also, here and there aggressive deep oboe register (with bassoon in unison).

> "Oboakoncert" rövid, középgyors. Hangrepeticios-stacc- óramüvek, preciziós mekanizmus, poliritm-polimetr, benne egyéb elegáns legato-stacatto, váltakozásu manirirt oboaszólók is, helyenként agressiv mély oboaregiszter (fag-gal unis.)

In this typed text, there are clear references to the repeated-note meccanico style and its possible changes in character with different registers or articulations. In handwritten annotations next to this passage, Ligeti added the description "Couperin figuration" (Couperin-figuració).[14] The abstract

---

13. *LiC*, 50. Martin Iddon, "Bartók's Relics: Nostalgia in György Ligeti's Second String Quartet," in *The String Quartets of Béla Bartók* (New York: Oxford University Press, 2014), 243–60, also discusses the complicated legacy of Bartók in this work.

14. The term "Couperin-figuració" also occurs in sketches for the Cello Concerto, where leggiero figures in this type of notation originate, and in sketches for the String

connection to the heavily ornamented character pieces of François Couperin contextualizes the oboe's figures, which emerge and become more ornate and elaborate as the piece progresses. Moreover, this recognition reveals a resemblance to ornamentation both in notation, similar to extended grace-note or cadenza passages, and in the way these passages often begin as trills or turns before spiraling out into less conventional patterns. The oboe solo sits at the crux of many of the movement's main concerns, as it emerges from the plain repeated notes of the ensemble and becomes the dominant voice, initiating changes as a classical soloist, changes—like the final transformation from pitch to noise as the players blow air through their instruments in a series of unpitched attacks—that also have a distinctly modern turn. With the acknowledgment of the oboe's Couperin figurations as the central image, the movement unfolds as a mixture of classical balance and contemporary chaos, presented through an ironic lens.

The eighth movement of the wind quintet also highlights Ligeti's concern with the immediate and historical contexts for his work, self-consciously combining his own techniques with concentrated references to the past, adapting them into a new and powerful means of expression. This movement is the mini-concerto for horn, but it begins with an extended introduction in the flute, clarinet, and bassoon, using the pattern-shifting techniques found in *Continuum*. Ligeti manipulates his pattern-meccanico techniques to achieve a softer, gentler atmosphere (expanding and contracting within the same general register), a softer dynamic, legato playing style, and conflicting subdivisions between the instruments. The canon between the voices becomes a peaceful and hypnotic texture, rather than carrying the associations of a broken-down machine.

Against this misty, nebulous background, the horn begins to emerge as the soloist and to evoke aspects of the traditional use of this instrument. The sketches mention two particular points of reference:

7) "Horn Concerto," initially slow solo horn introduction with echoes (= Mahler 7th Symphony, 1st Nachtstück), soon ex abrupto: fast (short) brutal, really a caccia piece, without the horn caccia in some places, caccia-like oboe (Pastorale scherzo) but only with short entrances.

7) "Kürtkoncert," elején lassu solo-Cor bevezetö echokkal (=Mahler 7. Symph. 1. Nachtstück), majd ex abrupto: gyors (rövid) brutális, igazi caccia-darab, Cor caccian kivül néhol Ob-caccia-szerü (Pastorale scherzo) de csak rövid bevetésekkel.

Quartet no. 2. Ligeti also discussed Couperin as a model for early composition exercises during his studies in Budapest (*GS*, 2:43 and 141), and also remarks on Couperin's influence on the "graphic, sharp-contoured character" of Bartók's piano writing in a discussion of the *Mikrokosmos* (*GS*, 1:319).

Handwritten near the typed excerpt are references to repetitions and echoes, harmonic glissandi, and the scherzo of Bruckner's Fourth Symphony (Bruckner IV Symph Scherzo, repeticiok, szignalok echok, harm-glissandok). In the finished score, as the horn enters "sounding as from the distance"[15] and gradually becomes more present, its gestures reference the decisive rhythms of hunting calls and fanfares. The references to the echo effects in Mahler's Seventh Symphony, however, are the clearest. These are seen toward the end of the work (although in the early planning stage of this sketch they were to be near the beginning). At measure 31 and following, the horn has repeated ascending gestures, first open, then half-stopped "quasi eco," and finally fully stopped "quasi eco di eco," imitating the call and answer of the open and muted horns at the opening of the second movement of Mahler's symphony. In talking to Joseph Häusler about the evocations of romantic music in *Lontano*, Ligeti recalled "a passage in Bruckner's Eighth Symphony, in the coda of the slow movement, where with great tranquility and gentleness the four horns suddenly play a passage that sounds almost like a quotation from Schubert, but seen through Bruckner's eyes."[16] Here, in turn, Ligeti is paraphrasing Mahler in the same distanced way—involving an ironic and temporal distance, as well as the evocation of physical distance provided by the soft, pattern-shifting introduction and the emergence and receding of the muted solo horn.

The bassoon mini-concerto is likewise expressive in suggestive ways. The bassoon has a long history of use as a comic instrument, and its combination with the piccolo—planned as a kind of burlesque in the sketches (Fagottkoncert piccoloval. Igen gyors, rövid, igen burleszk.) but limited to the end of the piece in realization—helps emphasize this by the use of incongruous registers.[17] The sketches also reference a "Miró-Klee balancing act, Circus" (Miró-Klee balanceakten, Zirkus) and the abrupt starts and stops of early comic film (Az egész minduntalan hirtelen megtorpan. [é]s ujra kezd. Trükkfilm). The inscription from Lewis Carroll's *Through the Looking Glass* found at the end of the score[18] places Humpty Dumpty's fall alongside the twiggy cartoonish figures of Joan Miró's painting *The Circus* (1937) or similarly frail and exaggerated figures by Paul Klee (e.g., *Die Sängerin der komischen Oper*, 1925) to suggest an atmosphere poised between comedy and danger, and these extramusical images work as analogies to the exaggerated registers and dynamic contrasts, the sudden presto sections interrupted by grand

15. György Ligeti, *Zehn Stücke für Bläserquintett* (Mainz: B. Schott's Söhne, 1969), 28.
16. *LiC*, 93.
17. The unusual combination of the piccolo and bassoon is used again in the slow movement of the Piano Concerto.
18. The quotation in György Ligeti, *Ten Pieces for Wind Quintet* (Mainz: Schott's Söhne, 1969) reads, "'. . . but—' There was a long pause. 'Is that all?' Alice timidly asked. 'That's all,' said Humpty Dumpty. 'Good-bye.'" (35)

pauses, an uncomfortable balancing act, always on the verge of tipping over or speeding out of control.

Along with the sketches, there are notes for a roundtable discussion or preconcert talk on this piece, and in them a comparison arises between this inscription and one of Schumann's most cryptic works, creating an involved chain of references:

> In some ways one could compare the ending section to Schumann's *Davidsbündlertanzen*: 'To top it off, Eusebius thought . . . ," but with the name of Eusebius perhaps changed to Humpty Dumpty!

> Den Schlussteil könnte man in etwa mit dem Schluss von Schumanns "Davidsbündlertänzen" vergleichen: "Ganz zum Überfluss meinte Eusebius . . .," wobei der Name Eusebius vielleicht durch Humpty Dumpty zu ersetzen wäre!

Although the remark may seem like a glib surface connection or a joke to warm the audience up to a difficult piece by comparing it to something better known, there are remarkable similarities between the sets. Schumann's work revels in its irregularities—a set of dance movements full of rhythmic displacements, unconventional phrasing, and stark contrasts between different introverted and extroverted movements, serious, humorous, joyful, and sorrowful. In Ligeti's *Ten Pieces for Wind Quintet*, these contrasts, distortions, and tongue-in-cheek references are expanded to border on the grotesque and kaleidoscopic.[19]

These verbal records, whether from sketches, interviews, or other writings, show the importance of the clear and unconfused characters that Ligeti demanded in "Metamorphoses of Musical Form." They are often developed in the verbal stage of composition, but they are also supported by the graphic stages, and together, they guide Ligeti's progressive refinement of musical details. We have seen how in the Requiem, for example, Ligeti worked out the broad motion from dark to light so critical for expressing the text, first through a graphic design for the Introitus that moved from low to high and to brighter instrumental timbres. This formal idea was followed by fixing entrance and exit points in musical notation and the more detailed working-out of individual blocks of text to get from one point to another. This general

19. In his discussion of the *Davidsbündlertänze* in *The Romantic Generation* (Cambridge, MA: Harvard University Press, 1995), 223–36, Charles Rosen points out several other features that could be compared to Ligeti: Schumann's tendency to use both internal and external references including the reuse of his own themes (the nostalgic theme of the second movement returning in the seventeenth), dance topics, the Clara Wieck motto, the characters of Florestan and Eusebius, and his ironic distortions of these elements in the work. Rosen also makes the comparison to Romantic landscape painting, and with Ligeti, too, there is a sense of the spatial helping unite the diverse elements of this set.

progression, in support of the initial conception of the work's character and shape, is present in Ligeti's works through the end of the period.

On one hand, graphic sketches were useful in conceptualizing original formal models, breaking away from the traditional forms he learned in Budapest.[20] On the other hand, in his Darmstadt lecture Ligeti acknowledged that "'unique forms,' however, acquire in retrospect, through history, . . . common characteristics which . . . turn the most varied individual formal realizations into members of a generic family of forms."[21] With this in mind, we can begin to discern some recurring formal principles in his music. In *Atmosphères*, we observed how individual parameters including dynamics, tone color, mobility, width, and register were listed separately and were not always coordinated with one another, having independent peaks and troughs, charted out graphically. Ligeti composed creatively with each parameter: in terms of register, for example, he might work with a ceiling or floor for a section of the work, or he might establish a normative direction, an expansion or contraction. The effect of density can be created horizontally by alteration of surface rhythm or vertically by harmonic structures that are more closely or widely spaced. The analysis of the pattern-meccanico compositions in chapter 6 showed some of the complex effects of these parameters: when nuanced and put into various combinations, they become a rich and multivalent system of tools for crafting potentially unique, yet intuitively recognizable forms.

Throughout Ligeti's form diagrams, however, register and density have come through as consistently important in defining formal landmarks. In the pieces that do not have explicit formal drawings, such as the brief movements of the *Ten Pieces*, analytically reconstructed harmonic skeletons and range graphs can show much the same. Although familiar constructs such as diatonic moments or recognizable interval signals sometimes serve as landmarks, the parameters of register and density are among the most palpable to the listener and are immediately comprehensible, written into our perception with broad strokes, without necessitating any reference to finely tuned systems such as serialism or tonality.

By tracing two common formal prototypes through Ligeti's oeuvre, we can observe some of the ways in which these different principles operate and develop meaning over time. Many of Ligeti's forms either develop from some sort of equilibrium or suggest a relatively regular process but then break off at some point. Score notations include the German indication to "stop suddenly as though torn off" (plötzlich aufhören wie abgerissen) and similarly in the

20. The depth to which traditional forms were ingrained in Ligeti during his schooling can be seen in his reaction—shortly after his arrival in Cologne—to Debussy's *Jeux*, a piece celebrated by Stockhausen and others for its nonconformance to any "'officially acceptable' form" (*LiC*, 42); the Paul Sacher Foundation also contains his notes for an analytical lecture on *Jeux*.

21. Ligeti, "Form in New Music," 788.

sketches, the Hungarian "break off" (abbamarad) appears frequently. In one particular family of forms, this abrupt cessation of activity is accompanied by a sudden move to the upper register, often at the golden section of the work or otherwise initiating the ending section of the piece. *Pièce électronique no. 3* is one of the earliest of this type, but the first movement of *Apparitions* is in the same mold. *Continuum* and *Coulée* also feature dramatic upward-shifting finales, as does the first movement of the *Ten Pieces*. There is variety within this family of forms. In some of these works—*Coulée*, for example—the process of upward motion is suggested slowly at first, but then accelerates out of control, as if by its own internal motivation. In *Pièce électronique no. 3*, *Apparitions*, and other works, impulsive "events" seem to arise from outside the process and work to bring about the change. Ideas of dynamic contrast, acceleration and corresponding increase in density, and the rate of pitch change over time all contribute to this basic rhetorical type, and the particulars are slightly different in each work.

Another family of forms involves the distortion of a symmetrical shape; *Harmonies* is a model, analyzed in chapter 6 with regard to its symmetrical registral plan, which is subjected to rhythmic liberties and distortions of both timbre and intonation. This idea, however, can be traced even further back, to *Glissandi*, whose two-part, prime-plus-retrograde design also entailed a symmetrical background complicated by superimposition of layers and filtering out of much of the material. The harmonic skeleton for the second movement of the Chamber Concerto also reveals a quasi-symmetrical contraction and expansion of register, which defines much of the form, but is articulated in different ways by the timbral and textural changes in how the instruments reveal this design. The distorted symmetries, however, have in common with the broken-off forms a principle of transformation, or metamorphosis, often from equilibrium to more chaotic states, or otherwise a process of inexorable deterioration, which is fundamental to Ligeti's compositional thought and which, through time, has come to resonate as an essential part of the pathos of his music.

In these two formal types, the idea of a wedge-like registral expansion is essential in sculpting the recognizable shapes and formal articulations, which in turn are the basis for expressive potential within the music. These constructions also provide a window into the way form and technique feed one another through stylistic changes. The wedge was first seen as a purely melodic idea in works from the earliest period of this book: *Invenció*, the *Omaggio a Girolamo Frescobaldi* from *Musica ricercata*, and the earliest works that began to explore the more systematic use of all twelve tones. Later, with the Kyrie of the Requiem and *Lux aeterna*, choral movements are built from the same type of expanding melodies placed in micropolyphonic imitation, but their effect is less melodic and more tied to the textural expansion of a cluster or sound mass. Now taken up as registral idea, the wedge can also be articulated by other polyphonic structures, including Type IV chorales within the *Dies irae*, and in many of the ensemble movements of the wind quintet, where the individual melodic lines are no longer wedge-shaped themselves, but work together to express this characteristic expansion. Finally, having developed a range of techniques that can be put to similar purpose, Ligeti was able to use these in combination with his harmonic networks to compose the sweeping registral gestures that define sections of the Second String Quartet and the Chamber Concerto.

Having examined the evolution of Ligeti's techniques and the way they supported his aesthetic vision in the works from the end of the 1960s, two works from the early 1970s help establish the continuity of Ligeti's method. *Clocks and Clouds* and *San Francisco Polyphony*—the last two major works composed before his opera, *Le Grand Macabre*—bear more imaginative titles than the String Quartet no. 2, *Ten Pieces for Wind Quintet*, or Chamber Concerto, but they operate in much the same way, amalgamating diverse sources of inspiration into a characteristic formal type and modifying a repertoire of more detailed techniques through stages of sketching that are now quite familiar. As such, these works serve to demonstrate far-reaching implications of the developments seen in this study.

The extramusical inspiration for *Clocks and Clouds* comes from a lecture by the philosopher Karl Popper in which these images represent two unattractive extremes: the "nightmare" of physical determinism on one side and the chaos of unbridled indeterminism on the other.[22] Popper described a continuum between these poles and theorized about a model of "plastic control," able to rein in the randomness of indeterminism without implying the hard control of complete determinism. Moreover, he followed these models of physical systems to their wider implications for human rationality and evolution, making frequent analogies to art and music, including the rules of counterpoint. In fact, there is not much of a stretch between Popper's ideas and the way that Ligeti conceptualized his own position between the polar extremes of the total predetermination of integral serialism and the total chance operations of Cage. Moreover, this debate had similarly profound implications for Ligeti, as one can tell by the rhetoric he used in critiquing these dogmatic approaches.

22. Karl Popper, "Of Clouds and Clocks," in *Objective Knowledge* (Oxford: Clarendon, 1972): 206–55 (esp. 217). At times Ligeti claimed that it was mostly the title of the lecture that was his inspiration for the piece (e.g., *LiC*, 64), but at other times (*Träumen Sie in Farbe?" Gyŏrgy Ligeti im Gespräch mit Eckhard Roelcke* [Vienna: Paul Zsolnay Verlag, 2003], 143–45) he showed a greater familiarity with Popper's ideas, even telling the story of meeting him in person and being disappointed by his conservative tastes in music. Nevertheless, there is a compelling parallel between Ligeti and Popper in aspects of their thought as well as in their life experiences as emigrants from Central Europe to the West who often felt like outsiders in their new environments.

In musical terms, Ligeti represents this pliable continuum between the rigid and the amorphous by the most gradual transitions between compositional techniques, as described above. The formal design, however, also takes a major role in shaping this expressive goal. Ligeti planned out the form graphically, as shown in example C.1. The registral expansions shown in the sketch are clear in the final work, as well. The lines and arrows seen in the second half of the diagram indicate some contraction of the initial plan that is evident in the final piece. Ligeti expanded the initial wedge to become the first seventy measures of the piece and simplified the second part of the expansion into a more succinct, unified gesture. The essential features—including the initial and final expansion, the emptying out (ür) of the middle register, and fading out of the bass and then the treble parts at the end—all remain.

The initial expansion is worked out in more detail in the diagram and is quite clear in the score. The diagram of the form includes note names, anchoring the wedge-like expansion from D4 to E4 down to D♭ and up to B♭ and then B, at which point the lower part of the wedge drops out, revealing the bare tritone F–B. More striking, though, is the fact that this initial expansion—shown as a single gesture in the graph—is realized with the combination of techniques described in chapter 6: pattern-meccanico figures in the instrumental parts expands from D down to D♭ (and even C) but only up to G, at which point the choir enters and begins the micropolyphonic expansion from their unison G up to B♭ and eventually the tritone F–B in measure 70. The fact that different techniques combine to articulate this first registral gesture points to the complex interactions of form and technique. The degree of plastic control over parameters including density and rate of change that Ligeti developed separately now enables him to blend techniques together smoothly into a single unified gesture. Not only do these techniques work together to articulate the wedge, one of Ligeti's characteristic formal types, but by doing so, they also help express the continuum between clocklike and cloudlike textures, giving voice to the initial inspiration of the work.

San Francisco Polyphony shows many of the same stages of composition put to fuller use and taking on, in many ways, more ambitious expressive goals. The extant sketches for this work seem to be more complete than those for other works, and they represent all the stages of the process. There are three separate iterations of form diagrams, one of which consists of three pages, laid out lengthwise and running to an approximate duration of eighteen minutes.[23]

23. This version of the form diagram, most likely the earliest, is reproduced in part in Louise Duchesneau and Wolfgang Marx, eds., *György Ligeti: Of Foreign Lands and Strange Sounds* (Woodbridge, UK: Boydell, 2011), color plate no. 1, and more fully in figure 3 of Richard Steinitz's article "The Study of Composers' Sketches, and an Overview of Those by Ligeti," *Contemporary Music Review* 31, nos. 2–3 (April–June 2012), 115–34.

Example C.1. *Clocks and Clouds*, sketch of the form. Reproduced with kind permission from the György Ligeti Collection of the Paul Sacher Foundation, Basel

Another version condenses much of the middle and end of the movement into a sixteen-minute work, shown in example C.2. Finally, Ligeti seems to have created a form drawing retrospectively, with text in German indicating that it was most likely used as an example for a talk.

Ligeti described the work as having three parts: an exposition that filters out a dense chromatic space, "as if someone went through it with a comb;" a middle section with expressive melodies that gradually move toward extreme registers, both low and high; and a coda, "a kind of perpetuum mobile machine-like music."[24] Along with the extensive verbal indications on the form drawings, there are other sheets of prose and pages devoted to working out each of the three main sections. Filtering diagrams made for the first section that show how a three-octave cluster from G2 to G5 is gradually separated out into bands, each the width of a fourth, with approximately a fourth between each. This filtering diagram resembles a looser version of the score to *Pièce électronique no. 3*, with horizontal lines showing the duration and endpoint of each note of the chromatic cluster. The end of the exposition, where everything begins shifting chromatically upward, is worked out on staff paper. The middle section, likewise, is plotted through sprawling semitonal voice leading, beginning with the C–Db–F#–G (0167) signal harmony in multiple octaves and continuing according to a harmonic skeleton. These harmonic structures are then articulated by different kinds of melodies—some rather straightforward, like those of *Melodien*, and others quite irregular and expressive. The melodies in the Chamber Concerto's second movement were not always complete expressions of the harmony in play, but in *San Francisco Polyphony* this incompleteness is taken to a greater extreme. Generally speaking, as notes shift, enter, or are filtered out of the underlying clusters, individual melodies stop using those pitches, yet no single melody uses all of the available pitches; this practice ensures a greater diversity in the melodic lines spread throughout the large orchestral ensemble.[25] Finally, the fast repeated figures of the closing section are also sketched out on staff paper, through a series of pattern transformations starting from D–Eb and expanding by the usual repertoire of primary transformations, shifting and adding notes a semitone away.

24. *LiC*, 44.

25. Jonathan Bernard analyzes passages from the ending section of *San Francisco Polyphony* in more detail in his article "Ligeti's Restoration of Interval and Its Significance for His Later Works" *Music Theory Spectrum*, 21, no 1 (Spring 1999), 1–31. Bernard describes some of the small-scale symmetrical interval combinations and their transformations, which I account for as effects of the same types of semitonal voice-leading transformations found in the harmonic skeletons discussed above. Bernard also points out the role of the G4 as the midpoint of the sound mass (which, as we may also note, appears as the upper boundary of the first section, and can be seen in the form diagram as a large-scale registral demarcation) and instances where the melodies anticipate pitches in the harmonic grid or otherwise stretch and skew the underlying ideal—something also seen in the Chamber Concerto, but taken farther here.

Example C.2. *San Francisco Polyphony*, sketch of the form. Reproduced with kind permission from the György Ligeti Collection of the Paul Sacher Foundation, Basel

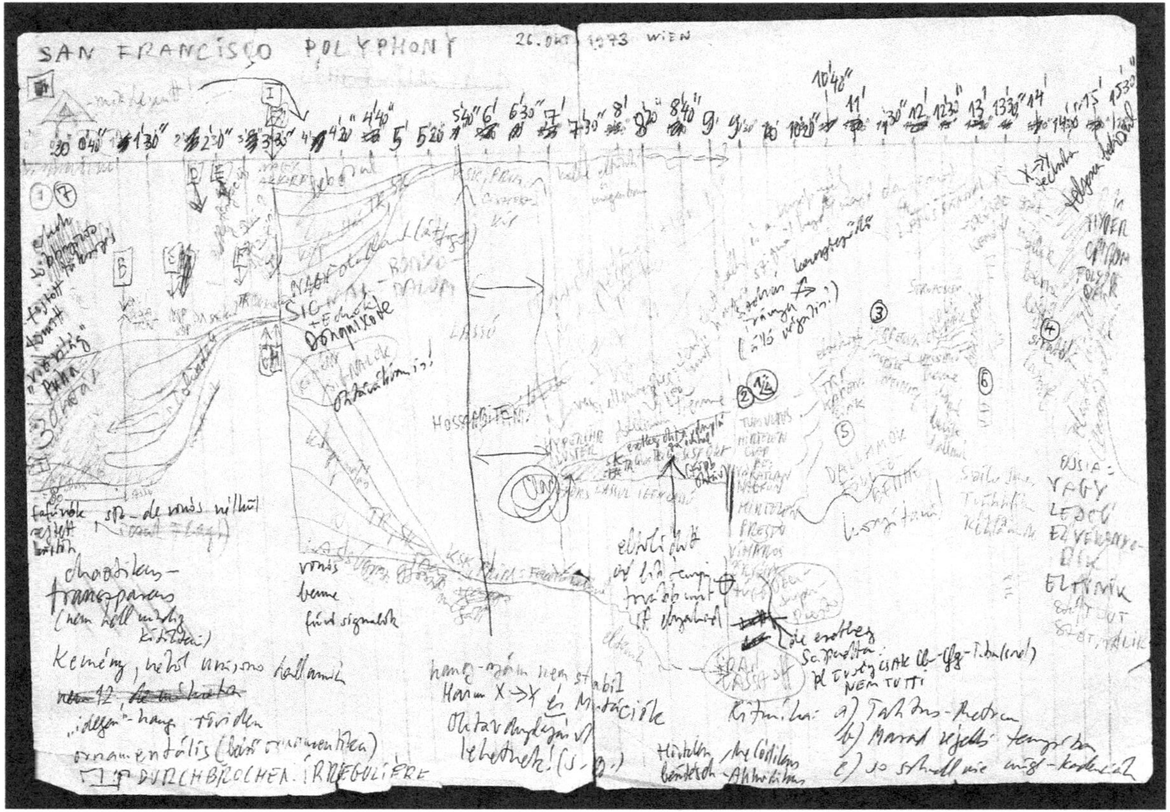

These technical features and compositional procedures are now quite familiar, but Ligeti continually adapted their use to new expressive means, responding to new experiences and stimuli. While stressing that the work is not in any way programmatic, Ligeti explained many of the inspirations for *San Francisco Polyphony*, which we may trace back to this network of musical features. Conversing with Péter Várnai, Ligeti discussed many of the charming features of San Francisco that struck him while he was in residence at Stanford University. Among them were the anachronistic and cosmopolitan features of the city, including the cable cars that reminded him of Budapest, the Victorian architecture from just after the 1906 earthquake, and the various ethnic neighborhoods reflecting waves of immigration in the city's history and refusing to completely integrate or amalgamate with the rest of the metropolis. The city's layout was also a source of charm for Ligeti, the regular grid of streets superimposed on an irregular landscape, resulting in the absurdly hilly inclines. Most significant of all, though, was the way the fog rolled in and out, and with it, how the visible landscape seemed to submerge and reemerge from its dense, fast-moving clouds.

Each of these sources of inspiration seems to be reflected in Ligeti's formal plan, and its execution in the composition draws on all the experience gained in his previous works. The idea of imposing a grid over irregular features was also seen in *Pièce électronique no. 3* (see chapter 2) and the dynamics between order and disorder have been discussed with regard to many of Ligeti's works. San Francisco's charming anachronisms can be seen in the expressive character of the melodies, which are more individual, have greater dynamic range, and show more sweeping contours than those in the Chamber Concerto. They are, as Ligeti said in retrospect, "reminiscent of Alban Berg or Mahler."[26] These melodies are not canonic or imitative but stand out as distinctive, and their heterogeneity also creates the sense of isolated objects or different characters intermingling in a bustling polyphonic environment.

The density of the polyphony, with the underlying clusters that make up the harmonic network behind it, seems an apt representation of the fog; Ligeti implied as much in his comments: "The backdrop is the fog ... the piece starts with a cluster full of various tunes that you cannot make out, as they are intertwined like creepers. Then slowly a very clear melodic pattern emerges from this dense texture, it is discernible for a while before it sinks back into the billowing mass. That is the overall structural principle of the work." As in *Lontano*, individual instrumental timbres may come through at different points as the "tunes emerge from the fog and then sink back into it."[27]

It is the last section of the work that Ligeti viewed as most American, saying that "only the end of the piece, the prestissimo section, with its machine-like,

26. See *LiC*, 67 and 44, for comments on the diverse melodies.
27. Ibid., 67.

hectic quality makes you think of a big American city."[28] Several points of reference go into this statement: the busy nature of the pattern-meccanico figures, the associations that they may have with American minimalist music, which had come increasingly into Ligeti's awareness during his visit to the United States, and, more generally, a renewed interest in tape music after having been in contact with John Chowning and the electronic music center at Stanford. Beyond the conspicuous similarity between the attenuation of chromatic clusters in the work and the schematic "modes" of *Pièce électronique no. 3* and filtering in studio practice more generally, there are similarities to Reich's tape-loops and phasing in the last section of the piece, where patterns shift, first in lockstep with one another, then separating and blurring into different strands. In a prose sketch planning some of the developments for the presto section, including descriptions of how it would widen and fill out, diverge, spread, and reconverge, there is an indication for the cymbal strike at the very end of the work reading: "cut off, like a magnetic tape" (elszakad mint egy magnószalag).[29]

By the time György Ligeti returned from the United States in 1972 much had changed, and though he continued to split his time between Vienna and various German cities, he found himself to be a very different composer than the refugee who escaped Hungary in 1956. He had achieved success after success, and the offer of a permanent position in Hamburg in 1973 granted him more stability than ever; he had worked out a compositional language with great expressive potential and had used it to write increasingly ambitious works. And yet this stability proved to be short-lived. His visit to America exposed him to the minimalism of Steve Reich and Terry Riley, the microtonality of Harry Partch, and eventually the rhythmic innovations of Conlon Nancarrow, all of which stimulated his creativity to move in new directions. His teaching in Hamburg, moreover, brought him in closer contact with new compositional ideas. Many of his students were interested in popular music and world music, which Ligeti heard in recordings, and which began to make an impact on his style. Some of his students also composed in neo-Romantic styles, which Ligeti spurned and saw as a reactionary, although there have been attempts to read his music as being in greater sympathy with this movement.[30] Moreover, in November 1973, the death of Bruno Maderna—Ligeti's friend and a champion of his music since his arrival in Cologne—cut one of the last threads connecting him to the Darmstadt avant-garde. Once again,

28. Ibid.
29. The writing in this sketch is very faint, and it is possible to read the word as "elszabad" (break loose, escape, run out of control) rather than "elszakad" (cut off, break, snap, tear, separate).
30. See Toop, *György Ligeti* (London: Phaidon, 1999), 152, and Richard Steinitz, *György Ligeti: Music of the Imagination* (Boston: Northeastern University Press, 2003), 244–45 and 270–71, for a discussion of the dynamic between Ligeti and the neo-Romantics.

Ligeti was dissatisfied. In retrospect, he looked at *Clocks and Clouds* as "one of my least complex compositions,"[31] and he found the early performances of *San Francisco Polyphony* unsatisfactory, failing to do justice to the score, with its intricate balance of soloistic lines in a large ensemble setting.[32]

Most of all, however, his work on *Le Grand Macabre* had become all-consuming, and it is this work that divides his stylistic periods. If the large works of the early 1970s expanded his compositional craft, pushing the limits of expressive potential, the demands of the opera brought the composer to a new point of crisis.[33] From 1974 to 1977 Ligeti devoted most of his time to the opera and produced little else. Having arrived at what seemed to be the limits of his repertoire of techniques, yet still struggling to synthesize new experiences, ideas, and influences, the composer made a decisive turn in his style with the eclectic mix found in the opera.

The relatively gradual changes from the late 1950s to the turn of the 1970s that have been the subject of this book define not so much a stable stylistic period as a general trajectory through the phases of Ligeti's musical metamorphosis, a path guided in parallel by aesthetic goals and the exploration of compositional techniques used to achieve them. Though the techniques themselves changed and developed over time, Ligeti's conception of musical form and expression remained quite consistent, and the framework of his compositional procedure gradually crystallized over the years. The composer's overarching vision and its detailed execution in individual works illustrate the meaning of his artistic credo:

Technique and imagination influence one another in a constant interchange. Every artistic innovation in the craft of composition ferments the whole spiritual edifice, and every change in this edifice demands constant revision of compositional procedure.[34]

The seamless counterpoint of *Lux aeterna* had its origins in the expression of eternal light but is also employed in the foggy distance of *Lontano*, the aggressive presence of the ninth piece for Wind Quintet, and cloudy sections of *Clocks and Clouds*. The pattern-meccanico works, starting with *Continuum* and *Coulée*, similarly range far from their original inspirations. Yet each time a technique shifts in its associations, it works toward the invention of a new character, a new imagination of sound and form. There is a distinctive plurality

31. *LiC*, 64.
32. Steinitz, *Ligeti*, 202–6, discusses the problematic place of *San Francisco Polyphony* in Ligeti's career and recounts many of the problems with early performances of this work.
33. Michael Searby addresses this period of Ligeti's creative work as such in his book, *Ligeti's Stylistic Crisis: Transformation in His Musical Style, 1974–1985* (Lanham, MD: Scarecrow, 2010).
34. Ligeti, "Metamorphoses," 5.

in Ligeti's techniques; not only can each be used for different effects, but different techniques can also work together toward a unified expression. Unlike the monolithic exploration of internally consistent techniques that he criticized in *Structures Ia* and elsewhere as a "fetish of technique,"[35] Ligeti's experimentalism never followed the implications of a technique to a singular end but, rather, looked for the greatest diversity within his methods. When the exploration of the techniques themselves inspired innovation, this innovation fed back into the imagination of musical characters, of formal and expressive potential, and the process began anew.

Ultimately, the techniques and the influences they synthesize—from his Bartókian roots and early experiences with serialism to the statistical ideas and greater awareness of psychoacoustics developed in Cologne; from Fluxus-inspired absurdity to his dramatic, satirical, and critical distance; and from his emulations of and reactions to other figures in the avant-garde to his growing independence and ultimate flourishing—serve this creative and unpredictable amalgamation of experience into musical form. Beyond the explication of individual pieces, a study of the sketches provides a fundamental key, revealing the full meaning of Ligeti's statement about technique and imagination, the aesthetic stance it entails, and the way he substantiated it in his compositions. Ligeti's wide-ranging career touched on many of the main currents of the second half of the century; he stands out as representative of his time, acutely aware of his personal journey, its intersections with the paths of his contemporaries, and their collective position in the historical tradition. Perhaps, then, we can even see in this book, not merely the chronicle of a composer finding his own voice, but a case study of someone navigating the changing tides between the high-modernist position of his upbringing and the emergence of postmodernist concerns around him.

35. See his wording in "Pierre Boulez: Decision and Automatism in Structure 1a," trans. Leo Black, in *Young Composers: Die Reihe* 4, English ed., 36–62 (Bryn Mawr, PA: Presser; London: Universal Edition, 1960), 39–40, and "Metamorphoses," 10. This issue is also taken up in my article "'Rules as Strict as Palestrina's': The Regulation of Pitch and Rhythm in Ligeti's Requiem and *Lux aeterna*," *Twentieth Century Music* 10, no. 2 (2013), 203–30.

BIBLIOGRAPHY

Adorno, Theodor W. *Philosophy of New Music*. Translated and edited by Robert Hullot-Kentor. Minneapolis: University of Minnesota Press, 2006.

Adorno, Theodor W. *Essays on Music*. Edited by Richard Leppert, translated by Susan H. Gillespie, et al. Berkeley: University of California Press, 2002.

Adorno, Theodor W. *Sound Figures*. Translated by Rodney Livingstone. Stanford: Stanford University Press, 1999.

Adorno, Theodor W. *Quasi una Fantasia: Essays on Modern Music*. Translated by Rodney Livingstone. London: Verso, 1992.

Adorno, Theodor W. *Dissonanzen; Einleitung in die Musiksoziologie*, Gesammelte Schriften 14. Edited by Rolf Tiedemann. Frankfurt: Suhrkamp, 1973.

Adorno, Theodor W. *Negative Dialectics*. Translated by E. B. Ashton. New York: Seabury, 1971.

Anhalt, Istvan. *Alternative Voices: Essays on Contemporary Vocal and Choral Composition*. Toronto: University of Toronto Press, 1984.

Antokoletz, Elliott. *The Music of Béla Bartók: A Study of Tonality and Progression in Twentieth-Century Music*. Berkeley: University of California Press, 1984.

Auner, Joseph, and Judy Lochhead, eds. *Postmodern Music/Postmodern Thought*. Studies in Contemporary Music and Culture 4, edited by Joseph Auner. New York: Routledge, 2002.

Babbitt, Milton. "The String Quartets of Bartók." *Musical Quarterly* 25 (July 1949): 377–85.

Bartók, Béla. *Essays*. Edited by Benjamin Suchoff. Lincoln: University of Nebraska Press, 1976.

Bartók, Béla. *Rumanian Folk Music*, vol. 2. The Hague: Nijhoff, 1967.

Bauer, Amy. *Ligeti's Laments: Nostalgia, Exoticism, and the Absolute*. Burlington, VT: Ashgate, 2011.

Bauer, Amy. "'Tone-Color, Movement, Changing Harmonic Planes:' Cognition, Constraints and Conceptual Blends in Modernist Music." In *The Pleasure of Modernist Music: Listening, Meaning, Intention, Ideology*, edited by Arved Ashby, 121–52. Rochester: University of Rochester Press, 2004.

Bauer, Amy. "'Composing the Sound Itself': Secondary Parameters and Structure in the Music of Ligeti." *Indiana Theory Review* 22, no. 1 (spring 2001): 37–64.

Bauer, Amy. "Compositional Process and Parody in the Music of György Ligeti." Ph.D. diss., Yale University, 1997.

Bayley, Amanda, ed. *The Cambridge Companion to Bartók*. New York: Cambridge University Press, 2001.

Beal, Amy. *New Music, New Allies: American Experimental Music in West Germany from the Zero Hour to Reunification*. Berkeley: University of California Press, 2006.

Beckles Willson, Rachel. *Ligeti, Kurtág, and Hungarian Music during the Cold War*. New York: Cambridge University Press, 2007.

Beckles Willson, Rachel. *György Kurtág, The Sayings of Péter Bornemisza, op. 7: A "concerto" for Soprano and Piano*. Burlington, VT: Ashgate, 2004.

Bernard, Jonathan. "Rules and Regulation: Lessons from Ligeti's Compositional Sketches." In *György Ligeti: Of Foreign Lands and Strange Sounds*, edited by Louise Duchesneau and Wolfgang Marx, 149–67. Woodbridge, UK: Boydell, 2011.

Bernard, Jonathan. "A Key to Structure in the Kyrie of György Ligeti's Requiem." *Mitteilungen der Paul Sacher Stiftung* 16 (2003): 42–47.

Bernard, Jonathan. "Ligeti's Restoration of Interval and Its Significance for His Later Works." *Music Theory Spectrum* 21, no. 1 (spring 1999): 1–31.

Bernard, Jonathan. "Voice Leading as a Spatial Function in the Music of Ligeti." *Music Analysis* 13, nos. 2–3 (July–October 1994): 227–53.

Bernard, Jonathan. "Inaudible Structures, Audible Music: Ligeti's Problem, and His Solution." *Music Analysis* 6, no. 3 (October 1987): 207–36.

Boehmer, Konrad. "Koenig, Sound Composition, *Essay*." In *Electroacoustic Music: Analytical Perspectives*, edited by Thomas Licata, 59–72. Westport, CT: Greenwood, 2002.

Borio, Gianmario. "Komponieren um 1960." In *Die Geschichte der Musik, III: Musik der Moderne*, edited by Matthias Brzoska and Michael Heinemann, 293–311. Laaber: Laaber Verlag, 2001.

Borio, Gianmario. "L'Eredità Bartókiana nel Secondo Quartetto de G. Ligeti, Sul Concetto di tradizione nella Musica Contemporanea." *Studi Musicali* 13 (1984): 289–307.

Borio, Gianmario, and Hermann Danuser, eds. *Im Zenit der Moderne: Die Internationalen Ferienkurse für neue Musik Darmstadt, 1946–1966*. Freiburg im Breisgau: Rombach, 1997.

Boulez, Pierre. *Stocktakings from an Apprenticeship*. Edited by Paule Thévenin, translated by Stephen Walsh. New York: Oxford University Press, 1991.

Burde, Wolfgang. *György Ligeti: Eine Monographie*. Zurich: Atlantis Musikbuch, 1993.

Cage, John. *Silence: Lectures and Writings*. Middletown, CT: Wesleyan University Press, 1961.

Caplin, William, James Hepokoski, and James Webster. *Musical Form, Forms, and Formenlehre: Three Methodological Reflections*. Edited by Pieter Bergé. Leuven: Leuven University Press, 2009.

Cardew, Cornelius. *Stockhausen Serves Imperialism and Other Articles*. London: Latimer New Dimensions, 1974.

Carr, Maureen. *Stravinsky's Pulcinella: A Facsimile of the Sources and Sketches*. Middleton, WI: A-R Editions, 2010.

Carr, Maureen. *Multiple Masks: Neoclassicism in Stravinsky's Works on Greek Subjects*. Lincoln: University of Nebraska Press, 2002.

Cerha, Friedrich. *Schriften: Ein Netzwerk*. Österreichische Musikzeitedition 28. Vienna: Verlag Lafite, 2001.

Chadabe, Joel. *Electric Sound: The Past and Promise of Electronic Music*. Upper Saddle River, NJ: Prentice Hall, 1997.

Clendinning, Jane Piper. "Review/Article of Miguel A. Roig-Francoli's Article 'Harmonic and Formal Processes in Ligeti's Net-Structure Compositions." *Music Theory Online* 2, no. 5 (1996), accessed through http://www.mtosmt.org/issues/mto.96.2.5/mto.96.2.5.clendinning.html, June 11, 2017.

Clendinning, Jane Piper. "Structural Factors in the Microcanonic Compositions of György Ligeti." In *Concert Music, Rock, and Jazz since 1945: Essays and Analytical Studies*, edited by Elizabeth West Marvin and Richard Hermann, 229–56. Rochester: University of Rochester Press, 1995.

Clendinning, Jane Piper. "The Pattern-Meccanico Compositions of György Ligeti." *Perspectives of New Music* 31, no. 1 (winter 1993): 192–234.

Clendinning, Jane Piper. "Contrapuntal Techniques in the Music of György Ligeti." PhD diss., Yale University, 1989.

Cogan, Robert. *New Images of Musical Sound*. Cambridge, MA: Harvard University Press, 1984.

Cogan, Robert, and Pozzi Escot. *Sonic Design: The Nature of Sound and Music*. Englewood Cliffs, NJ: Prentice Hall, 1976.

Cohn, Richard. "Inversional Symmetry and Transpositional Combination in Bartók." *Music Theory Spectrum* 10 (spring 1988): 19–42.

Cuciurean, John. "Aspects of Harmonic Structure, Voice Leading, and Aesthetic Function in György Ligeti's *in Zart Fliessender Bewegung*." *Contemporary Music Review* 31, nos. 2–3 (April–June 2012): 221–38.

Czigány, Gyula, ed. *Contemporary Hungarian Composers*. Budapest: Editio Musica Budapest, 1970.

de Benedictis, Angela Ida, and Pascal Decroupet. "Die Wechselwirkung von Skizzenforschung und spektromorphologischer Höranalyse als Grundlage für das ästhetische Verständnis: Zu György Ligetis *Atmosphères*." *Musiktheorie* 27, no. 4 (2012): 322–35.

Decroupet, Pascal. "Timbre Diversification in Serial Tape Music and Its Consequence on Form." *Contemporary Music Review* 10, no. 2 (1994): 13–23.

Dibelius, Ulrich. *György Ligeti: Eine Monographie in Essays*. Mainz: Schott, 1994.

Dibelius, Ulrich. *Moderne Musik*. Munich: Piper, 1966.

Dodge, Charles, and Thomas Jerse. *Computer Music: Synthesis, Composition, and Performance*, 2nd ed. New York: Schirmer, 1997.

Drott, Eric. "Lines, Masses, Micropolyphony: Ligeti's Kyrie and the 'Crisis of the Figure.'" *Perspectives of New Music* 49, no. 1 (winter 2011): 4–46.

Drott, Eric. "Ligeti in Fluxus." *Journal of Musicology* 21, no. 2 (spring 2004): 201–40.

Duchesneau, Louise, and Wolfgang Marx, eds., *György Ligeti: Of Foreign Lands and Strange Sounds*. Woodbridge, UK: Boydell, 2011.

Eimert, Herbert. "How Electronic Music Began." *Musical Times* (April 1973): 347–49.

Eimert, Herbert. "What Is Electronic Music?" translated by Cornelius Cardew, in *Electronic Music: Die Reihe* 1, English ed., 1–10. Bryn Mawr, PA: Presser, 1958.

Eimert, Herbert, and Karlheinz Stockhausen, eds. *Reports: Analyses: Die Reihe* 5, English ed., translated by Leo Black and Ruth Koenig. Bryn Mawr, PA: Presser, 1961.

Eimert, Herbert, and Karlheinz Stockhausen, eds. *Young Composers: Die Reihe* 4, English ed., translated by Leo Black. Bryn Mawr, PA: Presser, 1960.

Eimert, Herbert, and Karlheinz Stockhausen, eds. *Musical Craftsmanship: Die Reihe* 3, English ed., translated by Cornelius Cardew and Leo Black. Bryn Mawr, PA: Presser, 1959.

Eimert, Herbert, and Karlheinz Stockhausen, eds. *Electronic Music: Die Reihe* 1, English ed., translation uncredited. Bryn Mawr, PA: Presser, 1958.

Escot, Pozzi. "'Charm'd Magic Casements,' Mathematical Models in Ligeti." *Sonus* 9, no. 1 (1988): 17–37.

Floros, Constantin. *György Ligeti: Jenseits von Avantgarde und Postmoderne*. Vienna: Verlag Lafite, 1996.

Fosler-Lussier, Danielle. *Music Divided: Bartók's Legacy in Cold War Culture*. Berkeley: University of California Press, 2007.

Frobenius, Wolf. "Gottfried Michael Koenig als Theoretiker der seriellen Musik." In *Gottfried Michael Koenig*. Musik-Konzepte 66, 77–104. Munich: Edition Text+Kritik, 1989.

Geck, Martin. *Johann Sebastian Bach: Life and Work*, translated by John Hargraves. Orlando: Harcourt, 2006.

Geck, Martin. "Richard Wagner und die ältere Musik." In *Die Ausbreitung des Historismus über die Musik*, edited by Walter Wiora, 123–46. Regensburg: Bosse, 1969.

Gillies, Malcolm. "Bartók Analysis and Authenticity." *Studia Musicologica Academiae Scientarum Hungaricae* 36, nos. 3–4 (1995): 319–27.

Gillies, Malcolm. "Review Article: Ernő Lendvai: *The Workshop of Bartók and Kodály*." *Music Analysis* 5, nos. 2–3 (July–October 1986): 285–95.

Gollin, Edward. "Multi-Aggregate Cycles and Multi-Aggregate Serial Techniques in the Music of Béla Bartók." *Music Theory Spectrum* 29, no. 2 (fall 2007): 143–76.

Gottwald, Clytus. "*Lux aeterna*: Ein Beitrag zur Kompositionstechnik György Ligetis." *Musica* 25, no. 1 (1971): 12–17.

Griffiths, Paul. *György Ligeti*, 2nd ed. London: Robson, 1997.

Hall, Patricia. *A View of Berg's* Lulu *through the Autograph Sources*. Berkeley: University of California Press, 1996.

Hall, Patricia, and Friedemann Sallis, eds., *A Handbook to Twentieth-Century Musical Sketches*. New York: Cambridge University Press, 2004.

Hambraeus, Bengt. *Aspects of Twentieth-Century Performance Practice: Memories and Reflections*. Uppsala: Royal Swedish Academy of Music, 1997.

Harvey, Jonathan. *The Music of Stockhausen*. Berkeley: University of California Press, 1975.

Heikinheimo, Seppo. *The Electronic Music of Karlheinz Stockhausen: Studies on the Aesthetic and Formal Problems of Its First Phase*. Acta musicologica fennica 6. Helsinki: Suomen Musikkitieteellinen, 1972.

Heile, Björn. *The Music of Mauricio Kagel*. Burlington, VT: Ashgate, 2006.

Hicks, Michael. "Interval and Form in Ligeti's *Continuum* and *Coulée*." *Perspectives of New Music* 31, no. 1 (winter 1993): 172–90.

Holmes, Thom. *Electronic and Experimental Music: Technology, Music, and Culture*, 3rd ed. New York: Routledge, 2008.

Howat, Roy. "Bartók, Lendvai and the Principles of Proportional Analysis." *Music Analysis* 2, no. 1 (March 1983): 69–95.

Iddon, Martin. "Bartók's Relics: Nostalgia in György Ligeti's Second String Quartet." In *The String Quartets of Béla Bartók*, edited by Dániel Péter Biró and Harald Krebs, 243–60. New York: Oxford University Press, 2014.

Institute of Sonology. *His Master's Noise*. The Hague: BVHAAST CD 06/0701, 2001.

Ionesco, Eugène. *The Bald Soprano and The Lesson*, translated by Tina Howe. New York: Grove, 2006.

Ionesco, Eugène. *Rhinoceros and Other Plays*, translated by Derek Prouse. New York: Grove, 1960.

Iverson, Jennifer. "Ligeti's Dodecaphonic Requiem." *Tempo* 68, no. 270 (October 2014): 31–47.

Iverson, Jennifer. "Shared Compositional Techniques between György Ligeti's *Pièce électronique No. 3* and *Atmosphères*." *Mitteilungen der Paul Sacher Stiftung* 22 (April 2009): 29–33.

Iverson, Jennifer. "The Emergence of Timbre: Ligeti's Synthesis of Electronic and Acoustic Music in *Atmosphères*." *Twentieth-Century Music* 7, no. 1 (March 2010): 61–89.

Jarry, Alfred. *The Ubu Plays*. Translated by Cyril Connolly and Simon Watson Taylor. New York: Grove Weidenfield, 1969.

Jarvlepp, Jan. "Pitch and Texture Analysis of Ligeti's Lux Aeterna." *ex tempore* 2, no. 1 (1982): 16–32, accessed through http://www.ex-tempore.org/jarvlepp/jarv-lepp.htm, March 12, 2012.

Jelinek, Hanns. *Anleitung zur Zwölftonkomposition*, 2nd ed. Vienna: Universal Edition, 1967.

Jeppesen, Knud. *Counterpoint: The Polyphonic Vocal Style of the Sixteenth Century*. Translated by Glen Haydon. New York: Prentice Hall, 1939. Reprint, New York: Dover, 1992.

Jeppesen, Knud. *The Style of Palestrina and the Dissonance*. Translated by Margaret W. Hamerik. London: Oxford University Press, 1927.

Kafka, Franz. *Amerika*. Translated by Willa and Edwin Muir. New York: Schocken, 1996.

Karkoschka, Erhard. *Das Schriftbild der neuen Musik: Bestandsaufnahme neuer Notationssymbole, Anleitung zu deren Deutung, Realisation und Kritik*. Celle: Moeck, 1966. English ed., *Notation in New Music: A Critical Guide to Interpretation and Realisation*. Translated by Ruth Koenig. New York: Praeger, 1972.

Kárpáti, János. "Axis Tonality and Golden Section Theory Reconsidered." *Studia Musicologica Academiae Scientarum Hungaricae* 47, nos. 3–4 (September 2006): 417–26.

Kárpáti, János. *Bartók's Chamber Music*. Translated by Fred Macnicol and Mária Steiner, translation revised by Paul Merrick. Stuyvesant, NY: Pendragon, 1994.

Kassel, Matthias. "Das Fundament im Turm zu Babel: Ein weiterer Versuch, *Anagrama* zu lessen." In *Mauricio Kagel*. Musik-Konzepte 124, 4–26. Munich: Edition Text+Kritik, 2004.

Kaufmann, Harald. "Betreffend Ligetis Requiem." In *Von innen und aussen*, edited by Werner Grünzweig and Gottfried Krieger, 134–48. Hofheim: Wolke Verlag, 1993.

Kaufmann, Harald. "Ligetis Zweites Streichquartett." *Melos* 37, no. 5 (1970): 181–86.

Kaufmann, Harald. *Spurlinien: Analytische Aufsätze über Sprache und Musik*. Vienna: Verlag Lafite, 1969.

Kellein, Thomas. *The Dream of Fluxus, George Maciunas: An Artist's Biography*. London: Edition Hansjörg Mayer, 2007.

Kerékfy, Márton. "'A "new music" from nothing': György Ligeti's *Musica ricercata*." *Studia Musicologica* 49, nos. 3–4 (2008): 203–30.

Koblyakov, Lev. *Pierre Boulez: A World of Harmony*. Chur, Switzerland: Harwood Academic, 1990.

Koenig, Gottfried Michael. "Musik und Zahl." In *Gottfried Michael Koenig*, Musik-Konzepte 66, 13–34. Munich: Edition Text+Kritik, 1989.

Koenig, Gottfried Michael. "Ligeti und die elektronische Musik." In *György Ligeti: Personalstil, Avantgardismus, Popularität*, edited by Otto Kolleritsch, 11–26. Vienna: Universal Edition, 1987.

Koenig, Gottfried Michael. *Essay: Komposition für elektronische Klänge, 1957. Partitur zugleich technische Arbeitsanweisung*. Vienna: Universal Edition, 1960.

Kolleritsch, Otto, ed. *György Ligeti: Personalstil—Avantgardismus—Popularität*. Studien zur Wertungsforschung 19. Vienna: Universial Edition, 1987.

Kramer, Jonathan. *The Time of Music: New Meanings, New Temporalities, New Listening Strategies*. New York: Schirmer, 1988.

Kramer, Jonathan. "The Fibonacci Series in Twentieth-Century Music." *Journal of Music Theory* 17, no. 1 (spring 1973): 110–48.

Krebs, Harald. *Fantasy Pieces: Metrical Dissonance in the Music of Robert Schumann*. New York: Oxford University Press, 1999.

Krúdy, Gyula. *The Adventures of Sindbad* Edited and translated by George Szirtes. New York: Central European University Press, 1998.

Krúdy, Gyula. *Sunflower*. Translated by John Bátki, introduction by John Lukacs. New York: New York Review of Books, 1997.

Lendvai, Ernő. *The Workshop of Bartók and Kodály*. Budapest: Editio Musica Budapest, 1983.

Lendvai, Ernő. *Béla Bartók: An Analysis of His Music*. London: Kahn & Averill, 1971.

Levy, Benjamin R. "'Rules as Strict as Palestrina's': The Regulation of Pitch and Rhythm in Ligeti's Requiem and *Lux aeterna*." *Twentieth-Century Music* 10, no. 2 (2013): 203–30.

Levy, Benjamin R. "Shades of the Studio: Electronic Influences on Ligeti's *Apparitions*." *Perspectives of New Music* 47, no. 2 (2009): 59–87.

Levy, Benjamin R. "States of Balance and Turbulence: Ligeti's *Pièce électronique no. 3* in Concept and Realization." In *Musiktheorie als interdisziplinäres Fach*, musik. theorien der gegenwart 4, edited by Christian Utz. Saarbrücken: PFAU-Verlag, 2009.

Levy, Benjamin R. "The Electronic Works of György Ligeti and Their Influence on his Later Style," Ph.D. diss., University of Maryland, 2006.

Licata, Thomas, ed. *Electroacoustic Music: Analytical Perspectives*. Westport, CT: Greenwood, 2002.

Lichtenfeld, Monika. "György Ligeti, oder das Ende der seriellen Musik." *Melos* 39, no. 2 (1972): 74–80.

Lichtenfeld, Monika. "Zehn Stücke für Bläserquintett von György Ligeti." *Melos* 39, no. 6, (1972): 326–33.

Lichtenfeld, Monika. "'Requiem' von György Ligeti: Einleitung und Kommentar." *Wort und Wahrheit* 23, no. 4 (1968): 308–13.

Ligeti, György. *Gesammelte Schriften*, vols. 1 and 2. Edited by Monika Lichtenfeld. Publications of the Paul Sacher Foundation 10:1–2. Mainz: Schott, 2007.

Ligeti, György. Requiem. *rev. ed.*, vocal score by Zsigmond Szathmáry. New York: Litolff/C.F. Peters, 2006.

Ligeti, György. *"Träumen Sie in Farbe?" Gyorgy Ligeti im Gespräch mit Eckhard Roelcke*. Vienna: Paul Zsolnay Verlag, 2003.

Ligeti, György. "States, Events, Transformations," translated by Jonathan Bernard. *Perspectives of New Music* 31, no. 1 (winter 1993): 164–71.

Ligeti, György. *Continuum, Zehn Stücke für Bläserquintett, Artikulation, Glissandi, Etüden für Orgel, Volumina*. Wergo WER 60161-50, 1988.

Ligeti, György. "Form." In *Contemplating Music*, vol. 3, *Essence*, edited by Carl Dahlhaus and Ruth Katz, 781–96. New York: Pendragon, 1987.

Ligeti, György. *Ligeti in Conversation*. Translated by Gabor J. Schabert, Sarah E. Soulsby, Terence Kilmartin, and Geoffrey Skelton. London: Ernst Eulenburg, 1983.

Ligeti, György. *Kammerkonzert für 13 Instrumentalisten*. Mainz: B. Schott's Söhne, 1974.

Ligeti, György. *Volumina,* rev. ed. with English translation by Eugene Hartzell. New York: Litolff/C.F. Peters, 1973.

Ligeti, György. *Zehn Stücke für Bläserquintet.* Mainz: Schott's Söhne, 1969.

Ligeti, György. *Zwei Etüden für Orgel.* Mainz: Schotts Söhne, 1969.

Ligeti, György. "Spielanweisungen zur Erstfassung des zweiten Satzes der 'Apparitions.'" *Musica* 22 (1968): 177–79.

Ligeti, György. "Metamorphoses of Musical Form," translated by Cornelius Cardew. In *Form—Space: Die Reihe* 7, English ed., 5–19. Bryn Mawr, PA: Presser, 1965.

Ligeti, György. "Pierre Boulez: Decision and Automatism in Structure 1a," translated by Leo Black. In *Young Composers: Die Reihe* 4, English ed., 36–62. Bryn Mawr, PA: Presser; London: Universal Edition, 1960.

Ligeti, György. *A klasszikus harmóniarend.* Budapest: Zeneműkiadó, 1956.

Ligeti, György. *Klasszikus összhangzattan: Segédkönyv.* Budapest: Zeneműkiadó, 1954.

Lobanova, Marina. *György Ligeti: Style, Ideas, Poetics.* Translated by Marc Shuttleworth. Berlin: Kuhn, 2002.

Luchese, Diane. "Levels of Infrastructure in Ligeti's *Volumina.*" *Sonus* 9, no. 1 (1988): 38–58.

Maconie, Robin. *The Works of Karlheinz Stockhausen,* 2nd ed. New York: Oxford University Press, 1990.

Mahler, Gustav. *Symphonies nos. 3 and 4 in Full Score.* New York: Dover, 1989 (reprint of Universal Edition, [n.d.].

Mahler, Gustav. *Symphony no. 8 in Full Score.* New York: Dover, 1989 (reprint of Izdatel'stvo "Muzyka," Moscow, 1976).

Manning, Peter. *Electronic and Computer Music,* revised and expanded edition. New York: Oxford University Press, 2004.

Marshall, Kimberly. "György Ligeti." In *Twentieth-Century Organ Music,* edited by Christopher S. Anderson, 262–85. New York: Routledge, 2012.

Marx, Wolfgang. "'Make Room for the Grand Macabre!' The Concept of Death in György Ligeti's Oeuvre." In *György Ligeti: Of Foreign Lands and Strange Sounds,* edited by Louise Duchesneau and Wolfgang Marx, 71–84. Woodbridge, UK: Boydell, 2011.

Mason, Colin. "An Essay in Analysis: Tonality, Symmetry, and Latent Serialism in Bartók's Fourth Quartet." *Music Review* 18 (1957): 189–201.

McAdams, Stephen. "Perspectives on the Contribution of Timbre to Musical Structure." *Computer Music Journal* 23, no. 3 (fall 1999): 85–102.

Metzger, Heinz-Klaus, and Rainer Riehn, eds. *Dieter Schnebel,* Musik-Konzepte 16. Munich: Edition Text + Kritik, 1980.

Michel, Pierre. *György Ligeti: Compositeur d'aujourd'hui.* Paris: Minerve, 1985.

Mirka, Danuta. "To Cut the Gordian Knot: The Timbre System of Krzysztof Penderecki." *Journal of Music Theory* 45, no. 2 (autumn 2001): 435–56.

Morrison, Charles. "Stepwise Continuity as a Structural Determinant in György Ligeti's *Ten Pieces for Wind Quintet.*" *Perspectives of New Music* 24, no. 1 (1985): 158–82.

Nattiez, Jean-Jacques, ed. *The Boulez-Cage Correspondence.* Translated by Robert Samuels. New York: Cambridge University Press, 1993.

Nordwall, Ove. *György Ligeti: Sketches and Unpublished Scores, 1938–1958.* Stockholm: Royal Sweedish Academy of Music, 1976.

Nordwall, Ove. *György Ligeti: Eine Monographie.* Mainz: Schott's Söhne, 1971.

Nordwall, Ove. "György Ligeti (Two Hungarian Composers, 2)." *Tempo,* n.s., no. 88 (spring 1969): 22–25.

Nordwall, Ove. "Der Komponist, György Ligeti." *Musica* 22 (1968): 173–77.

Nordwall, Ove. *Det omojligas konst.* Stockholm: n.p., 1966.

Piencikowski, Robert T. "Inschriften: Ligeti–Xenakis–Boulez." *Musiktheorie* 12, no. 1 (1997): 7–16.

Piencikowski, Robert T. "Fonction relativ du timbre." In *Le Timbre, metaphore pour la composition*, 82–89. Paris: Bourgois, 1991.

Piencikowski, Robert. "Les points sur les i: Le Concerto de Chambre de Ligeti." *InHarmoniques* 2 (1978): 211–16.

Popper, Karl. "Of Clocks and Clouds." In *Objective Knowledge: An Evolutionary Approach*, 206–55. Oxford: Clarendon, 1972.

Pulido, Alejandro. "Differentiation and Integration in Ligeti's Chamber Concerto III." *Sonus* 9, no. 1 (1988): 17–37.

Quinn, Ian. "A Unified Theory of Chord Quality in Equal Temperaments." PhD diss., Eastman School of Music, 2004.

Reich, Willi. *Alban Berg: Mit Bergs eigenen Schriften und Beiträgen von Theodor Wiesengrund-Adorno und Ernst Krenek*. Vienna: Herbert Reichner Verlag, 1937.

Reiprich, Bruce. "Transformation of Coloration and Density in György Ligeti's *Lontano*." *Perspectives of New Music* 16, no. 2 (spring–summer 1978): 167–80.

Roig-Francolí, Miguel. "Harmonic and Formal Processes in Ligeti's Net-Structure Compositions," *Music Theory Spectrum* 17, no. 2 (fall 1995): 242–67.

Rosen, Charles. *The Romantic Generation*. Cambridge, MA: Harvard University Press, 1995.

Ross, Alex. *The Rest Is Noise*. New York: Farrar, Straus, and Giroux, 2007.

Rourke, Sean. "Ligeti's Early Years in the West." *Musical Times* 130, no. 9 (1989): 532–35.

Sabbe, Herman. *György Ligeti: Studien zur kompositorischen Phänomenologie*. Musik-Konzepte 53. Munich: Edition Text + Kritik, 1987.

Sabbe, Herman. "Techniques médiévales en musique contemporaine: Histoire de la musique et sens culturel." *Revue belge de Musicologie* 34–35 (1980–81): 220–33.

Sallis, Friedemann. "We Play the Music and the Music Plays with Us: Sándor Veress and His Student György Ligeti." In *György Ligeti: Of Foreign Lands and Strange Sounds*, edited by Louise Duchesneau and Wolfgang Marx, 1–16. Woodbridge, UK: Boydell, 2011.

Sallis, Friedemann. *An Introduction to the Early Works of György Ligeti*. Berliner Musik Studien 6. Cologne: Studio, 1996.

Salmenhaara, Erkki. *Das musikalische Material und seine Behandlung in den Werken "Apparitions," "Atmosphères," "Aventures" und "Requiem" von György Ligeti*. Acta musicologica fennica 2. Regensburg: Bosse, 1969.

Schaarschmidt, Helmut. "G. Ligeti: Atmosphères." In *Werkanalyse in Beispielen*, edited by Siegmund Helms and Helmuth Hopf, 370–78. Regensburg: Bosse, 1986.

Scherzinger, Martin. "György Ligeti and the Aka Pygmies Project." *Contemporary Music Review* 25, no. 3 (2006): 227–62.

Schneider, David E. *Bartók, Hungary, and the Renewal of Tradition: Case Studies in the Intersection of Modernity and Nationality*. Berkeley: University of California Press, 2006.

Searby, Michael. *Ligeti's Stylistic Crisis: Transformation in His Musical Style, 1974–1985*. Lanham, MD: Scarecrow, 2010.

Searby, Michael. "Ligeti's Chamber Concerto: Summation or Turning Point?" *Tempo* 168 (1989): 30–34.

Seiber, Matyas. *The String Quartets of Béla Bartók*. London: Boosey & Hawkes, 1945.

Shepard, Roger N. "Circularity in Judgements of Relative Pitch." *Journal of the Acoustical Society of America* 36, no. 12 (1964): 2346–53.

Shultis, Christopher. "Cage and Europe." In *The Cambridge Companion to John Cage*, edited by David Nicholls, 20–40. New Yorke: Cambridge University Press, 2002.

Somfai, László. *Béla Bartók: Composition, Concepts, and Autograph Sources*. Berkeley: University of California Press, 1996.

Steinitz, Richard. "The Study of Composers' Sketches, and an Overview of Those by Ligeti." *Contemporary Music Review* 31, nos. 2–3 (April–June 2012): 115–34.

Steinitz, Richard. "À qui un hommage? Genesis of the Piano Concerto and the Horn Trio." In *György Ligeti: Of Foreign Lands and Strange Sounds*, edited by Louise Duchesneau and Wolfgang Marx, 169–214. Woodbridge, UK: Boydell, 2011.

Steinitz, Richard. *György Ligeti: Music of the Imagination*. Boston: Northeastern University Press, 2003.

Steinitz, Richard. "Weeping and Wailing." *Musical Times* 137, no. 1842 (August 1996): 17–22.

Stevens, Halsey. *The Life and Music of Béla Bartók*, 3rd ed. New York: Oxford University Press, 1993.

Stockhausen, Karlheinz. *Gesang der Jünglinge: Elektronische Musik (1955–56): Werk Nr. 8*. Kürten: Stockhausen Verlag, 2001.

Stockhausen, Karlheinz. *Elektronische Musik, 1952–60*. Stockhausen Complete Edition 3, 1991. Compact Disc.

Stockhausen, Karlheinz. *Stockhausen on Music*, edited by Robin Maconie. New York: Marion Boyars, 1989.

Stockhausen, Karlheinz. *Nr. 12 Kontakte: Elektronische Musik, Relisations Paritur*. London: Universal Edition (UE 13678 LW), 1968.

Stockhausen, Karlheinz. *Texte zur Musik*, vol. 1: *Texte zur elektronischen und instrumentalen Musik: Aufsätze 1952–1962 zur Theorie des Komponierens*. Edited by Dieter Schnebel. Cologne: M. DuMont Schauberg, 1963; vol. 2: *Texte zu eigenen Werken, zur Kunst Anderer, Aktuelles: Aufsätze 1952–1962 zur musikalischen Praxis*. Edited by Dieter Schnebel. Cologne: M. DuMont Schauberg, 1964; vol. 3: *Texte zur Musik (1963–1970): Einführungen und Projekte, Kurse, Sendungen, Standpunkte, Nebennoten*. Edited by Dieter Schnebel. Cologne: M. DuMont Schauberg, 1971.

Stockhausen, Karlheinz. "The Concept of Unity in Electronic Music." Translated by Elaine Barkin. *Perspectives of New Music* 1, no. 1 (1962): 39–48.

Stockhausen, Karlheinz. ". . . how time passes . . ." In *Musical Craftsmanship: Die Reihe* 3, English ed., 10–40. Bryn Mawr, PA: Presser, 1959.

Stockhausen, Karlheinz. "Actualia." Translation uncredited. In *Electronic Music: Die Reihe* 1, English ed., 45–51. Bryn Mawr, PA: Presser, 1958.

Straus, Joseph. *Introduction to Post-Tonal Theory*, 3rd ed. Upper Saddle River, NJ: Pearson, 2005.

Straus, Joseph. "A Primer for Atonal Set Theory." *College Music Symposium* 31 (1991): 1–26.

Stucky, Steven. *Lutosławski and His Music*. New York: Cambridge University Press, 1981.

Suchoff, Benjamin. *Béla Bartók: A Celebration*. Lanham, MD: Scarecrow, 2004.

Szathmáry, Zsigmond. "Die Orgelwerke von György Ligeti." In *György Ligeti: Personalstil—Avantgardismus—Popularität*, edited by Otto Kolleritsch, 213–21. Vienna: Universal Edition, 1987.

Taruskin, Richard. *Oxford History of Western Music*, vol. 5. New York: Oxford University Press, 2005.

Taylor, Stephen A. "Chopin, Pygmies, and Tempo Fugue: Ligeti's 'Automne a Varsovie.'" *Music Theory Online* 3, no. 3 (May 1997).

Taylor, Stephen A. "The Lamento Motif: Metamorphosis in Ligeti's Late Style." DMA diss., Cornell University, 1994.

Țiplea-Temeș, Bianca. "Ligeti's String Quartet no. 1: Stylistic Incongruence?" *Studia Universitatis Babes-Bolyai—Musica* 2 (2008): 187–203.

Toop, Richard. "'Are You *Sure* You Can't Hear It?' Some Informal Reflections on Simple Information and Listening." In *The Pleasure of Modernist Music: Listening, Meaning, Intention, Ideology*, edited by Arved Ashby, 223–49. Rochester: University of Rochester Press, 2004.

Toop, Richard. *György Ligeti*. London: Phaidon, 1999.

Toop, Richard. "On Complexity." *Perspectives of New Music* 31, no. 1 (winter 1993): 42–57.

Toop, Richard. "Stockhausen's Electronic Works: Sketches and Work-Sheets from 1952–1967. *Interface* 10 (1981): 149–97.

Toop, Richard. "Stockhausen and the Sine-Wave: The Story of an Ambiguous Relationship." *Musical Quarterly* 45, no. 3 (July 1979): 379–91.

Toop, Richard. "Stockhausen's *Konkrete Etüde*." *Music Review* (November 1976): 295–300.

Travis, Roy. "Tonal Coherence in the First Movement of Bartók's Fourth String Quartet." *Music Forum* 2 (1976): 298–371.

Treitler, Leo. "Harmonic Procedures in the 'Fourth Quartet' of Bela Bartók." *Journal of Music Theory* 3 (1959): 292–98.

Ungeheuer, Elena, ed. *Elektroakustische Musik*. Handbuch der Musik im 20. Jahrhundert 5. Laaber: Laaber Verlag, 2002.

Ungeheuer, Elena. "From the Elements to the Continuum: Timbre Composition in Early Electronic Music." *Contemporary Music Review* 10, no. 2 (1994): 25–33.

Ungeheuer, Elena. *Wie die elektronishce Musik 'erfunden' wurde . . .: Quellensudie zu Werner Meyer-Epplers musikalischem Entwurf zwischen 1949 und 1953*. Kölner Schriften zur Neuen Musik 2. Mainz: Schott, 1992.

Urban, Uve. "Serielle Technik und barocker Geist in Ligetis Cembalo-Stück *Continuum*." *Musik und Bildung* 5, no. 2 (1973): 63–70.

van den Toorn, Pieter C. Stravinsky and The Rite of Spring: *The Beginnings of a Musical Language*. Berkeley: University of California Press, 1987.

Varga, Bálint András, ed. *György Kurtág: Three Interviews and Ligeti Homages*. Rochester: University of Rochester Press, 2009.

Webern, Anton. *The Path to the New Music*. Edited Willi Reich, translated by Leo Black. Bryn Mawr, PA: Presser, 1963.

Wehinger, Rainer. *Ligeti—Artikulation: Electronische Musik, eine Hörpartitur*. Mainz: Schott, 1970.

Wehinger, Rainer, and Thomas Kabisch, eds. *Analysieren und Hören neuer Musik: Karkoschka Festschrift*. Musiktheorie 12 no. 1 (1997).

Wilson, Charles. "György Ligeti and the Rhetoric of Autonomy." *Twentieth-Century Music* 1, no. 1 (2004): 5–28.

Wilson, Paul. *The Music of Béla Bartók*. New Haven: Yale University Press, 1992.

Wörner, Karl Heinrich. *Stockhausen: Life and Work*. Edited and translated by Bill Hopkins. Berkeley: University of California Press, 1973.

Young, La Monte, and Jackson Mac Low, eds. *An Anthology*, 2nd ed. N.p.: Heiner Friedrich, 1970.

INDEX

indeterminacy. *See* aleatoric composition and indeterminacy
Institute of Sonology, 71
International Society for Contemporary Music (ISCM), 88–89
Ionesco, Eugène, 143, 150
   The Bald Soprano, 150
Isou, Isidore, 143
Iverson, Jennifer, 173

Jarry, Alfred, 143
Jelinek, Hanns, *Anleitung zur Zwölftonkomposition*, 33, 36–38, 44, 50
Jennings, Terry, 133
Jeppesen, Knud, 180
Joyce, James, *Finnegans Wake*, 51

Kadosa, Pál, 9–10
Kafka, Franz, *Amerika*, 259
Kagel, Mauricio, 6, 50, 73, 88–89, 129, 131, 134–35, 138, 143, 163, 209, 256n2
   Anagrama, 73, 88–89, 143
   Improvisation ajoutée, 135, 138
   Sonant, 209
Kaufmann, Harald, 2
Kerékfy, Márton, 18
Klee, Paul, *Die Sängerin der komischen Oper*, 263
Kodály, Zoltán, *Hegyi Éjszakák*, 41
Koenig, Gottfried Michael, 50, 52–53, 72, 79–80, 87–88, 102–3, 114, 129, 133
   Essay, 79–80, 87
Krebs, Harald, 241
Krúdy, Gyula, 150–51
   Adventures of Sindbad, 151
Kurtág, György, 18n22, 43

language, artificial, 73–75, 143–44
Leibowitz, René, *Introduction à la musique de douze sons*, 11, 33
Lendvai, Ernő, 17n20, 18–19, 32, 42, 92, 107
letterism, 143
Lichtenfeld, Monika, 89, 169
Lidholm, Ingvar, 135
Ligeti, György, life
   childhood in Cluj (Kolozsvár), 39, 85–86, 142, 149–51
   postwar Budapest, 9–13, 23, 31–33, 49, 106, 164
   as student at the Liszt Academy, 18, 44n68, 108–9, 164, 179–80, 262n14, 265

in Romania, 9, 17
in western Europe, 33, 50–52, 71–72, 83–84, 85–90, 128–30, 132–33, 163, 210, 256, 267n22, 273–75
teaching and lecturing, 135, 163, 195n38, 210, 273
in the United States, 71, 240n29, 272–73
Judaism, 164
reception, reputation, and legacy, 1, 5–6, 12, 84, 85, 88–89, 114, 127, 163, 273–75
Ligeti, György, works
   Apparitions, 4, 6, 7, 39, 42, 49, 67, 70–71, 77, 85, 87–88, 89–111, 113, 114, 117, 119, 124, 128, 132, 133, 135, 156, 163, 165, 195, 207, 210, 213, 216, 229, 261, 266, Exs. 3.1–3.10 (see also *Sötét és Világos*)
   Artikulation, 1, 52, 71–84, 85, 91, 101, 114, 143–44, 149, 156, 163, 195, 206, 211, 250, Exs. 2.7–2.9
   Atmosphères, 1, 2, 6, 7, 31, 62, 85, 86–88, 103, 105, 113–27, 128, 163, 164, 198, 202, 210–11, 214, 219–20, 221, 225, 243, 265, Exs. 3.15–3.21
   Aventures, 1, 4, 7, 39, 50, 105, 106, 132, 142–62, 163, 164, 177, 178, 188, 198, 205–6, 208–9, 210–11, 250–51, 261, Exs. 4.3–4.9, Ex. 5.8 (see also *Nouvelles Aventures*)
   Cello Concerto, 5, 7, 106, 164, 199, 205–9, 225, 247, 251, 252, 261, Ex. 5.20
   Cello Sonata, 10
   Chamber Concerto, 1, 4, 7, 8, 50, 142, 162, 179, 209, 210–11, 213–14, 218–20, 220–26, 227, 229–35, 235–36, 250–51, 254–55, 266–67, 270, 272, Exs. 6.6–6.9, 6.11–6.13
   Chromatische Phantasie, 6, 31, 34–36, 38–39, 109, 209, Ex. 1.11
   Clocks and Clouds, 8, 245, 246, 249–50, 250, 267–69, 274, Ex. C.1
   Concert Românesc, 10–11, 12, 17, 23
   Concerto for Violin and Orchestra, 15–16
   Continuum, 1, 7, 8, 211, 236, 238–39, 242, 244, 250, 262, 266, 274
   Double Concerto, 245, 246–47, Ex. 6.19
   Éjszaka and *Reggel*, 6, 40–43, 90, 109, 119, 165, Exs. 1.15–1.16
   Études for Piano, 142, 248
   Fragment, 7, 133–34